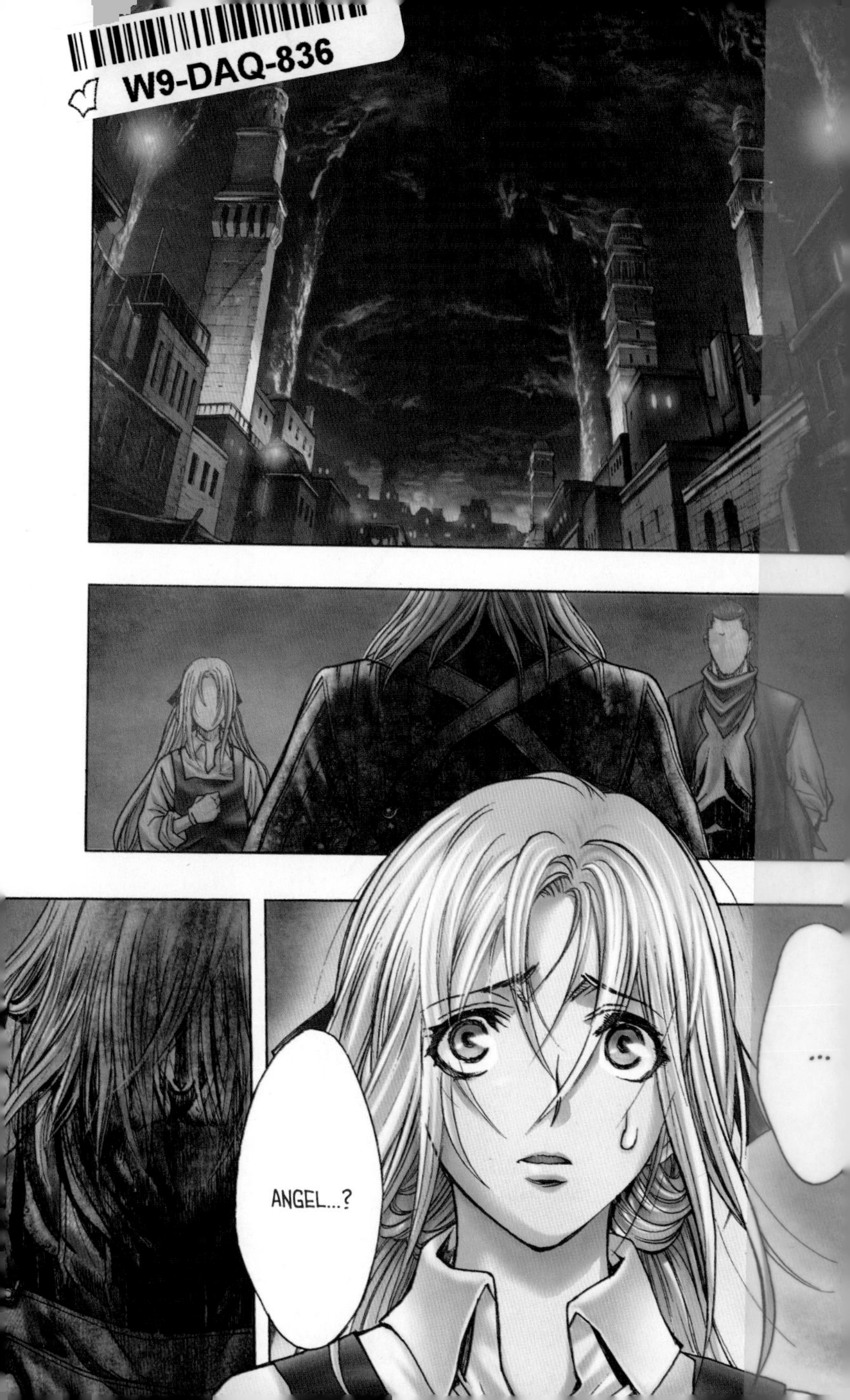
...
ANGEL...?

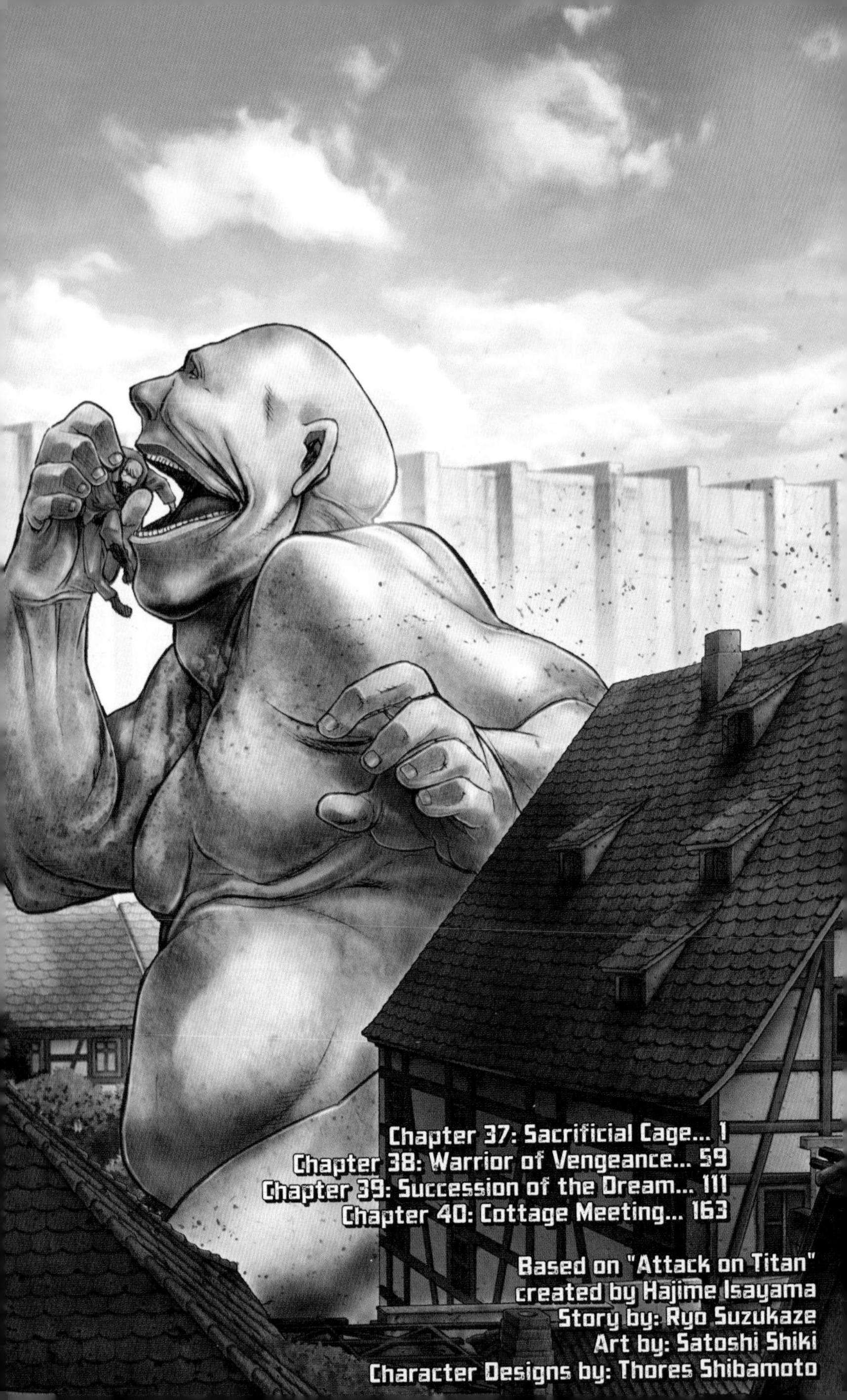

Based on "Attack on Titan"
created by Hajime Isayama
Story by: Ryo Suzukaze
Art by: Satoshi Shiki
Character Designs by: Thores Shibamoto

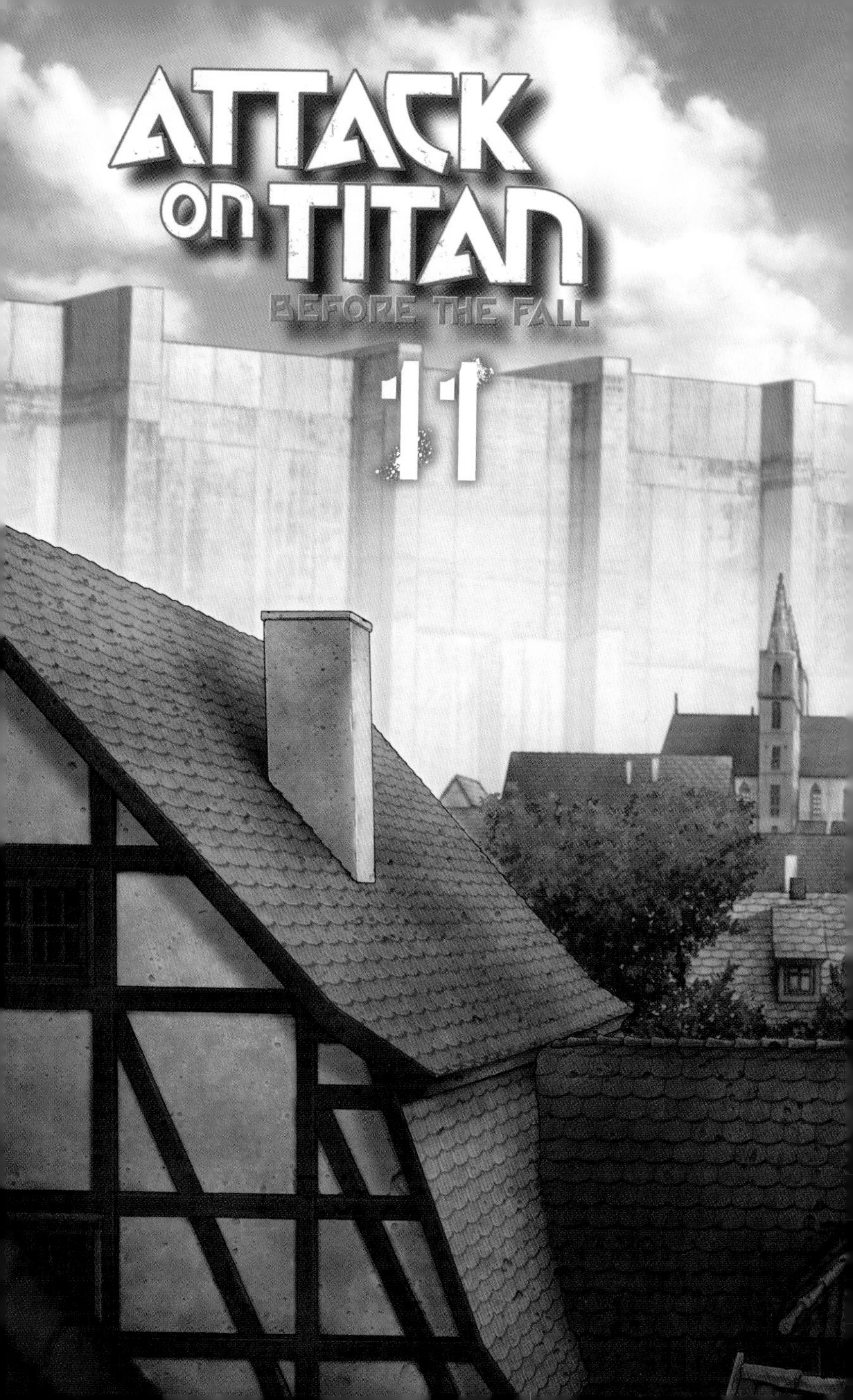
ATTACK on TITAN
BEFORE THE FALL
11

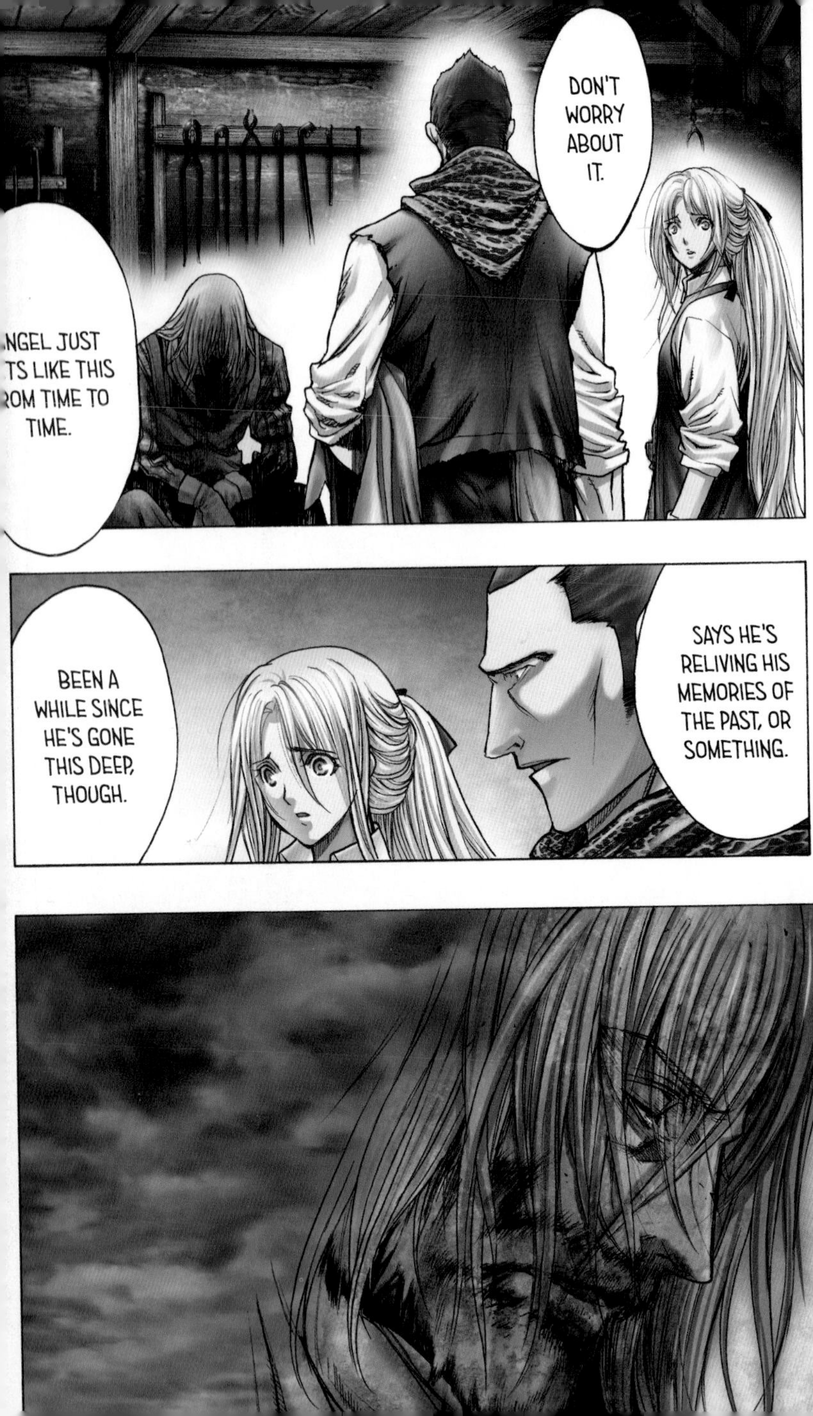
DON'T WORRY ABOUT IT.
NGEL JUST TS LIKE THIS ROM TIME TO TIME.
SAYS HE'S RELIVING HIS MEMORIES OF THE PAST, OR SOMETHING.
BEEN A WHILE SINCE HE'S GONE THIS DEEP, THOUGH.

Before the fall Character Profiles

Kuklo

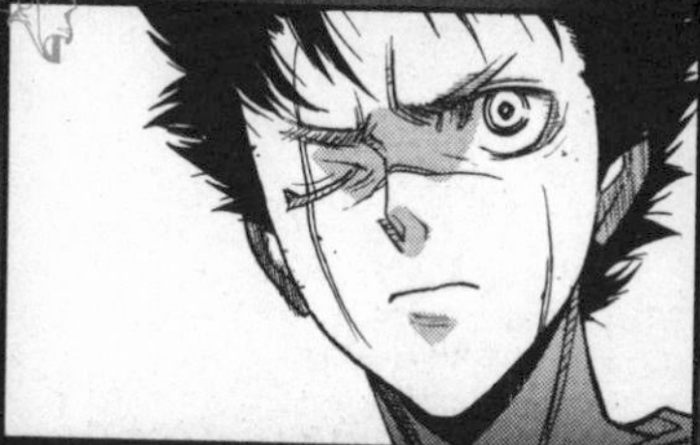

A 15-year-old boy born from a dead body packed into the vomit of a Titan, which earned him the moniker, "Titan's Son." He is fascinated with the Device as a means to defeat the Titans. The protagonist of this story. His current status is unknown, after he was defeated by Xavi.

Sharle Inocencio

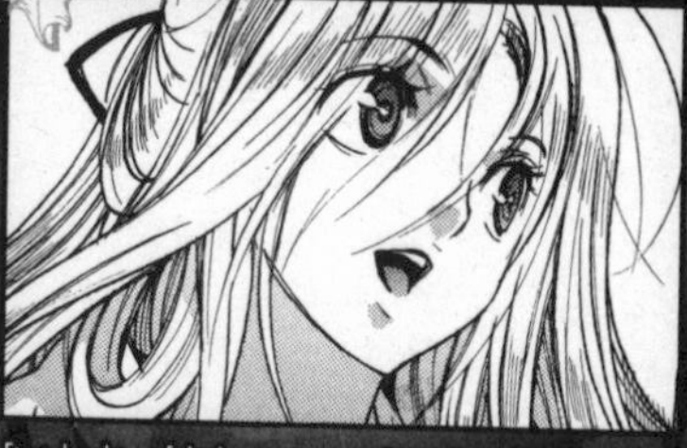

First daughter of the Inocencios, a rich merchant family within Wall Sheena. When she realized that Kuklo was a human, she taught him to speak and learn. She trained as an apprentice craftsman under Xenophon in the Industrial City, until Xavi dragged her back home.

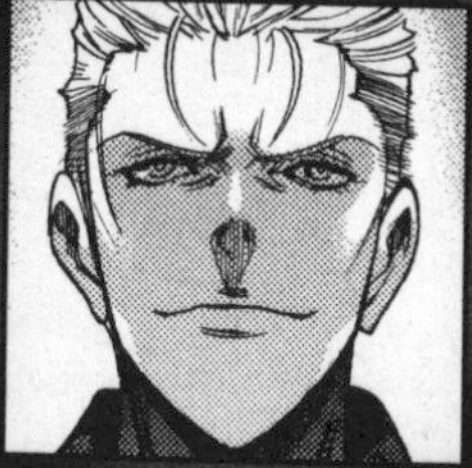

Xavi Inocencio

Head of the Inocencio family and Sharle's brother. Member of the Military Police in Shiganshina District.

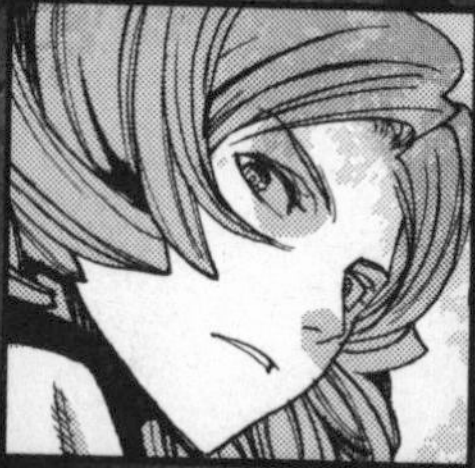

Cardina Baumeister

Kuklo's first friend in the outside world, and his companion in developing the Device.

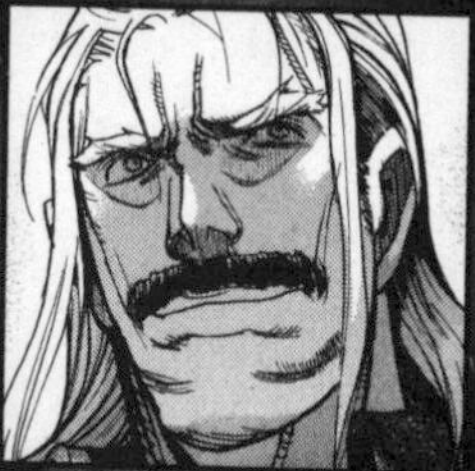

Jorge Pikale

Training Corps instructor. A former Survey Corps captain who was hailed as a hero for defeating a Titan.

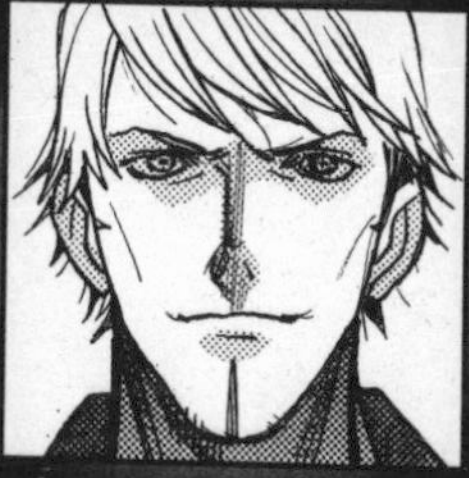

Carlo Pikale

Jorge's son and current captain of the Survey Corps. After they battled Titans together, he has great respect for Kuklo.

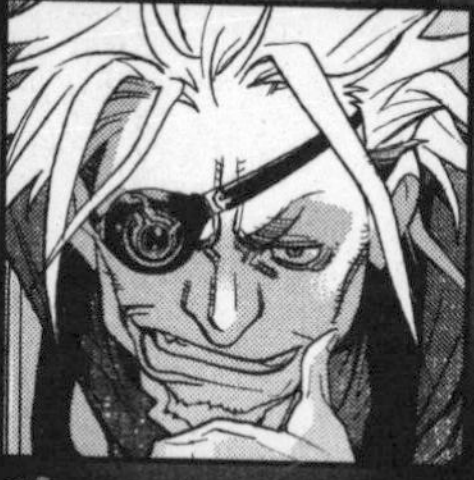

Xenophon Harkimo

Foreman at the Industrial City. He took over development of the Device from its inventor, Angel.

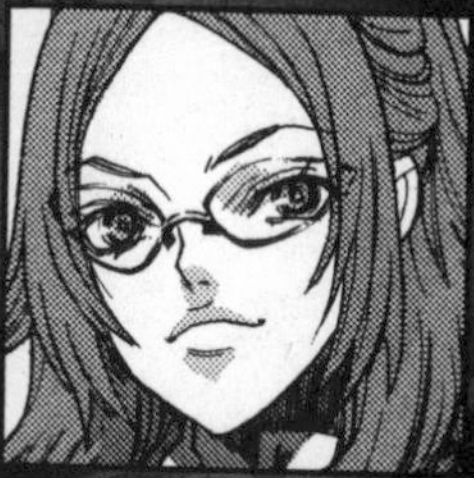

Gloria Bernhart

Captain of the Military Police in Shiganshina District. A powerful MP officer with a cold, tactical mind.

The Story So Far

When a Titan terrorized Shiganshina District and left behind a pile of vomit, a baby boy was miraculously born of a pregnant corpse. This boy was named Kuklo, the "Titan's Son," and treated as a sideshow ak. Eventually the wealthy merchant Dario Inocencio bought Kuklo to ve as a punching bag for his son, Xavi. On the other hand, when she rned he was human and not the son of a Titan, Xavi's sister Sharle ided to teach him the words and knowledge of humanity instead. Two rs later, Kuklo escaped from the mansion along with Sharle, who s being forced into a marriage she did not desire.

Shiganshina District, the Survey Corps was preparing for its first edition outside of the wall in 15 years. Kuklo snuck into the edition's cargo wagon, but the Titan they ran across was far worse a monster than he expected. He helped the Survey Corps survive, but ide the walls he was greeted by the Military Police, who wanted the tan's Son" on charges of murdering Dario. In prison, he met Cardina, young man jailed over political squabbles. They hoped to escape to fety when exiled beyond the Wall, but found themselves surrounded a pack of Titans. It was through the help of Jorge, former Survey rps captain and the first human to defeat a Titan, that the two boys caped with their lives. The equipment that Jorge used was the very evice" that was the key to defeating the Titan those 15 years ago.

klo and Cardina escaped the notice of the MPs by hiding in the dustrial City, where they found Sharle. It is there that the three ungsters learned the truth of the ill-fated Titan-capturing expedition years earlier, and swore to uphold the will of Angel, the inventor of e Device.

ext, Kuklo and Cardina headed back to Shiganshina to test out a new odel of the Device developed by Xenophon, Angel's friend and rival. ut while they were gone, a rebellion by anti-establishment dissidents roke out in the Industrial City. Kuklo was able to slip through the chaos rescue Sharle from the dissidents, but just as they started to elebrate their reunion, Sharle's brother Xavi arrived, and turned his word on Kuklo. Xavi won the battle by inflicting a grievous blow on uklo, who fell into the river. Sharle was taken back to the Inocencio ansion, but following her belief that Kuklo was still alive, she escaped nd headed underground to find Angel and ask for his help in improving he Device. But once she found him, she was surprised at his vehement esistance to the idea.

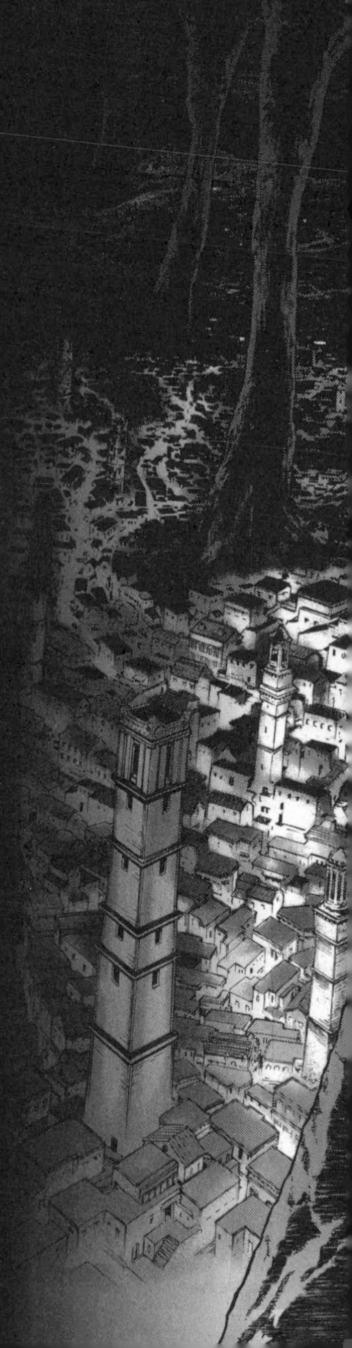

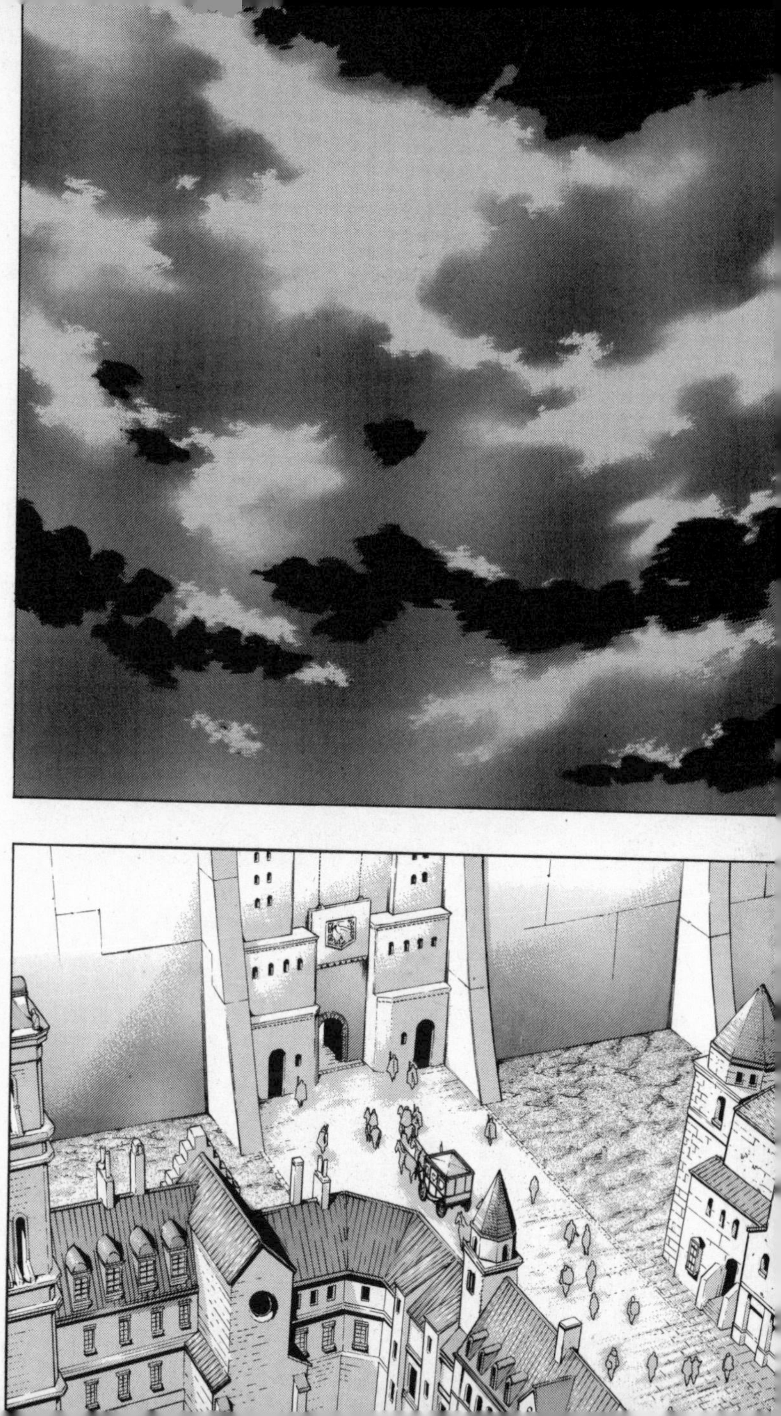

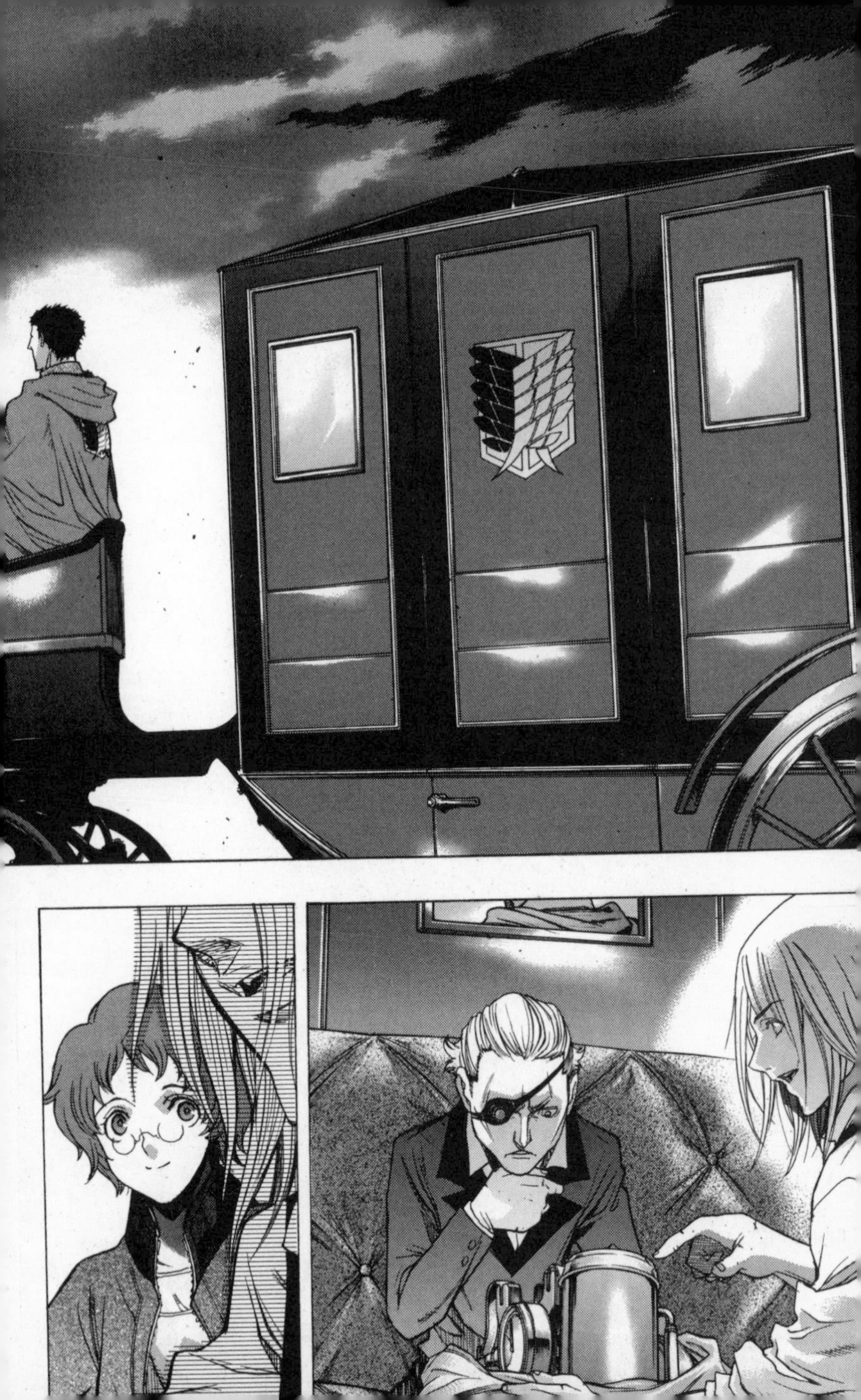

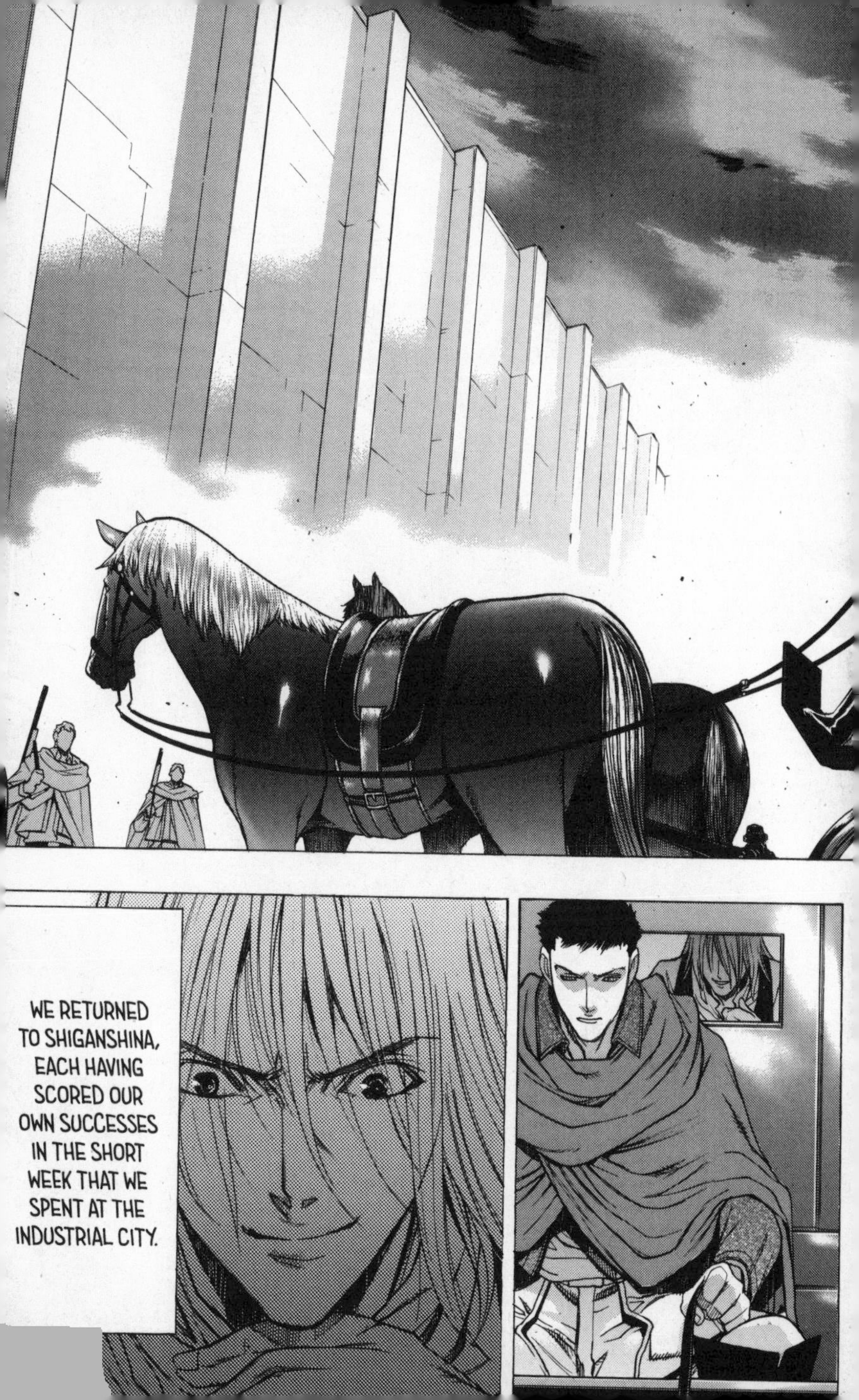
WE RETURNED TO SHIGANSHINA, EACH HAVING SCORED OUR OWN SUCCESSES IN THE SHORT WEEK THAT WE SPENT AT THE INDUSTRIAL CITY.

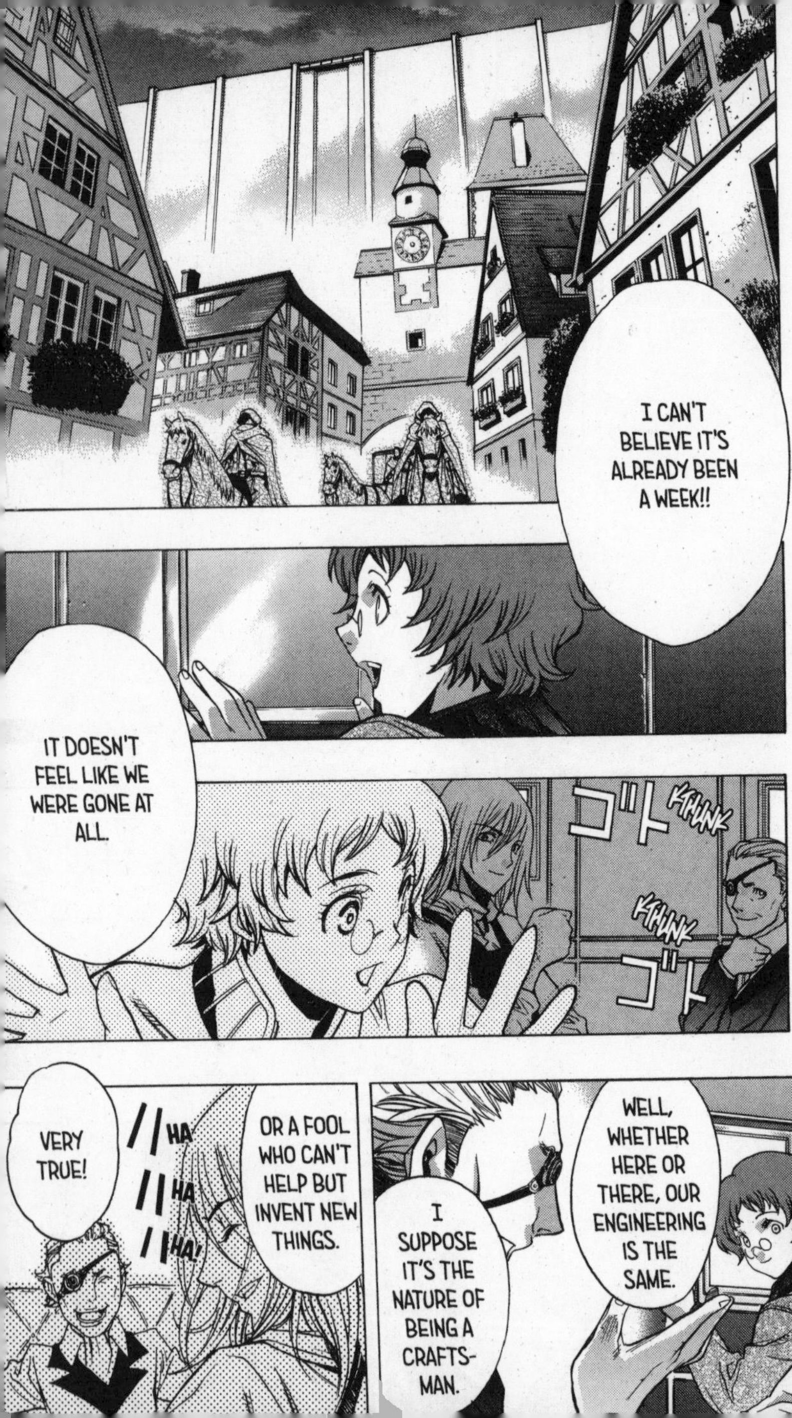
I CAN'T BELIEVE IT'S ALREADY BEEN A WEEK!!
IT DOESN'T FEEL LIKE WE WERE GONE AT ALL.
ゴト
KTHUNK
KTHUNK
ゴト
WELL, WHETHER HERE OR THERE, OUR ENGINEERING IS THE SAME.
I SUPPOSE IT'S THE NATURE OF BEING A CRAFTSMAN.
OR A FOOL WHO CAN'T HELP BUT INVENT NEW THINGS.
HA HA HA!
VERY TRUE!

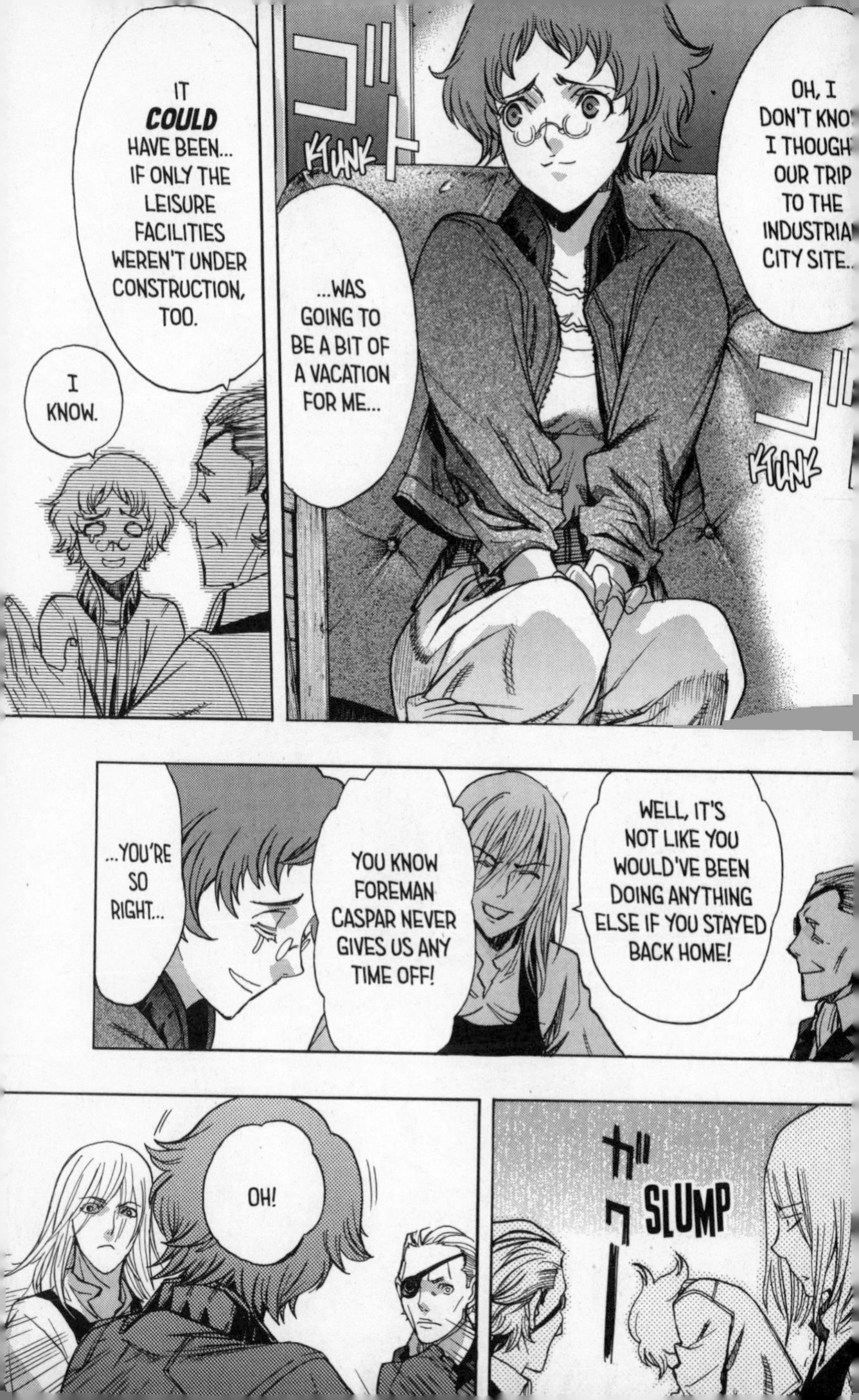

OH, I DON'T KNO I THOUGH OUR TRIP TO THE INDUSTRIA CITY SITE...
KTUNK
KTUNK
...WAS GOING TO BE A BIT OF A VACATION FOR ME...
IT **COULD** HAVE BEEN... IF ONLY THE LEISURE FACILITIES WEREN'T UNDER CONSTRUCTION, TOO.
I KNOW.
WELL, IT'S NOT LIKE YOU WOULD'VE BEEN DOING ANYTHING ELSE IF YOU STAYED BACK HOME!
YOU KNOW FOREMAN CASPAR NEVER GIVES US ANY TIME OFF!
...YOU'RE SO RIGHT...
SLUMP
OH!

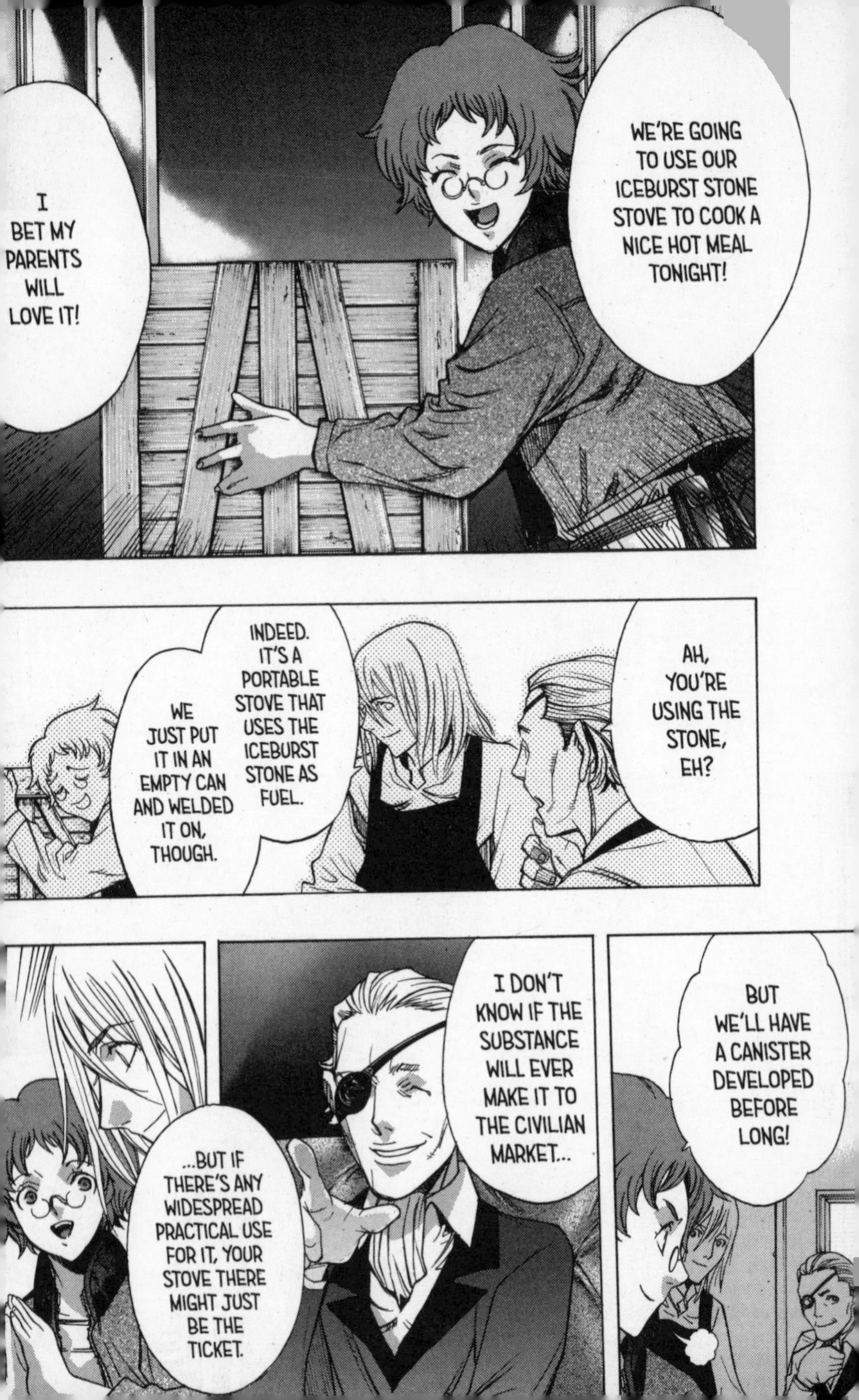
WE'RE GOING TO USE OUR ICEBURST STONE STOVE TO COOK A NICE HOT MEAL TONIGHT!
I BET MY PARENTS WILL LOVE IT!
AH, YOU'RE USING THE STONE, EH?
INDEED. IT'S A PORTABLE STOVE THAT USES THE ICEBURST STONE AS FUEL.
WE JUST PUT IT IN AN EMPTY CAN AND WELDED IT ON, THOUGH.
BUT WE'LL HAVE A CANISTER DEVELOPED BEFORE LONG!
I DON'T KNOW IF THE SUBSTANCE WILL EVER MAKE IT TO THE CIVILIAN MARKET...
...BUT IF THERE'S ANY WIDESPREAD PRACTICAL USE FOR IT, YOUR STOVE THERE MIGHT JUST BE THE TICKET.

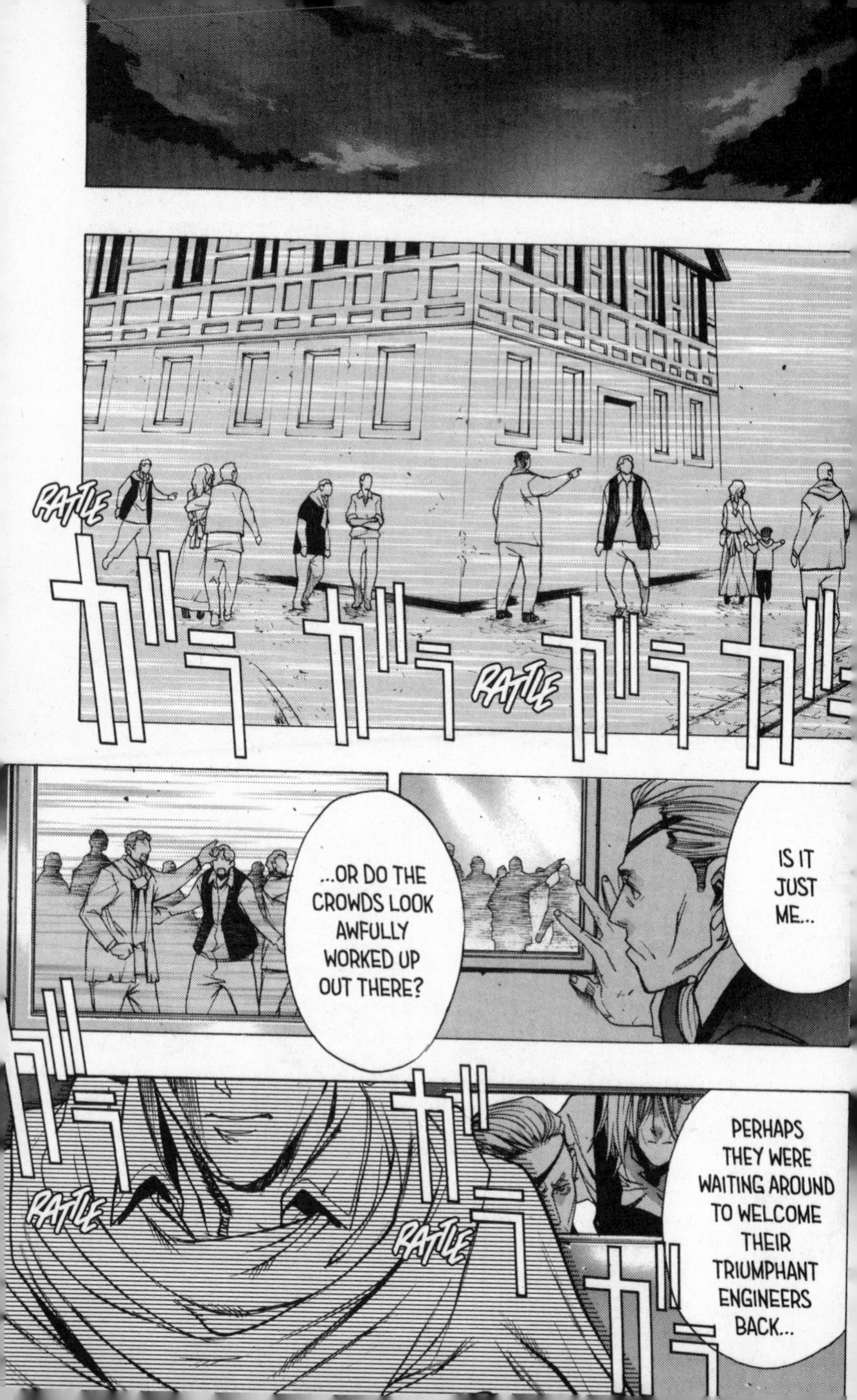
RATTLE
RATTLE
IS IT JUST ME...
...OR DO THE CROWDS LOOK AWFULLY WORKED UP OUT THERE?
PERHAPS THEY WERE WAITING AROUND TO WELCOME THEIR TRIUMPHANT ENGINEERS BACK...
RATTLE
RATTLE

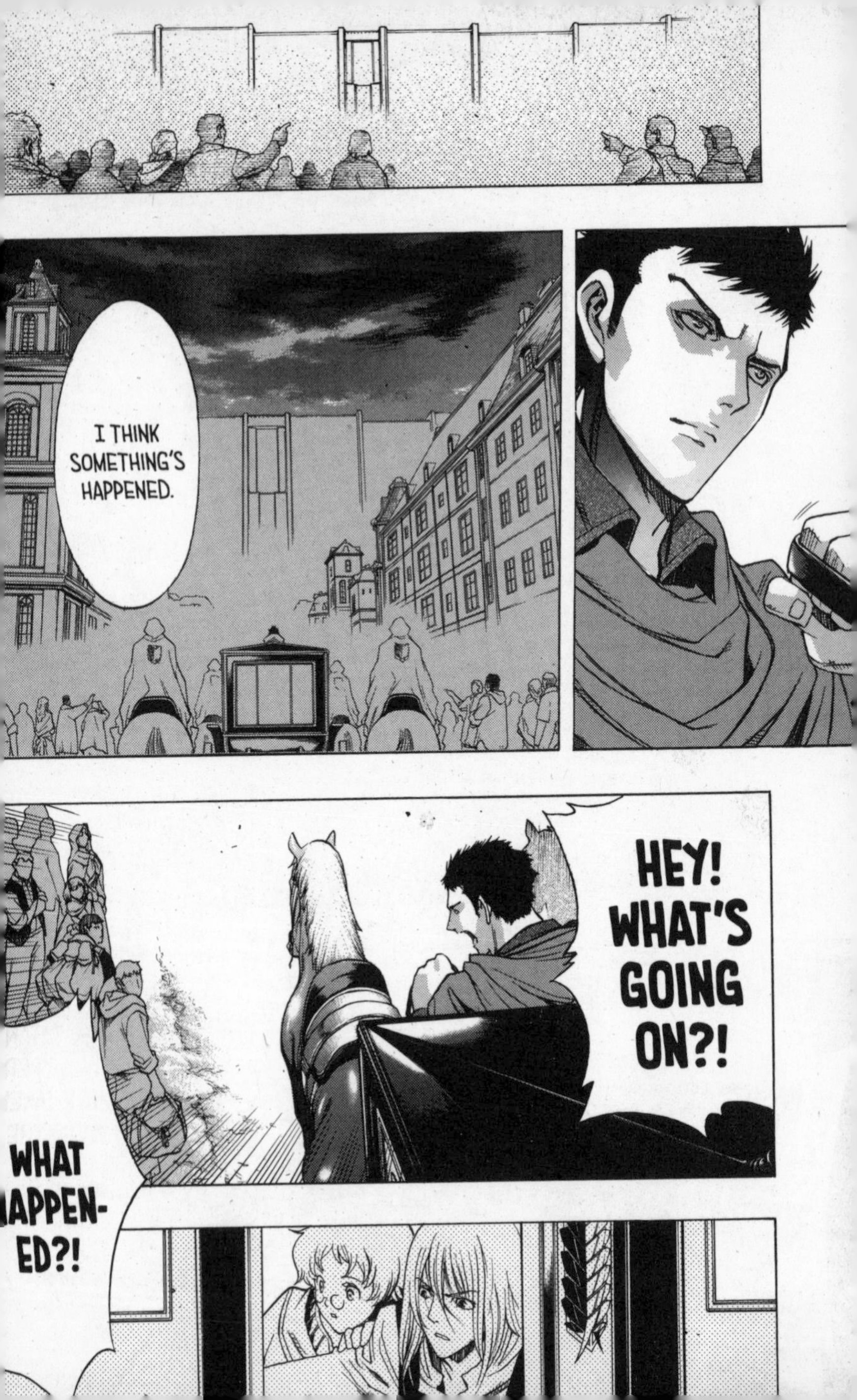
I THINK SOMETHING'S HAPPENED.
HEY! WHAT'S GOING ON?!
WHAT HAPPEN-ED?!

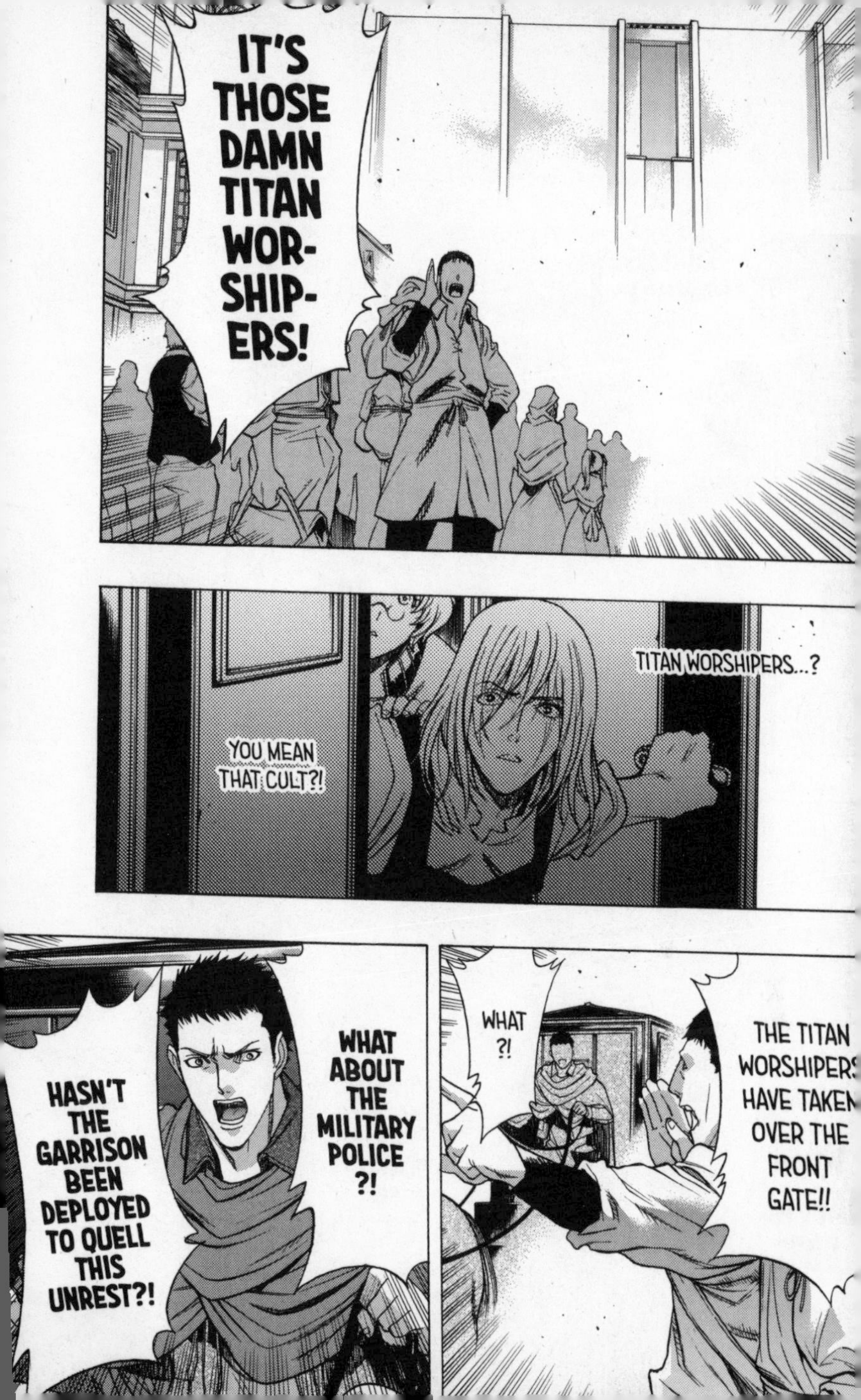
IT'S THOSE DAMN TITAN WOR-SHIP-ERS!
TITAN WORSHIPERS...?
YOU MEAN THAT CULT?!
THE TITAN WORSHIPERS HAVE TAKEN OVER THE FRONT GATE!!
WHAT ?!
WHAT ABOUT THE MILITARY POLICE ?!
HASN'T THE GARRISON BEEN DEPLOYED TO QUELL THIS UNREST?!

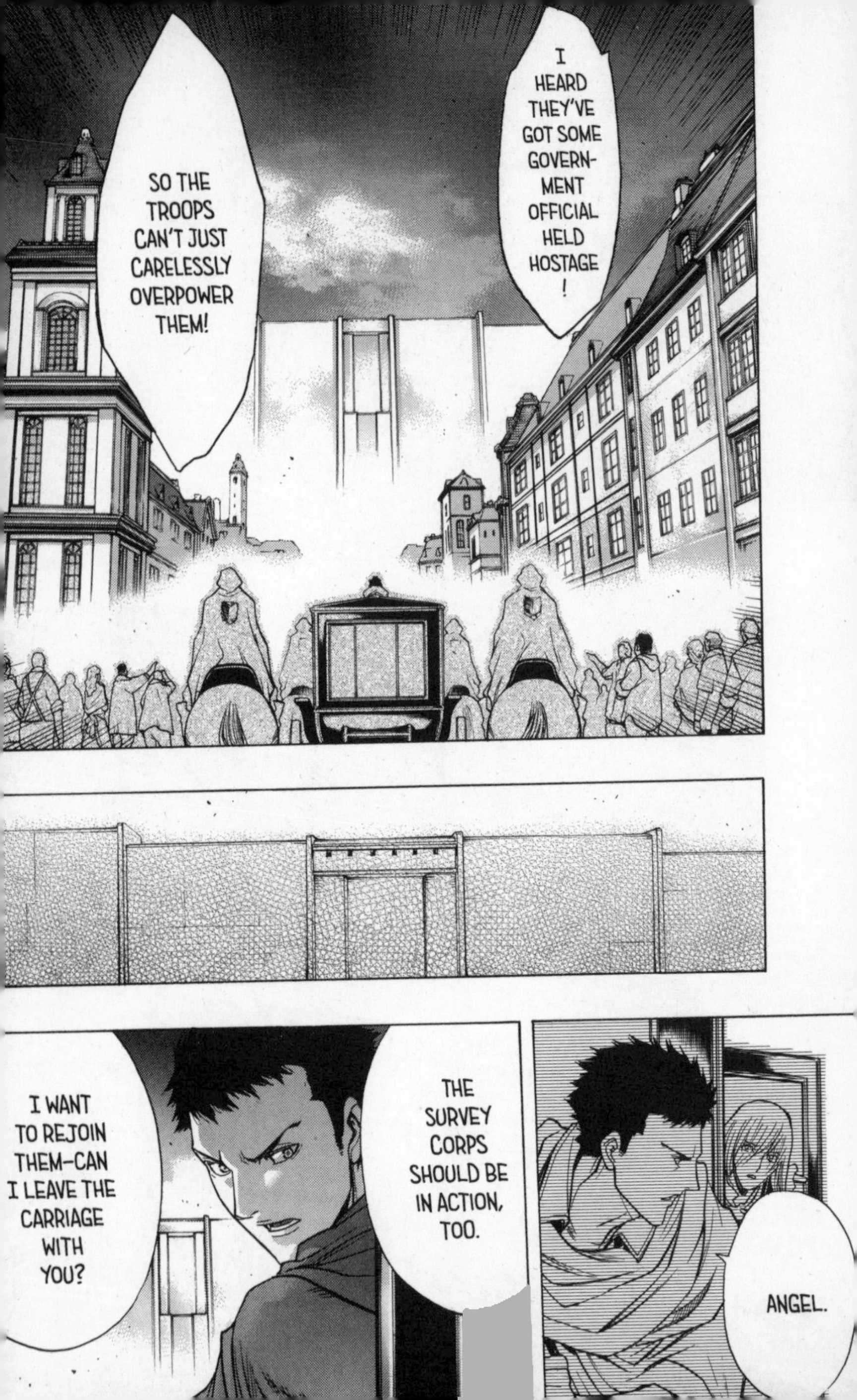
I HEARD THEY'VE GOT SOME GOVERN-MENT OFFICIAL HELD HOSTAGE!
SO THE TROOPS CAN'T JUST CARELESSLY OVERPOWER THEM!
ANGEL.
THE SURVEY CORPS SHOULD BE IN ACTION, TOO.
I WANT TO REJOIN THEM—CAN I LEAVE THE CARRIAGE WITH YOU?

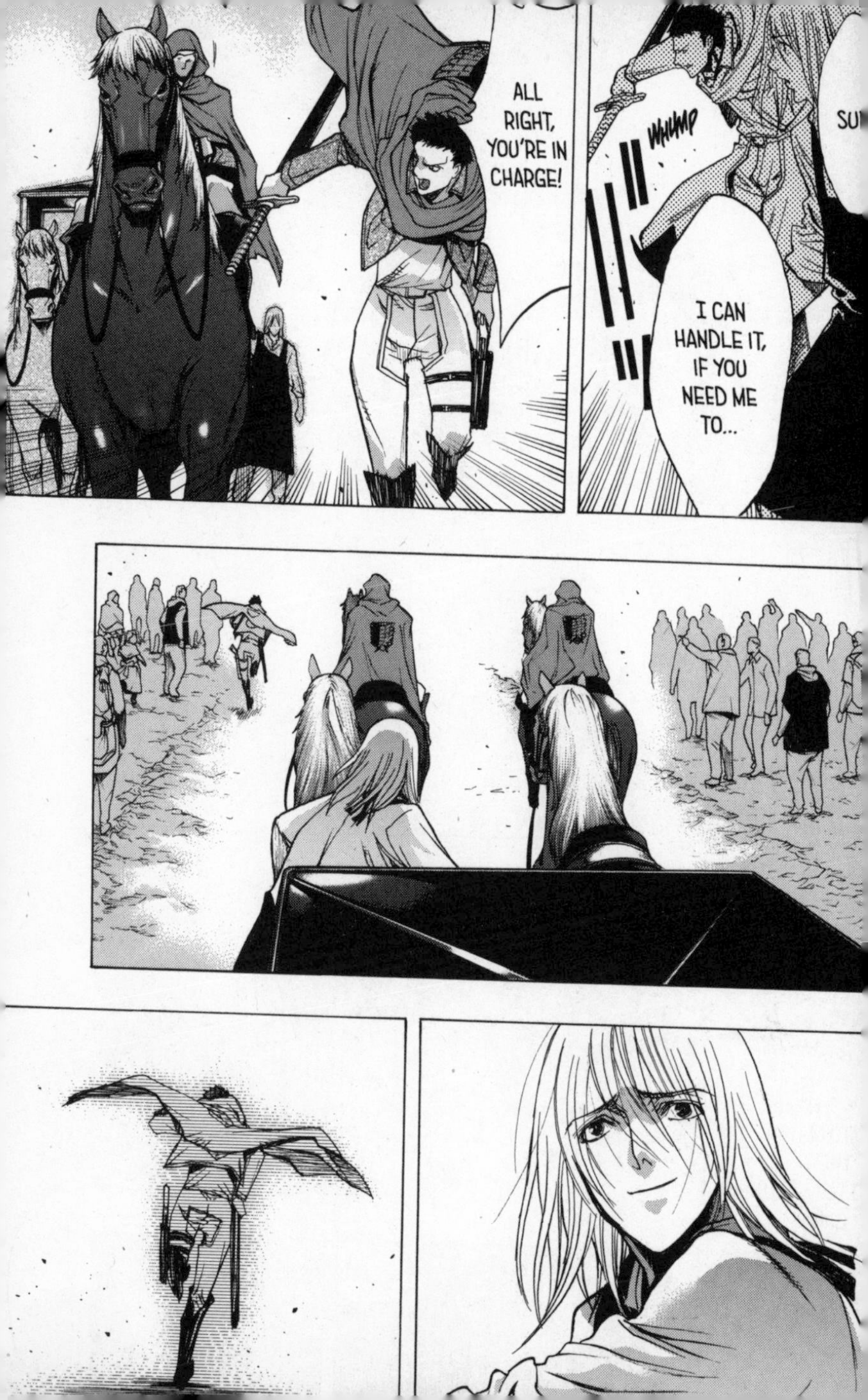
SU
WHUMP
I CAN HANDLE IT, IF YOU NEED ME TO...
ALL RIGHT, YOU'RE IN CHARGE!

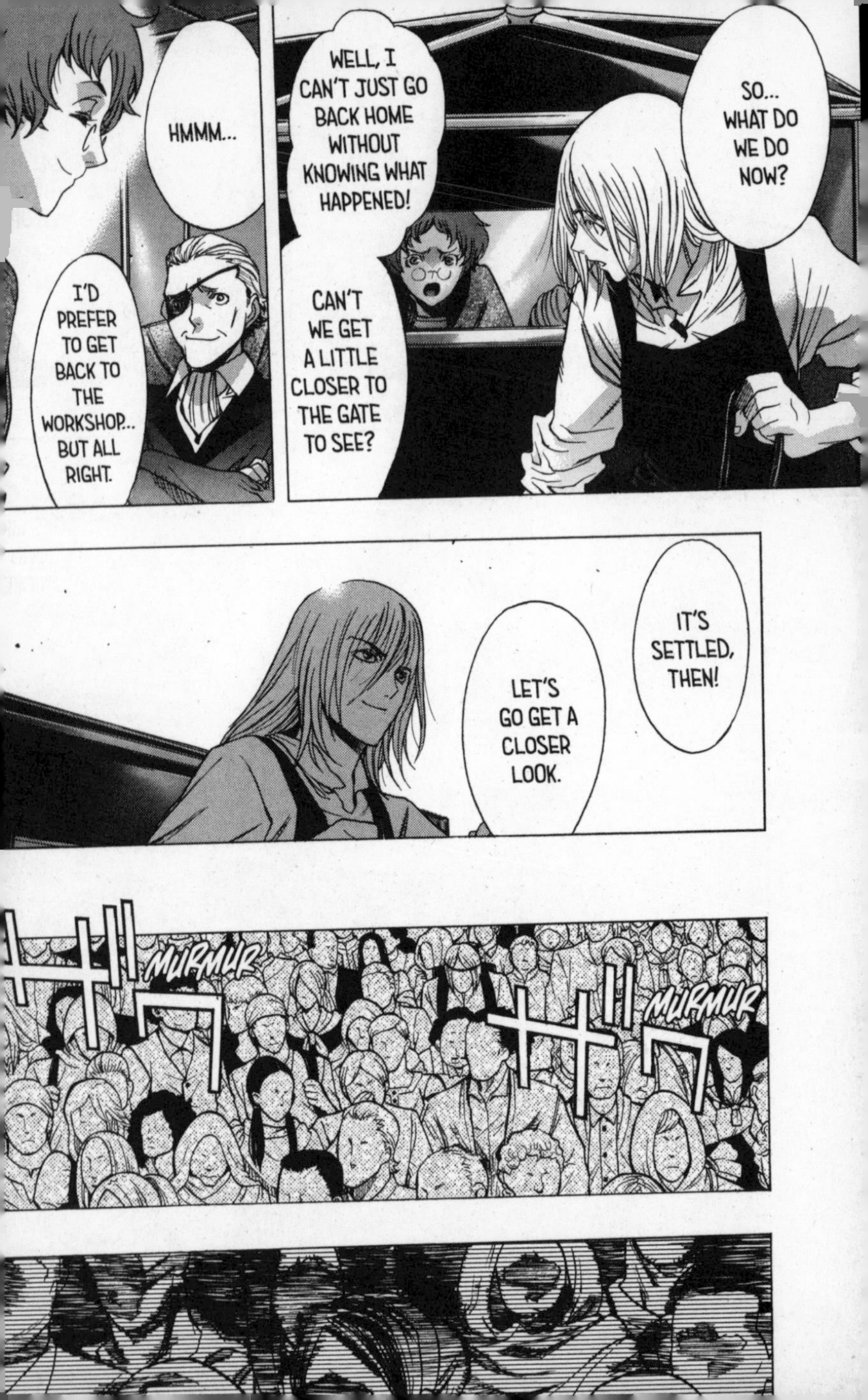
SO... WHAT DO WE DO NOW?
WELL, I CAN'T JUST GO BACK HOME WITHOUT KNOWING WHAT HAPPENED!
CAN'T WE GET A LITTLE CLOSER TO THE GATE TO SEE?
HMMM...
I'D PREFER TO GET BACK TO THE WORKSHOP... BUT ALL RIGHT.
IT'S SETTLED, THEN!
LET'S GO GET A CLOSER LOOK.
MURMUR
MURMUR

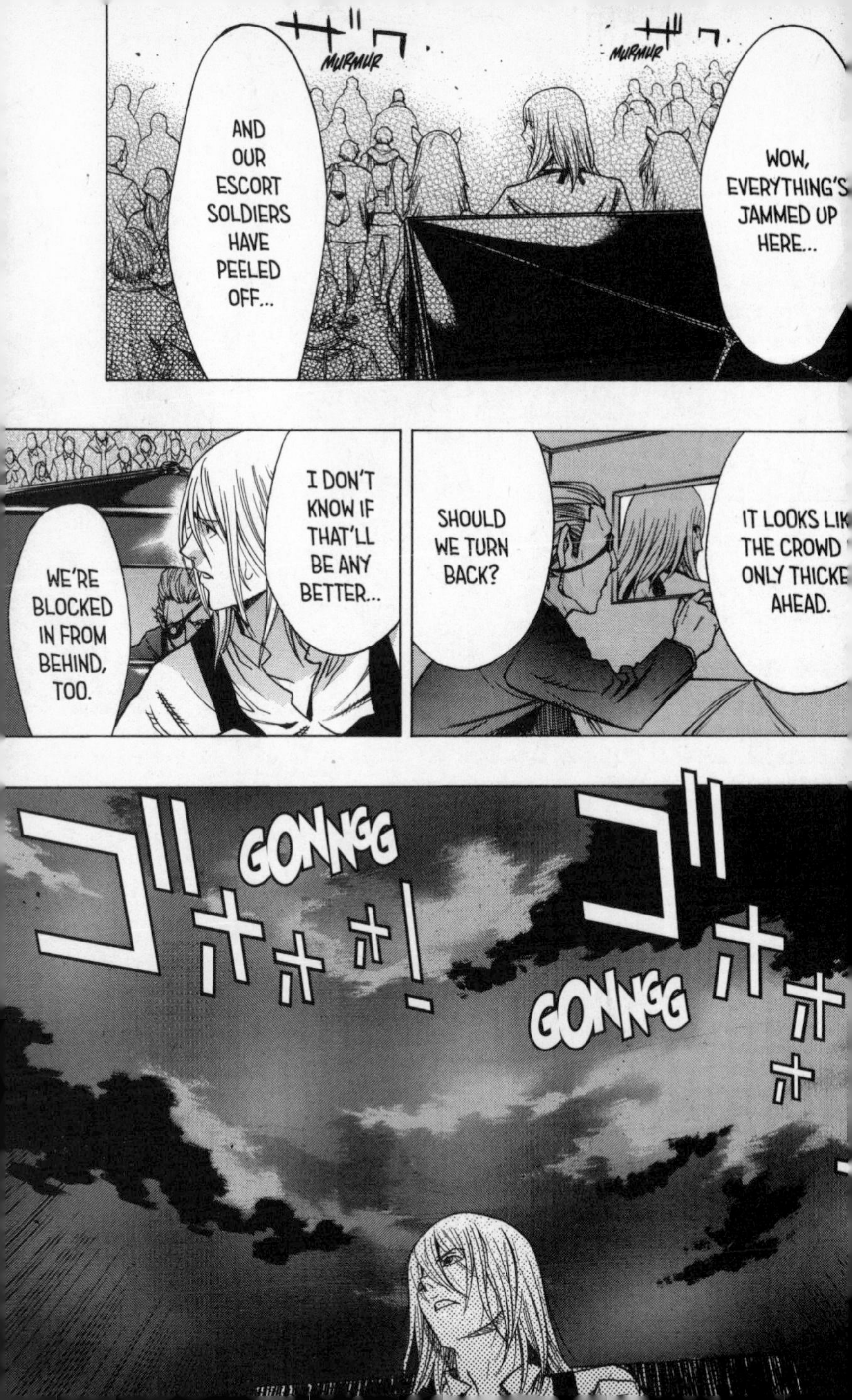

ザワ
MURMUR
ザワ
MURMUR
WOW, EVERYTHING'S JAMMED UP HERE...
AND OUR ESCORT SOLDIERS HAVE PEELED OFF...
IT LOOKS LIK THE CROWD ONLY THICKE AHEAD.
SHOULD WE TURN BACK?
I DON'T KNOW IF THAT'LL BE ANY BETTER...
WE'RE BLOCKED IN FROM BEHIND, TOO.
ゴォォォ
GONNGG
ゴォォォ!
GONNGG

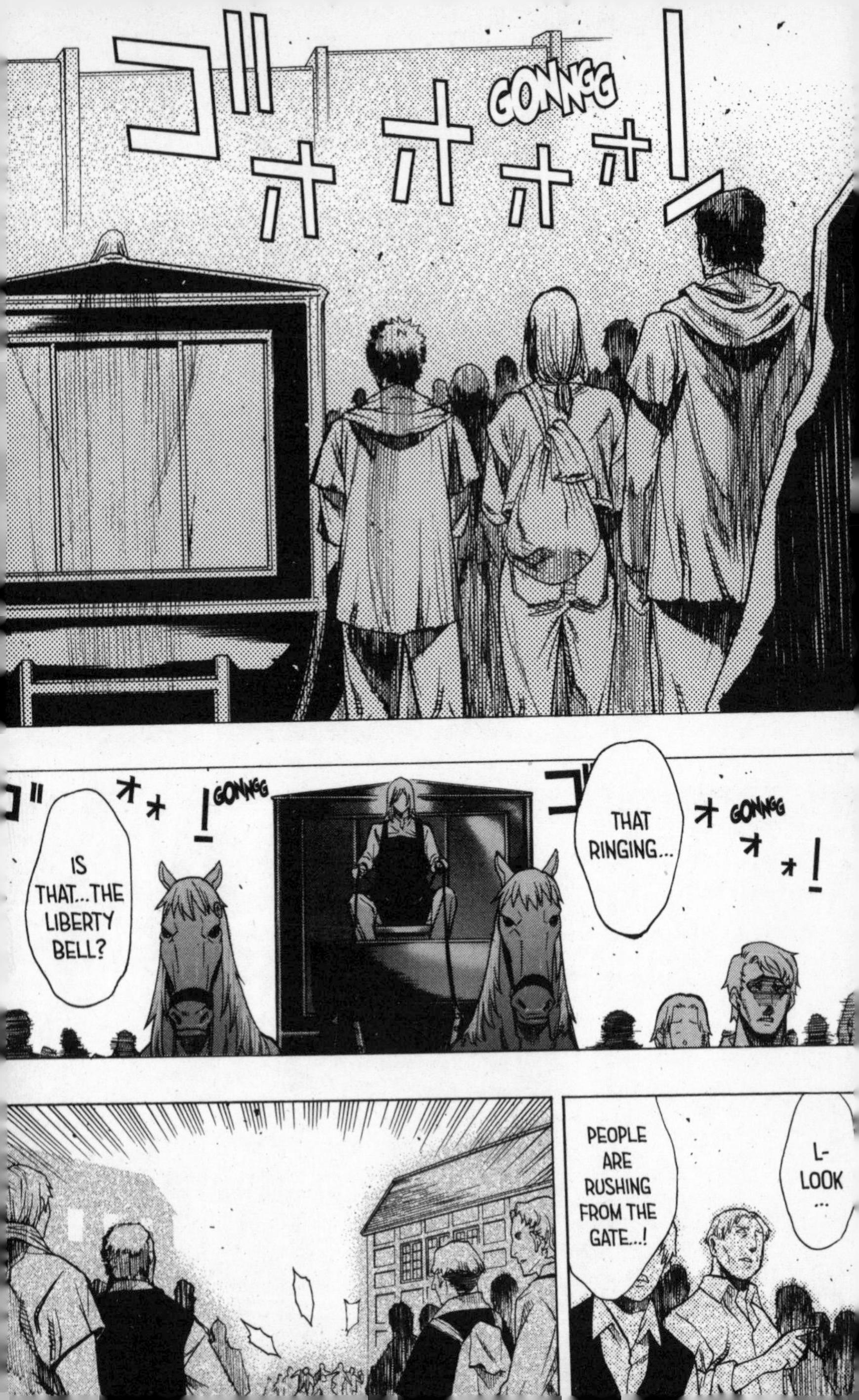

ゴオオォォー
GONNGG
THAT RINGING...
GONNGG
IS THAT...THE LIBERTY BELL?
GONNGG
L-LOOK...
PEOPLE ARE RUSHING FROM THE GATE...!

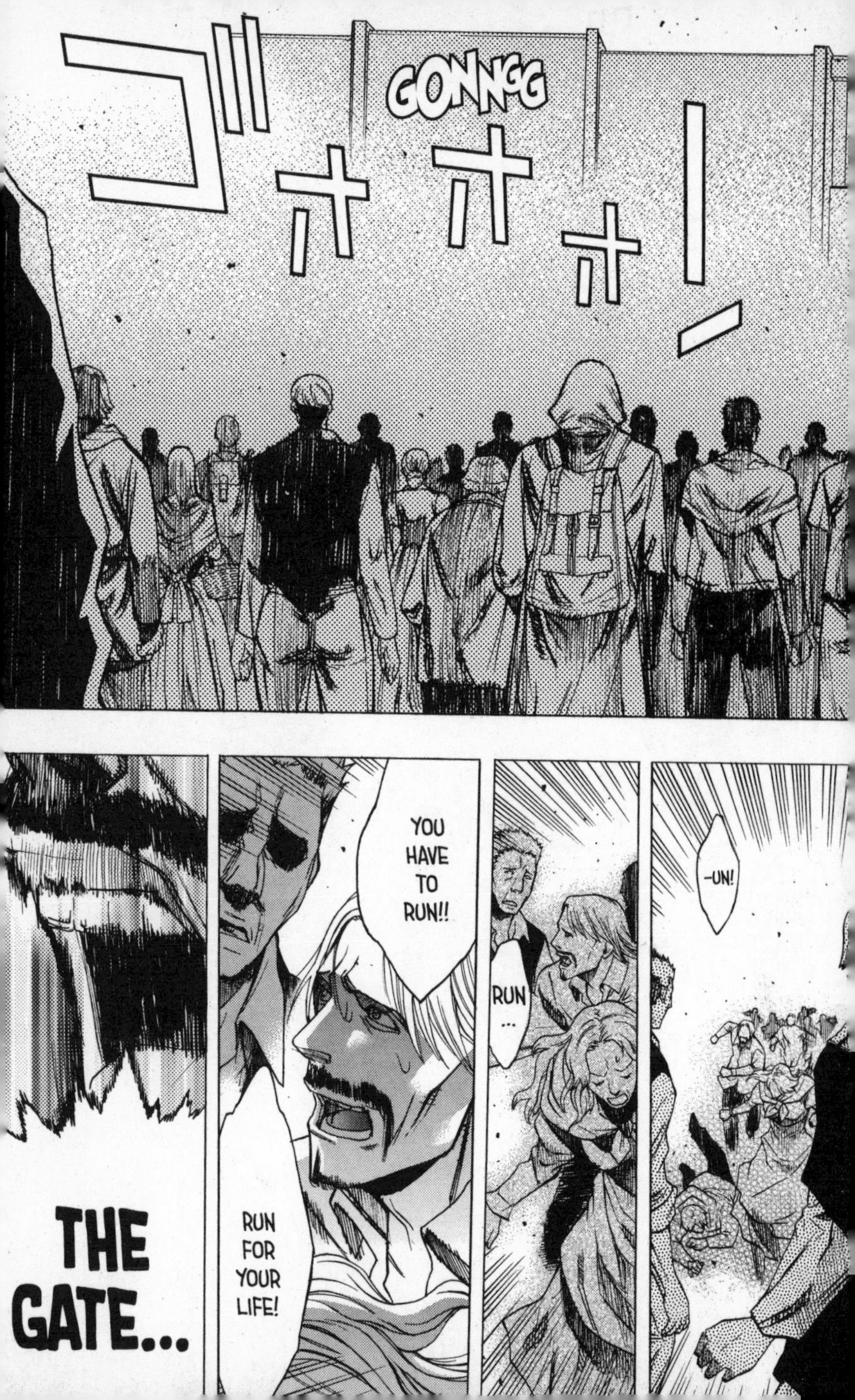
ゴォォォーン
GONNGG
–UN!
RUN...
YOU HAVE TO RUN!!
RUN FOR YOUR LIFE!
THE GATE...

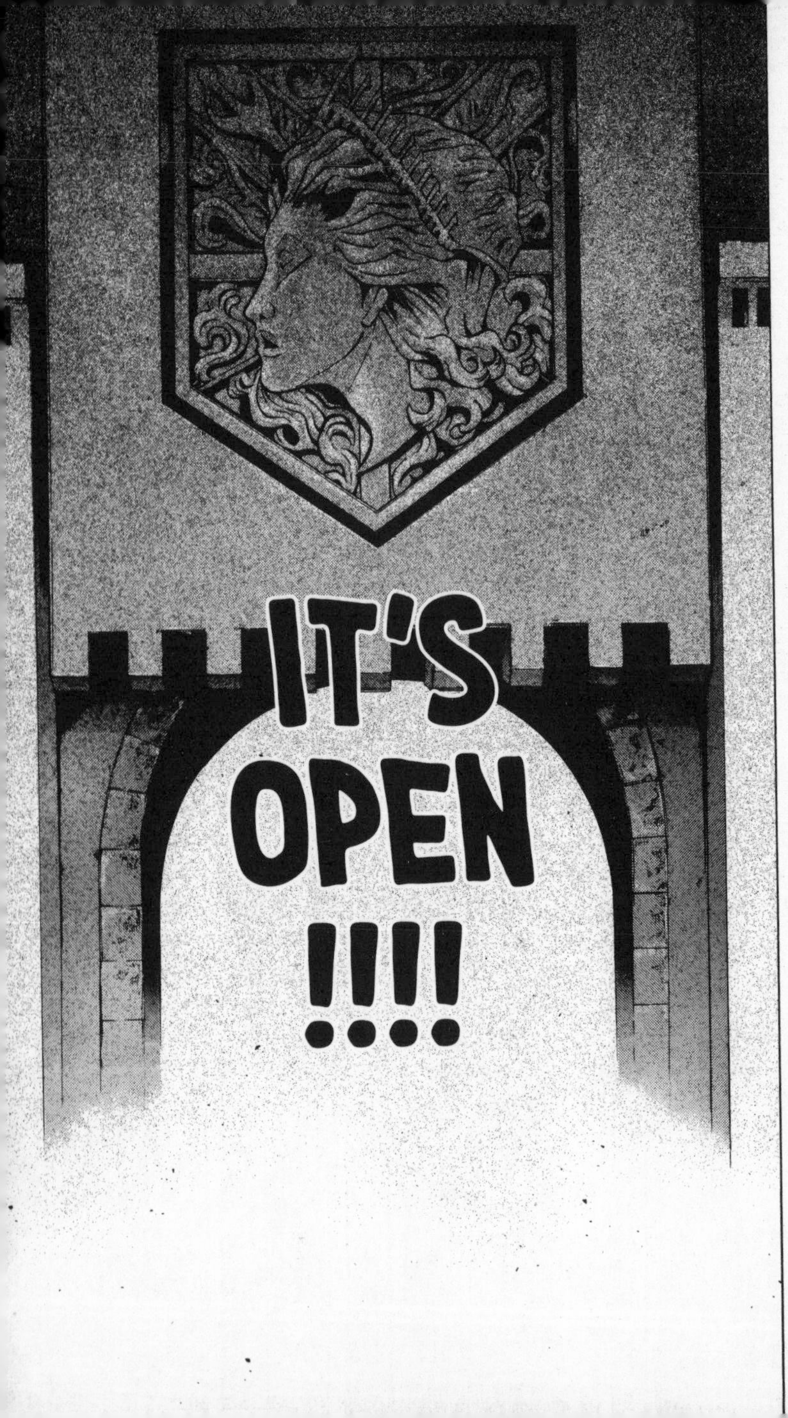
IT'S OPEN !!!!

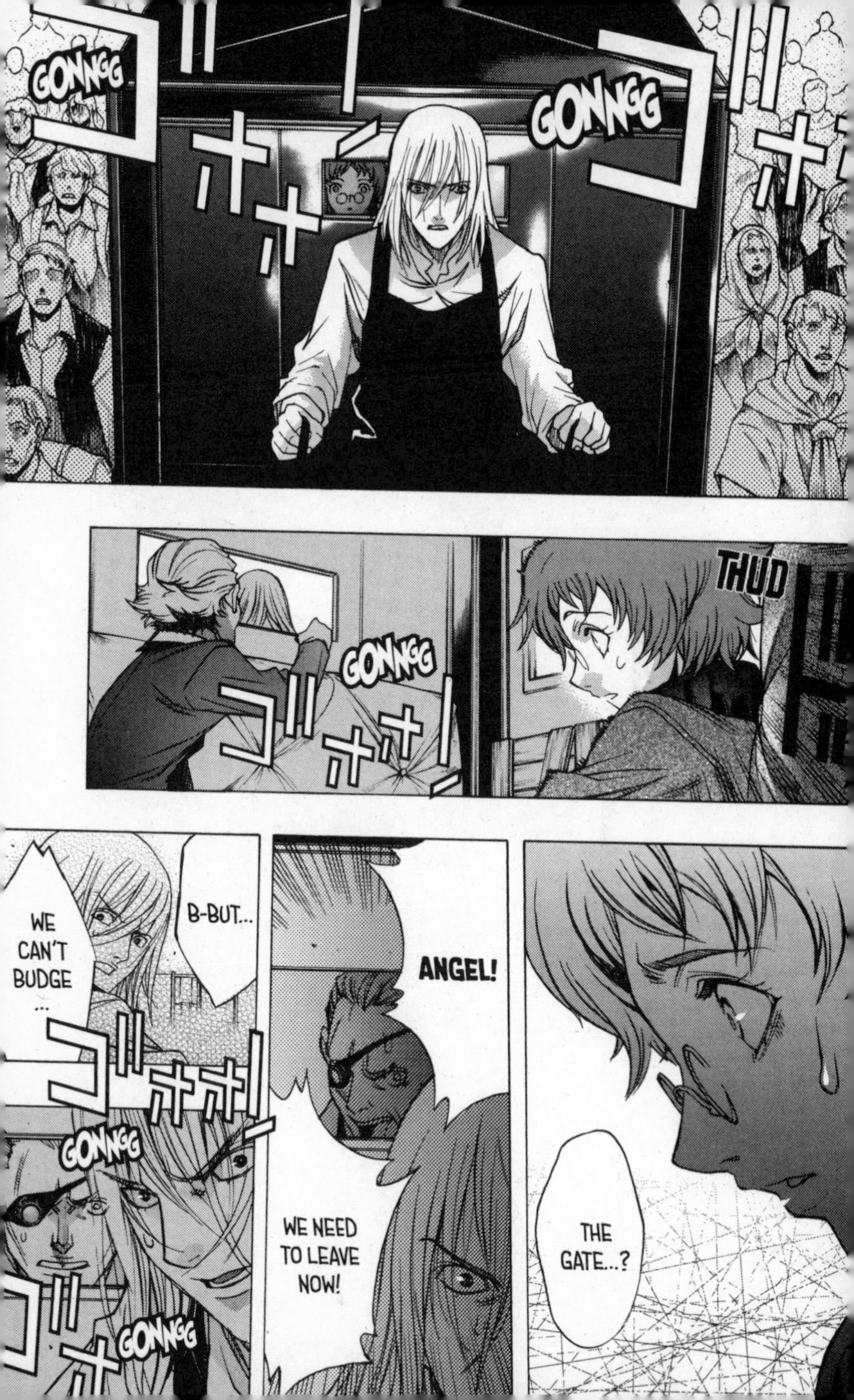
GONNGG
GONNGG
THUD
GONNGG
THE GATE...?
ANGEL!
WE NEED TO LEAVE NOW!
B-BUT...
WE CAN'T BUDGE...
GONNGG
GONNGG

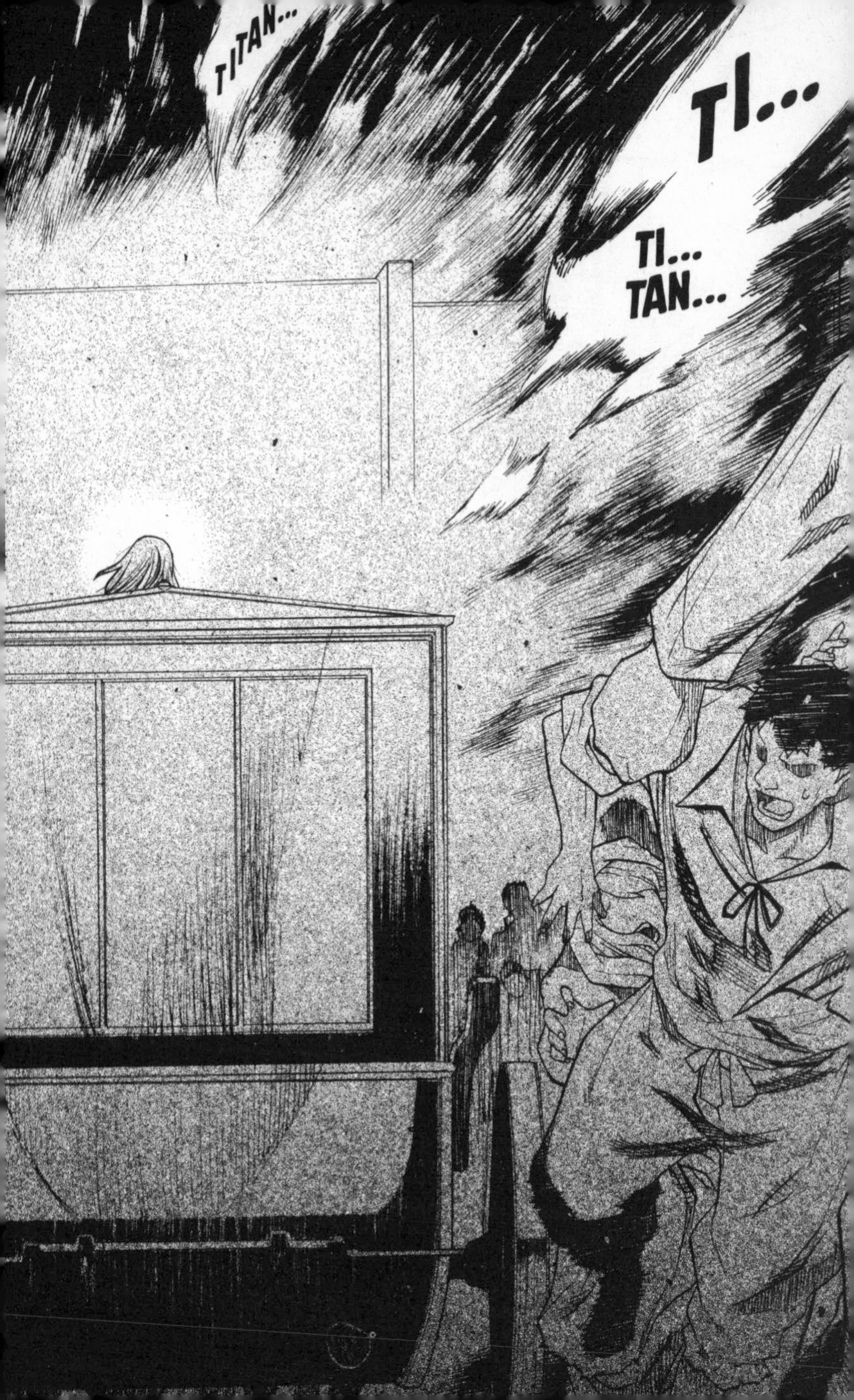
TI...
TITAN...
TI... TAN...

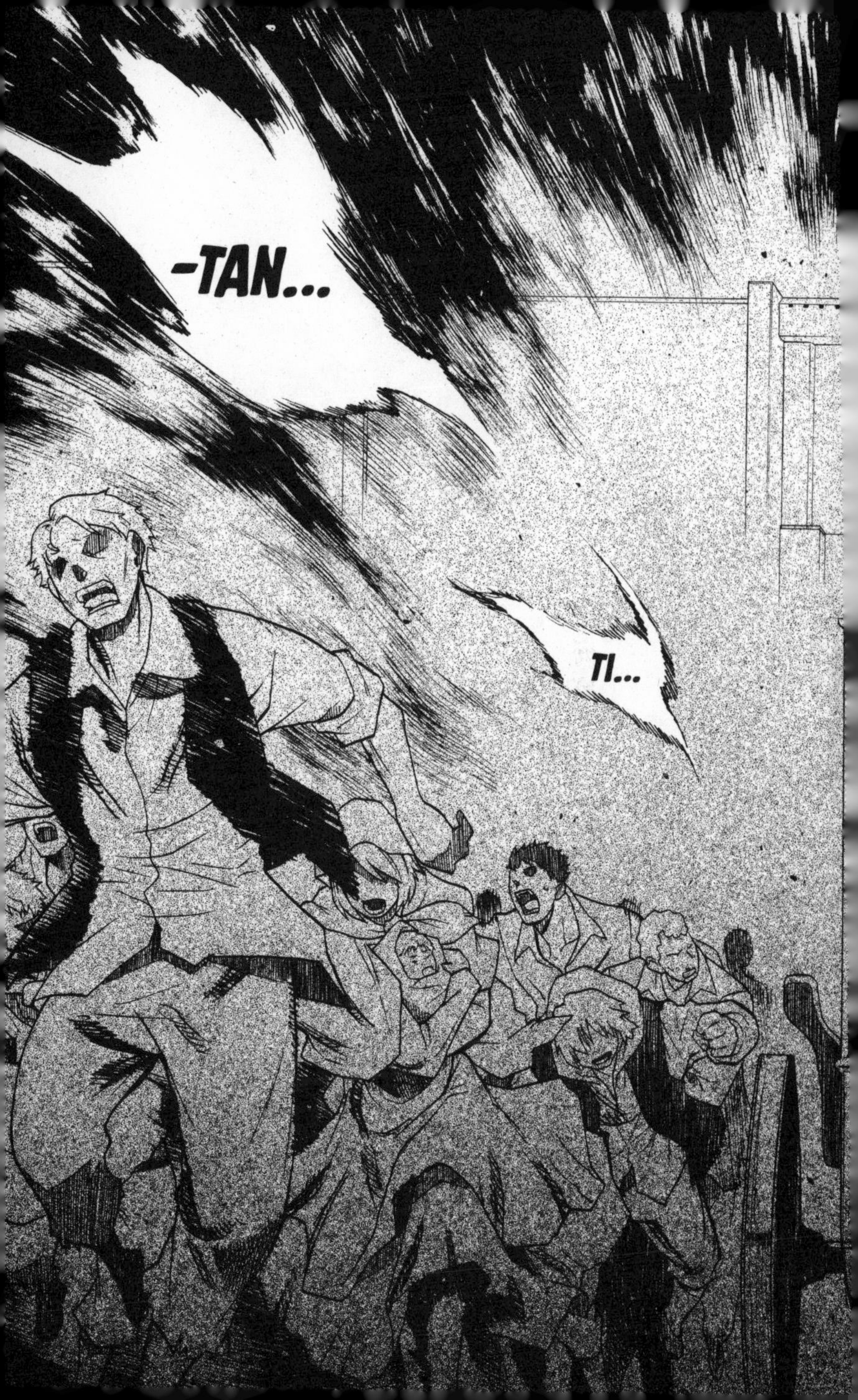
TI...
-TAN...

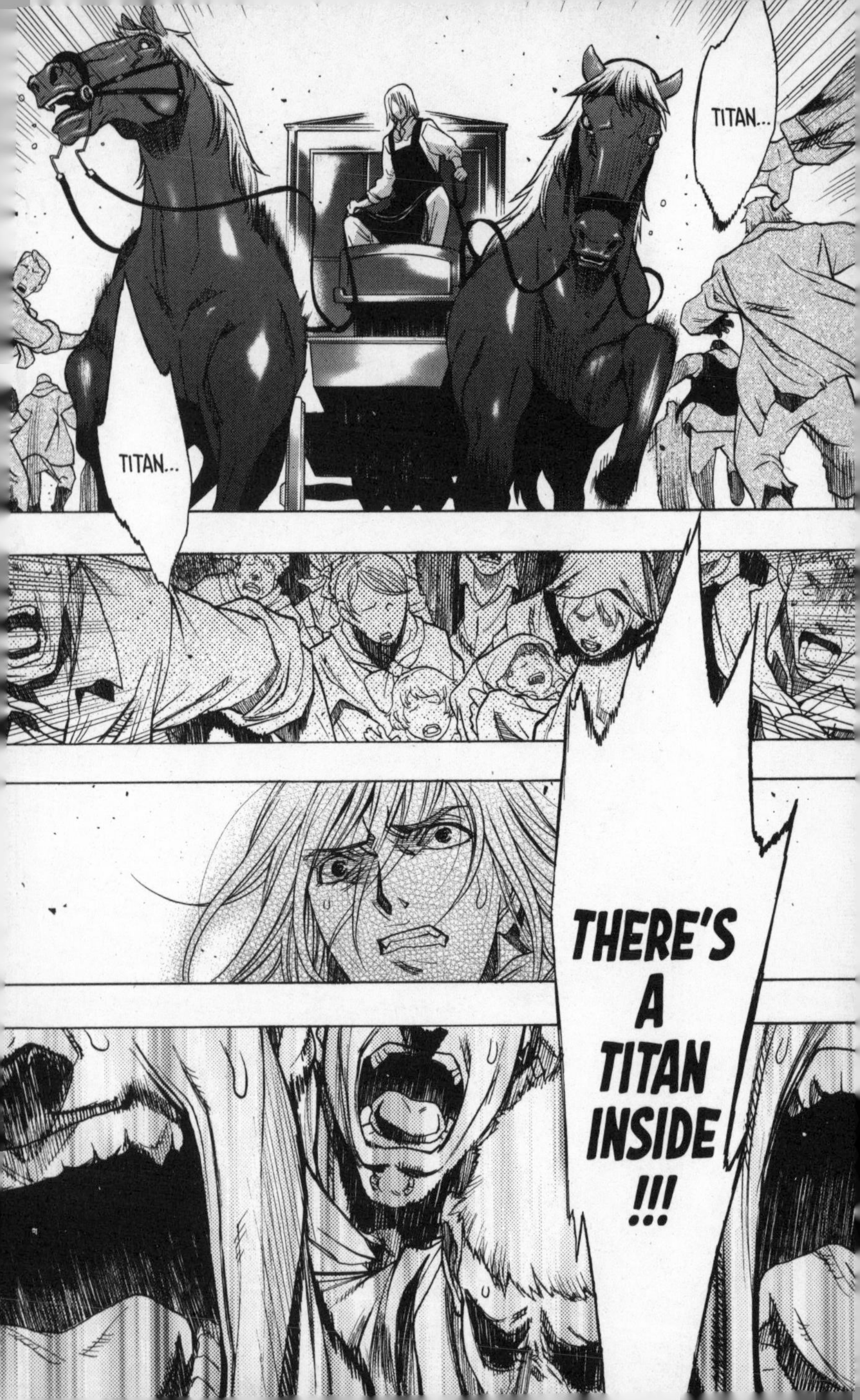
TITAN...
TITAN...
THERE'S A TITAN INSIDE !!!

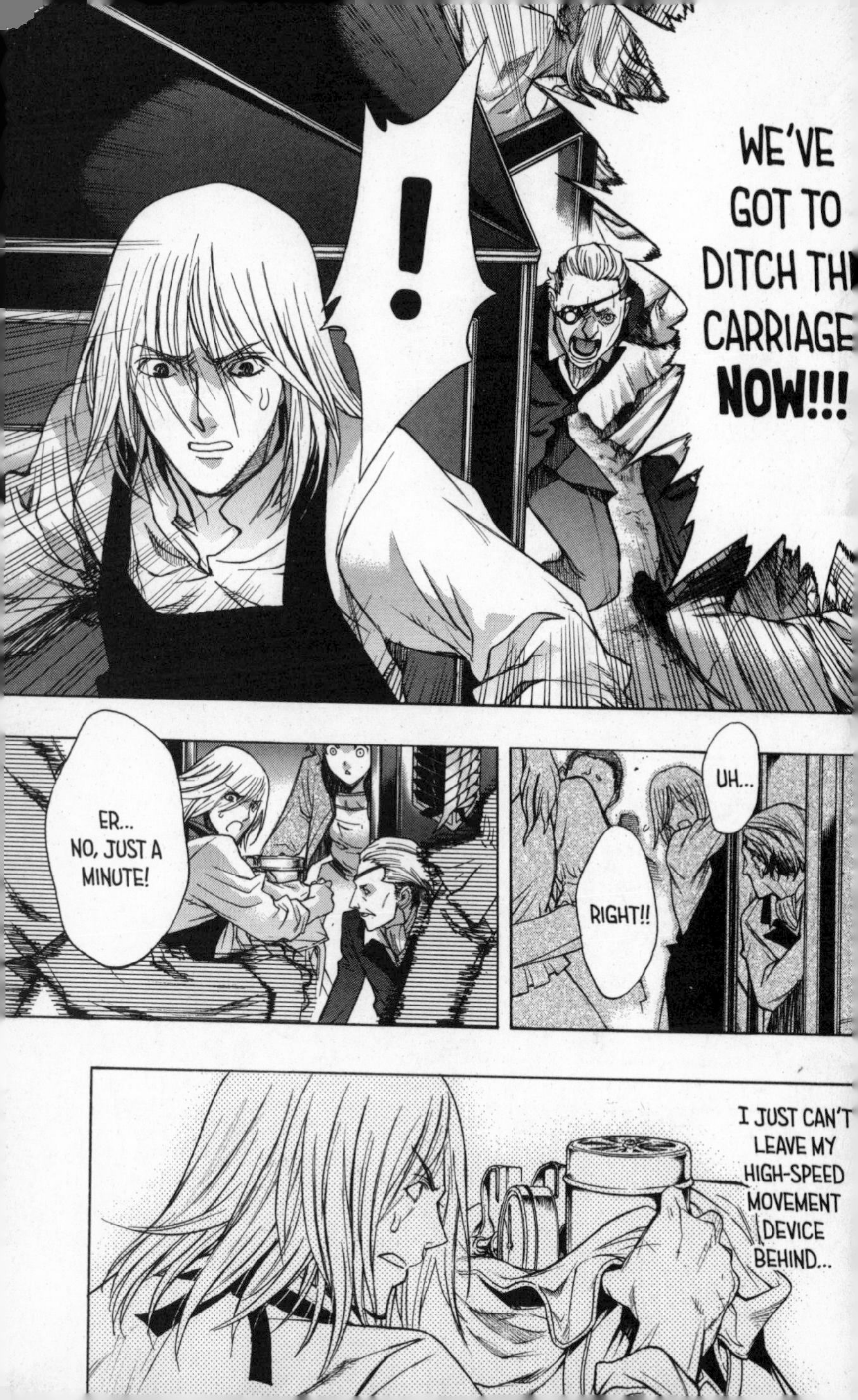
WE'VE GOT TO DITCH TH CARRIAGE NOW!!!
!
UH...
RIGHT!!
ER... NO, JUST A MINUTE!
I JUST CAN'T LEAVE MY HIGH-SPEED MOVEMENT DEVICE BEHIND...

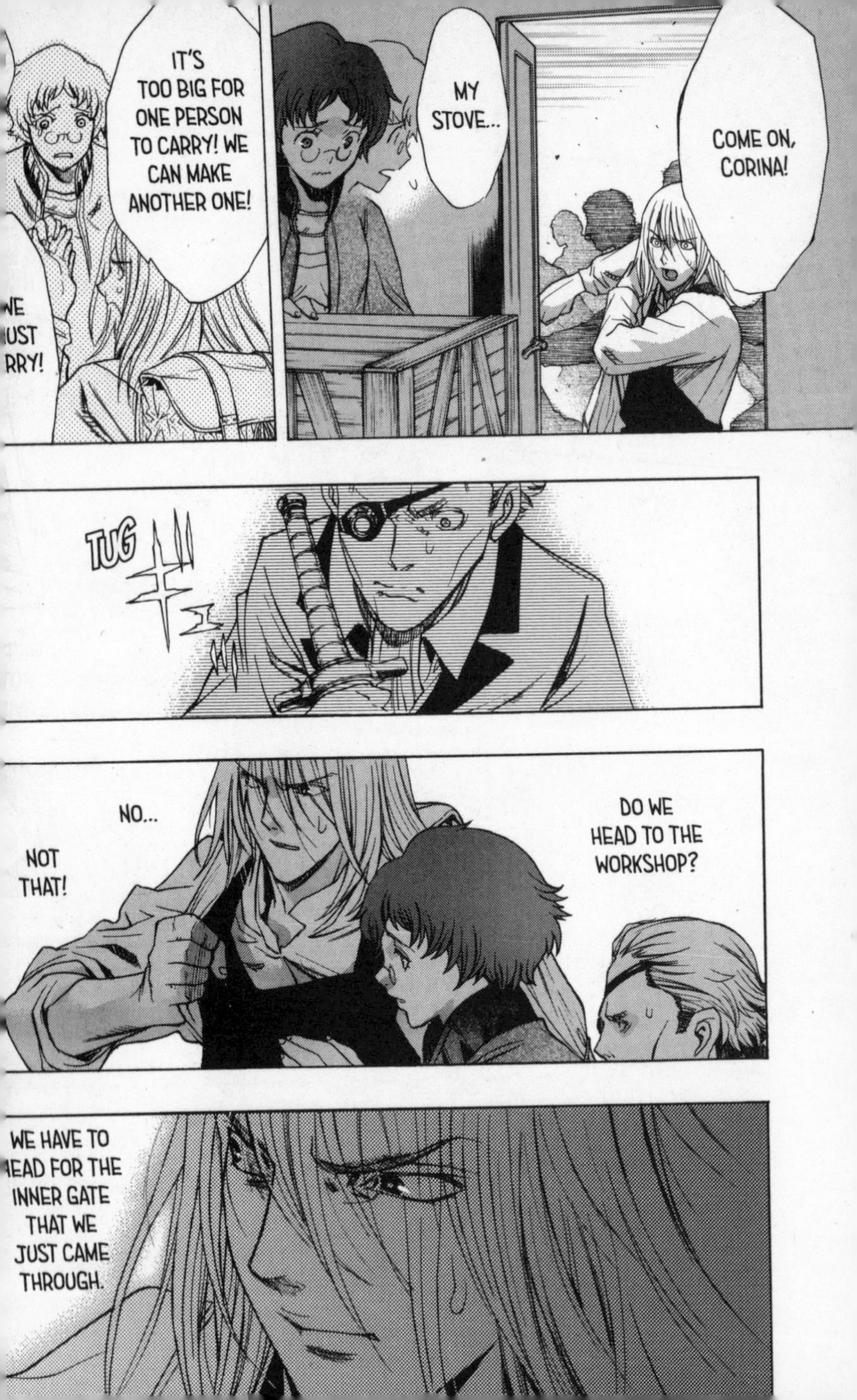
COME ON, CORINA!
MY STOVE...
IT'S TOO BIG FOR ONE PERSON TO CARRY! WE CAN MAKE ANOTHER ONE!
TUG
DO WE HEAD TO THE WORKSHOP?
NO...
NOT THAT!
WE HAVE TO HEAD FOR THE INNER GATE THAT WE JUST CAME THROUGH.

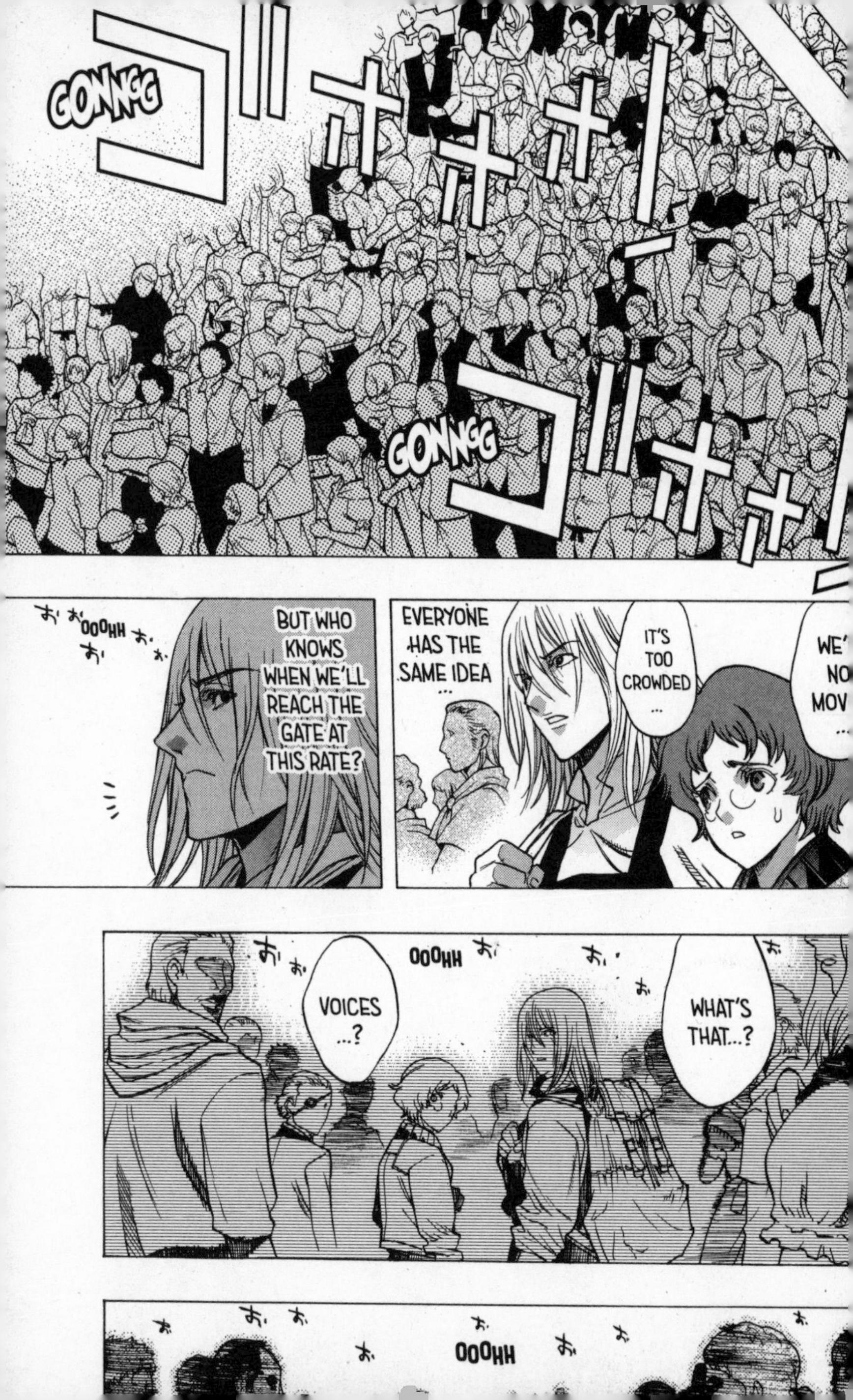
GONNGG
GONNGG
WE' NO MOV ...
IT'S TOO CROWDED ...
EVERYONE HAS THE SAME IDEA ...
BUT WHO KNOWS WHEN WE'LL REACH THE GATE AT THIS RATE?
OOOHH
WHAT'S THAT...?
OOOHH
VOICES ...?
OOOHH

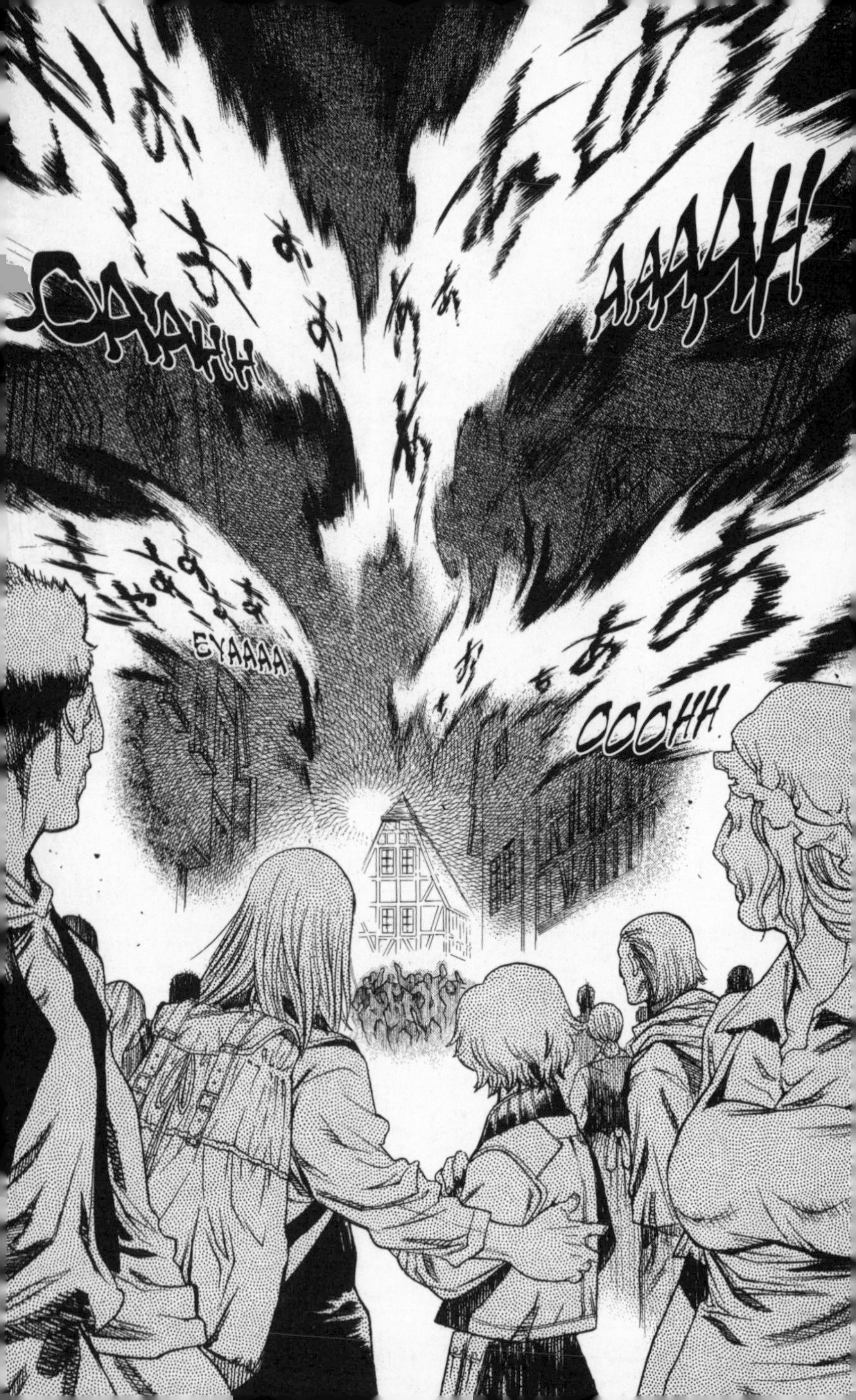
AAAAH
OAAHH
OOOHH
EYAAAA

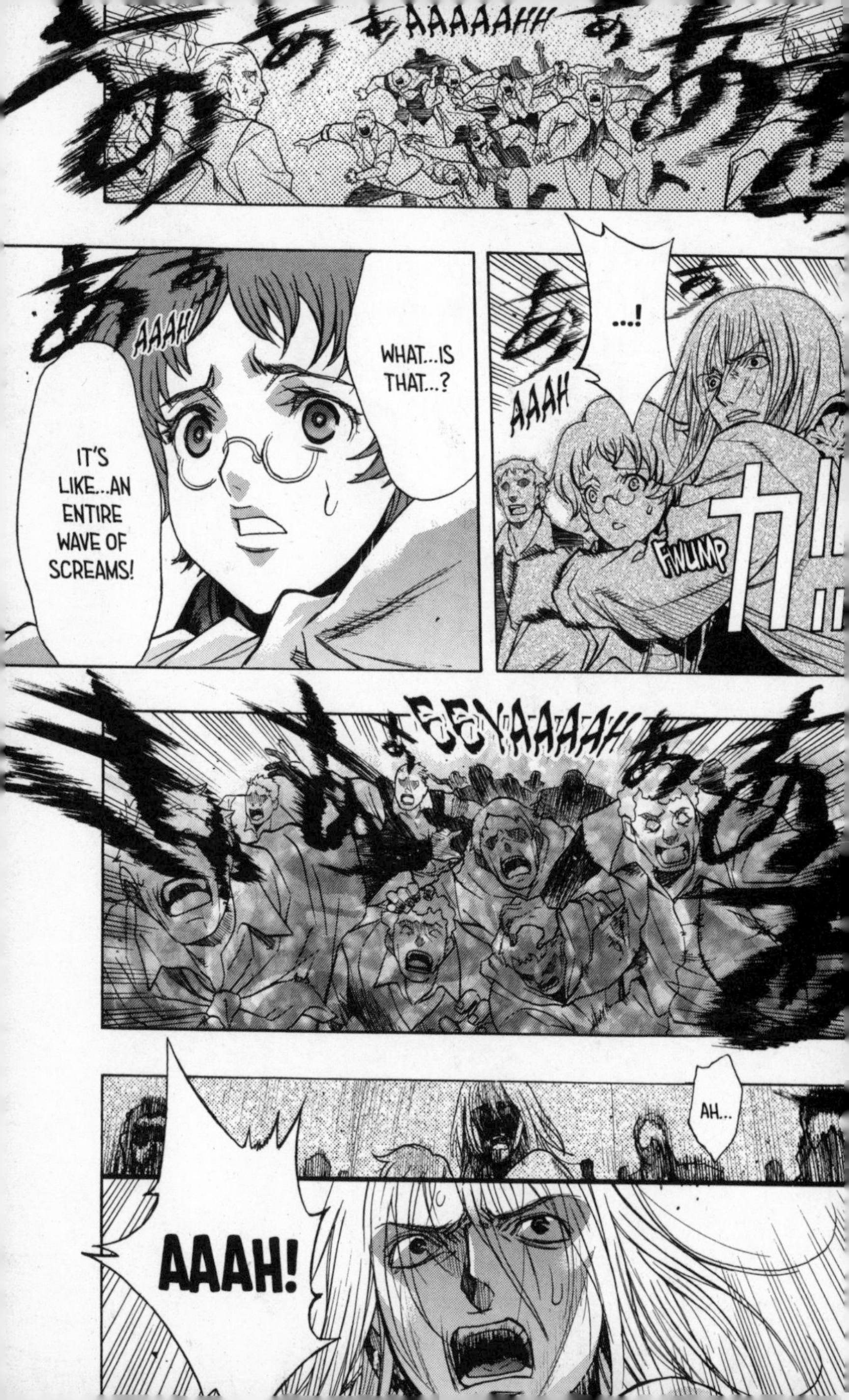
AAAAAHH
...!
AAAH
FWUMP
WHAT...IS THAT...?
AAAH!
IT'S LIKE...AN ENTIRE WAVE OF SCREAMS!
EEEYAAAAAH
AH...
AAAH!

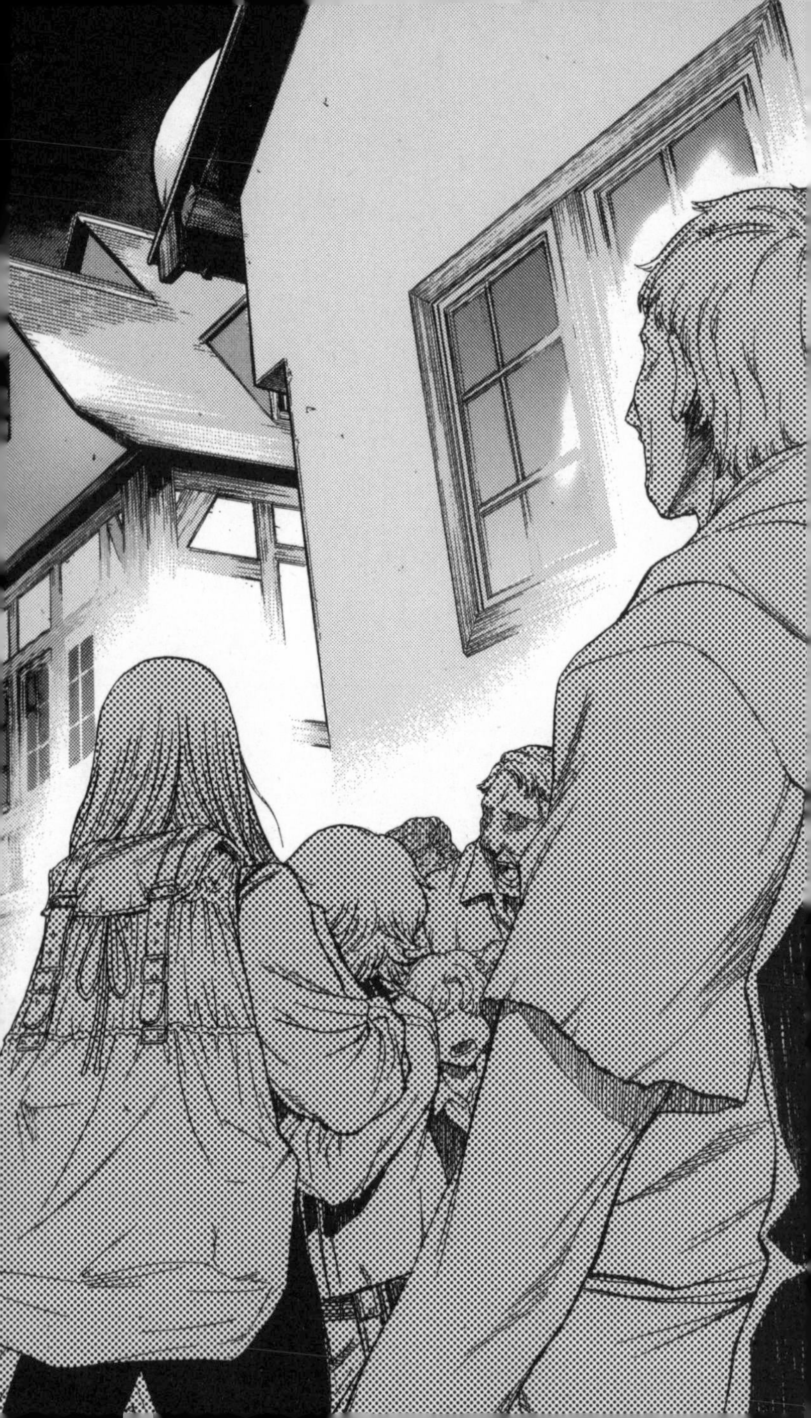

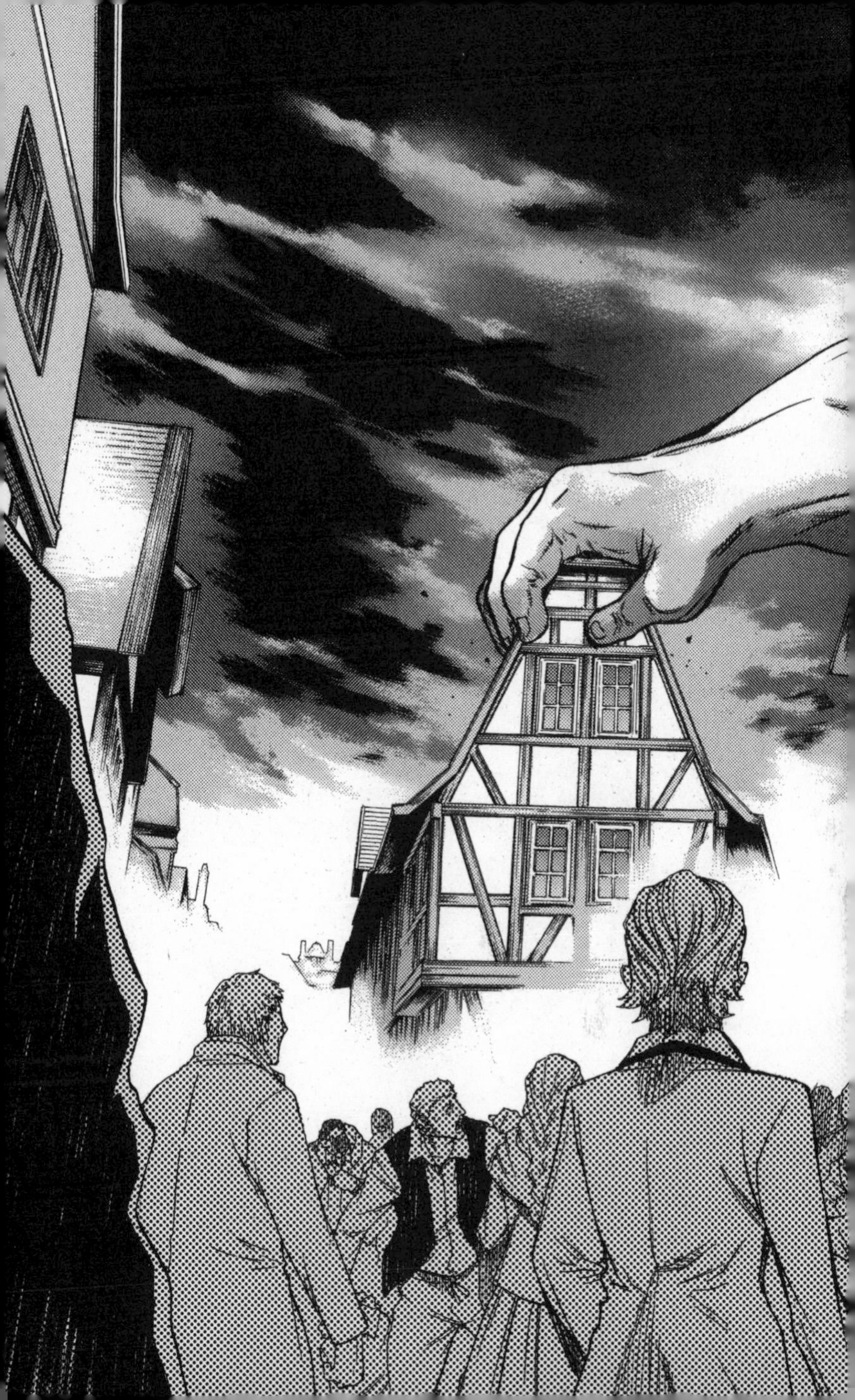

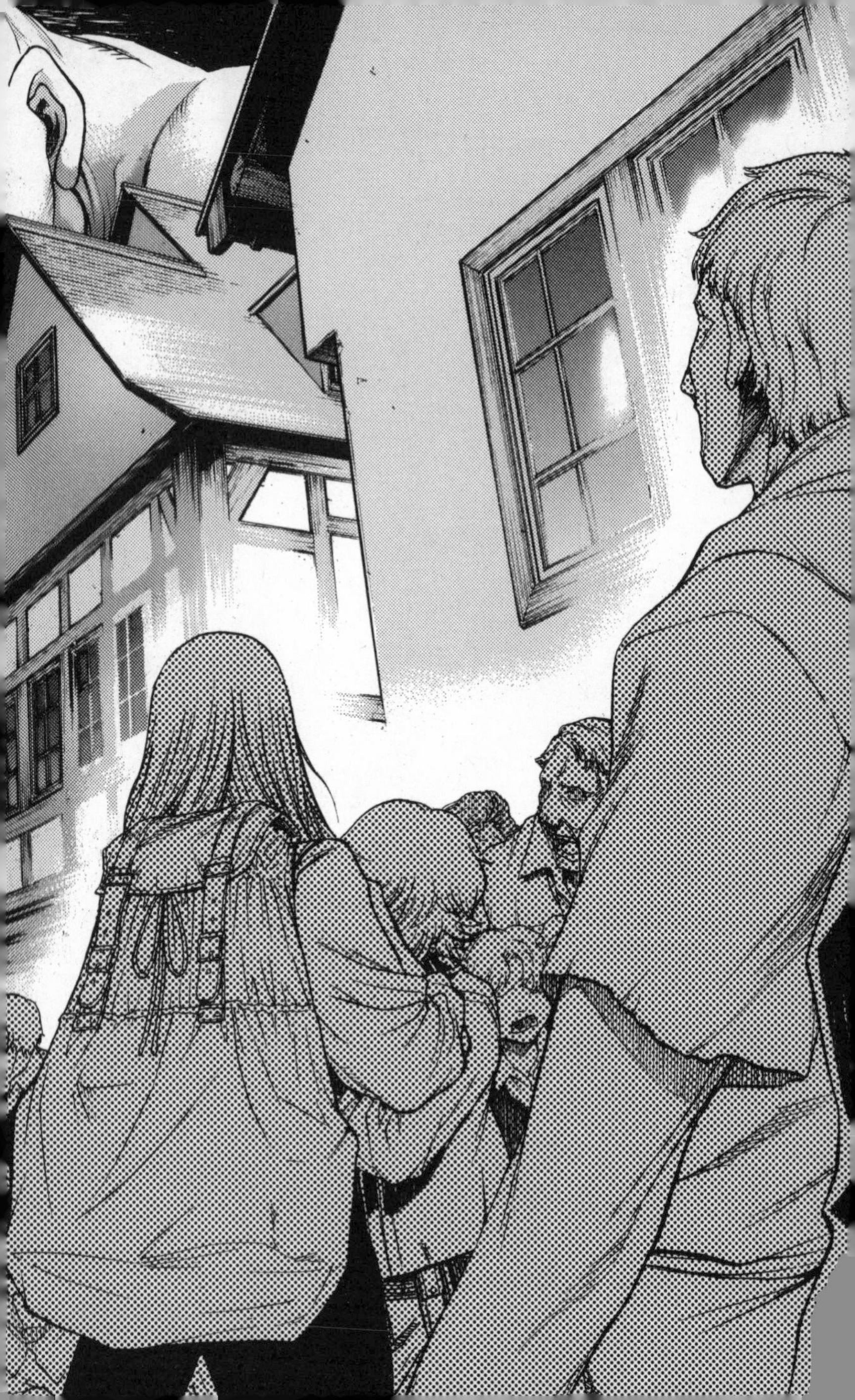

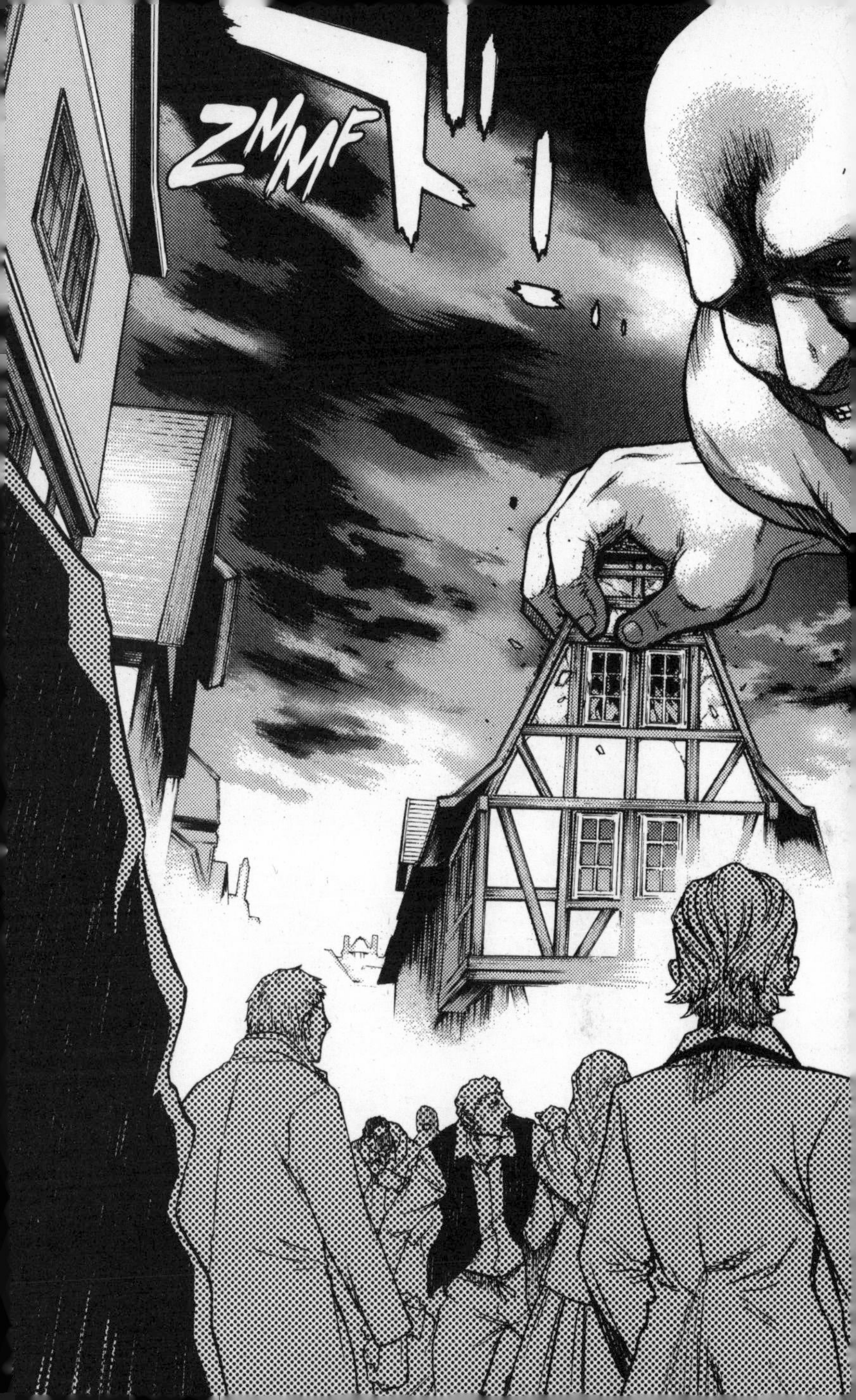
ZMMF

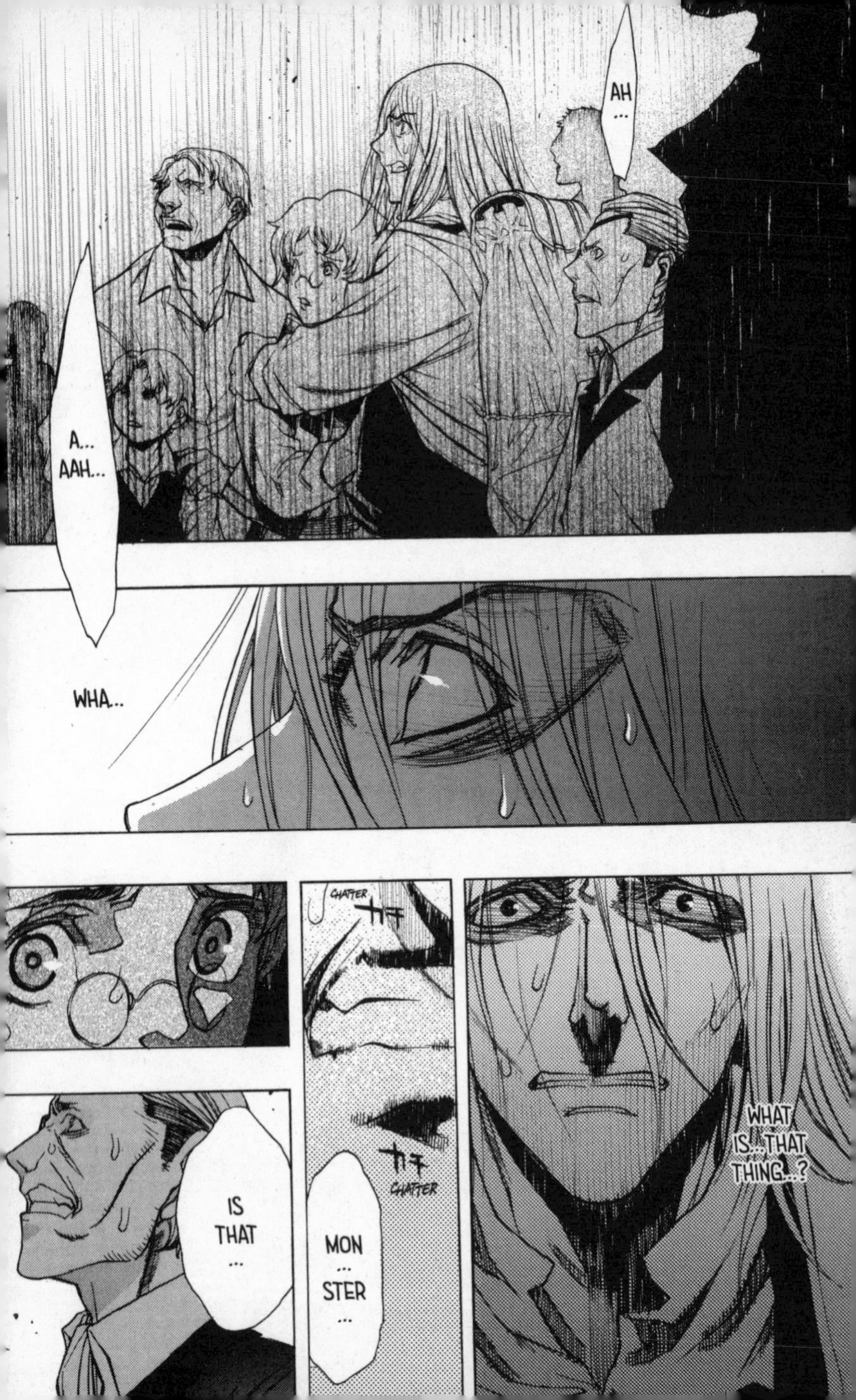
AH...
A... AAH...
WHA...
WHAT IS... THAT THING...?
CHATTER
カチ
カチ
CHATTER
MON... STER...
IS THAT ...

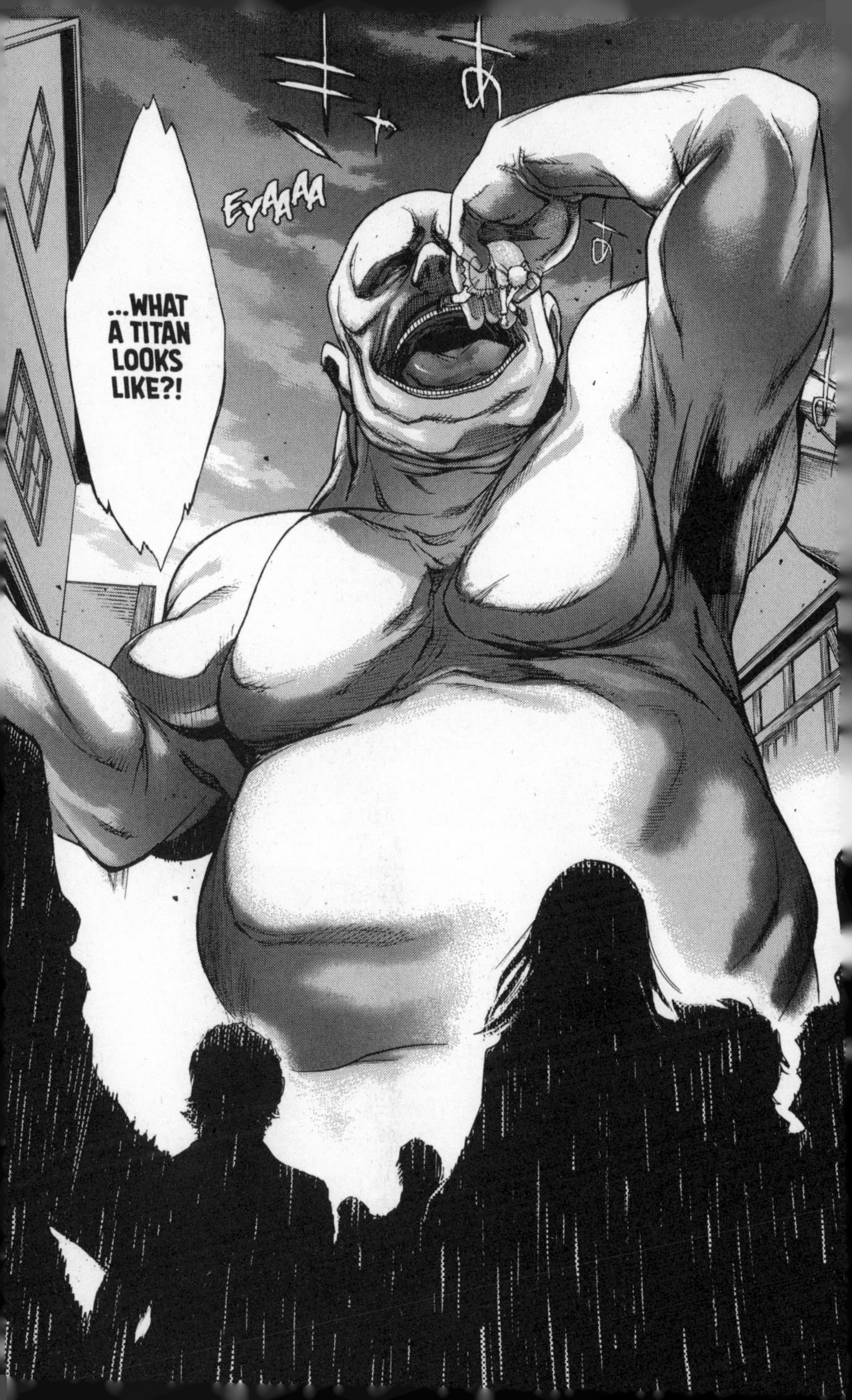
...WHAT A TITAN LOOKS LIKE?!
EYAAAAA

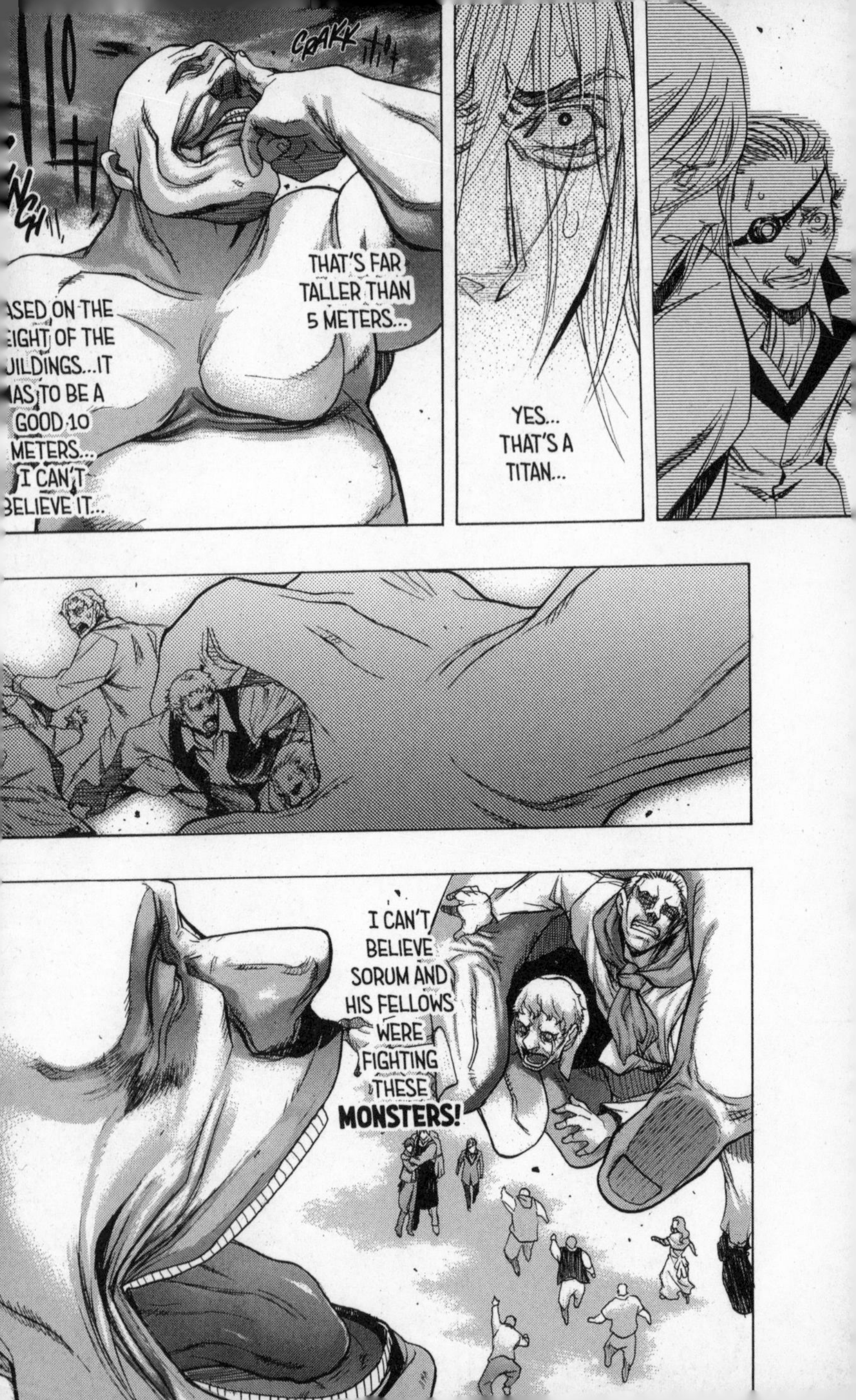
YES... THAT'S A TITAN...
CRAKK
THAT'S FAR TALLER THAN 5 METERS...
ASED ON THE EIGHT OF THE UILDINGS...IT HAS TO BE A GOOD 10 METERS... I CAN'T BELIEVE IT...
I CAN'T BELIEVE SORUM AND HIS FELLOWS WERE FIGHTING THESE **MONSTERS!**

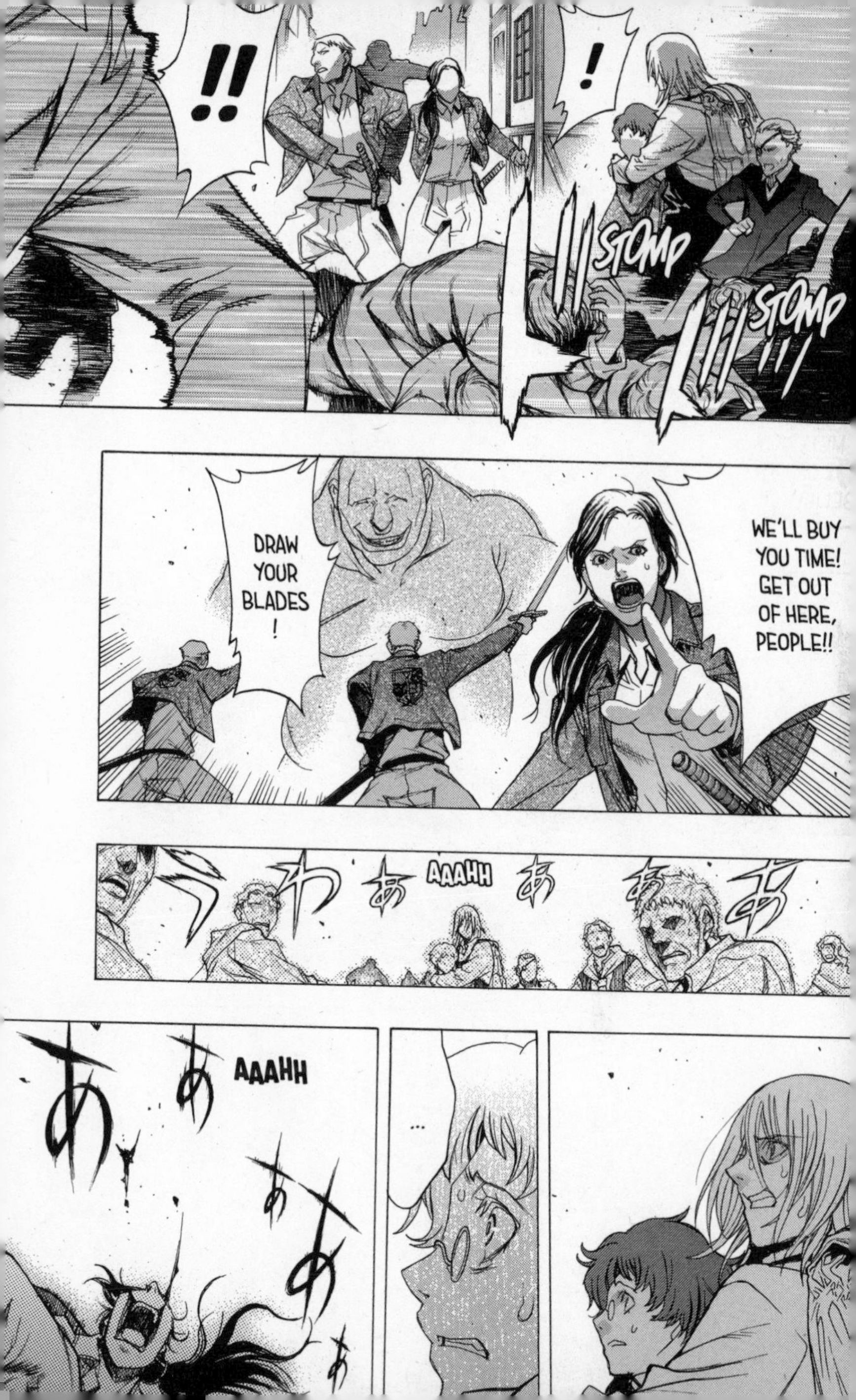
!
!!
STOMP
STOMP
WE'LL BUY YOU TIME! GET OUT OF HERE, PEOPLE!!
DRAW YOUR BLADES!
AAAHH
...
AAAHH

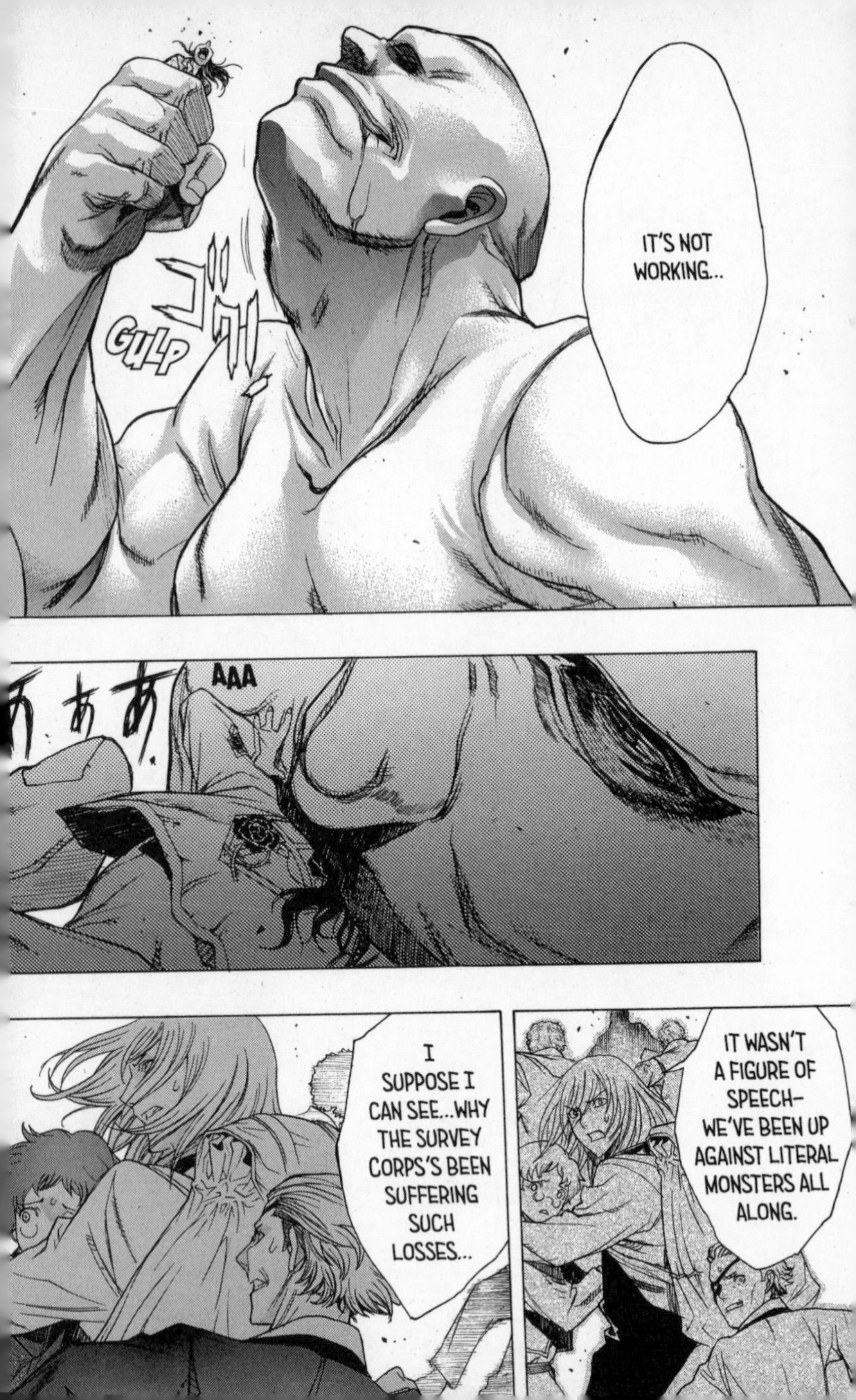
IT'S NOT WORKING...
GULP
AAA
IT WASN'T A FIGURE OF SPEECH— WE'VE BEEN UP AGAINST LITERAL MONSTERS ALL ALONG.
I SUPPOSE I CAN SEE...WHY THE SURVEY CORPS'S BEEN SUFFERING SUCH LOSSES...

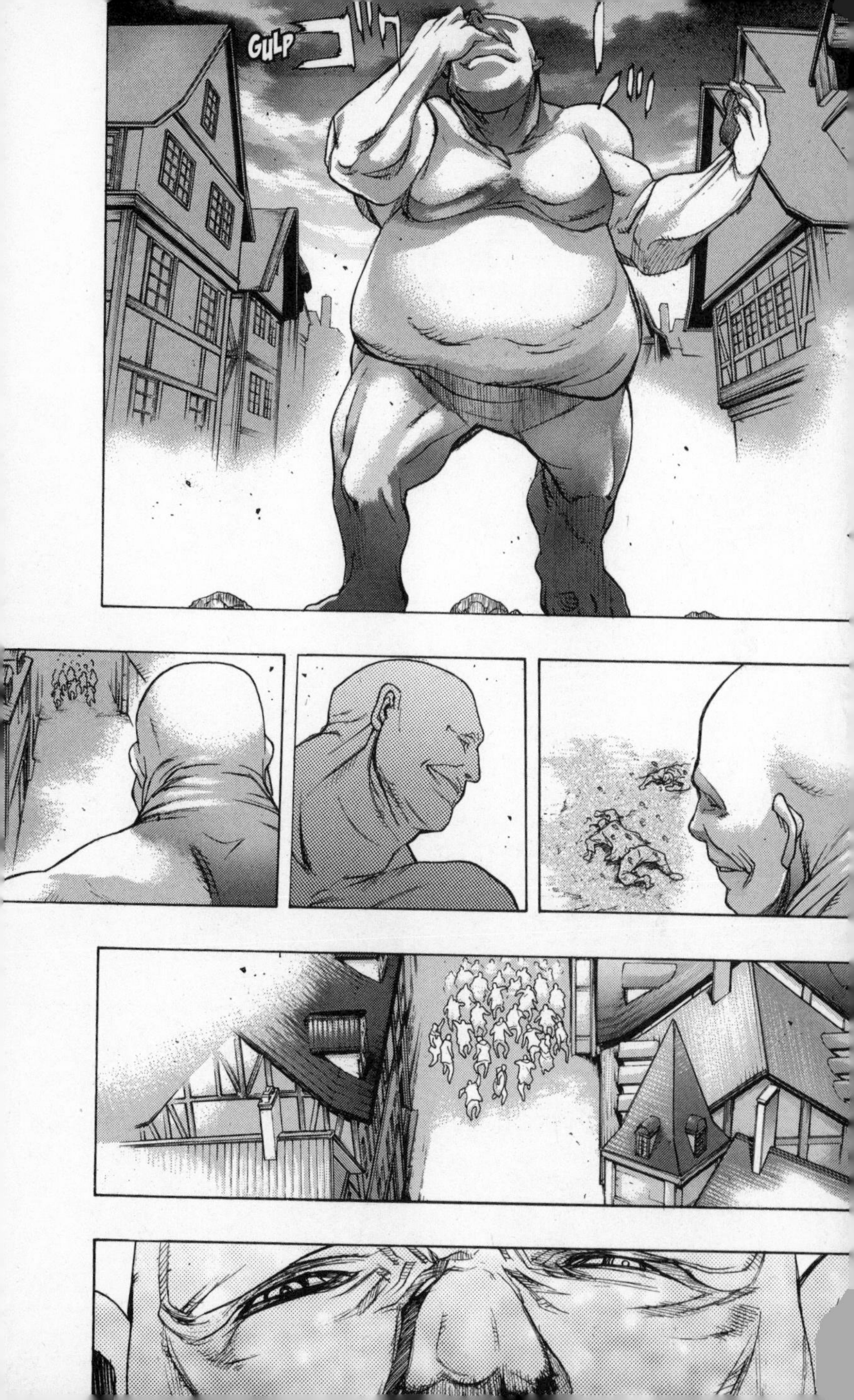
GULP

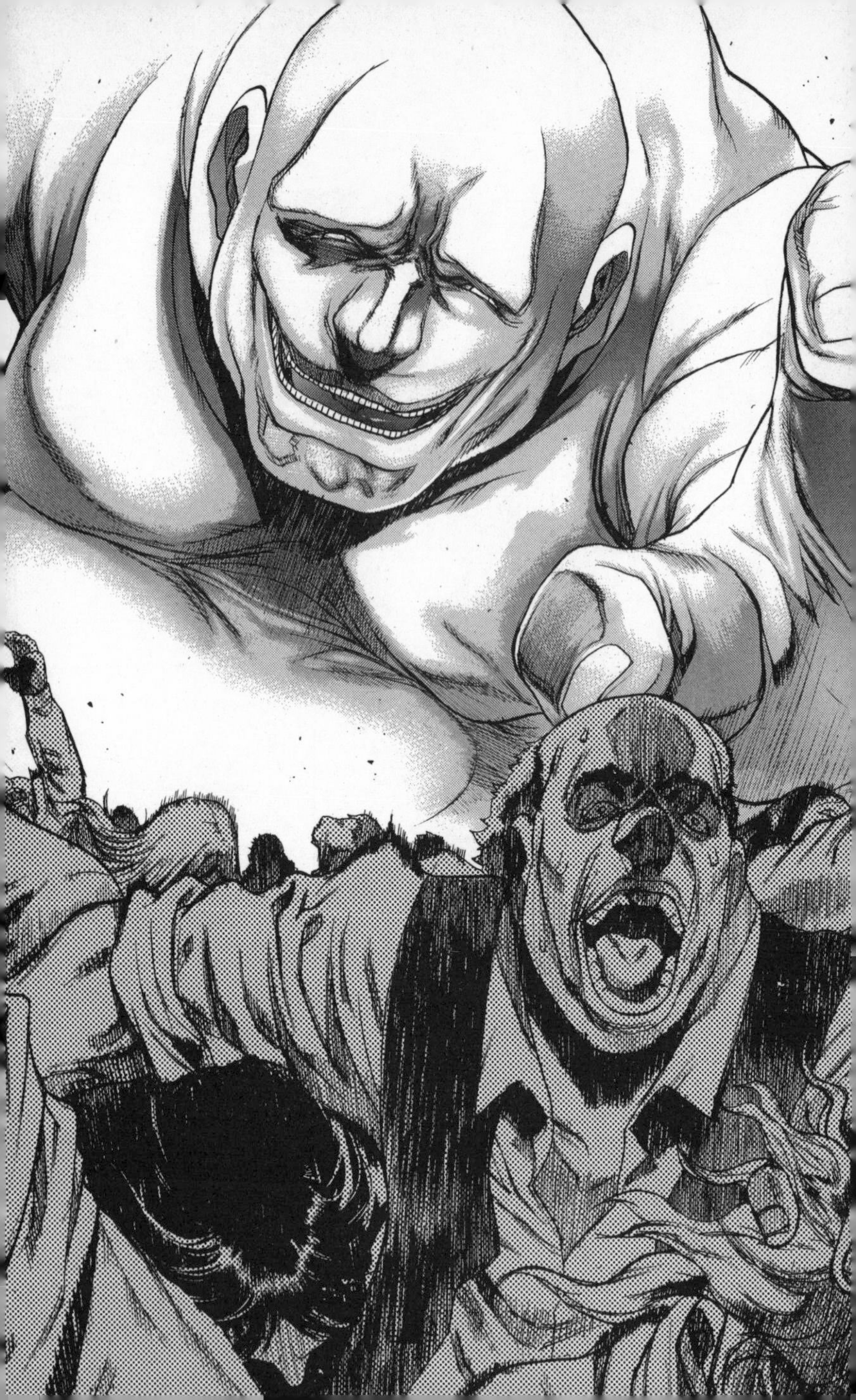

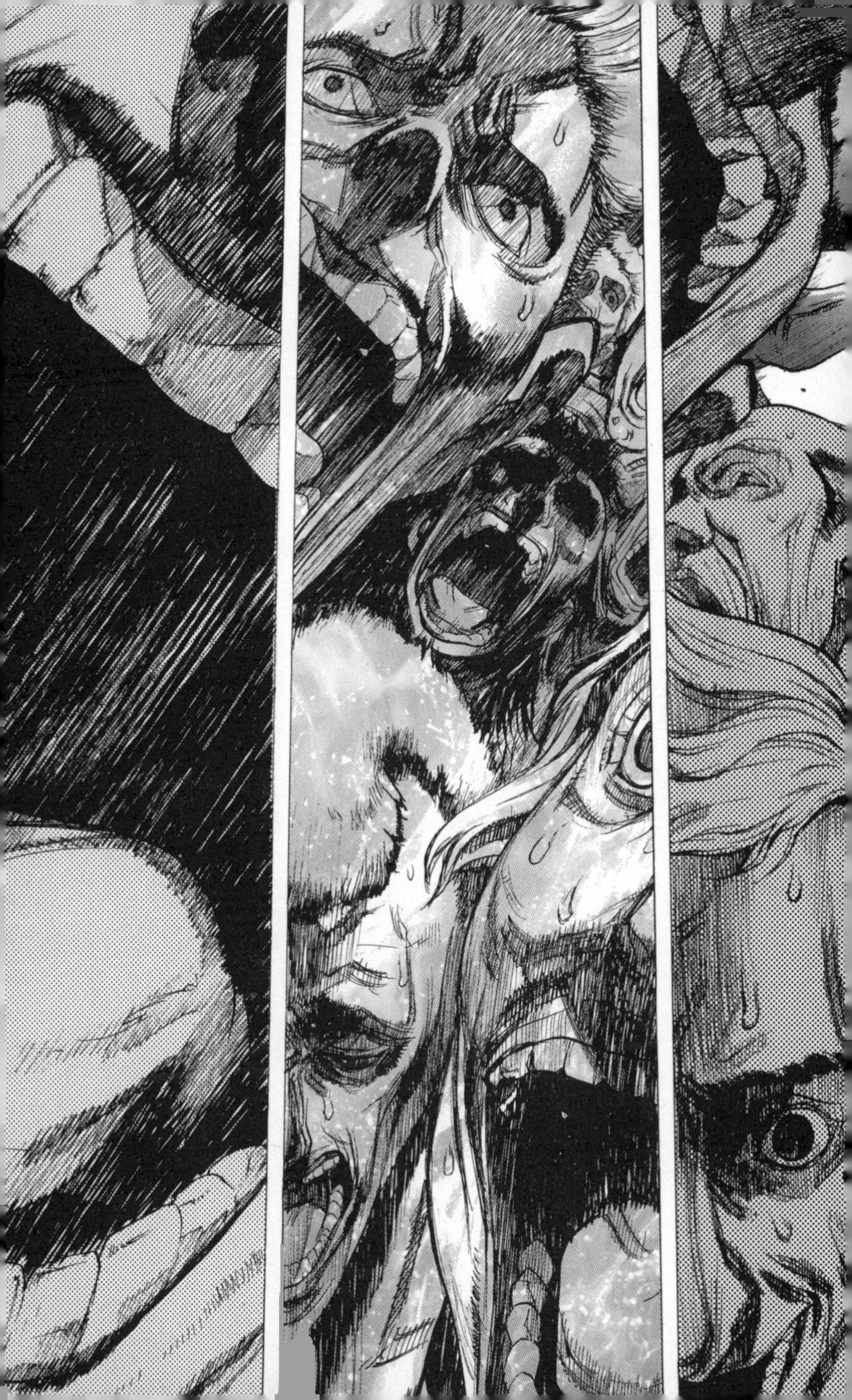

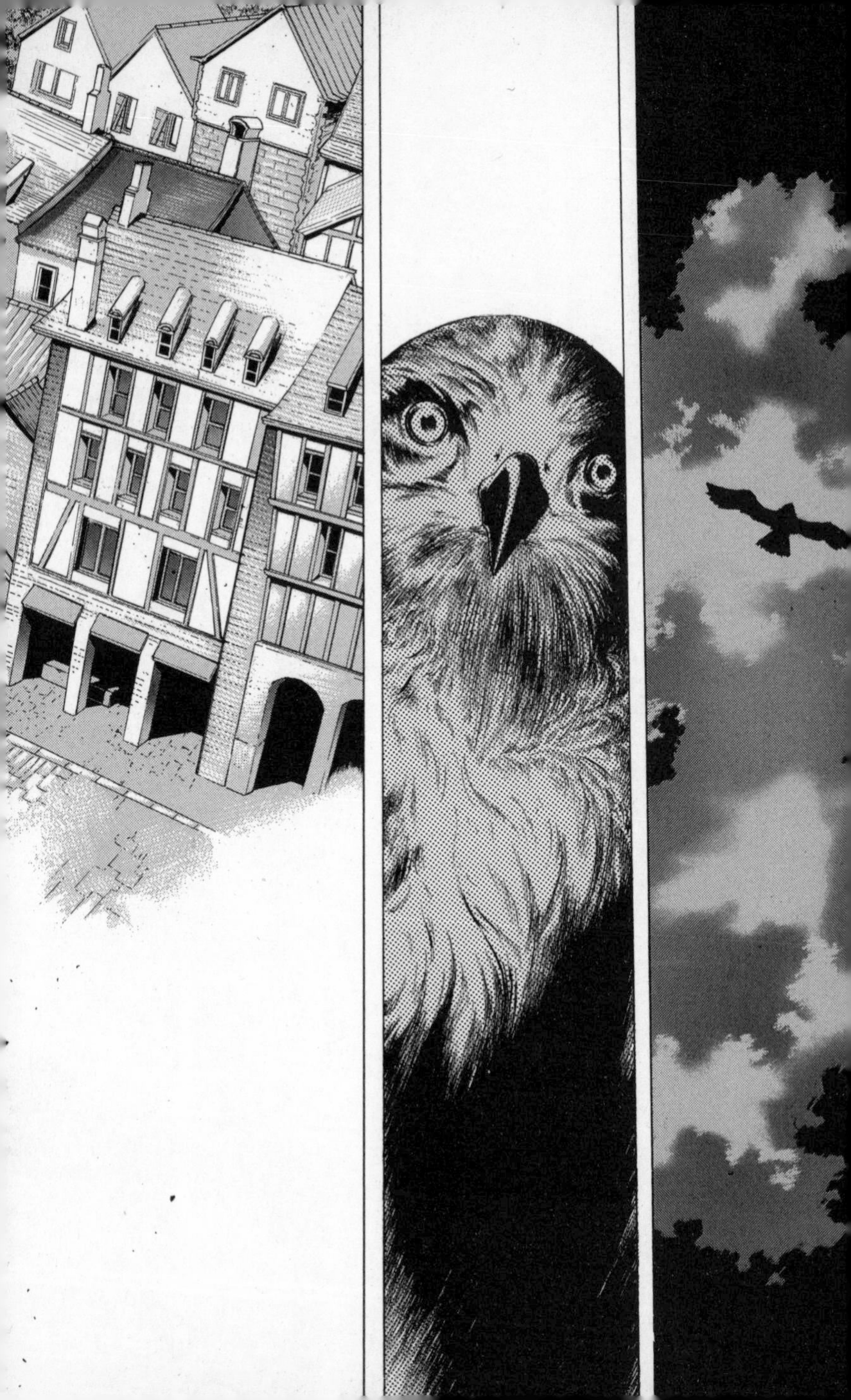

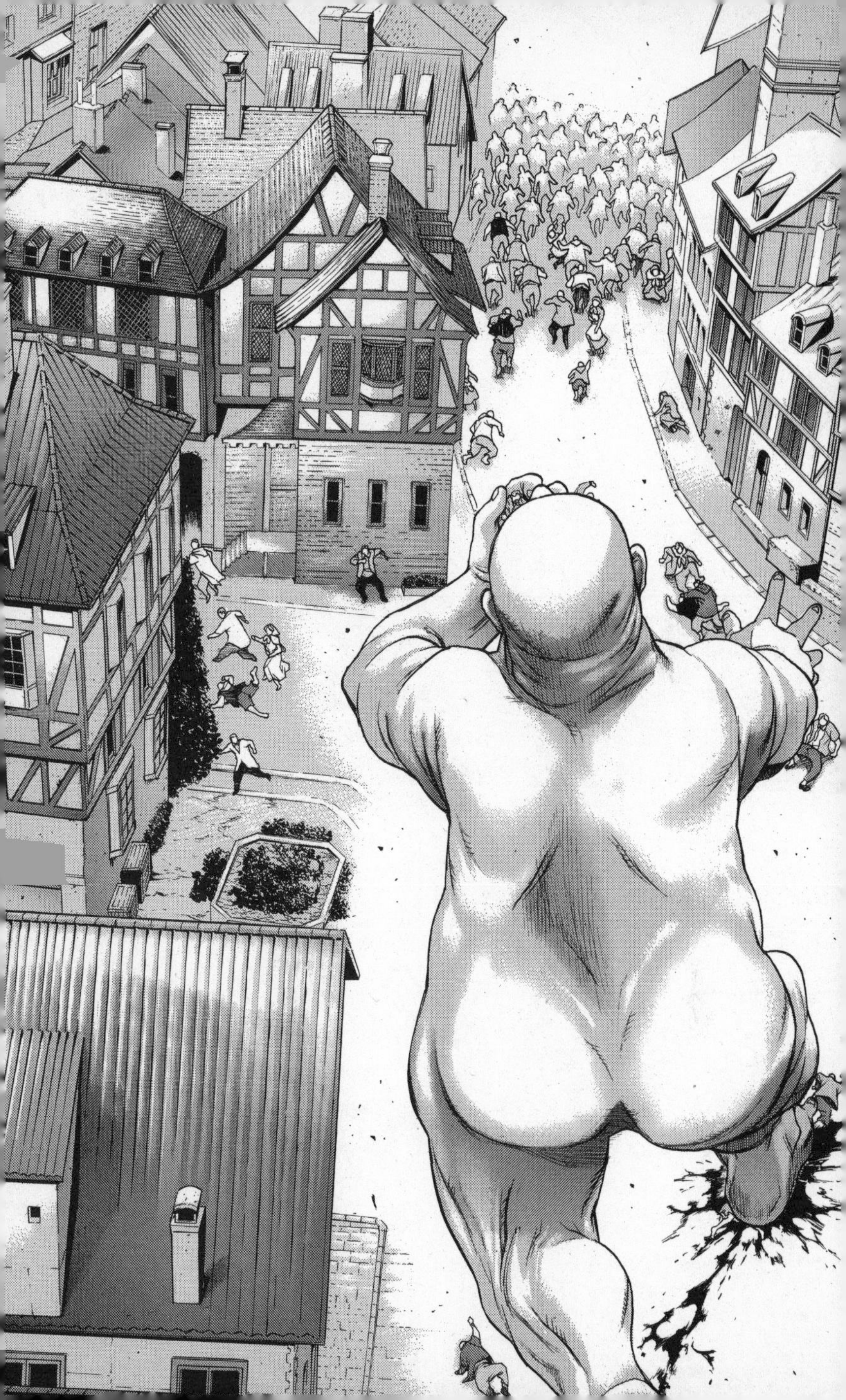

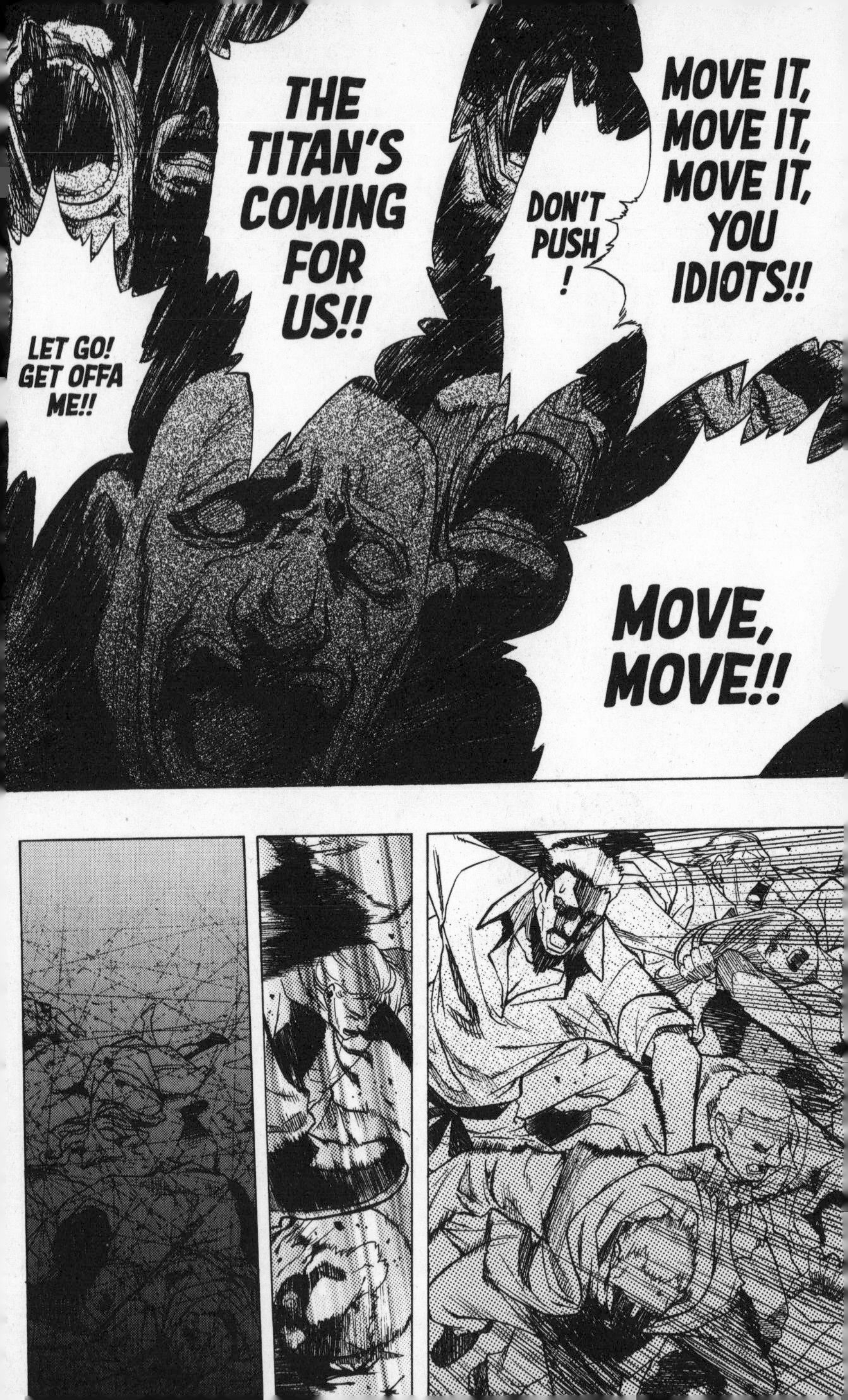
MOVE IT, MOVE IT, MOVE IT, YOU IDIOTS!!
DON'T PUSH!
THE TITAN'S COMING FOR US!!
MOVE, MOVE!!
LET GO! GET OFFA ME!!

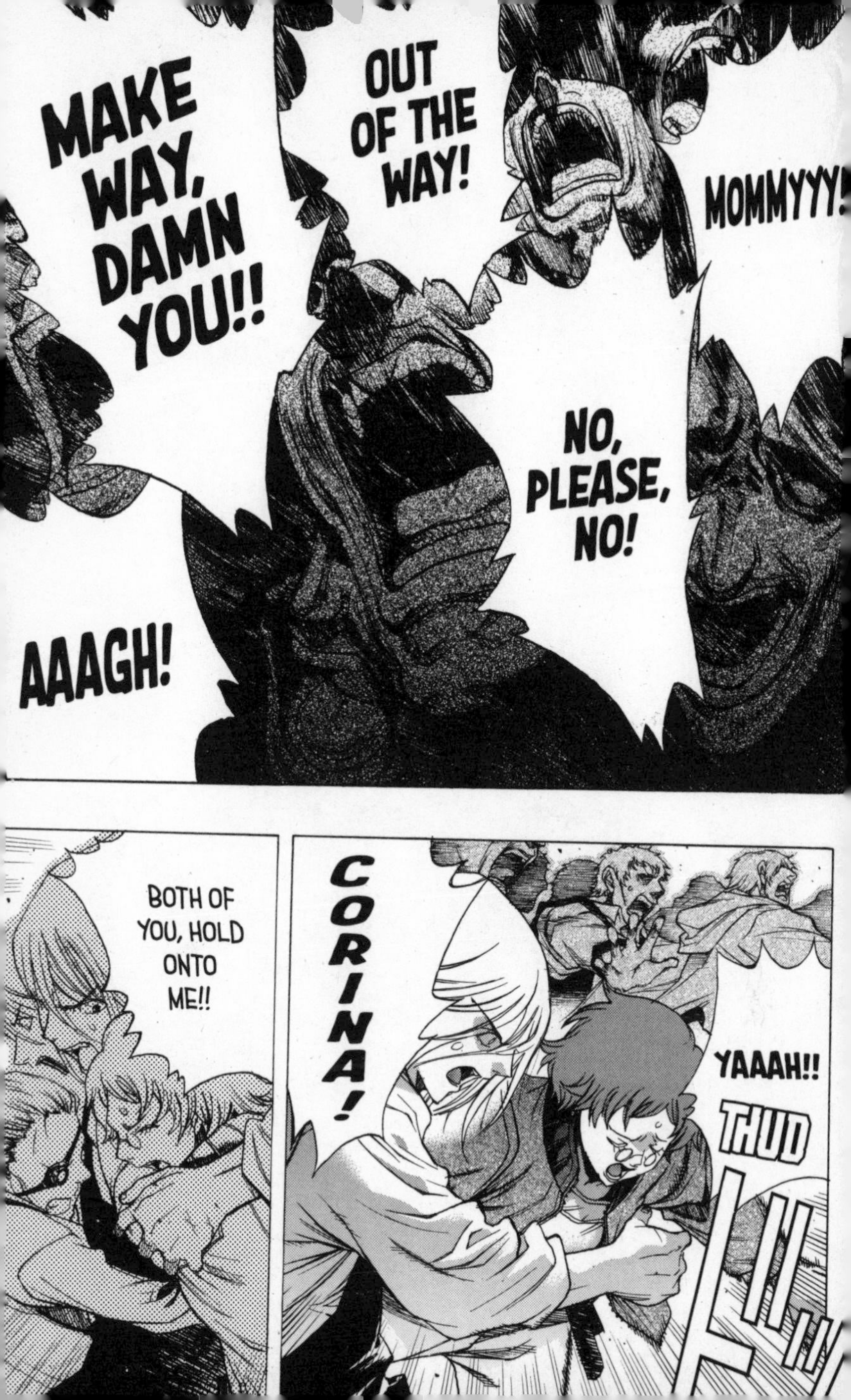
MOMMYYY!
OUT OF THE WAY!
MAKE WAY, DAMN YOU!!
NO, PLEASE, NO!
AAAGH!
CORINA!
YAAAH!!
THUD
BOTH OF YOU, HOLD ONTO ME!!

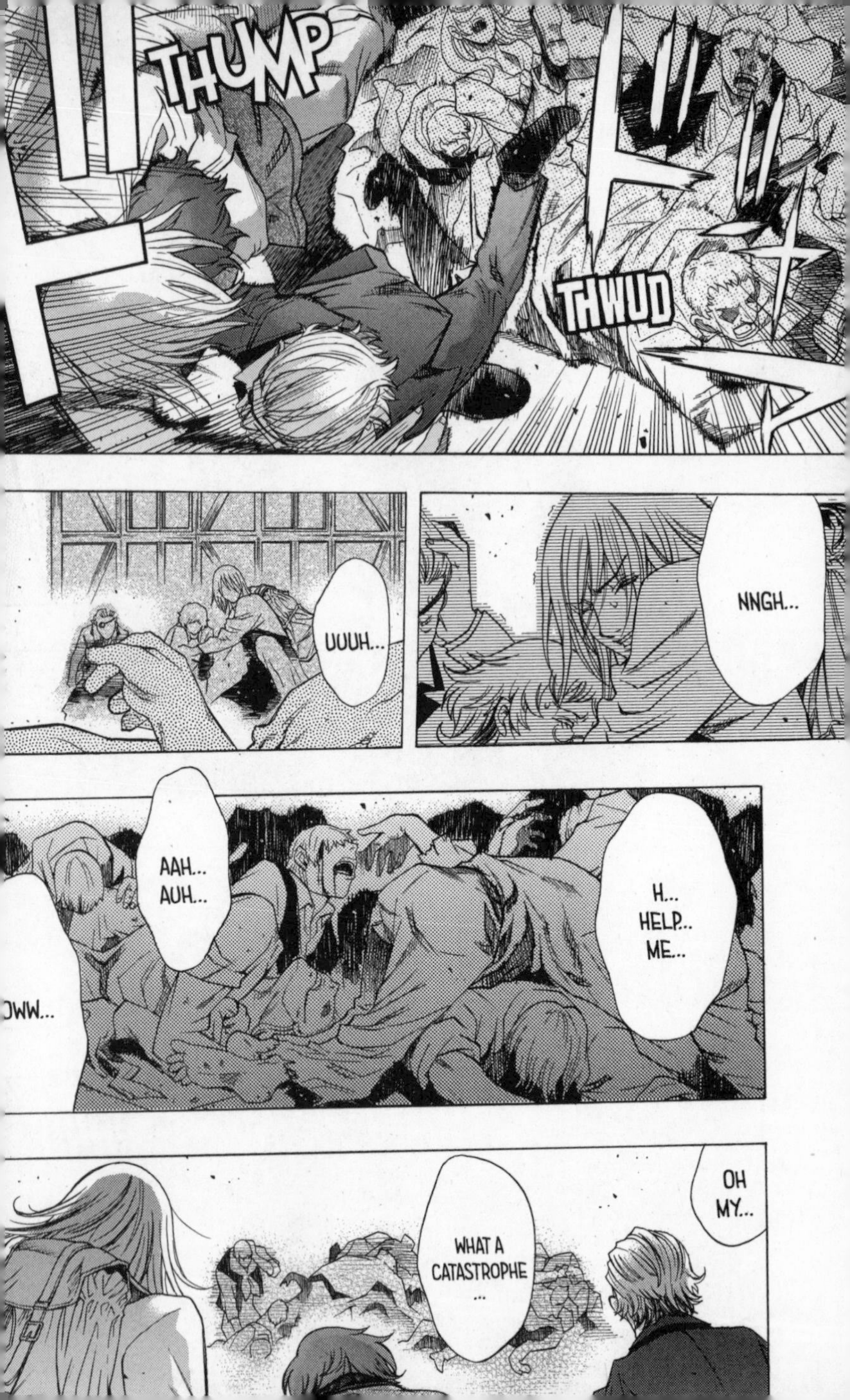
THUMP
THWUD
NNGH...
UUUH...
H... HELP... ME...
AAH... AUH...
OWW...
OH MY...
WHAT A CATASTROPHE ...

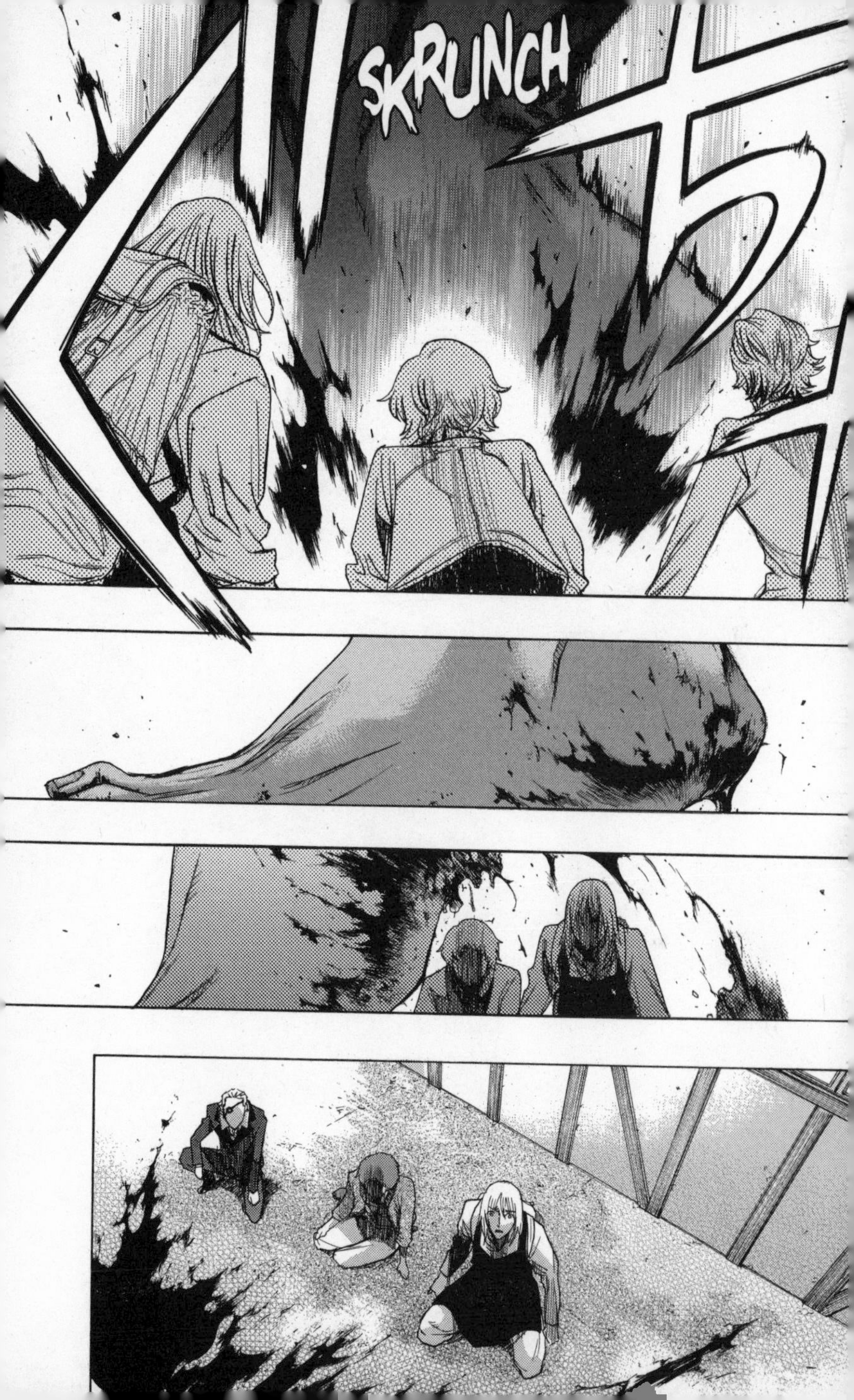
SKRUNCH

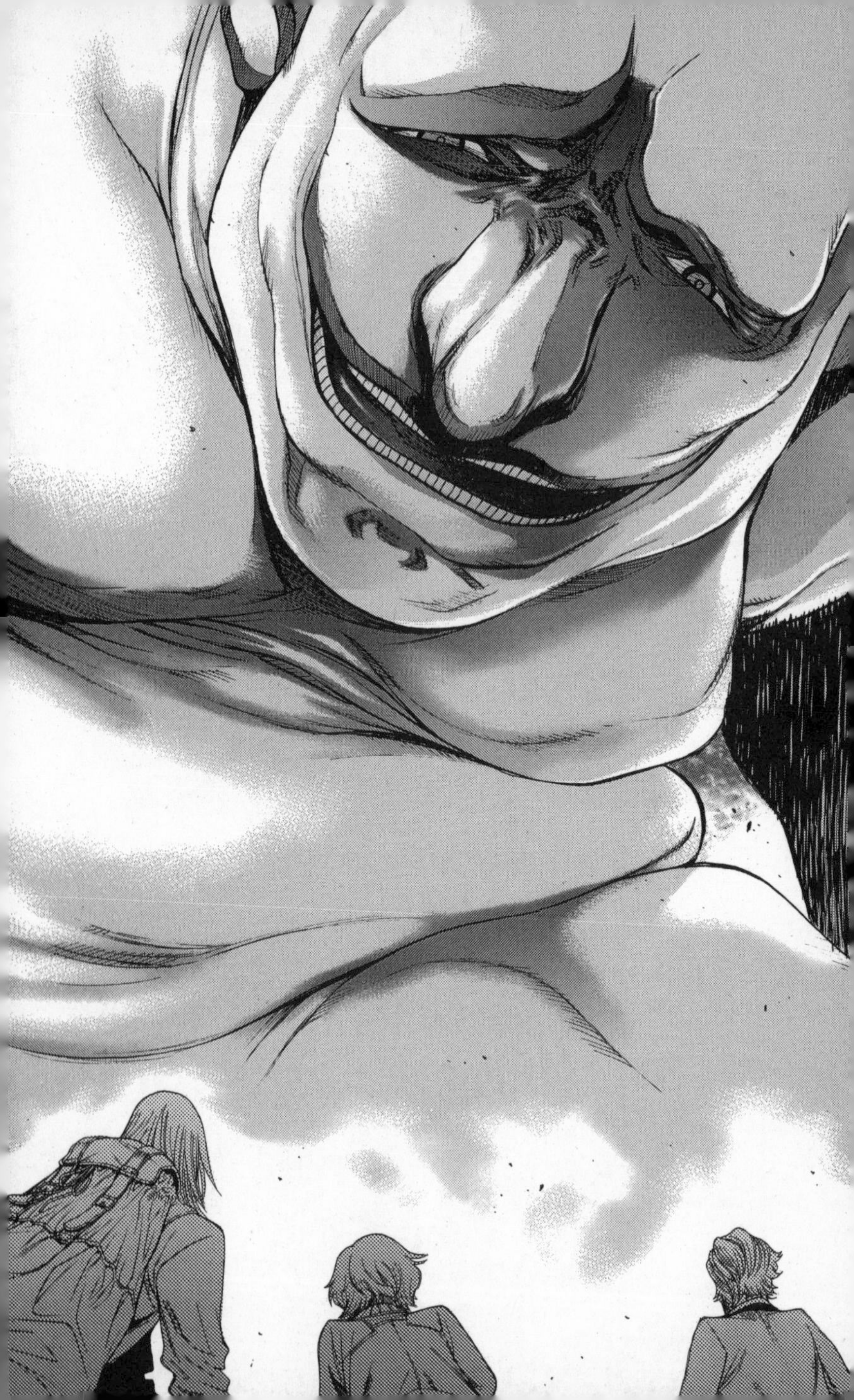

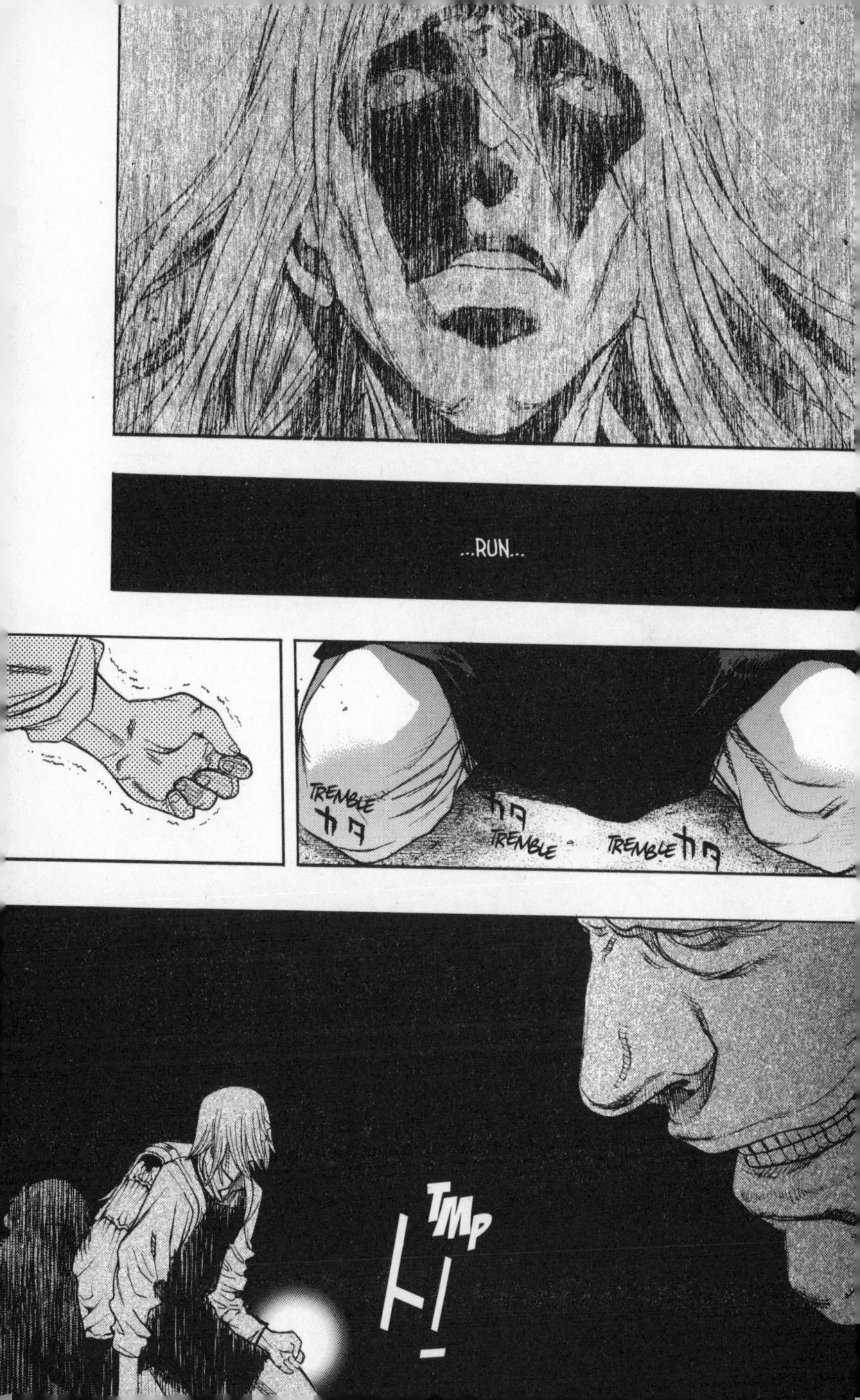
...RUN...
TREMBLE
TREMBLE
TREMBLE
TMP

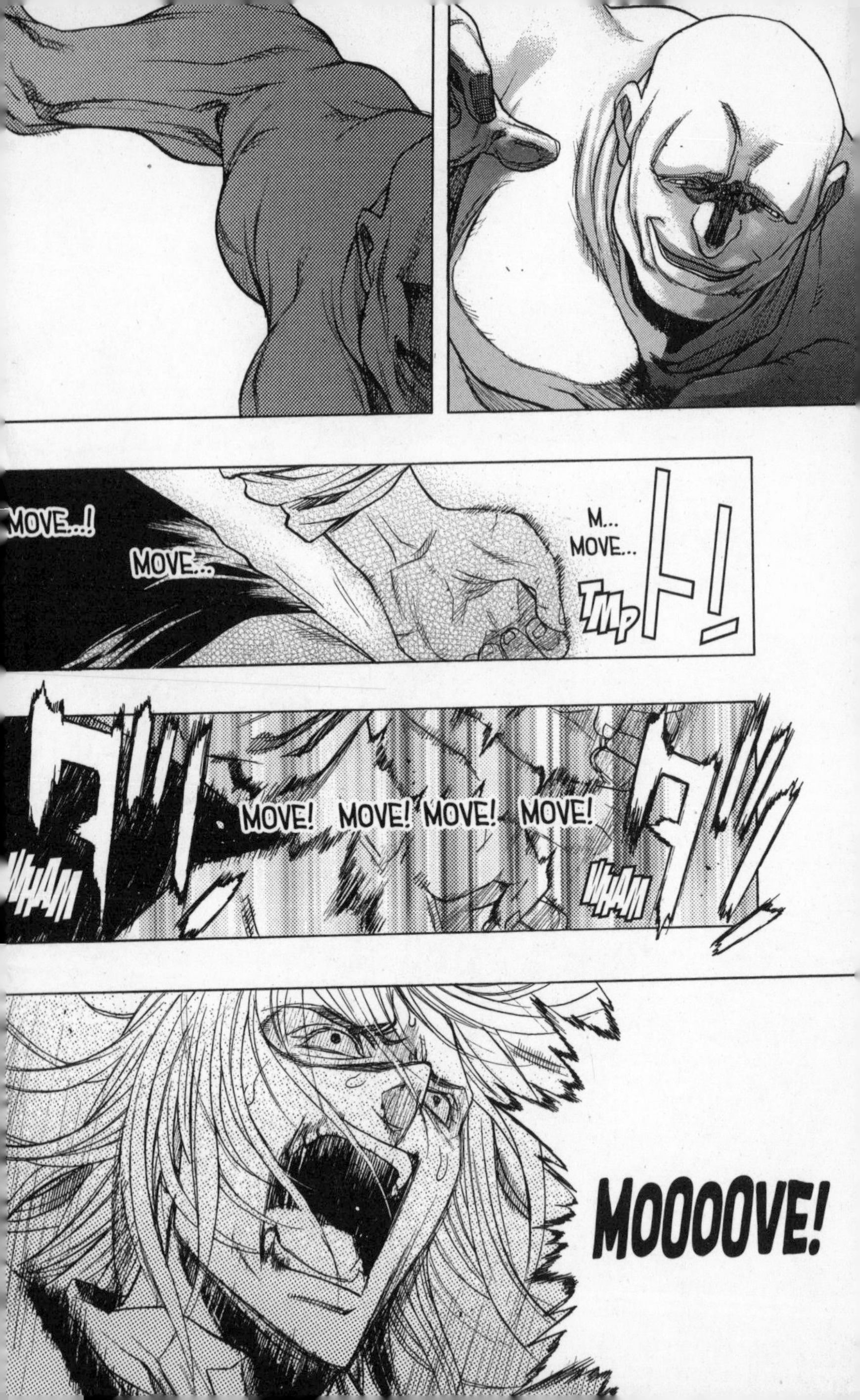
M... MOVE...
TMP
MOVE...
MOVE...!
WHAM
MOVE!
MOVE!
MOVE!
MOVE!
WHAM
MOOOOVE!

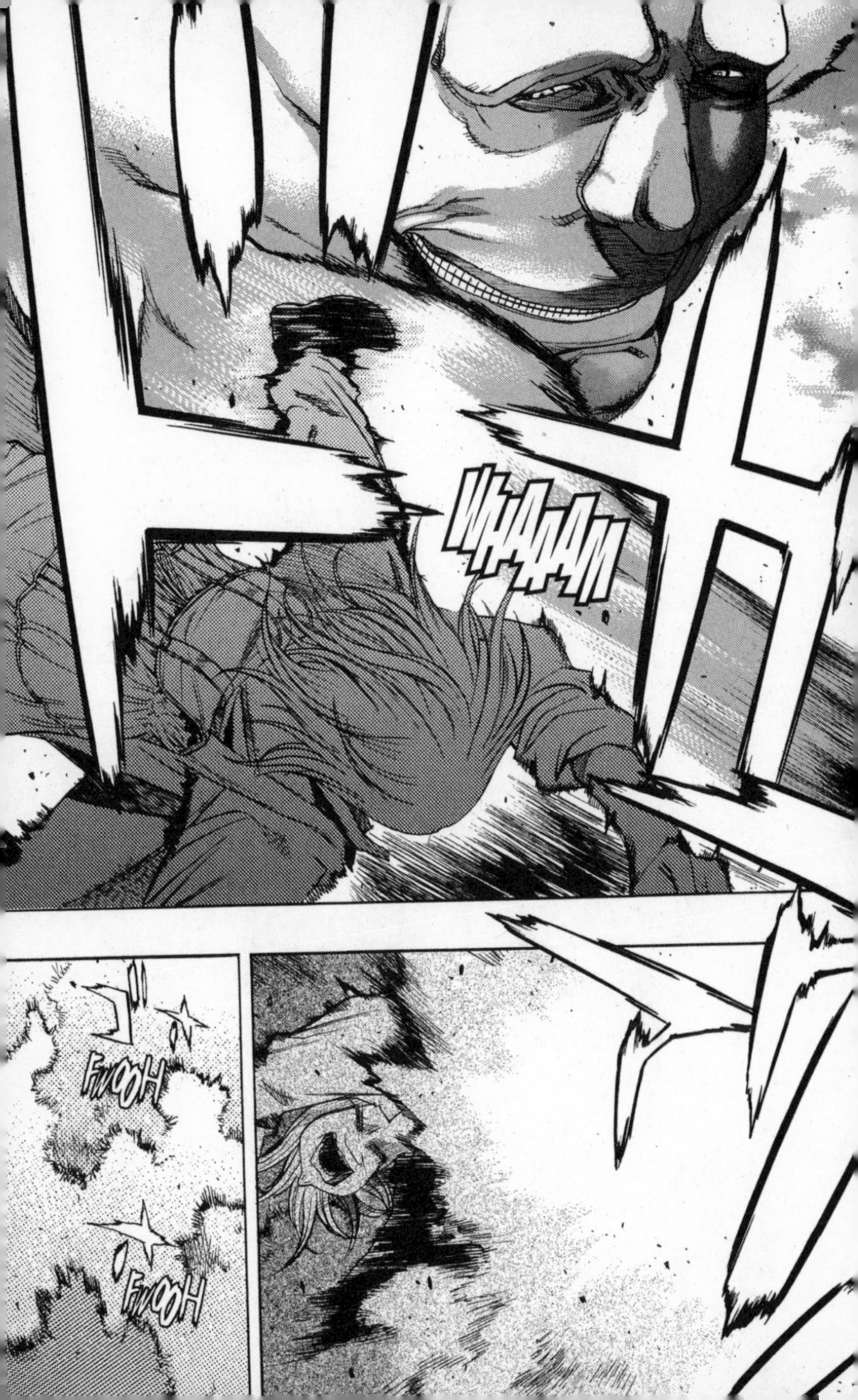
WHAAAM
FWOOH
FWOOH

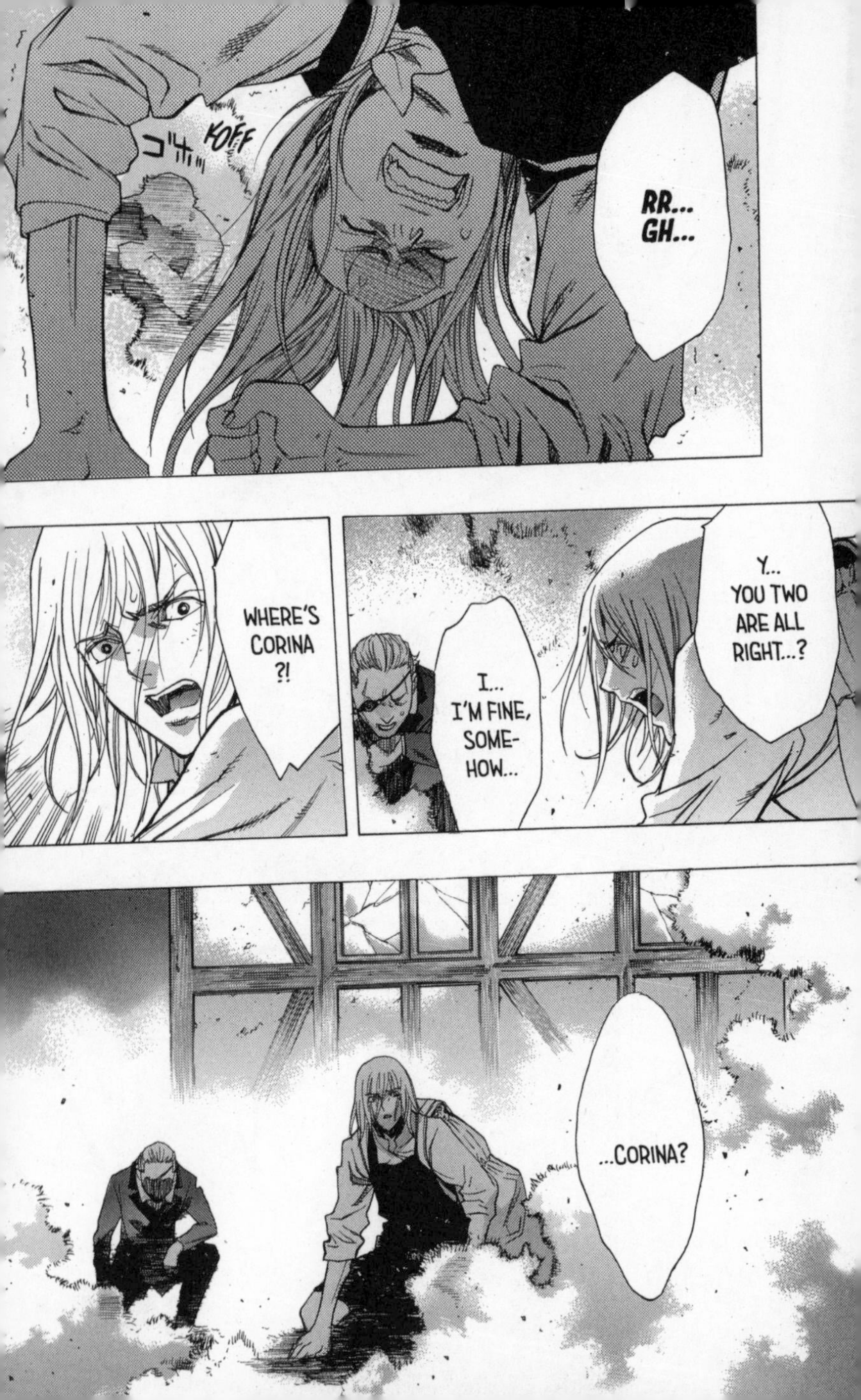
RR... GH...
ゴホッ
KOFF
Y... YOU TWO ARE ALL RIGHT...?
I... I'M FINE, SOME-HOW...
WHERE'S CORINA ?!
...CORINA?

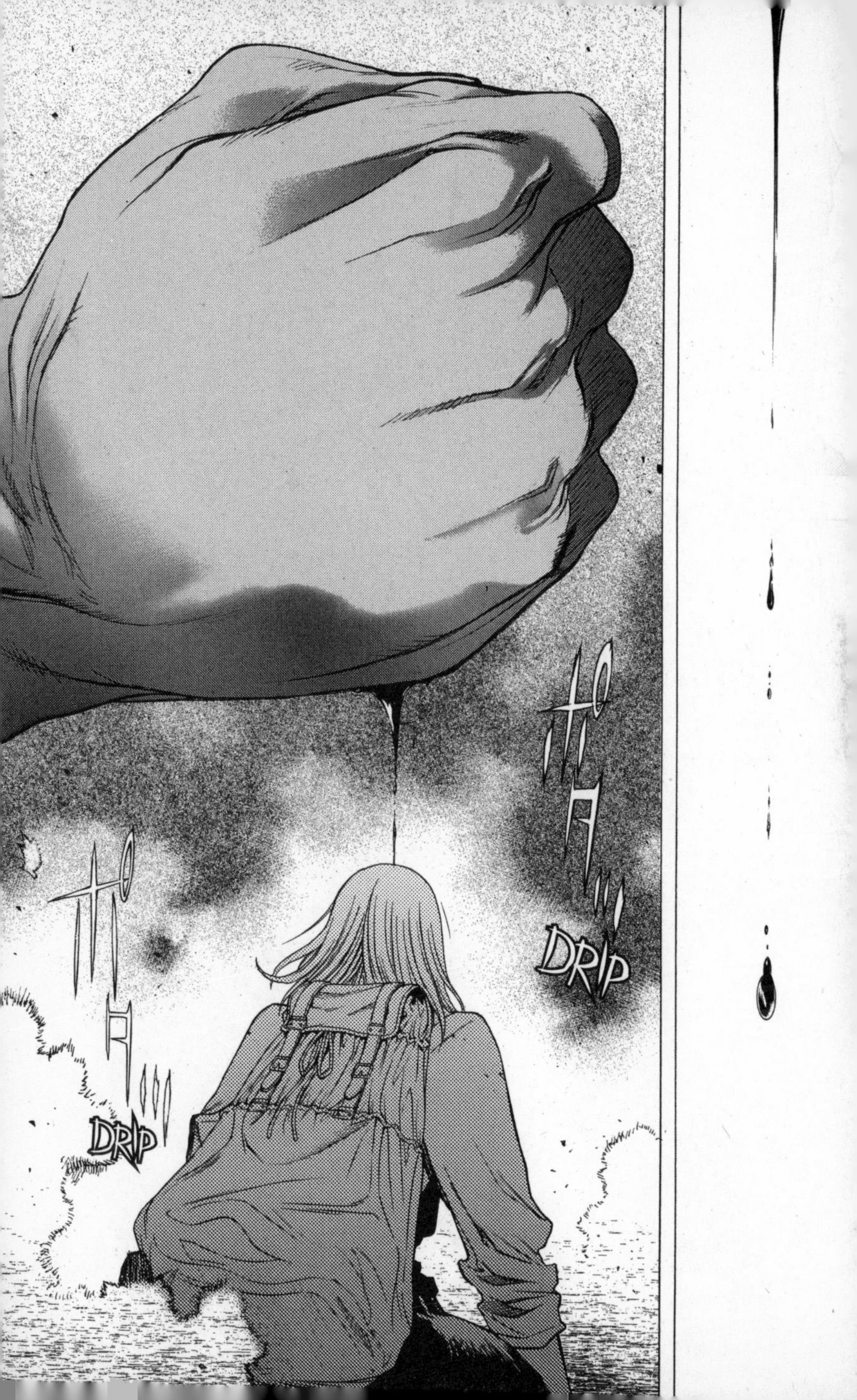
DRIP
DRIP

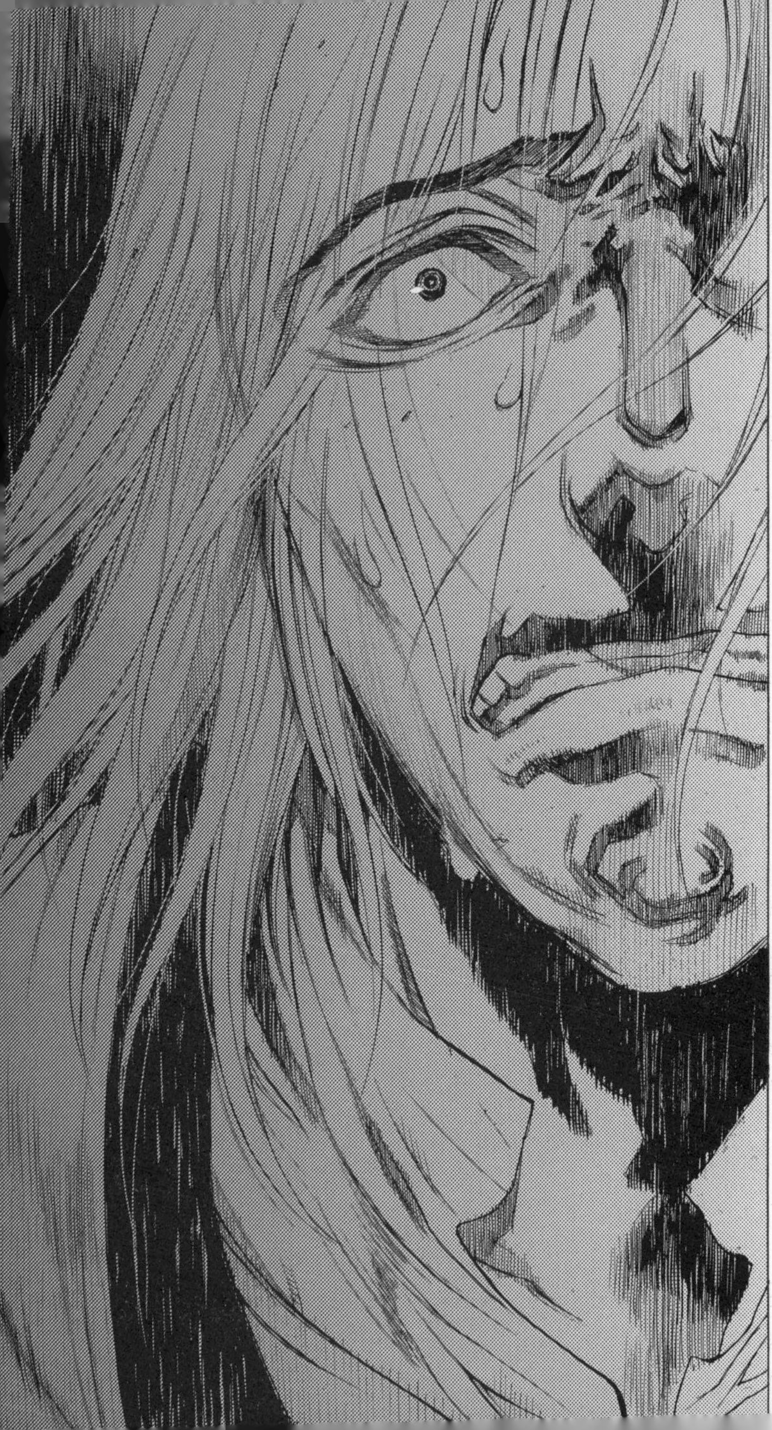

Chapter 37: Sacrificial Cage · End

ATTACK on TITAN
BEFORE THE FALL

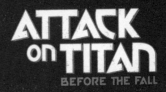

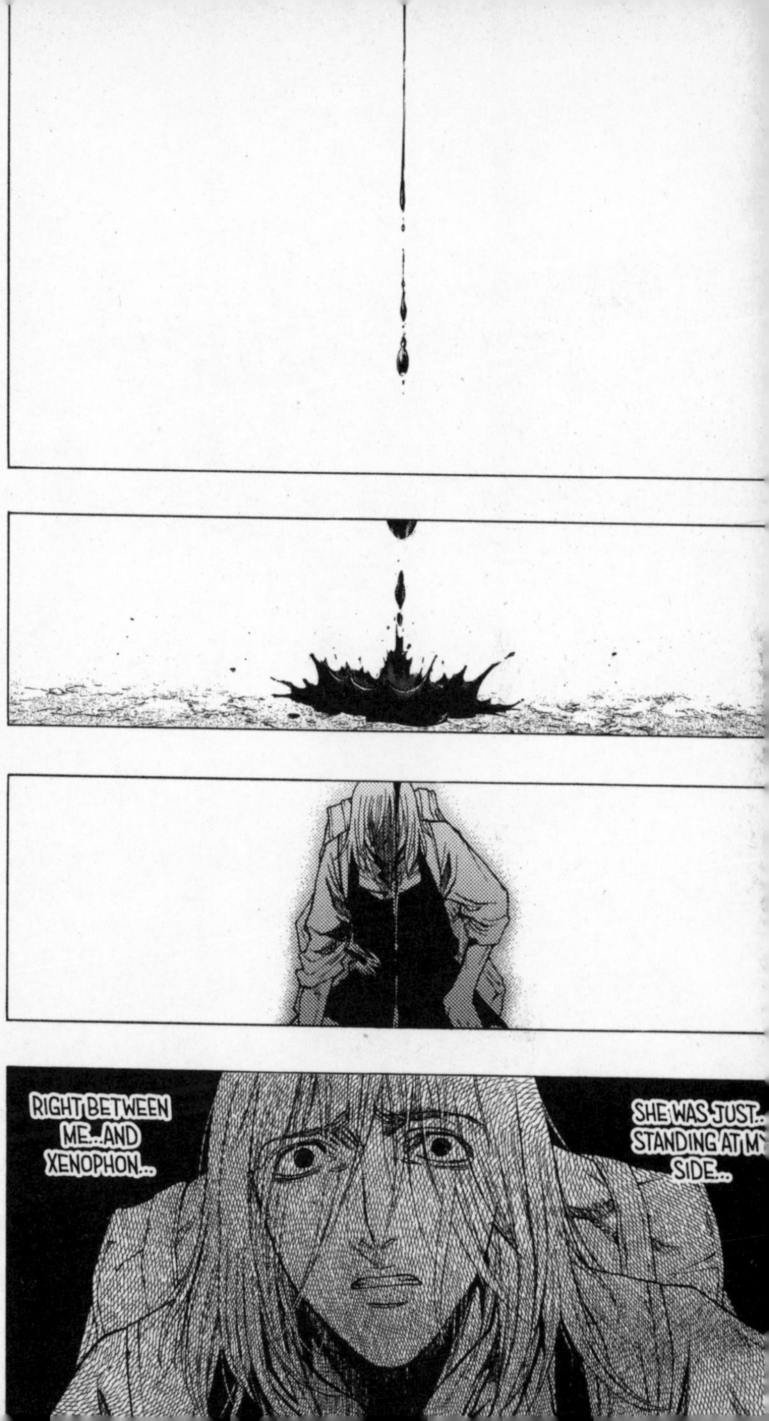
SHE WAS JUST... STANDING AT MY SIDE...
RIGHT BETWEEN ME...AND XENOPHON...

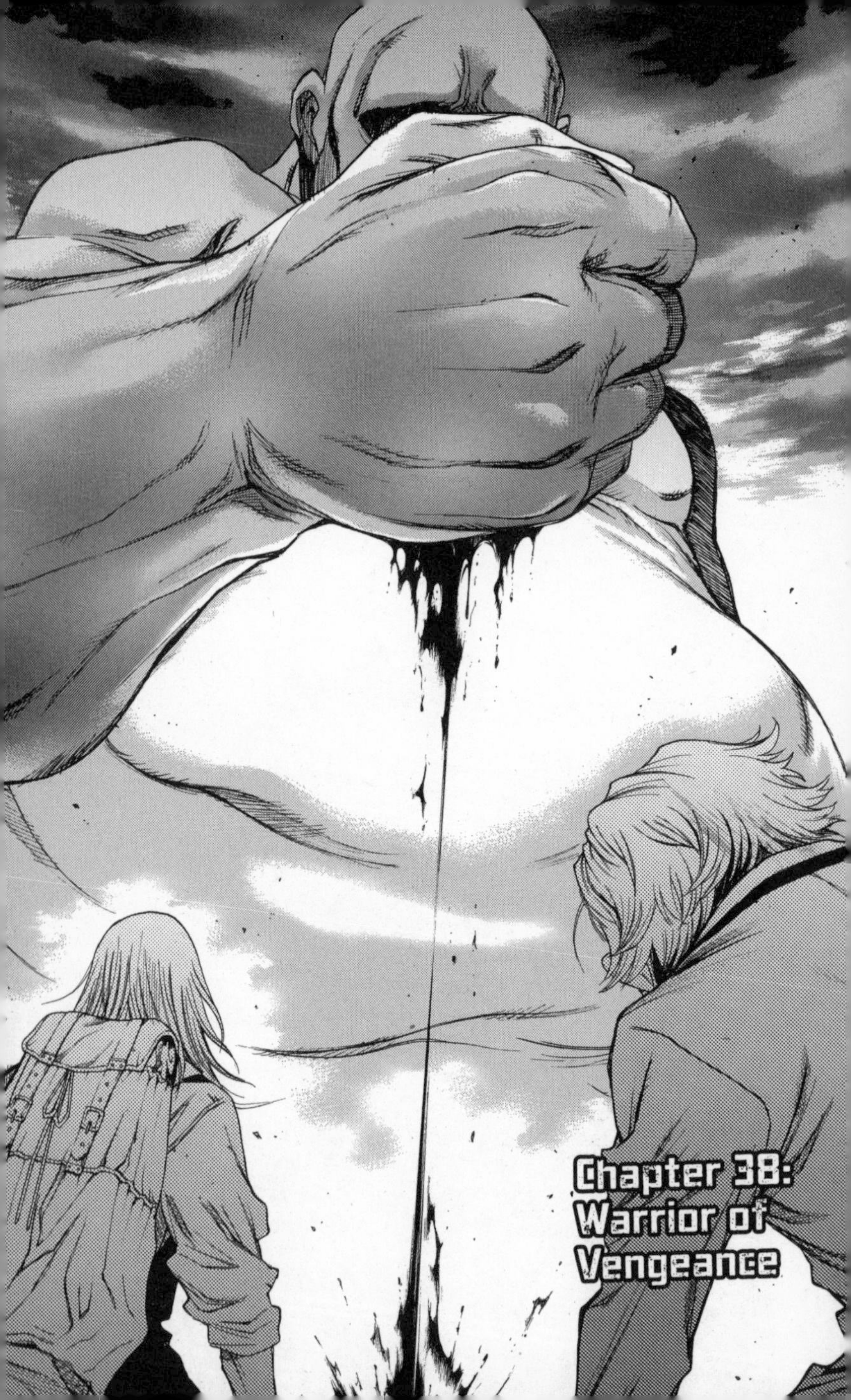
Chapter 38:
Warrior of
Vengeance

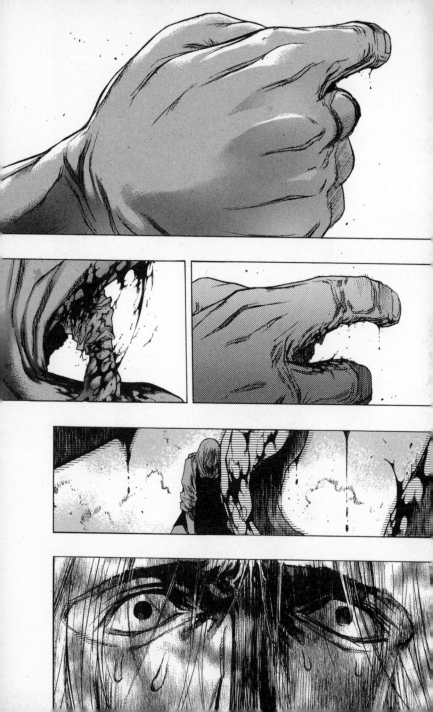

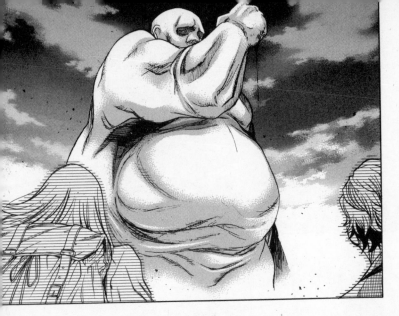

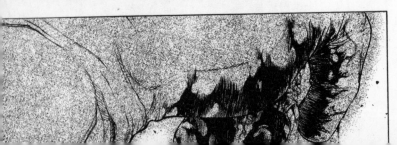

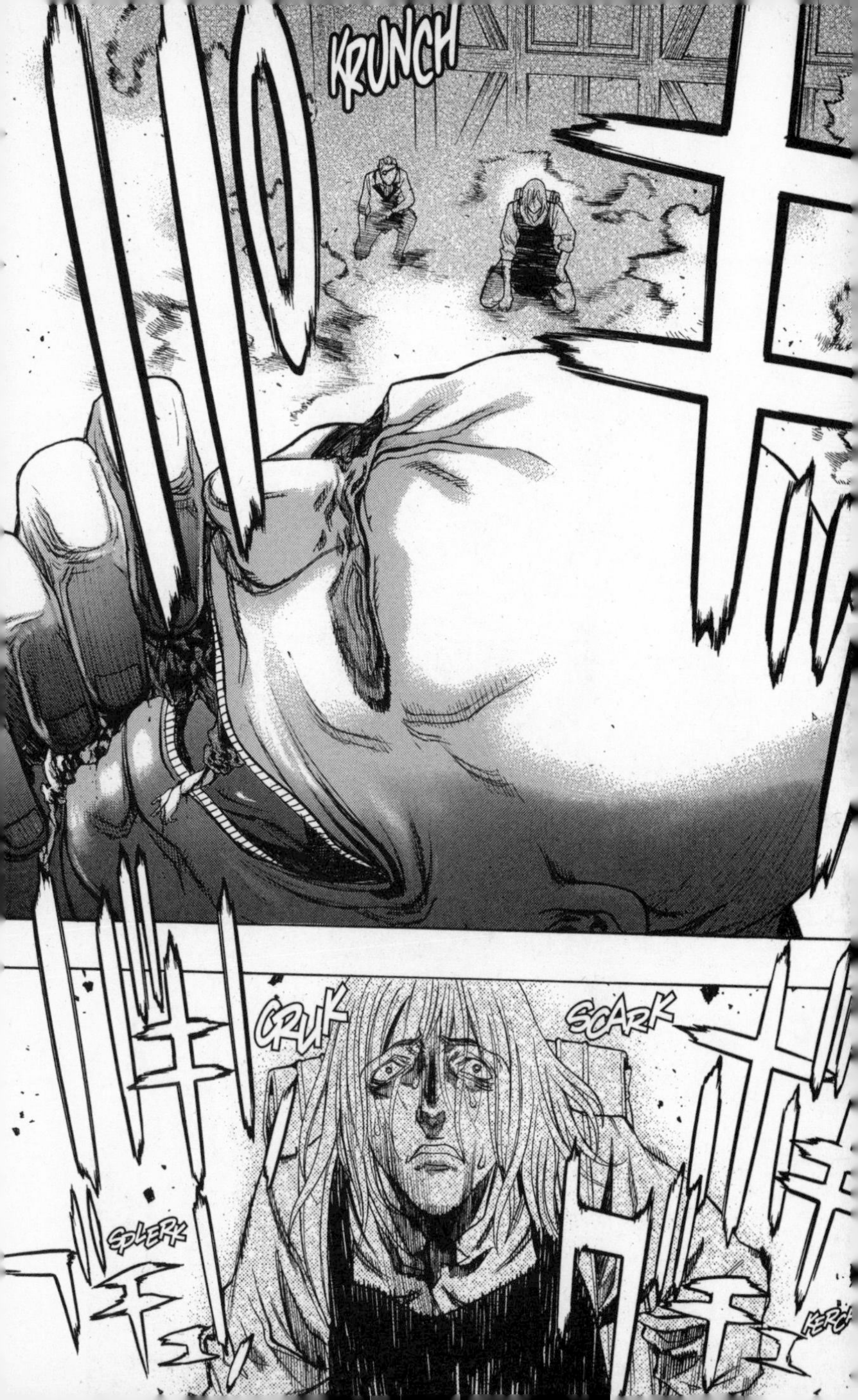
KRUNCH
SCARK
CRUK
KERC
SPLERK

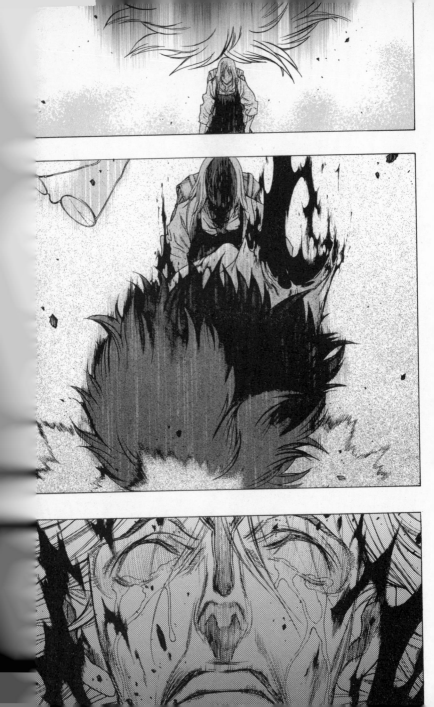

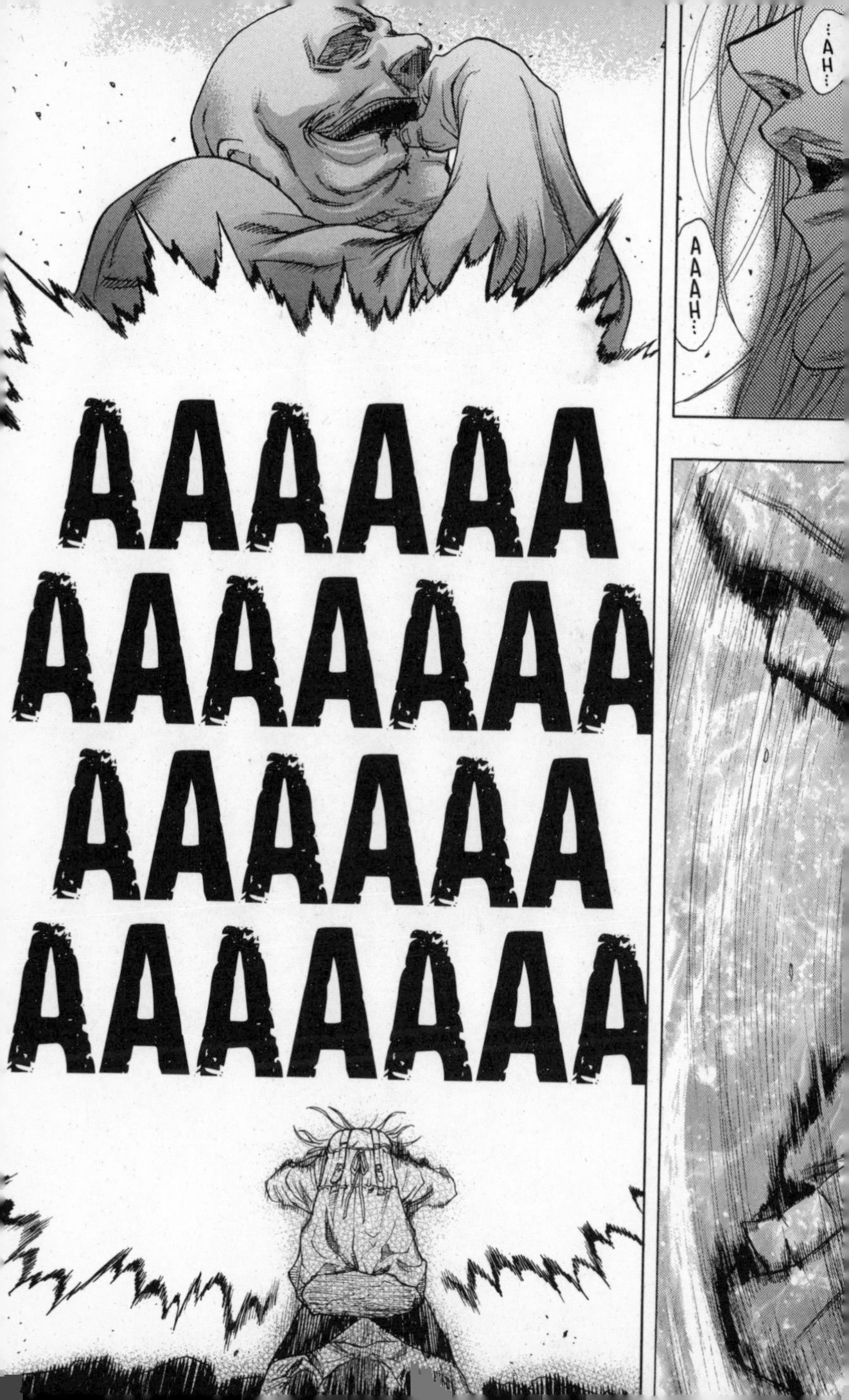
...AH...
AAAH...
AAAAAA
AAAAAAA
AAAAAA
AAAAAAA

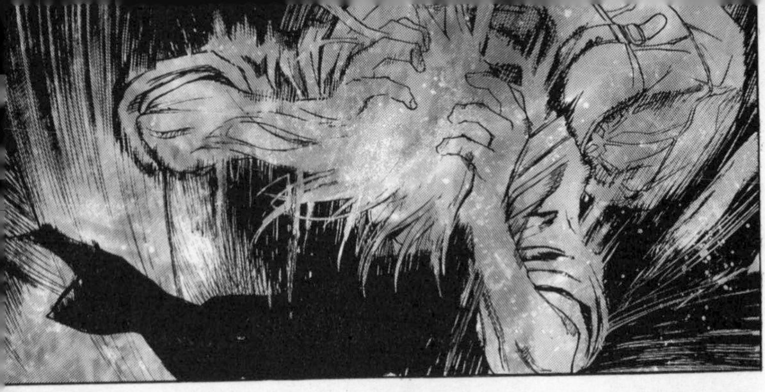

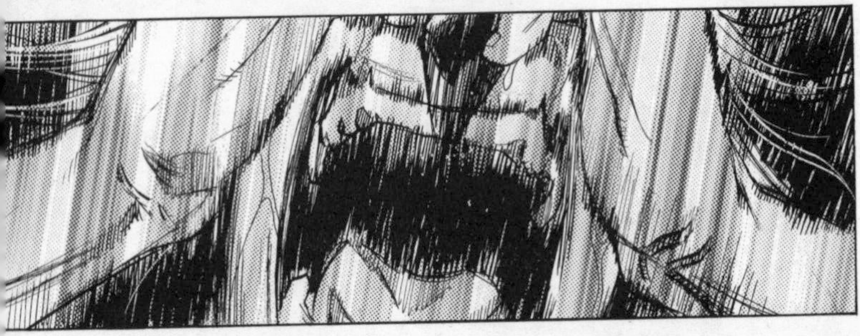

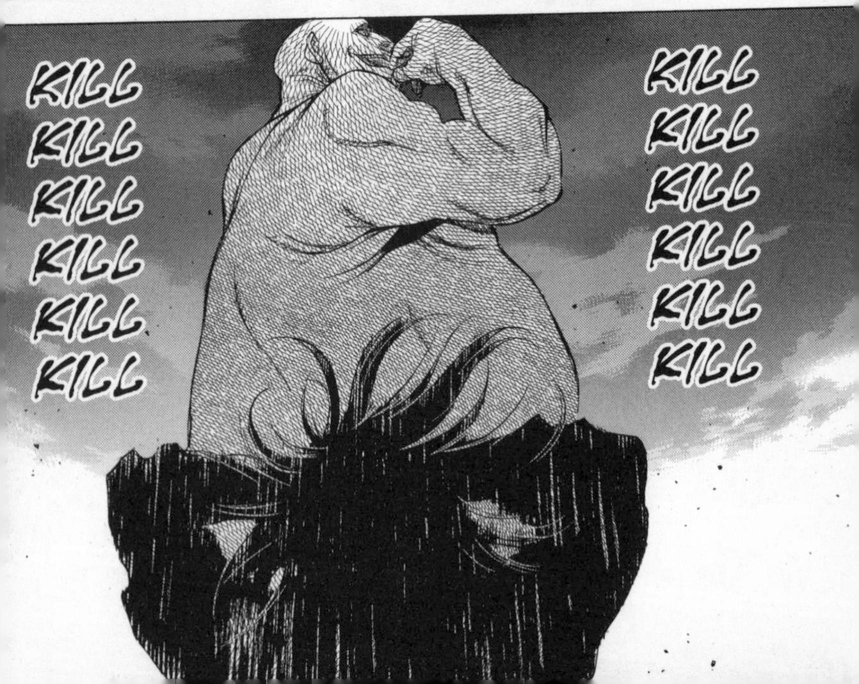
KILL
KILL
KILL
KILL
KILL
KILL
KILL
KILL
KILL
KILL
KILL
KILL

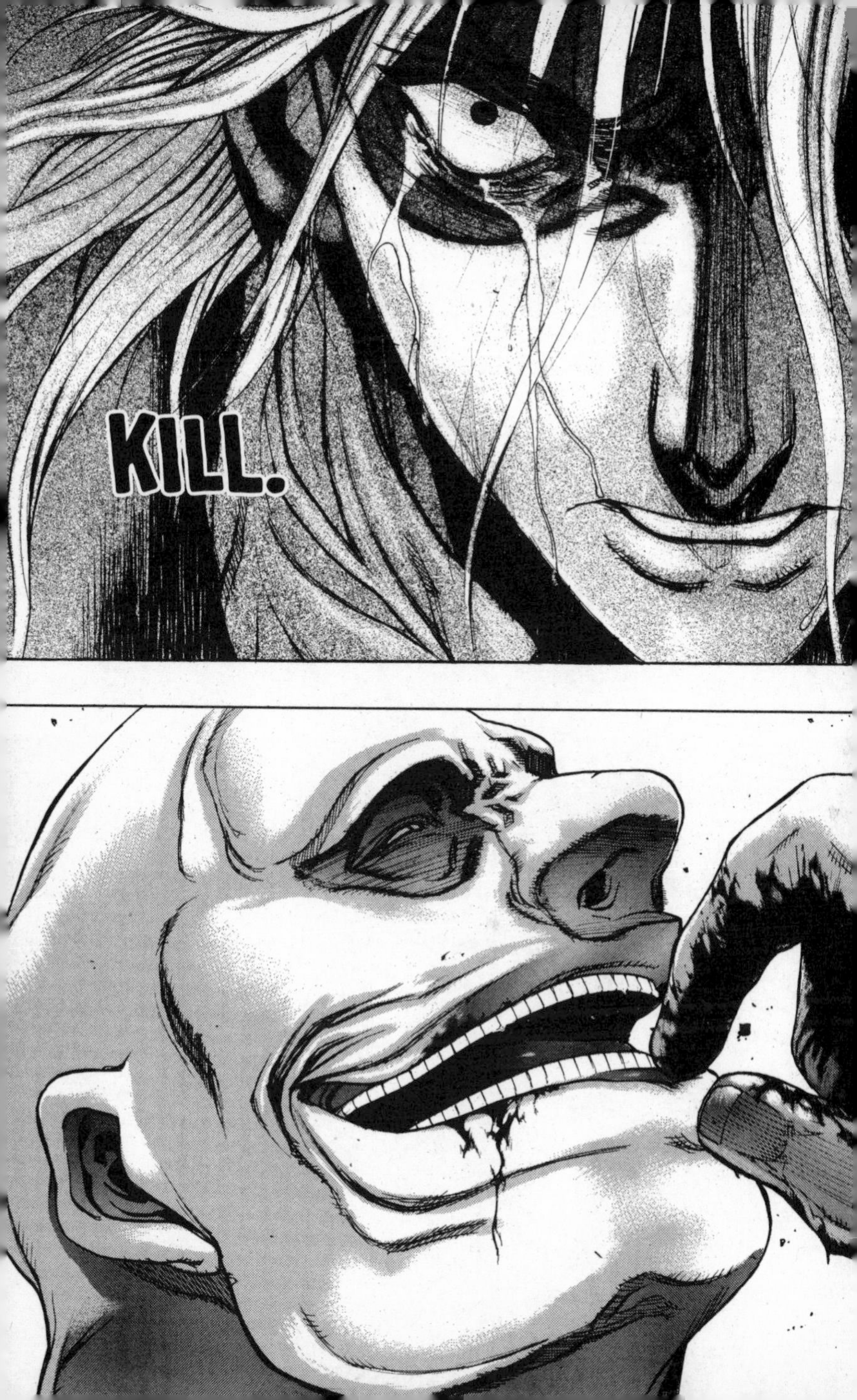
KILL.

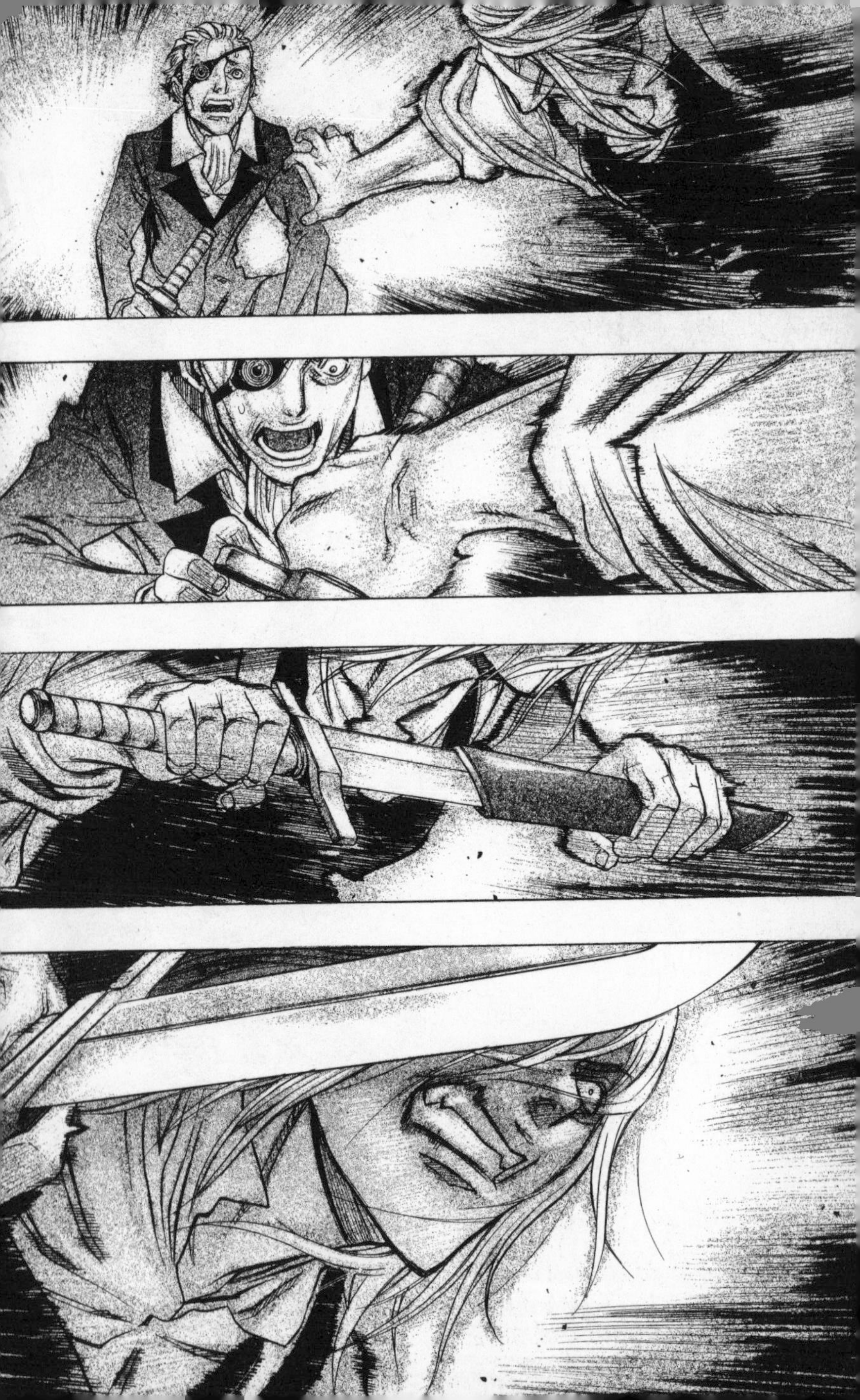

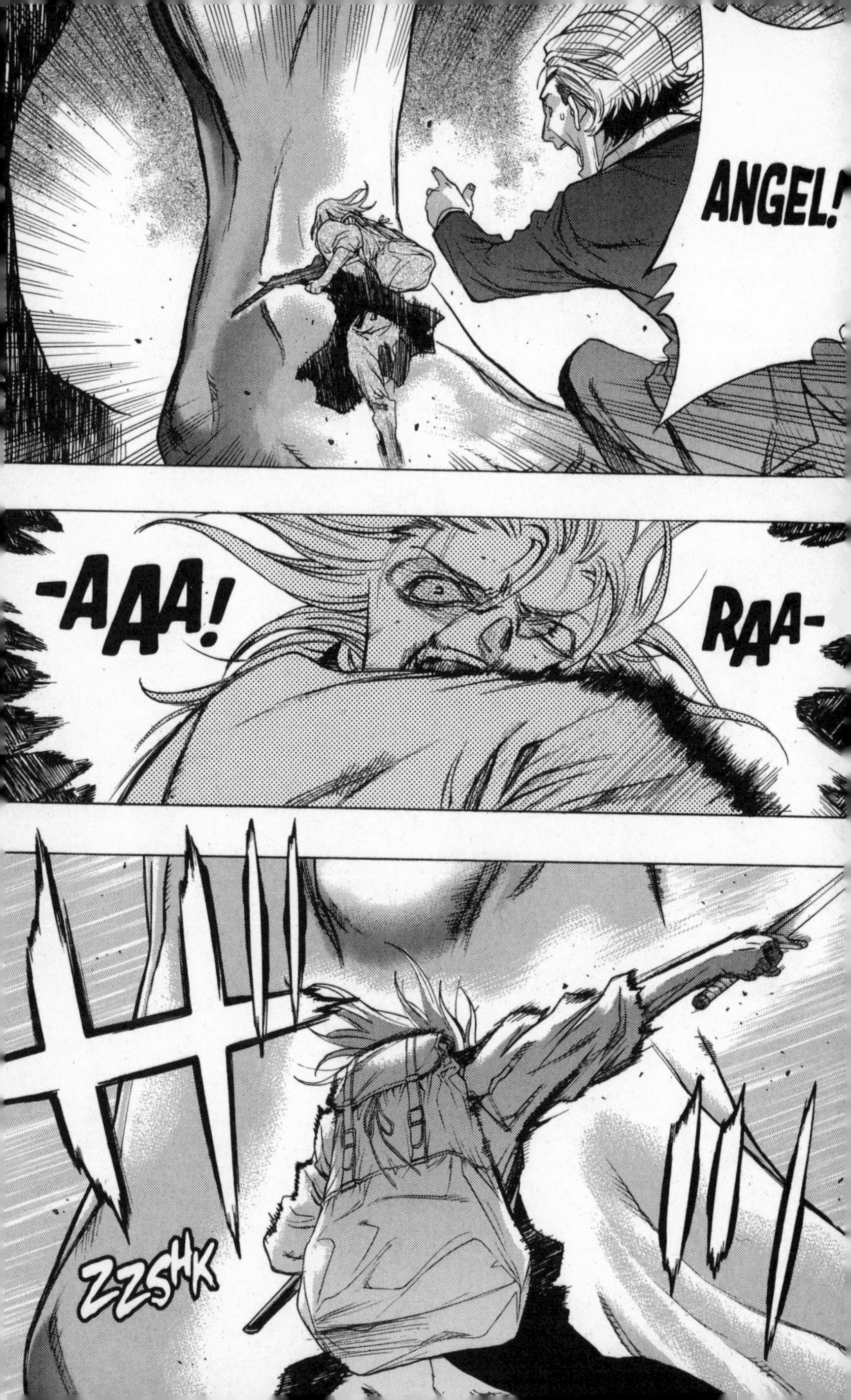
ANGEL!
RAA-
-AAA!
ZZSHK

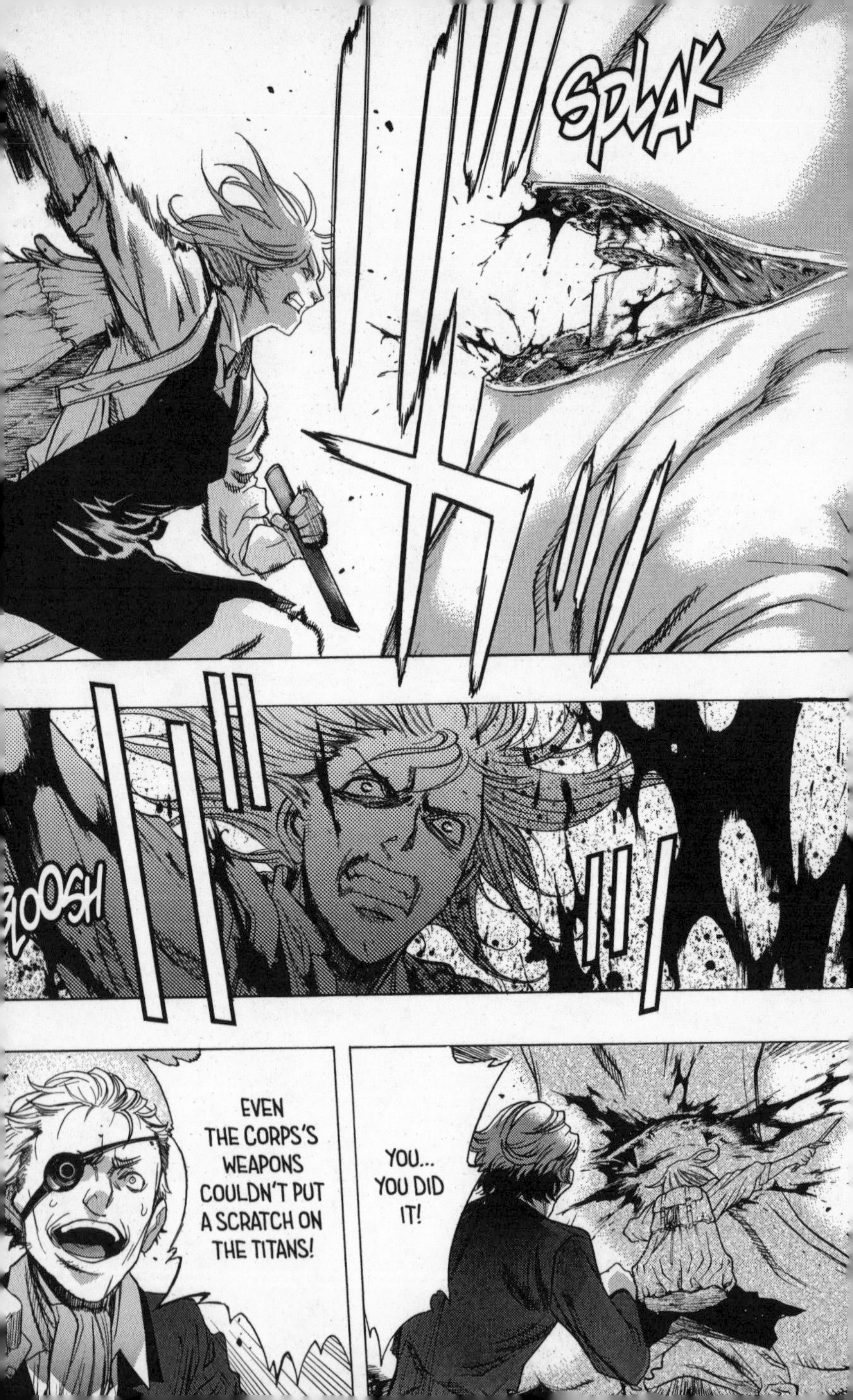
SPLAK
ZLOOSH
YOU... YOU DID IT!
EVEN THE CORPS'S WEAPONS COULDN'T PUT A SCRATCH ON THE TITANS!

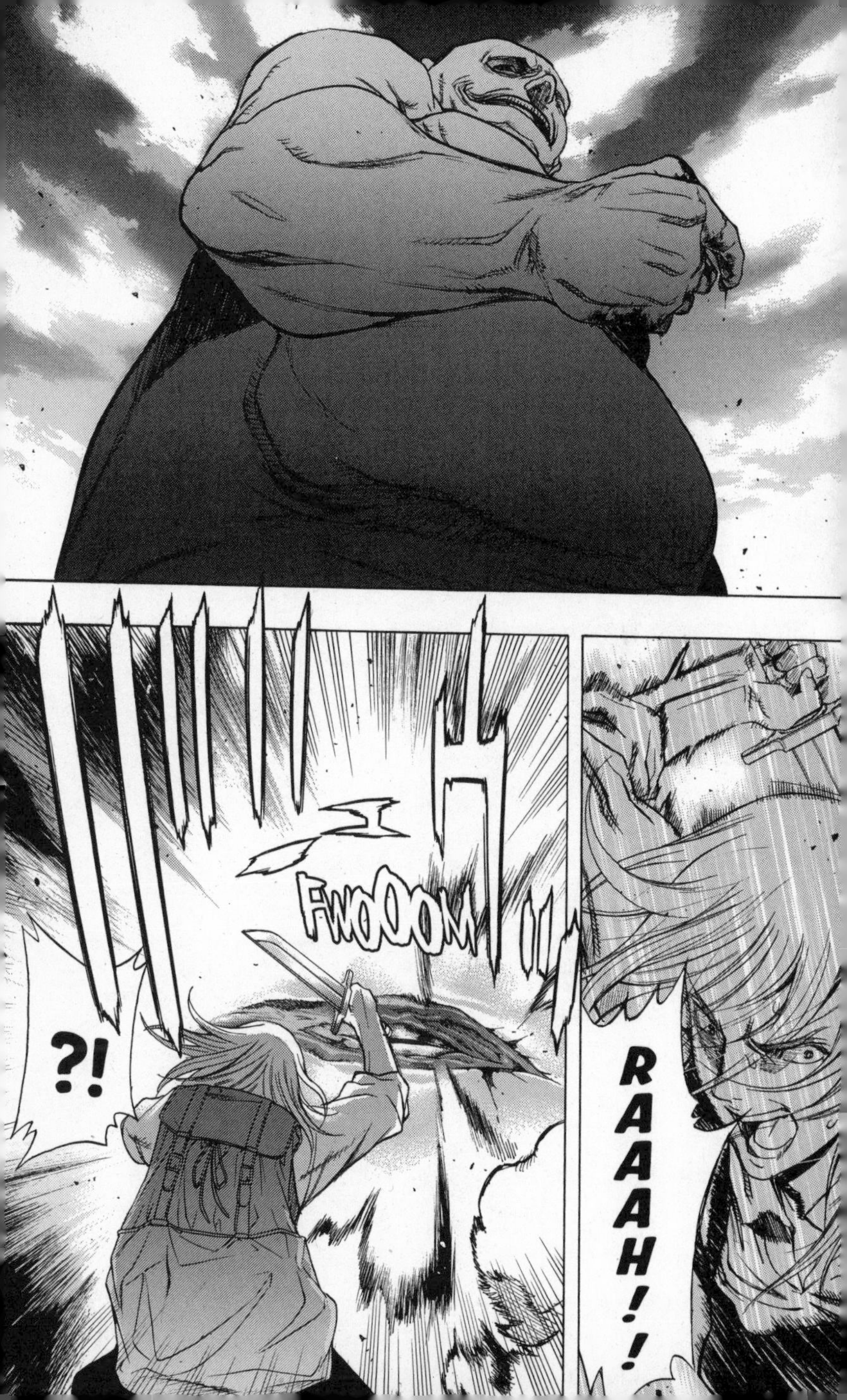
FWOOOM
?!
RAAAAH!!!

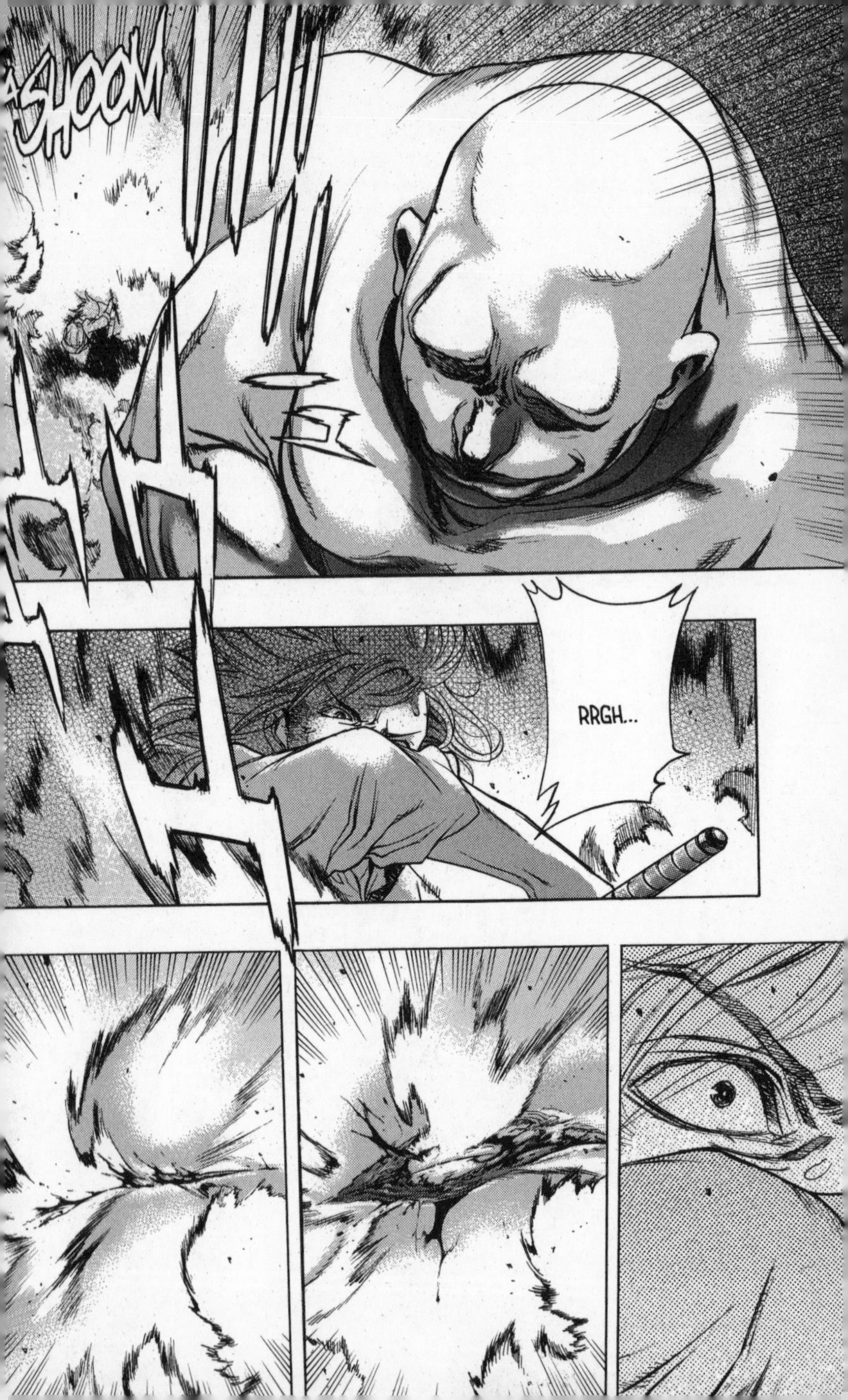
SHOOM
RRGH...

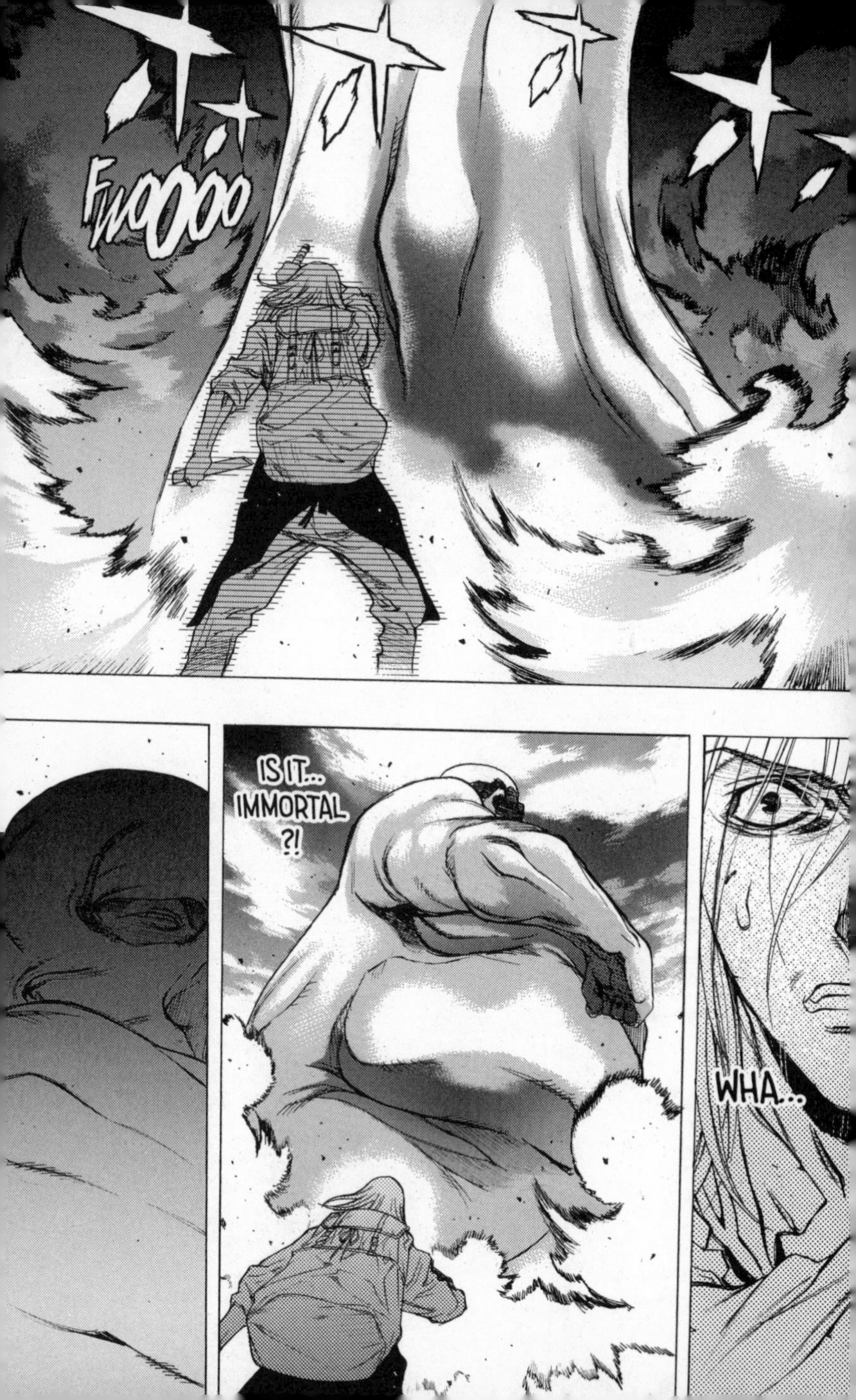
Fwoooo
WHA...
IS IT... IMMORTAL ?!

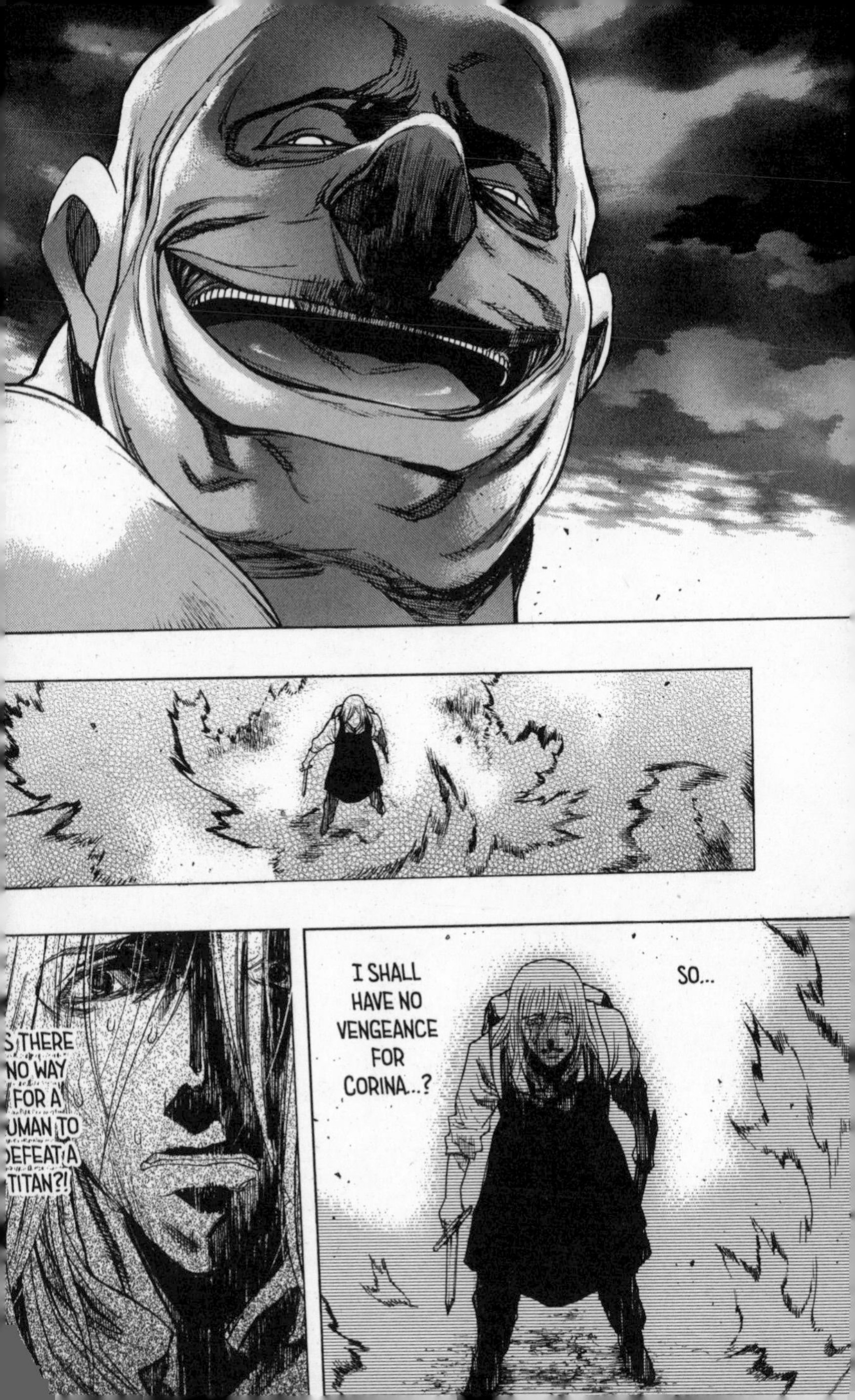
SO...
I SHALL HAVE NO VENGEANCE FOR CORINA..?
S THERE NO WAY FOR A UMAN TO DEFEAT A TITAN?!

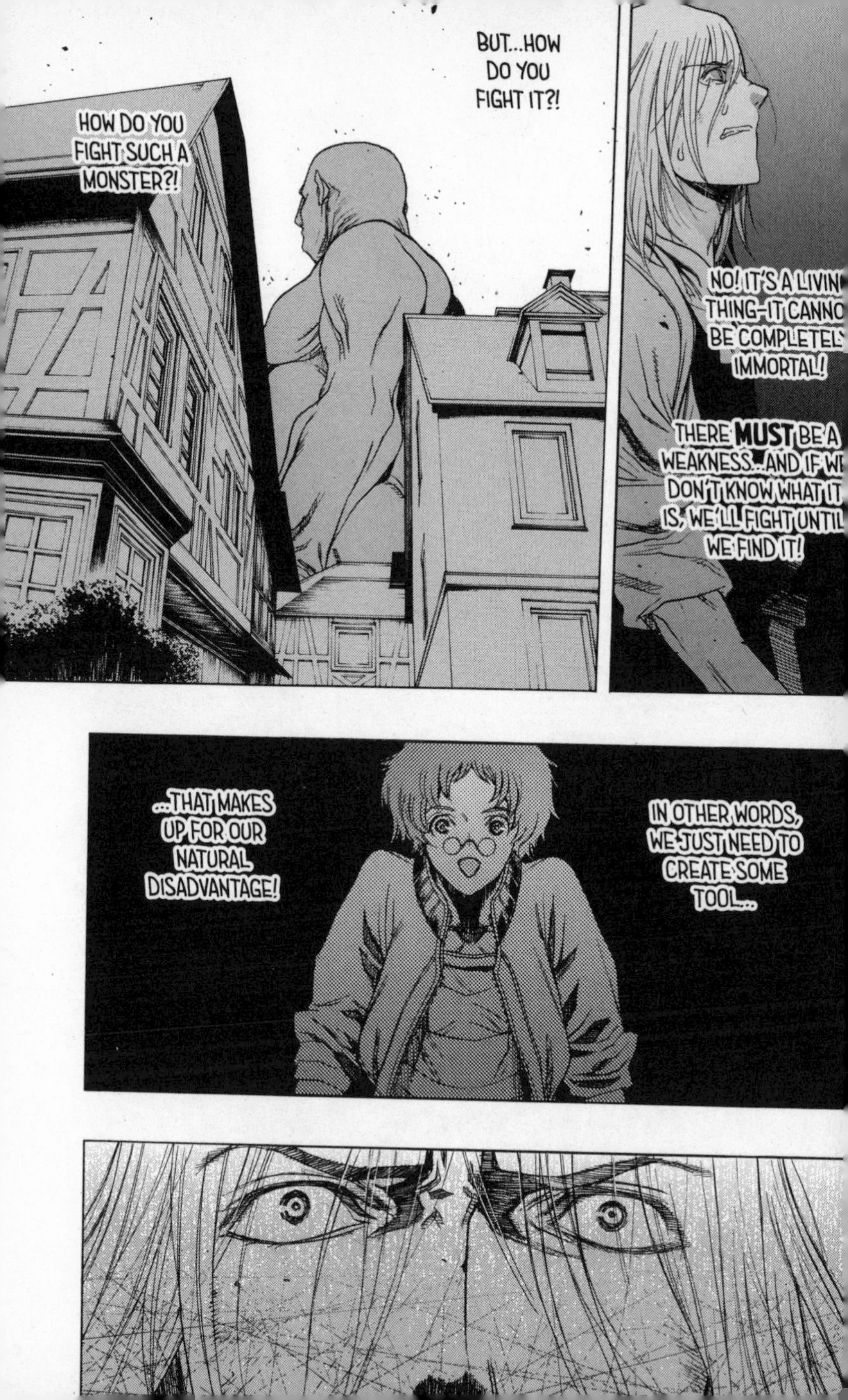
NO! IT'S A LIVIN THING–IT CANNO BE COMPLETEL IMMORTAL!
THERE **MUST** BE A WEAKNESS...AND IF W DON'T KNOW WHAT IT IS, WE'LL FIGHT UNTIL WE FIND IT!
BUT...HOW DO YOU FIGHT IT?!
HOW DO YOU FIGHT SUCH A MONSTER?!
IN OTHER WORDS, WE JUST NEED TO CREATE SOME TOOL...
...THAT MAKES UP FOR OUR NATURAL DISADVANTAGE!

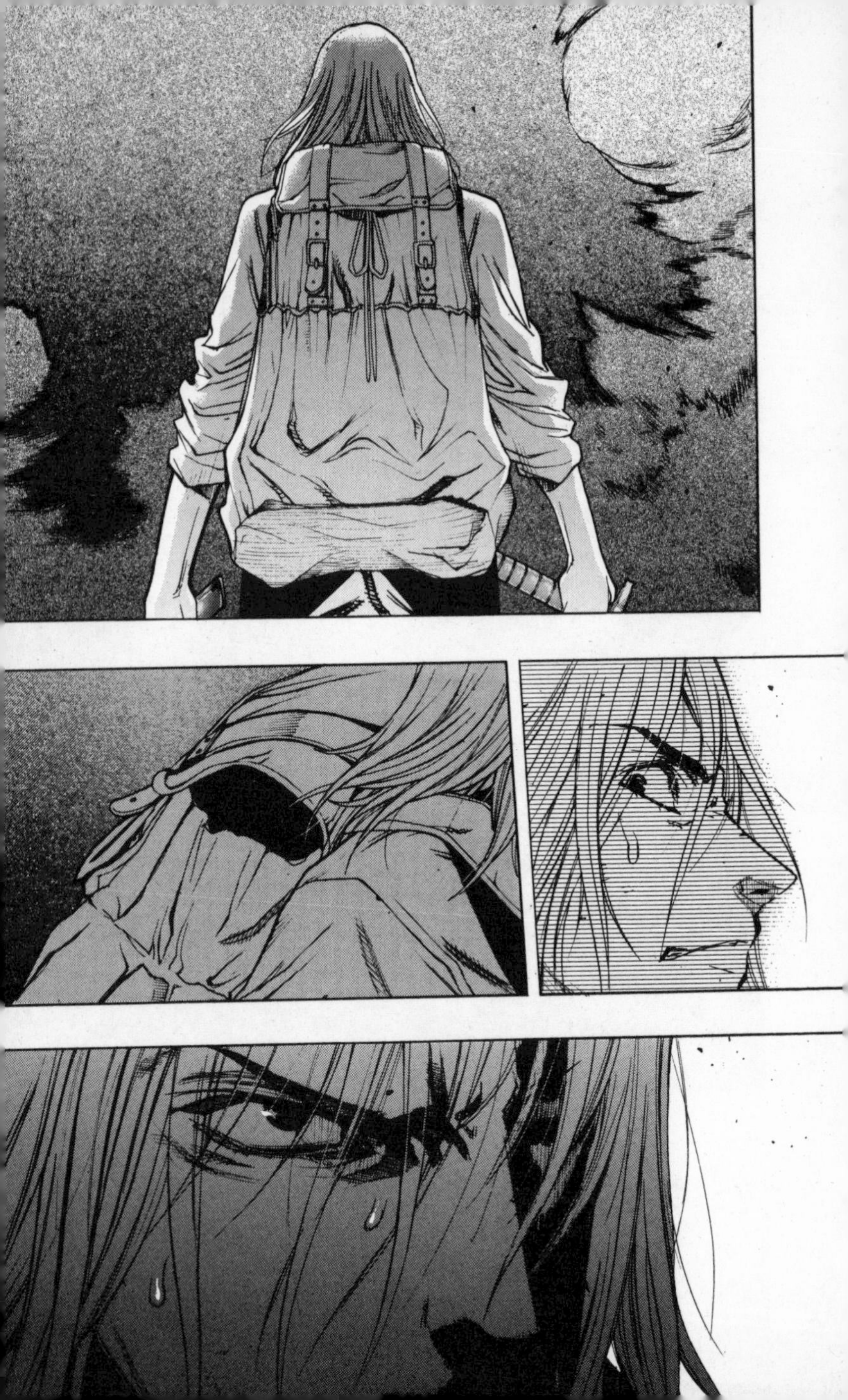

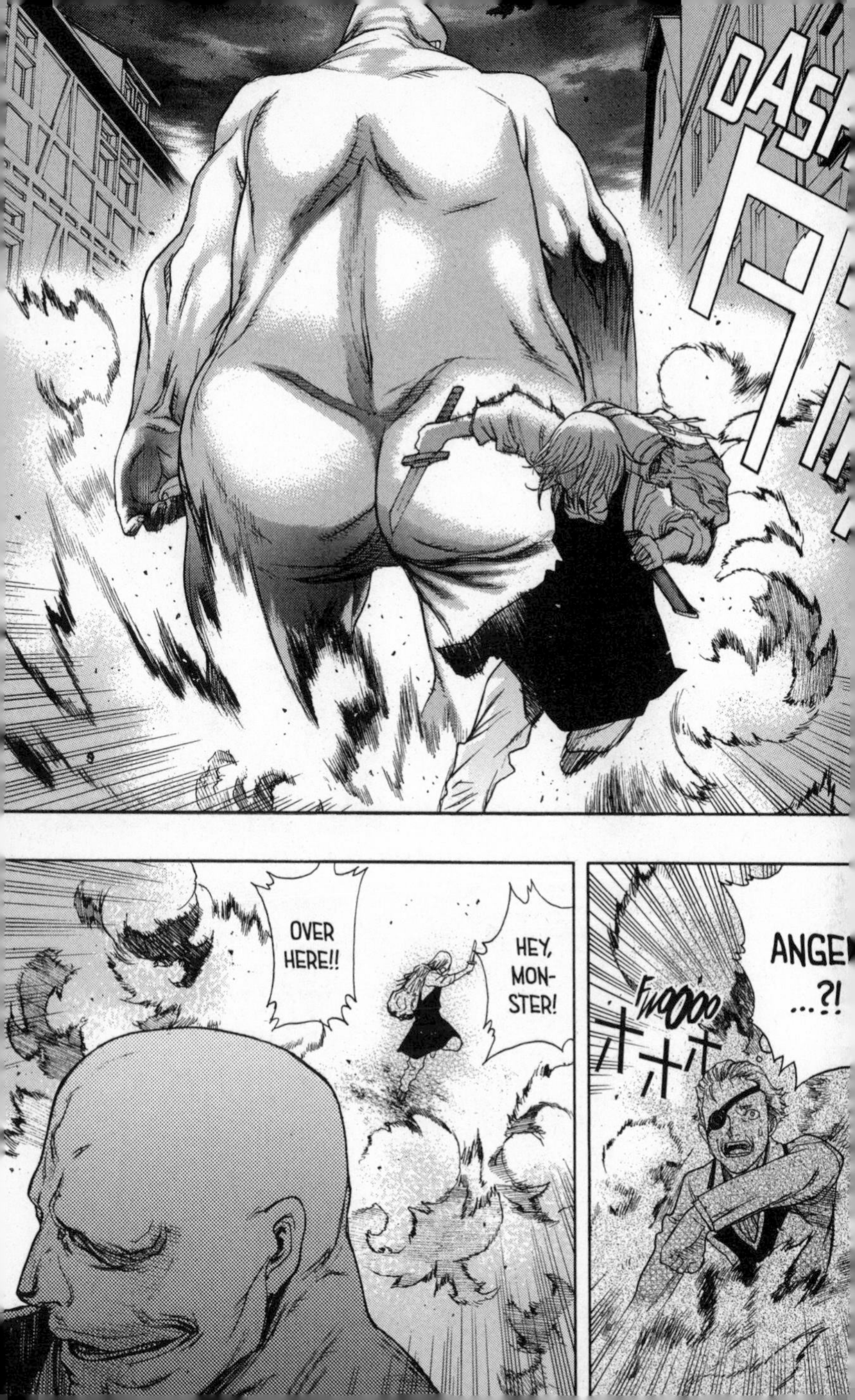

DASH
ダッ
ANGE
...?!
FWOOOO
HEY, MON-STER!
OVER HERE!!

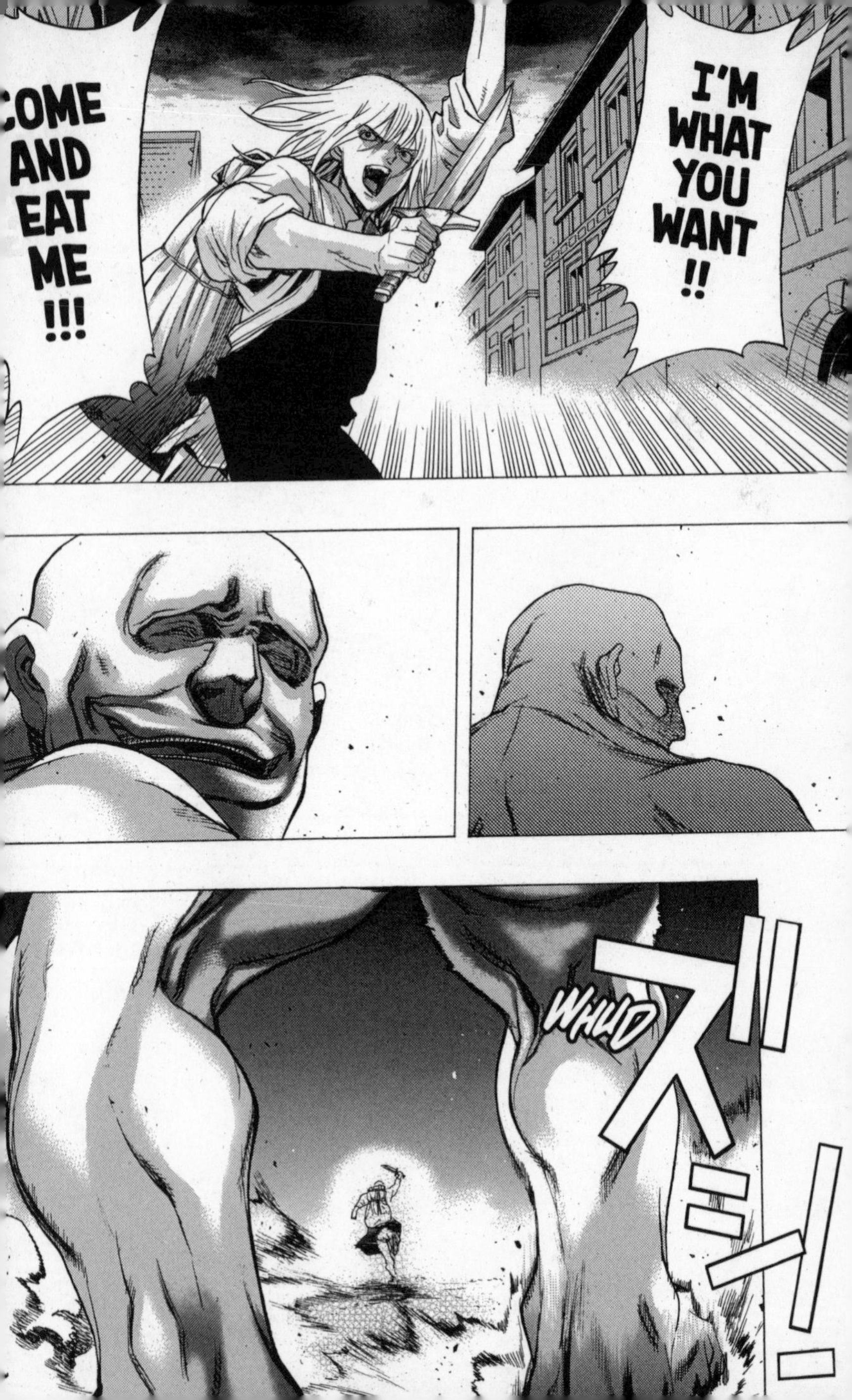
I'M WHAT YOU WANT!!
COME AND EAT ME!!!
WHUD

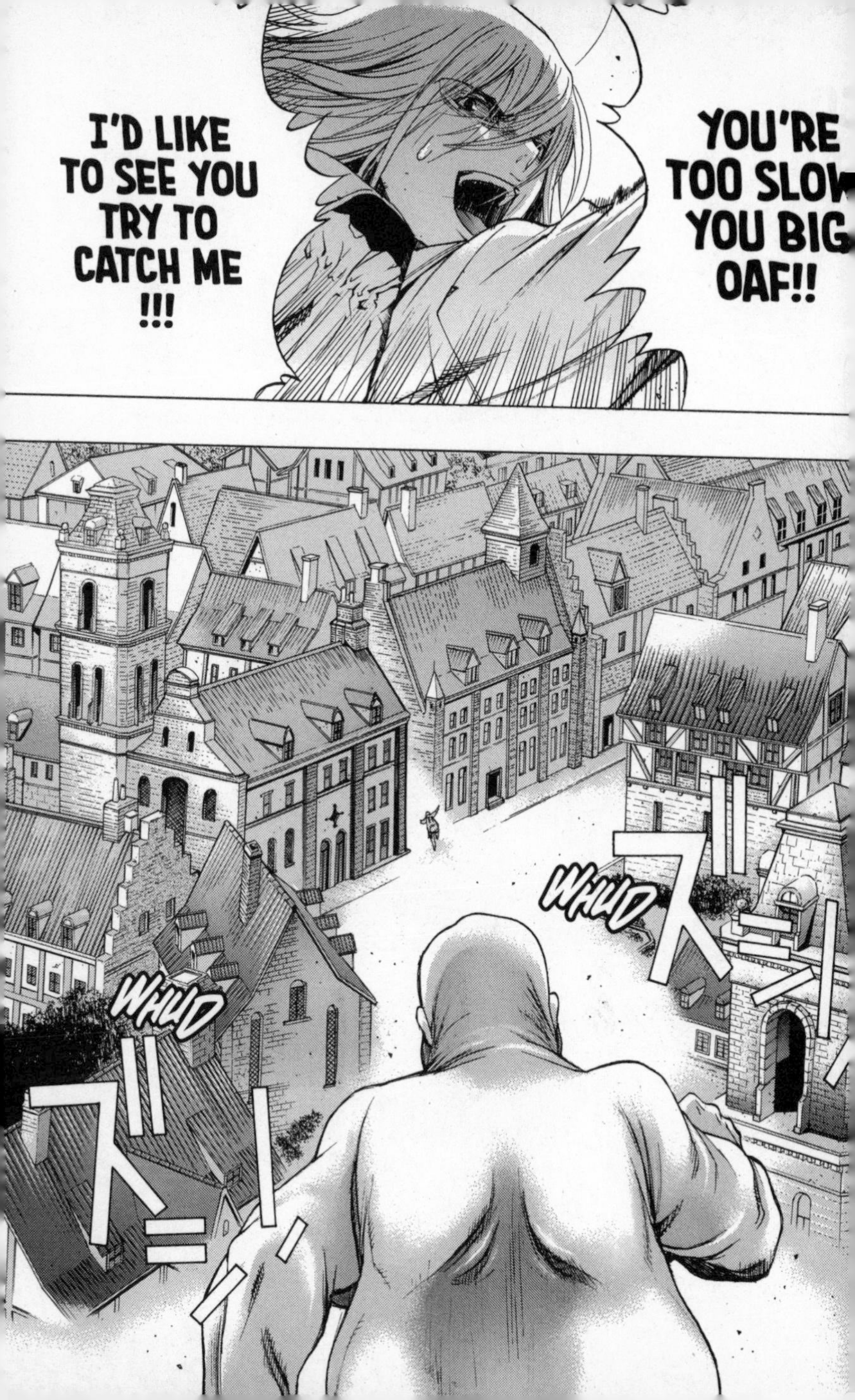
YOU'RE TOO SLOW YOU BIG OAF!!
I'D LIKE TO SEE YOU TRY TO CATCH ME !!!
WHUD
WHUD

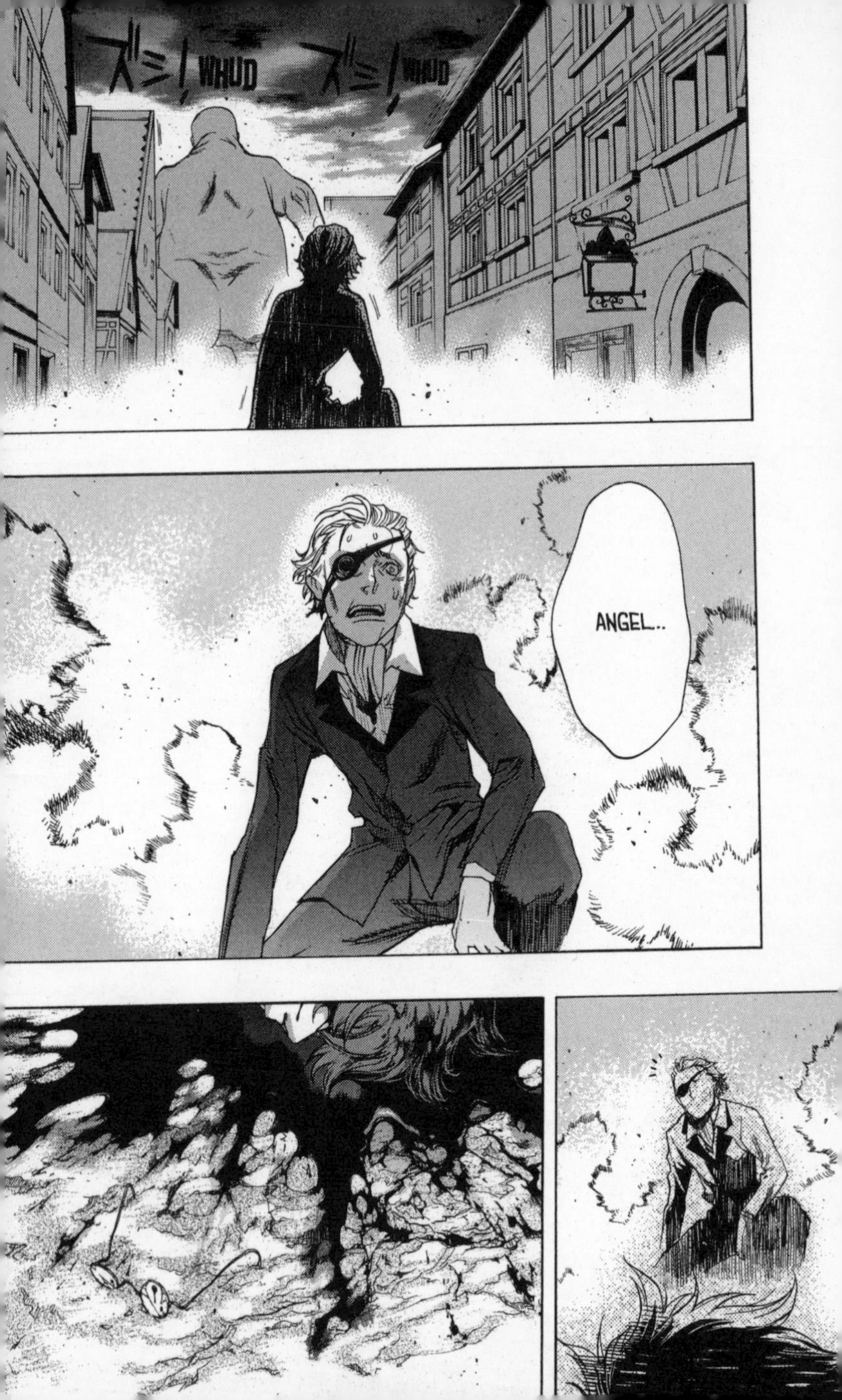
ズシ! WHUD
ズシ! WHUD
ANGEL..

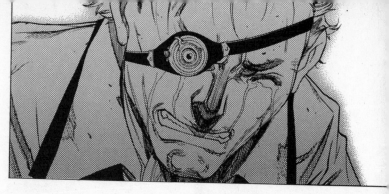

KCHAK

HUFF...

GRRK

GRRK

HUFF!

KCHAK

CLINK

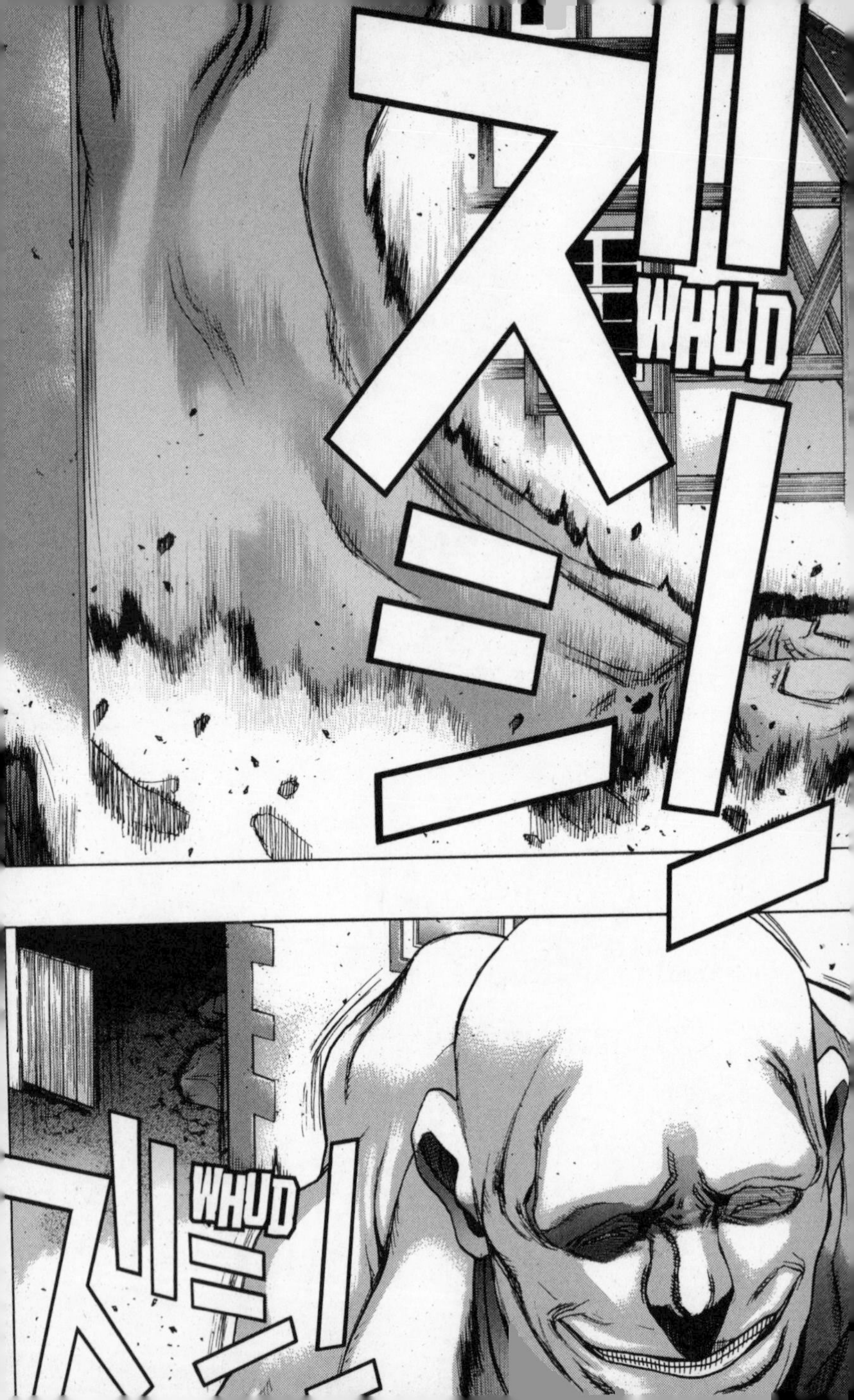
ズシ
WHUD
ズシ
WHUD

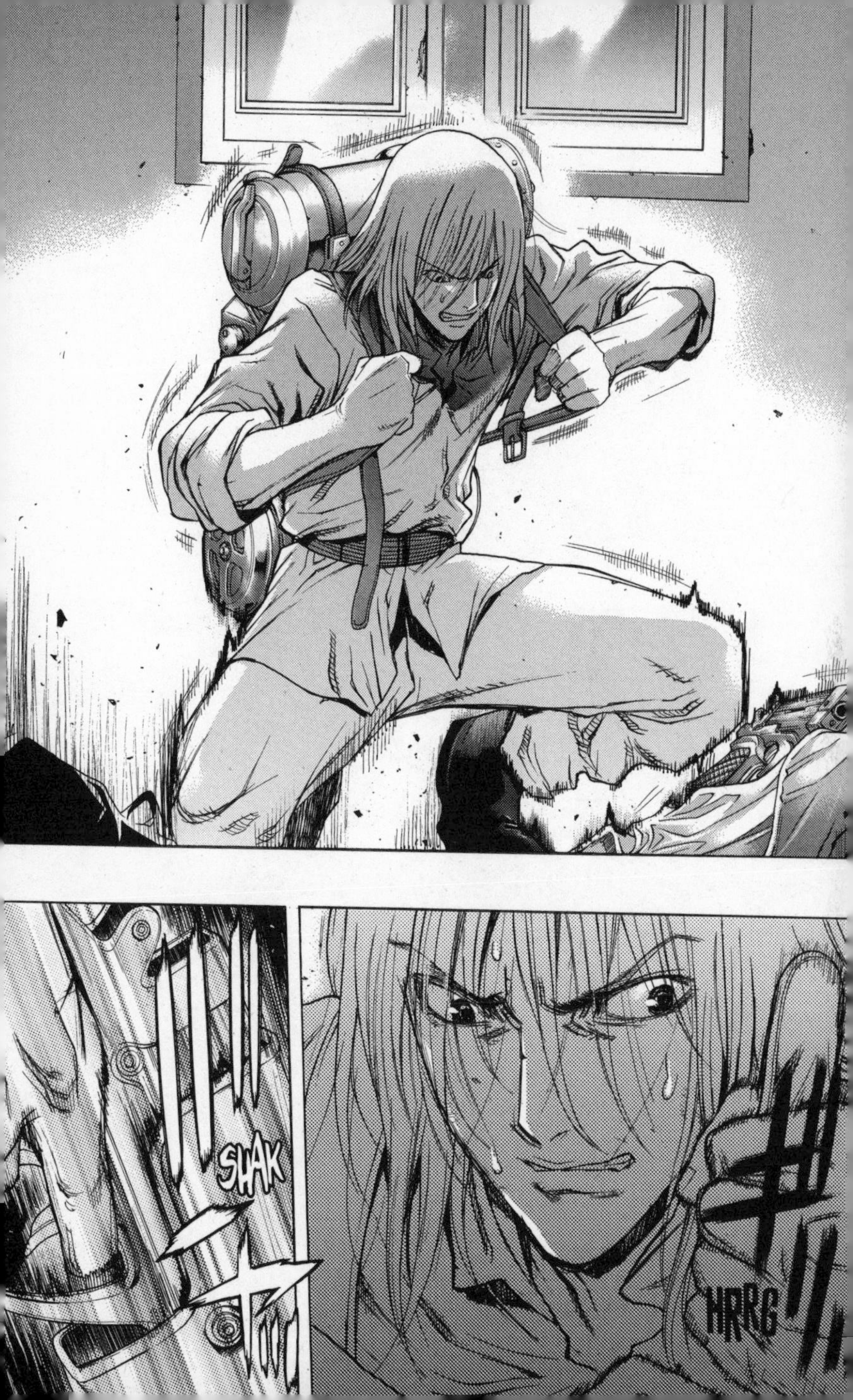
HRRG
SHAK

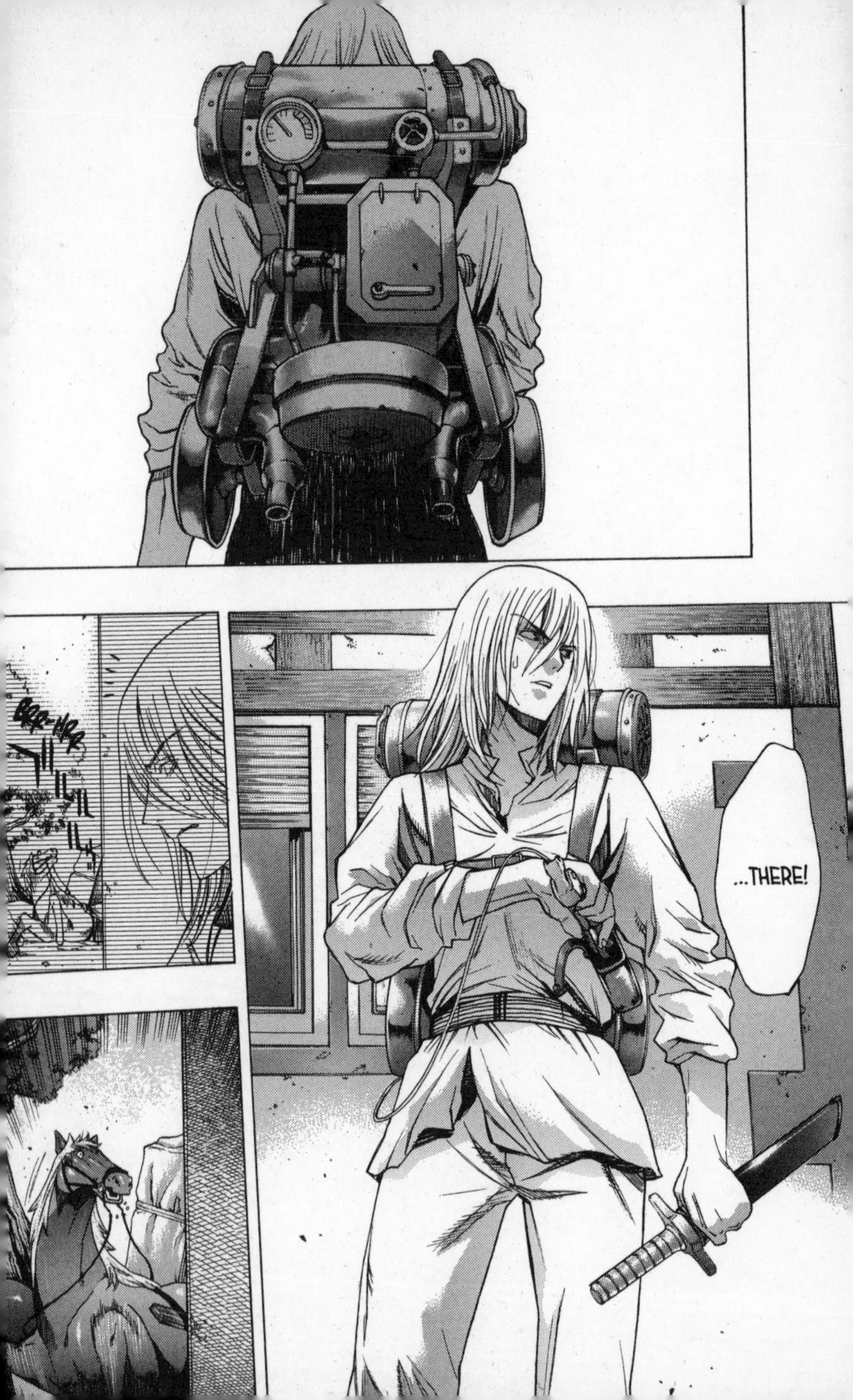
...THERE!
BRR-HRR

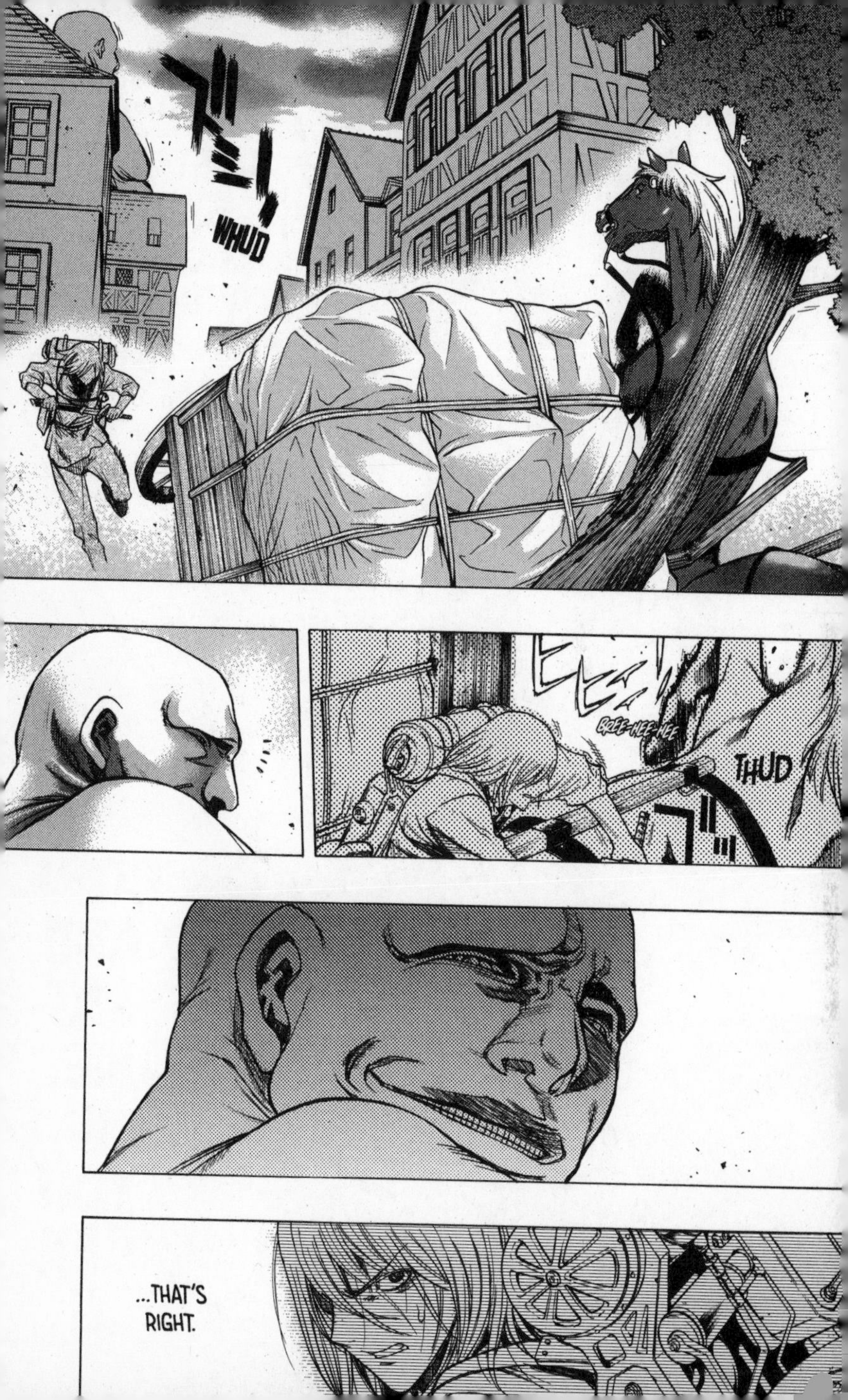
WHUD
BREE-HEE-HEE
THUD
...THAT'S RIGHT.

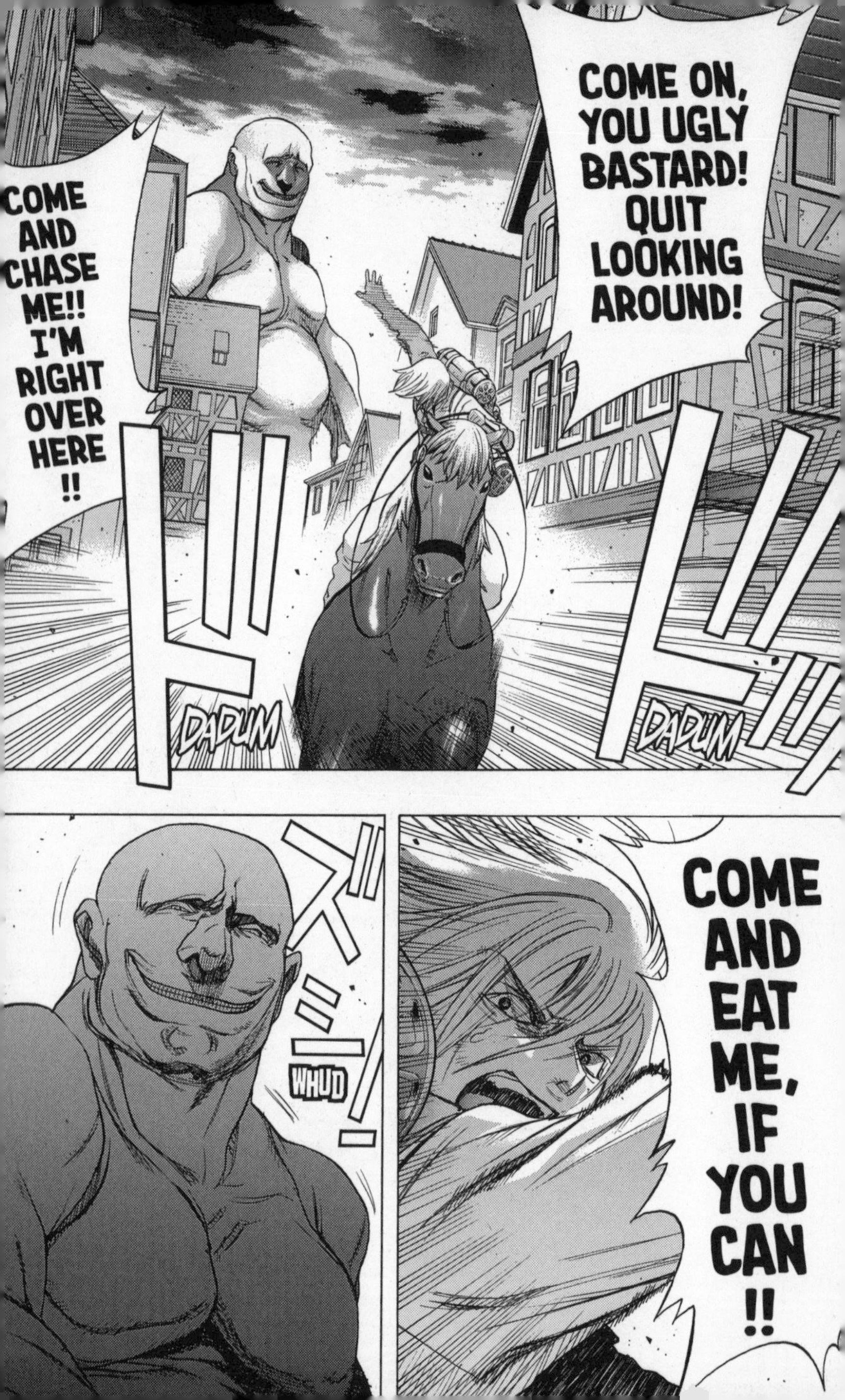
COME ON, YOU UGLY BASTARD! QUIT LOOKING AROUND!
COME AND CHASE ME!! I'M RIGHT OVER HERE!!
DADUM
DADUM
COME AND EAT ME, IF YOU CAN!!
WHUD

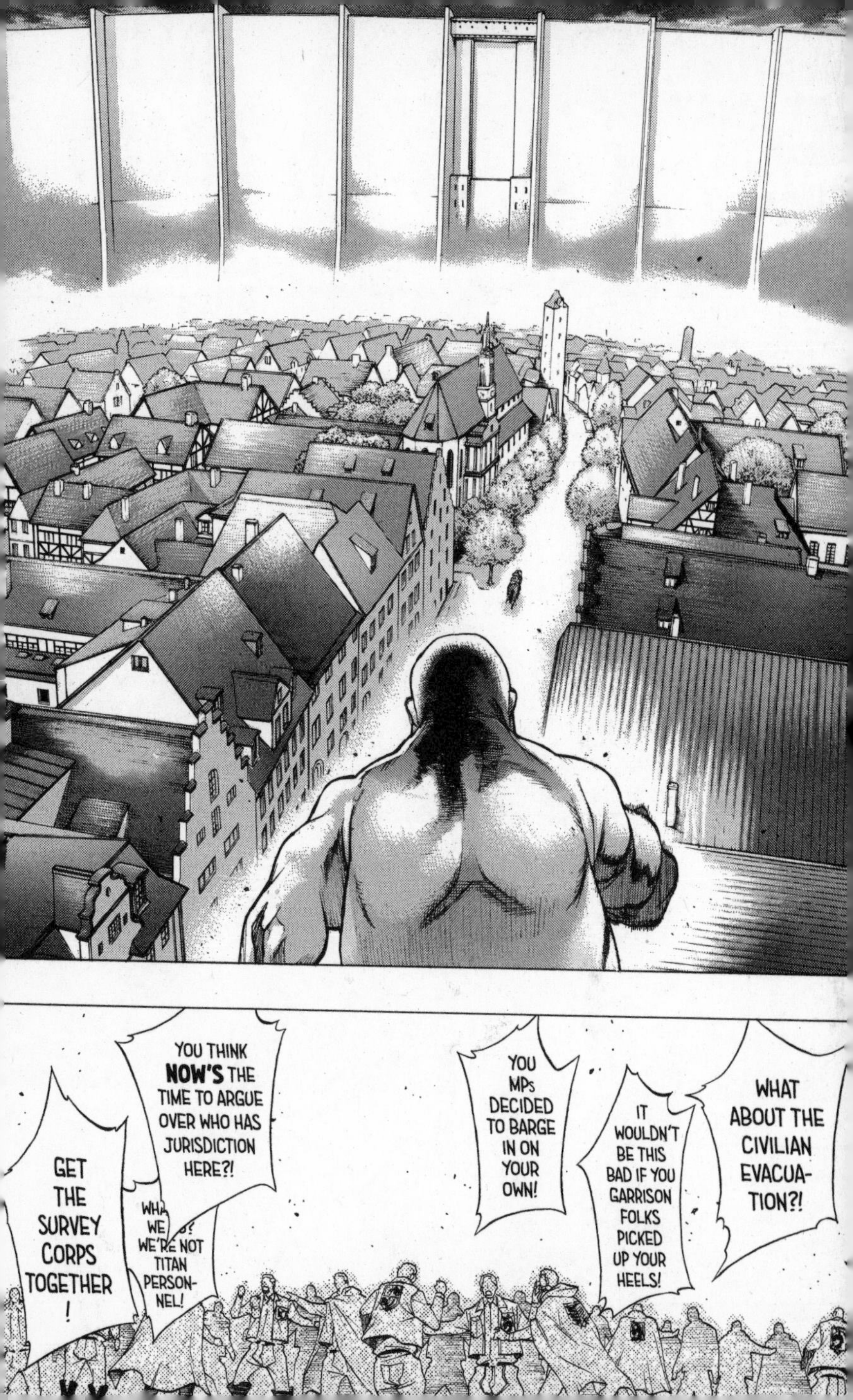
WHAT ABOUT THE CIVILIAN EVACUATION?!
IT WOULDN'T BE THIS BAD IF YOU GARRISON FOLKS PICKED UP YOUR HEELS!
YOU MPs DECIDED TO BARGE IN ON YOUR OWN!
YOU THINK NOW'S THE TIME TO ARGUE OVER WHO HAS JURISDICTION HERE?!
WE'RE NOT TITAN PERSONNEL!
GET THE SURVEY CORPS TOGETHER!

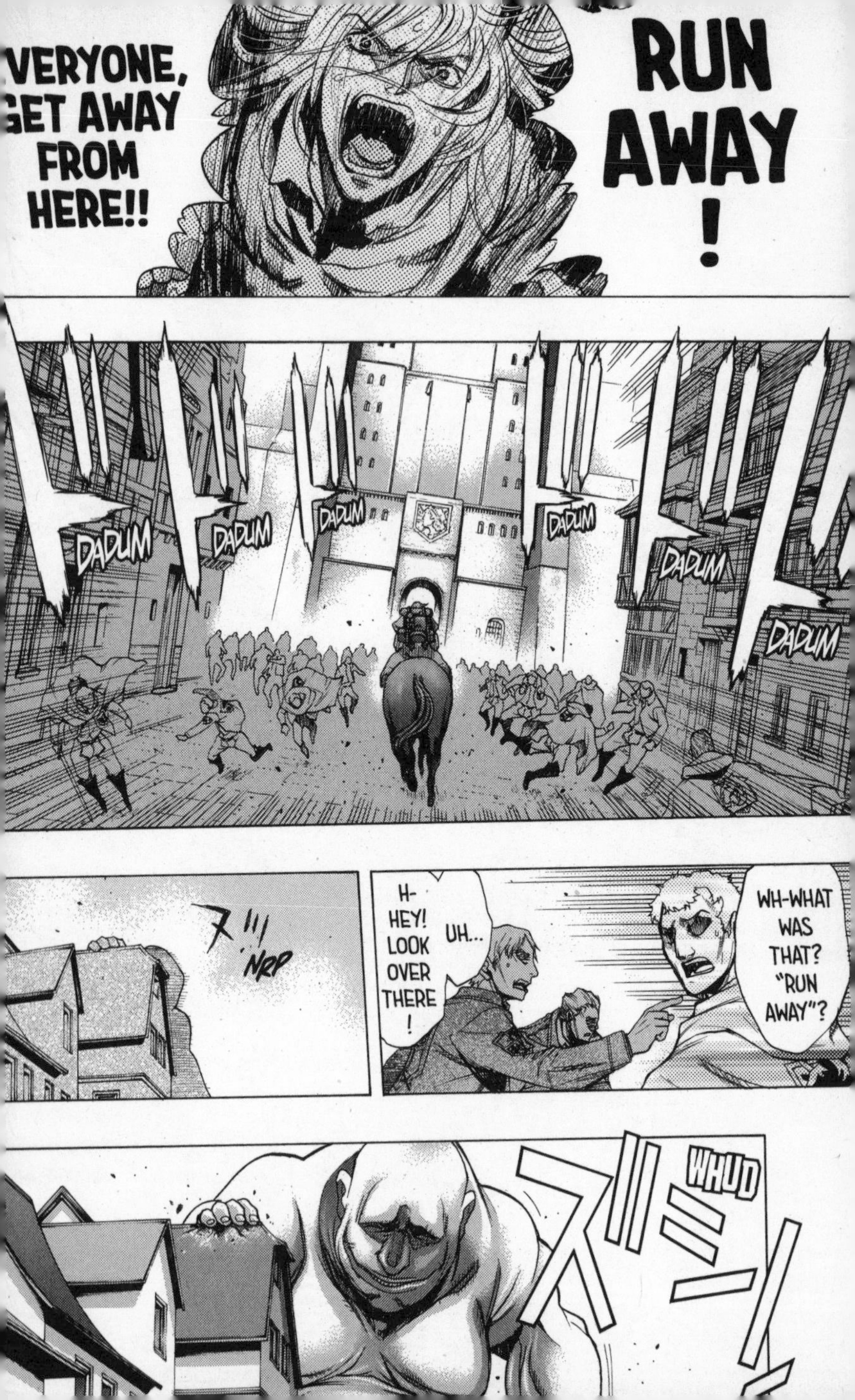
RUN AWAY!
VERYONE, GET AWAY FROM HERE!!
DADUM
DADUM
DADUM
DADUM
DADUM
DADUM
WH-WHAT WAS THAT? "RUN AWAY"?
UH...
H-HEY! LOOK OVER THERE!
NRP
WHUD

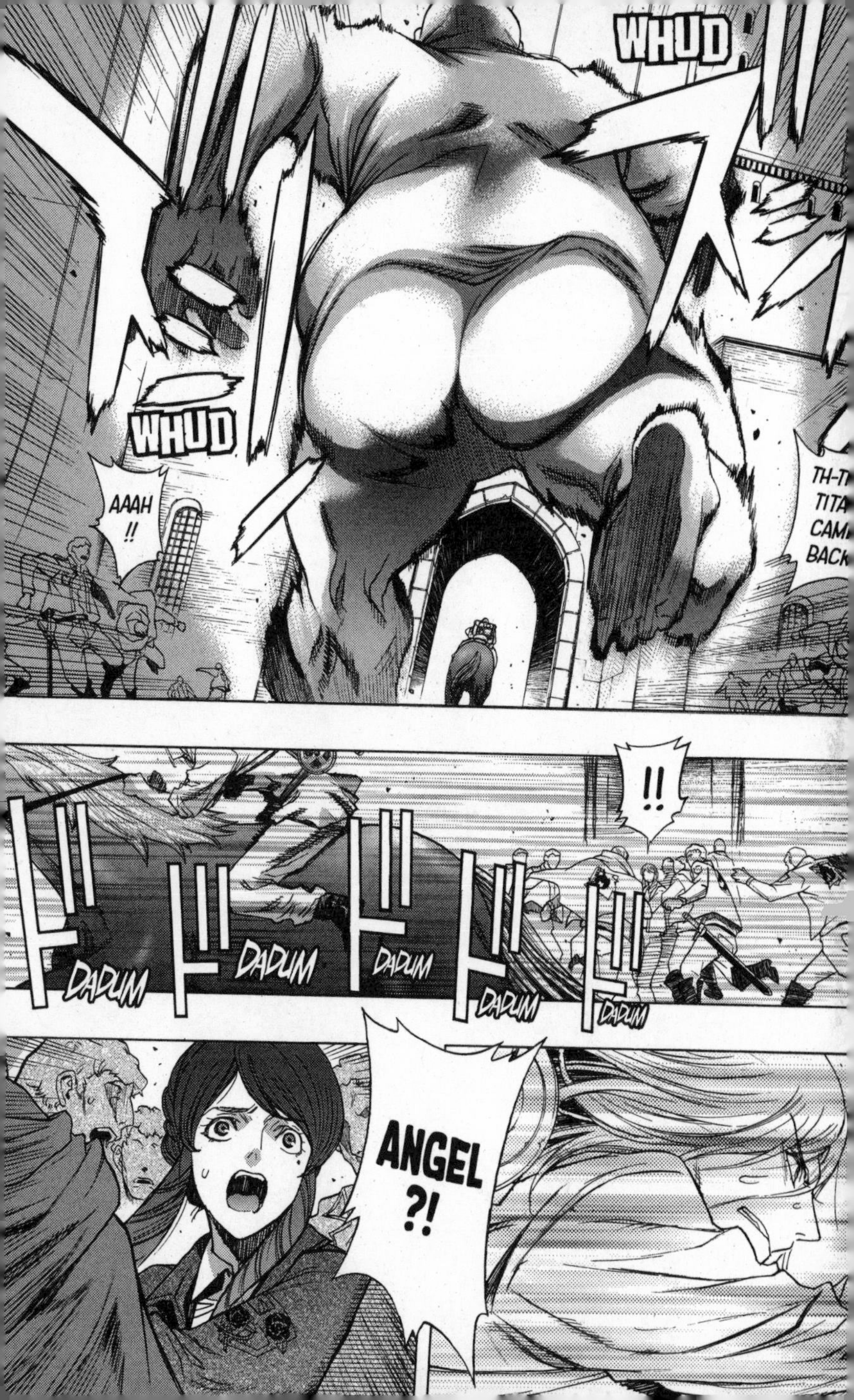
WHUD
TH-TI TITA CAM BACK
WHUD
AAAH !!
!!
DADUM
DADUM
DADUM
DADUM
DADUM
ANGEL ?!

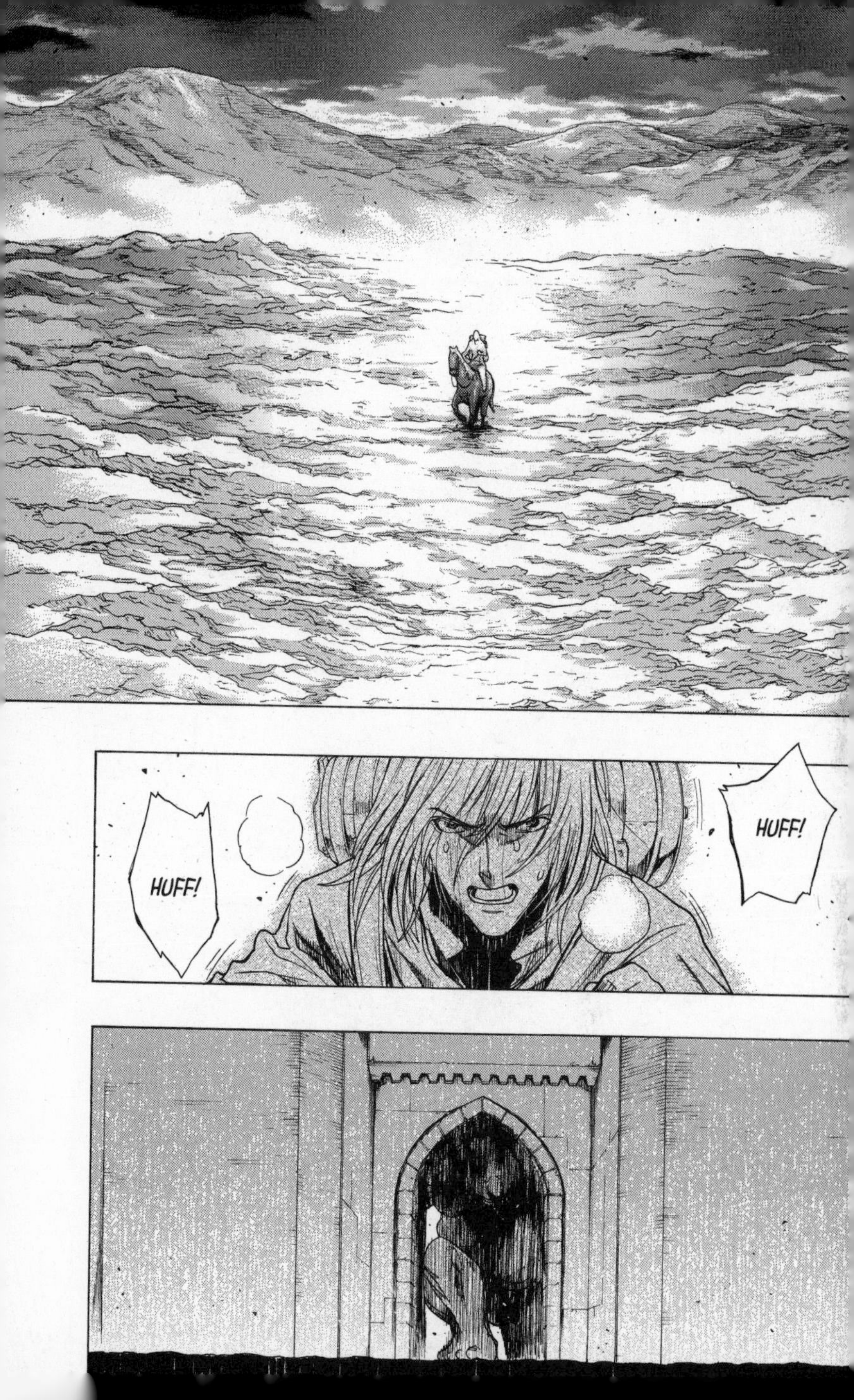
HUFF!
HUFF!

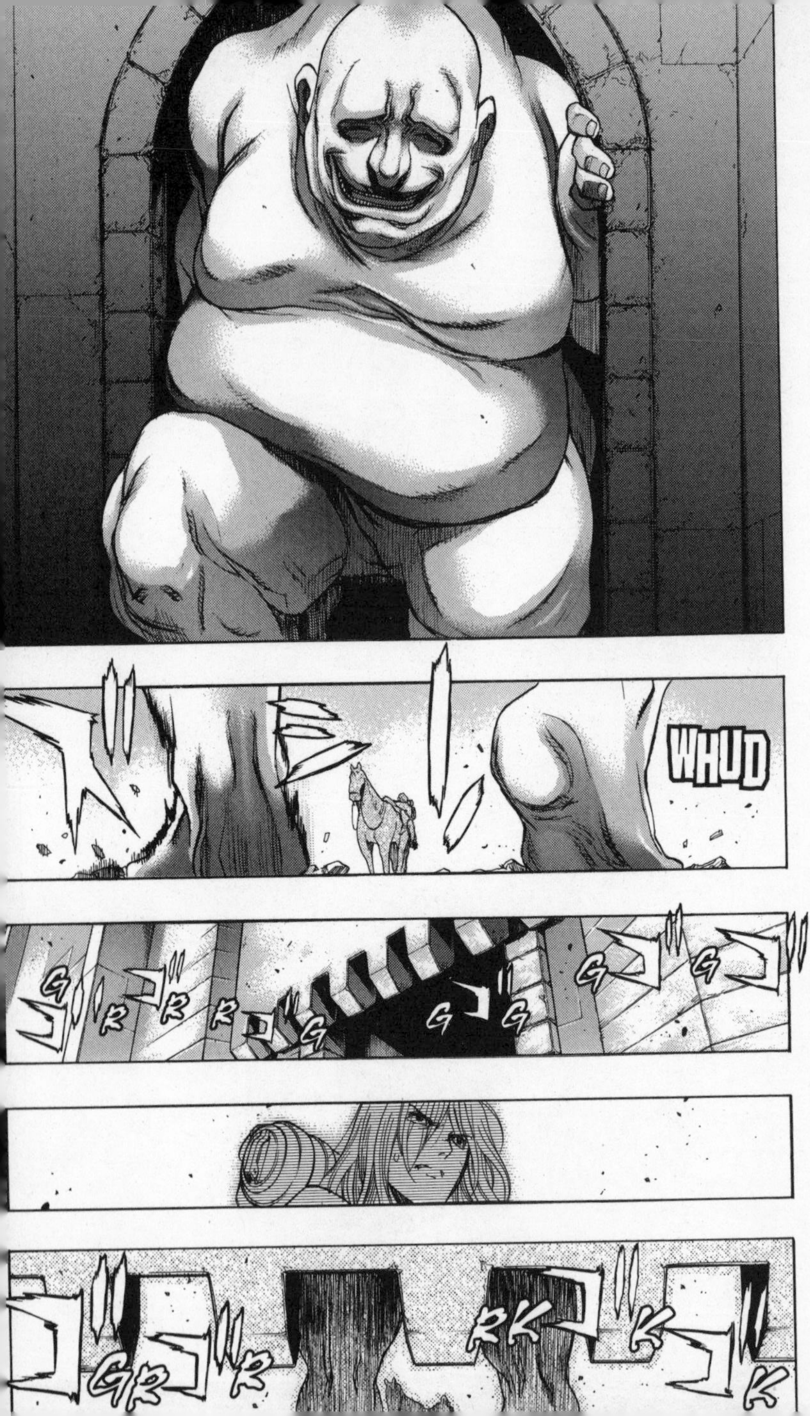
WHUD
G G
GRRRG
G G
RKKK
GRR

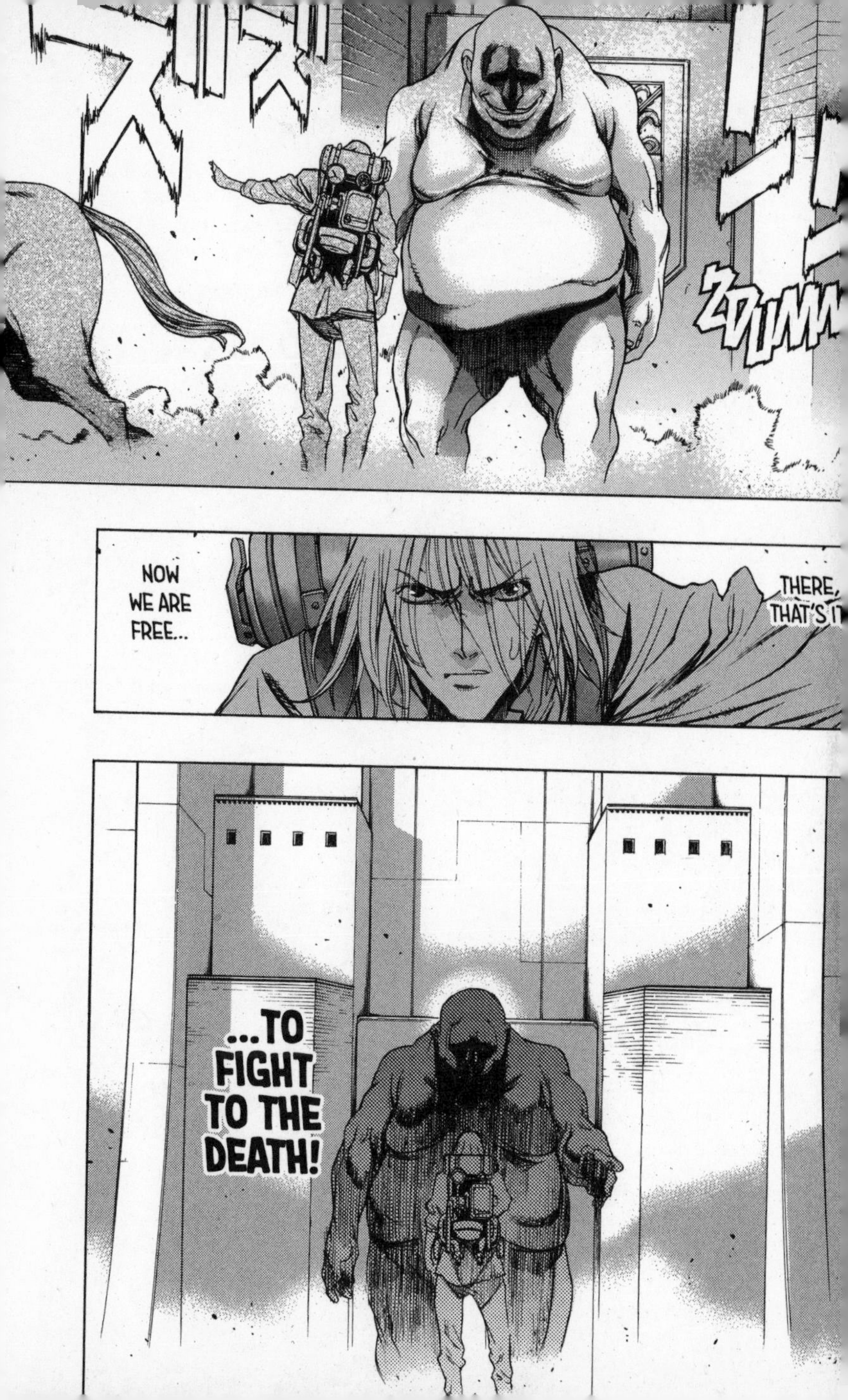
ZDUMM
THERE, THAT'S IT
NOW WE ARE FREE...
...TO FIGHT TO THE DEATH!

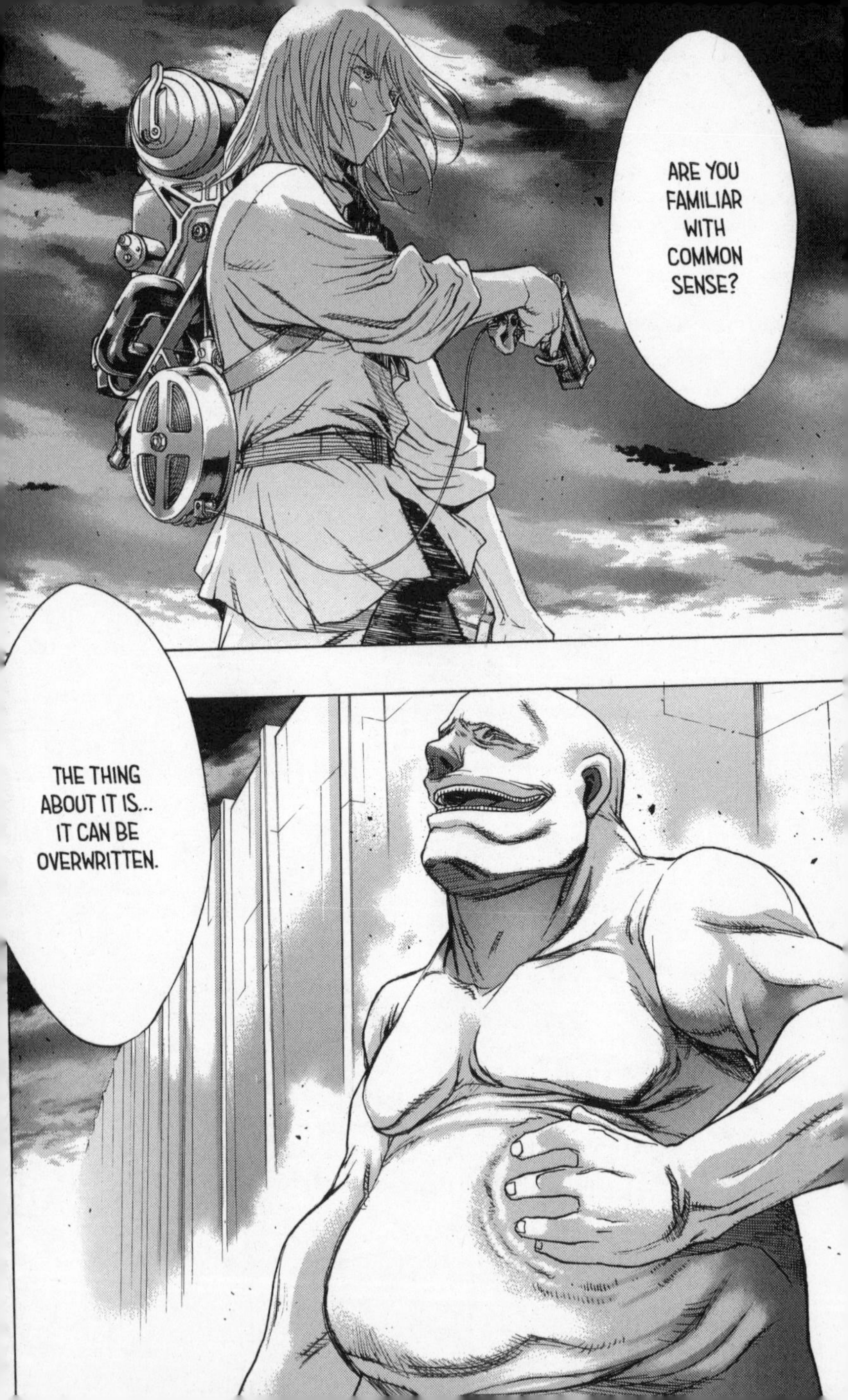
ARE YOU FAMILIAR WITH COMMON SENSE?
THE THING ABOUT IT IS... IT CAN BE OVERWRITTEN.

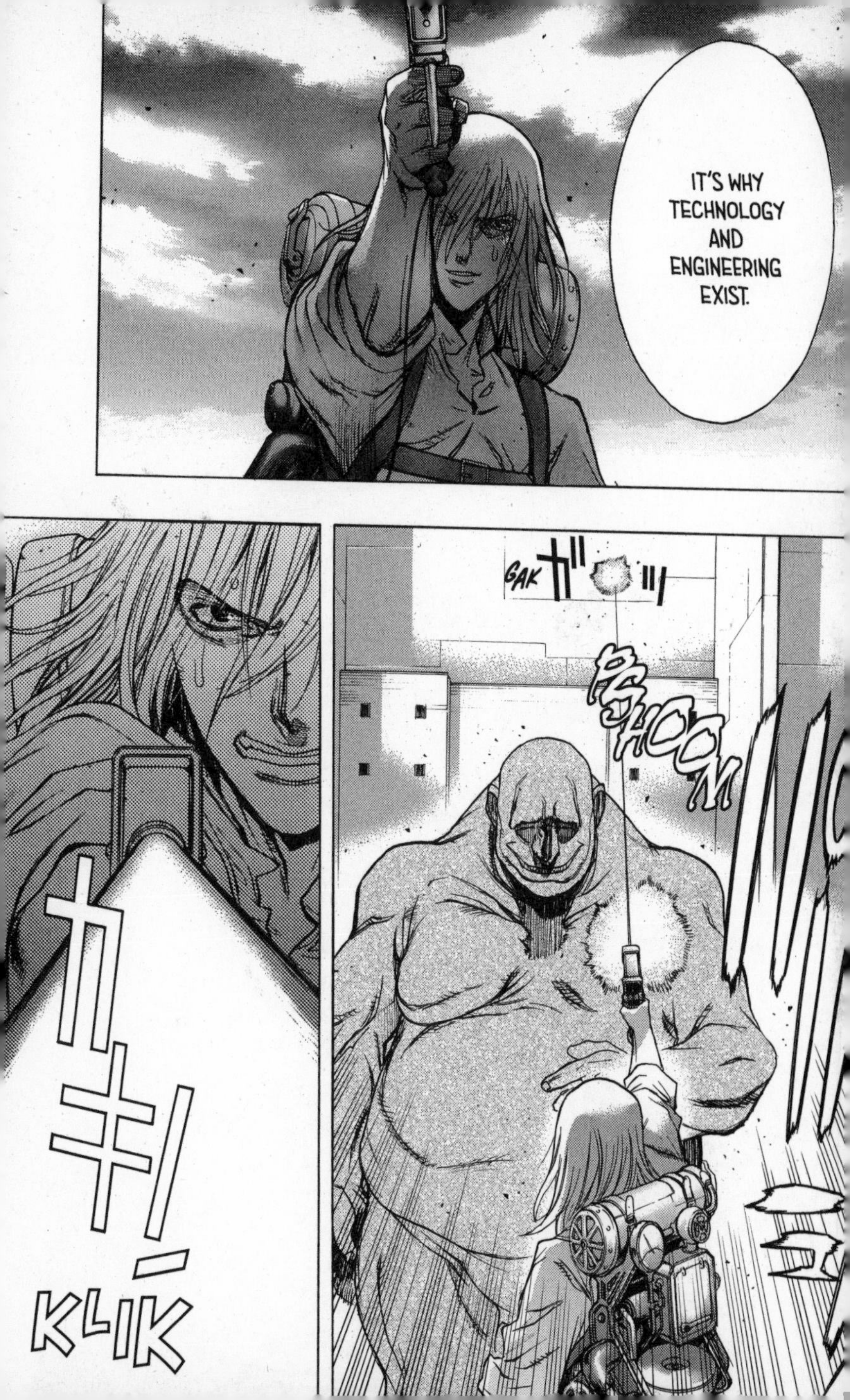
IT'S WHY TECHNOLOGY AND ENGINEERING EXIST.
GAK
PSHOOM
KLIK

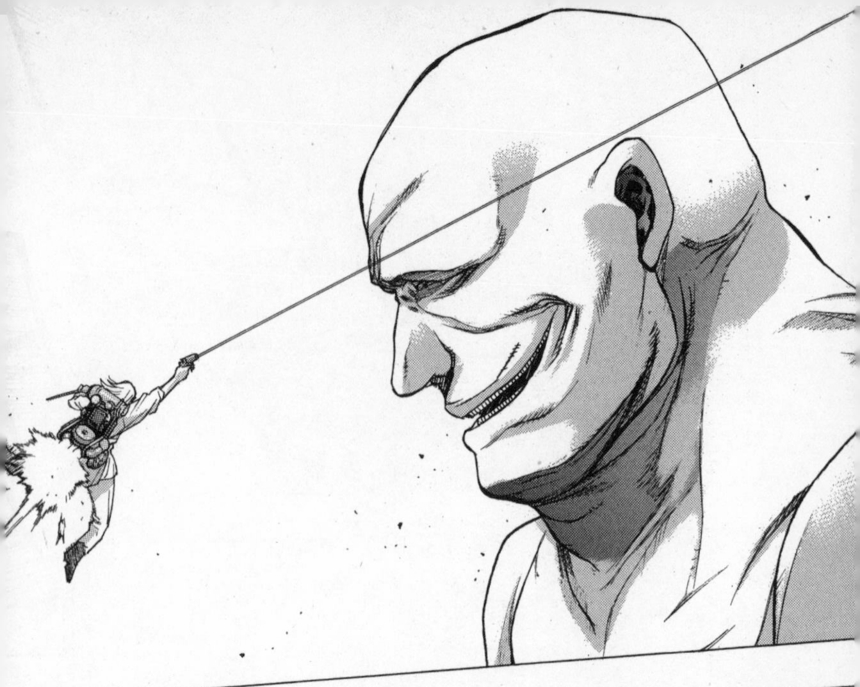
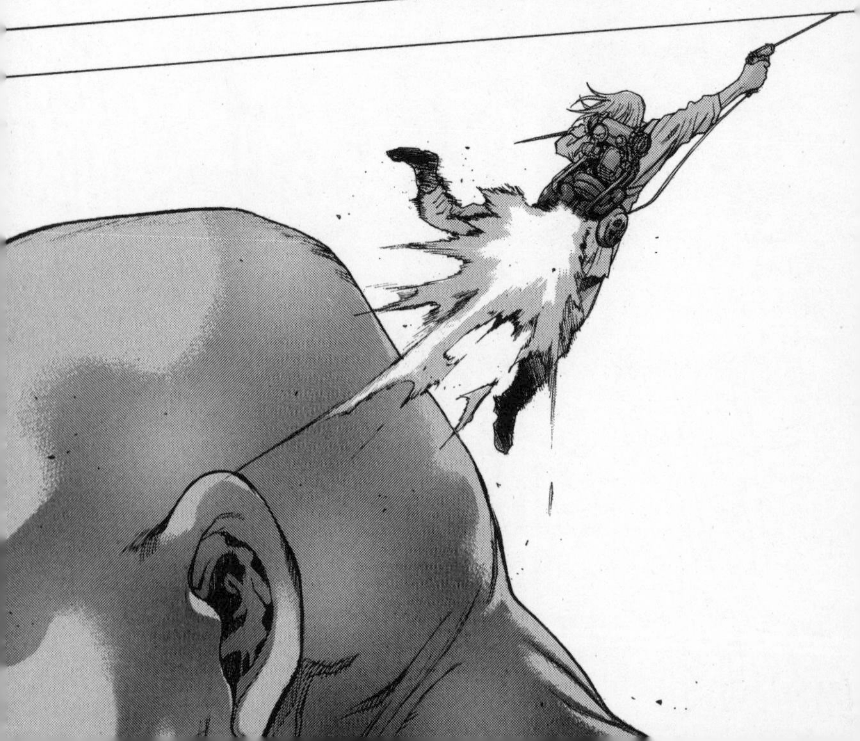

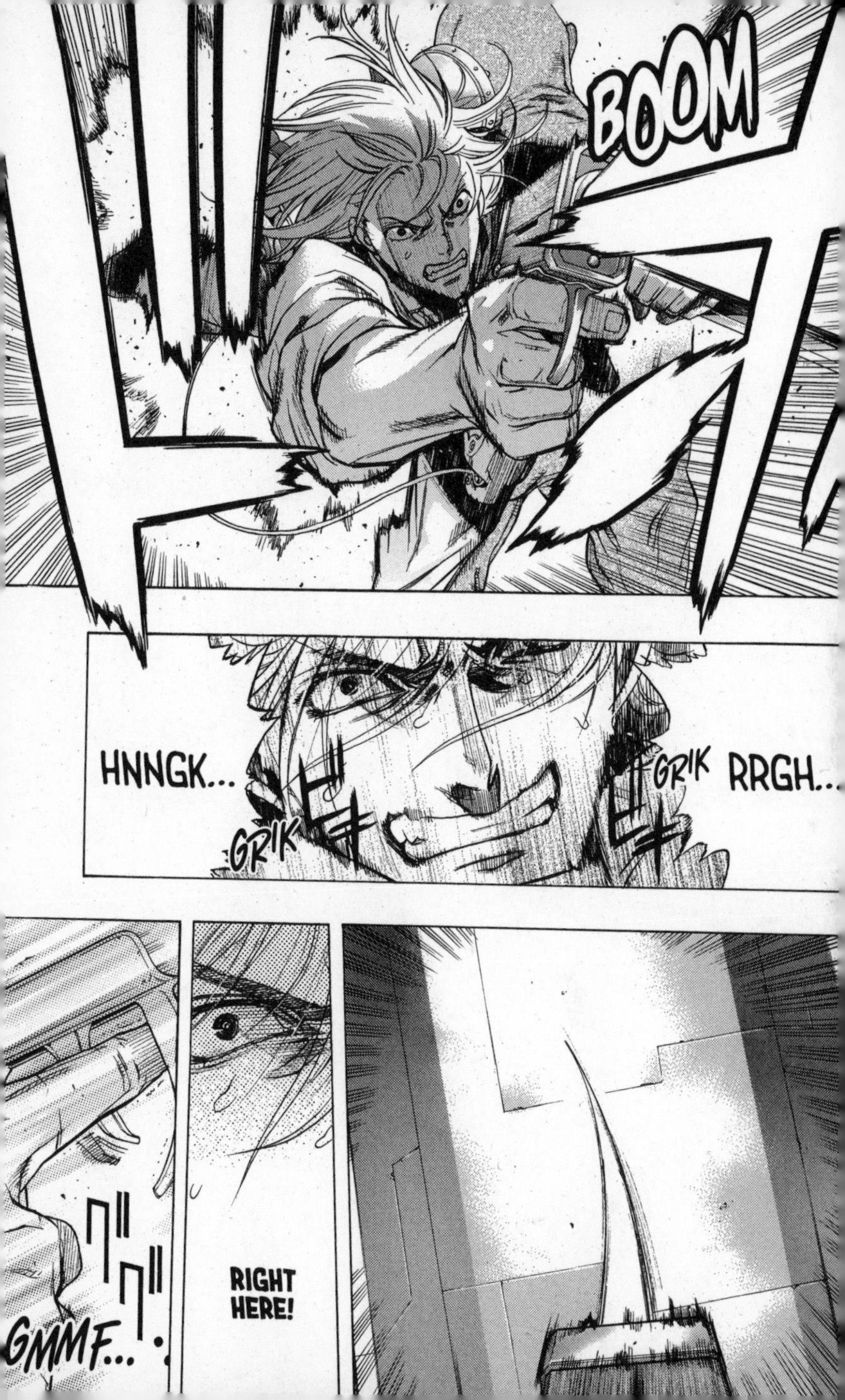
BOOM
RRGH...
GRIK
HNNGK...
GRIK
RIGHT HERE!
GMMF...

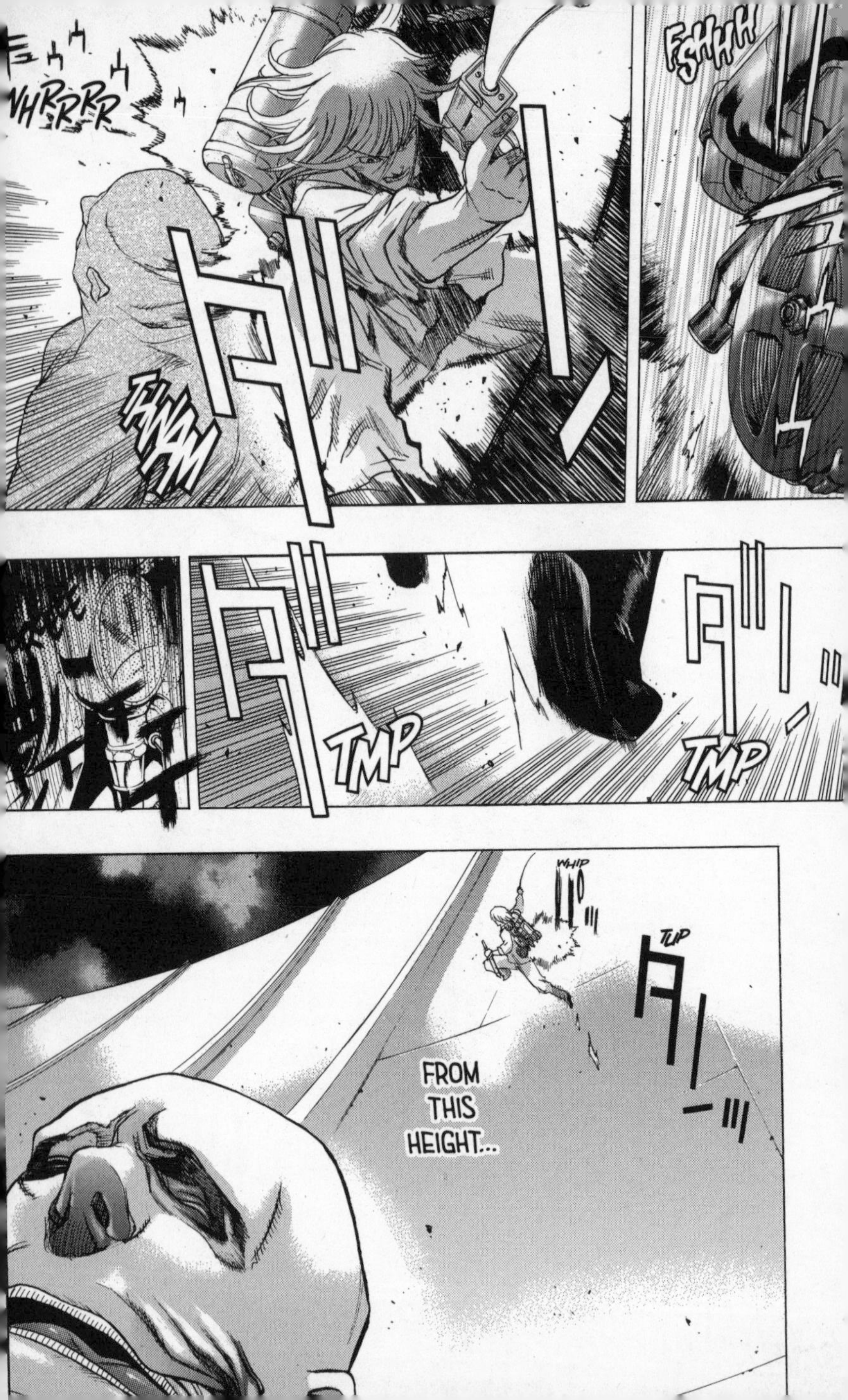
FSHHH
VHRRRR
THWAM
TMP
TMP
WHIP
TUP
FROM THIS HEIGHT...

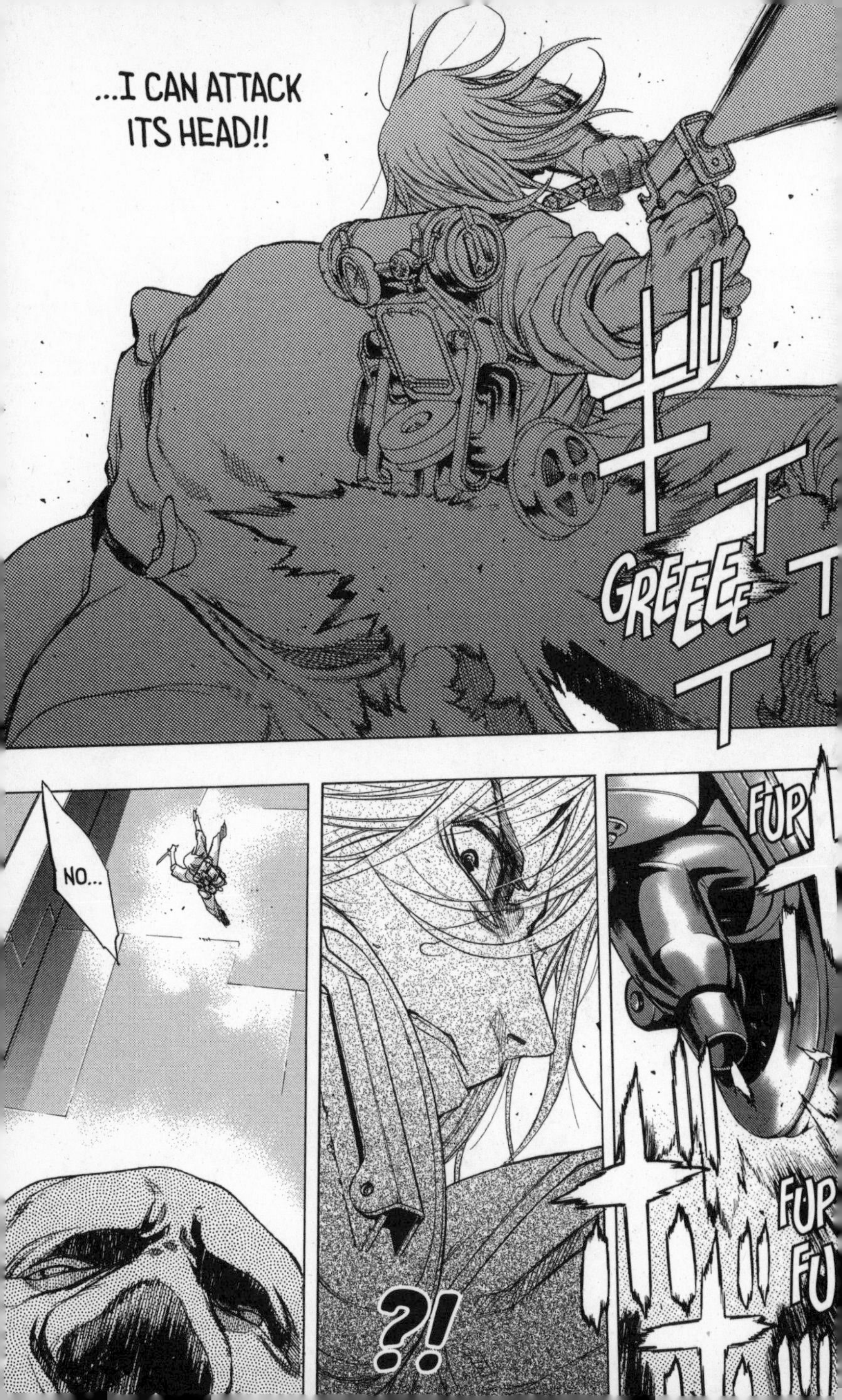
...I CAN ATTACK ITS HEAD!!
GREEEEE
FUP
FUP FU
?!
NO...

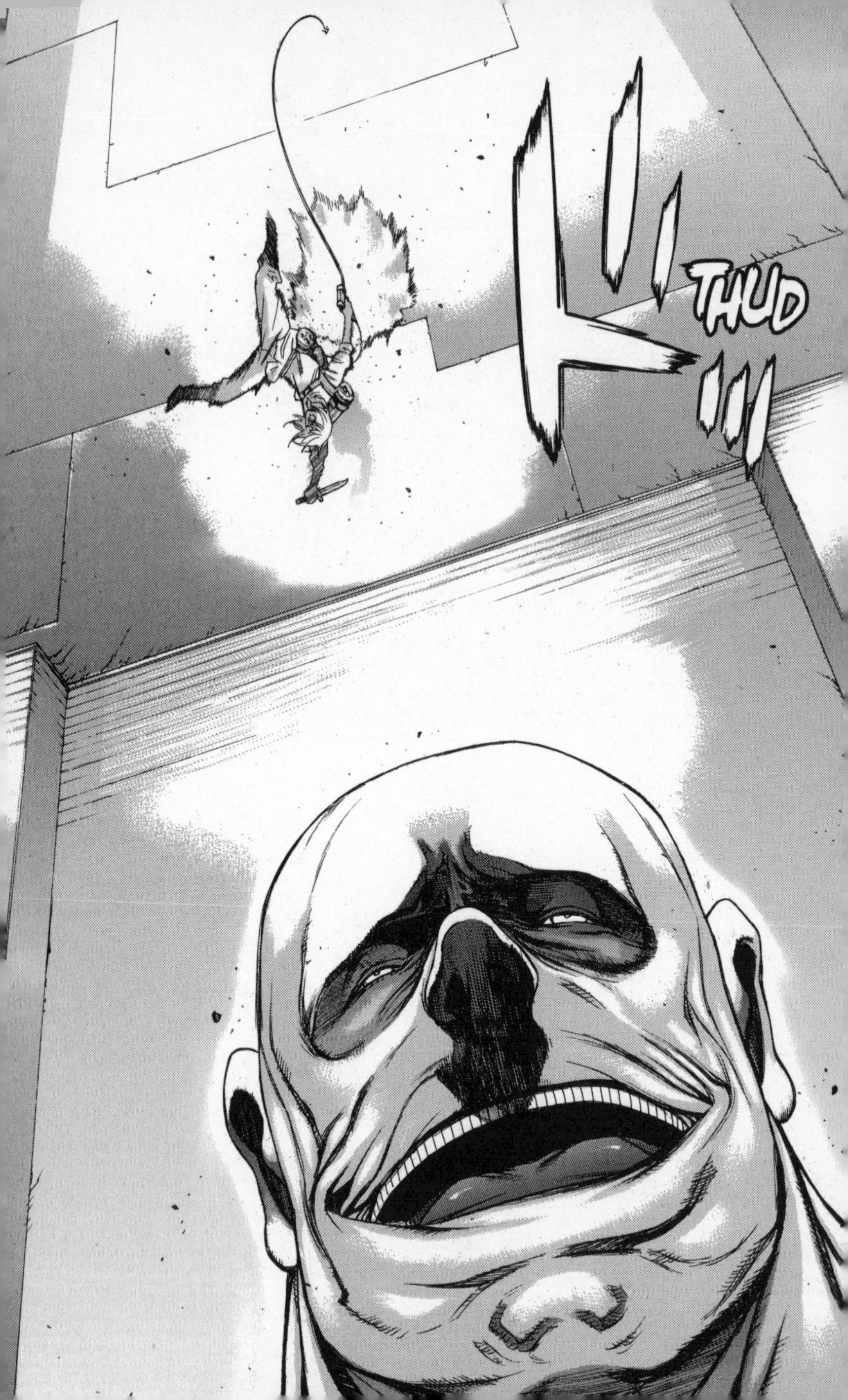
THUD

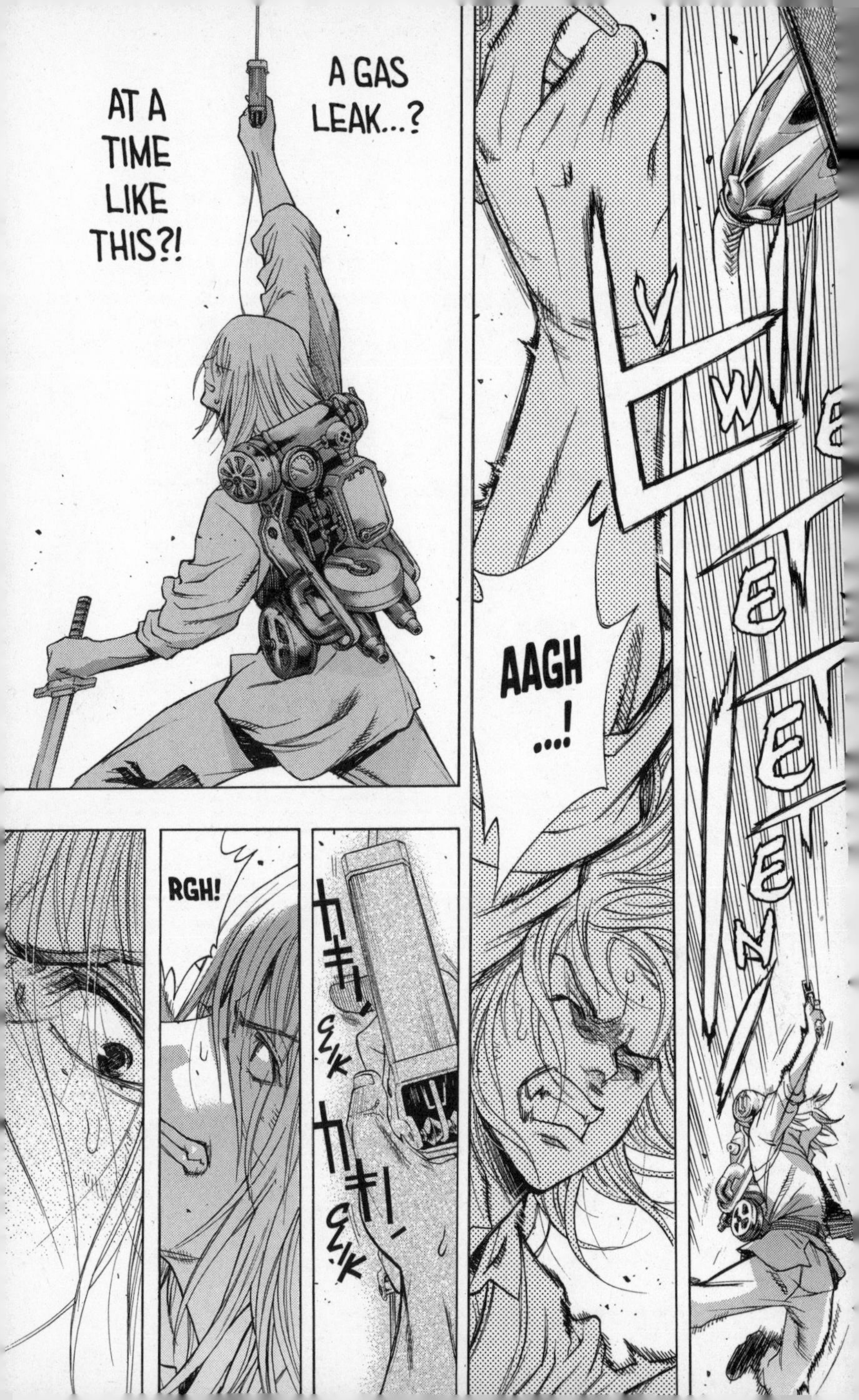
VWEEEEN
AAGH ...!
A GAS LEAK...?
AT A TIME LIKE THIS?!
CLIK
CLIK
RGH!

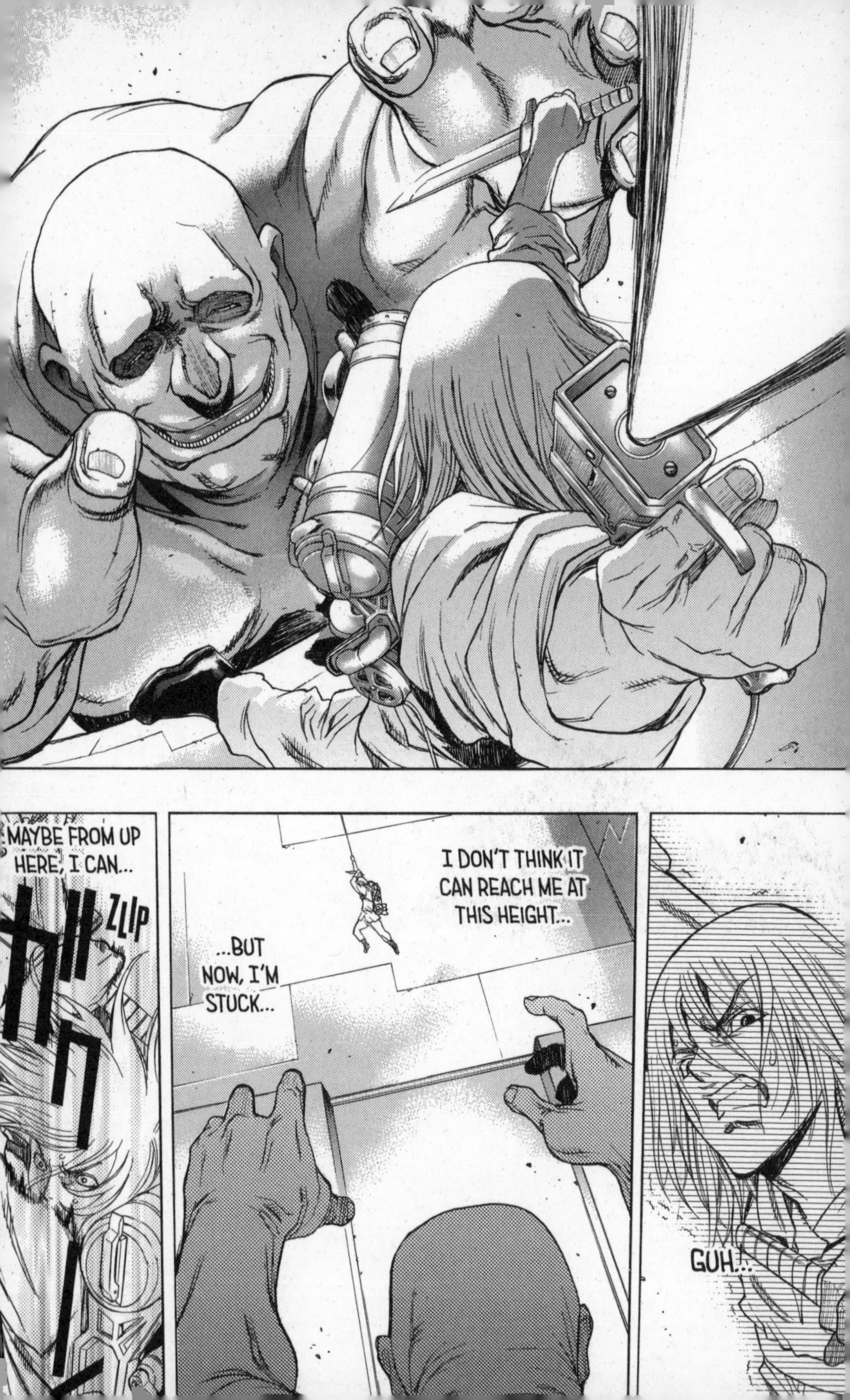
GUH...
I DON'T THINK IT CAN REACH ME AT THIS HEIGHT...
...BUT NOW, I'M STUCK...
MAYBE FROM UP HERE, I CAN...
ZLIP

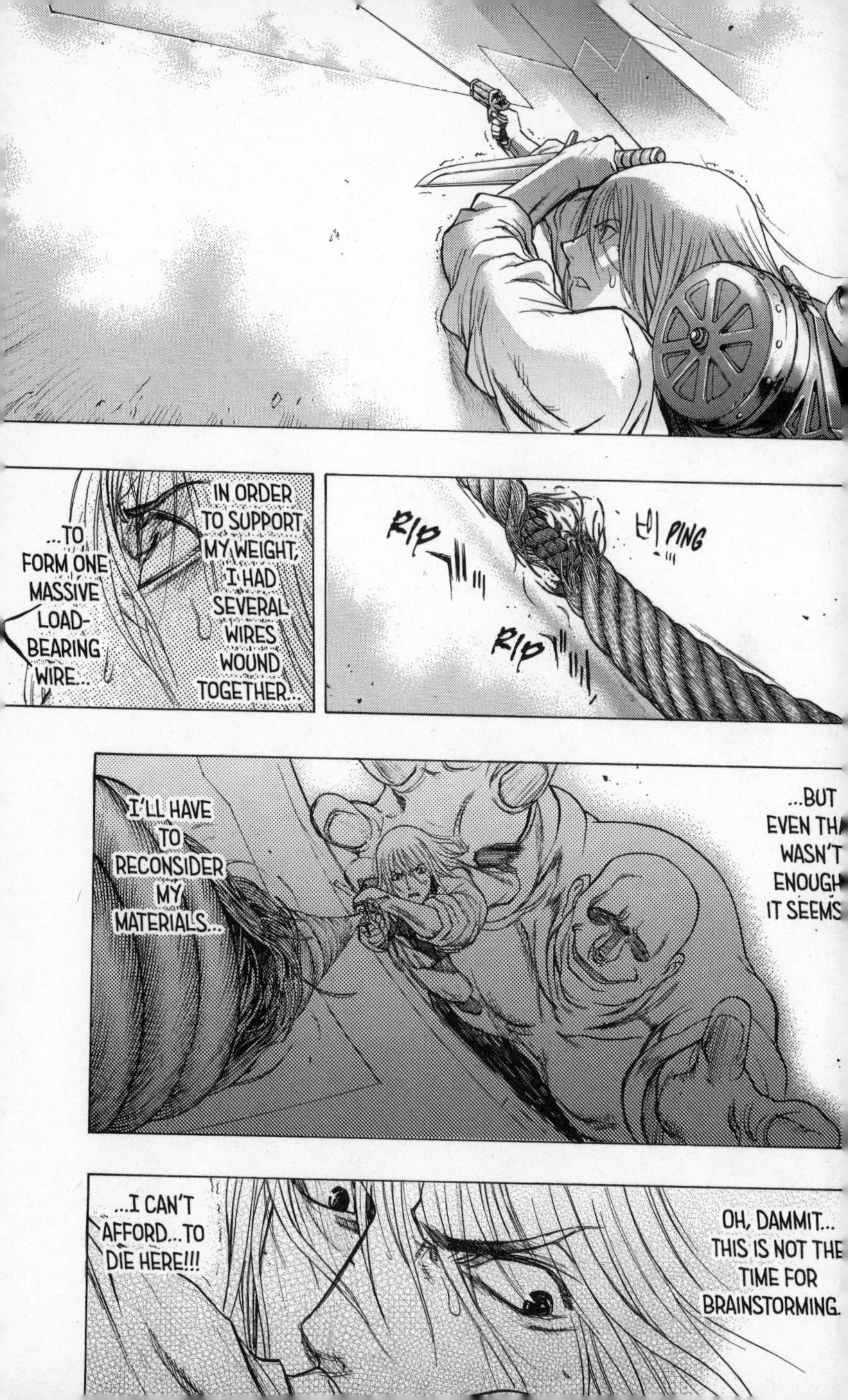
RIP
PING
RIP
IN ORDER TO SUPPORT MY WEIGHT, I HAD SEVERAL WIRES WOUND TOGETHER...
...TO FORM ONE MASSIVE LOAD-BEARING WIRE...
...BUT EVEN THA WASN'T ENOUGH IT SEEMS
I'LL HAVE TO RECONSIDER MY MATERIALS...
OH, DAMMIT... THIS IS NOT THE TIME FOR BRAINSTORMING.
...I CAN'T AFFORD...TO DIE HERE!!!

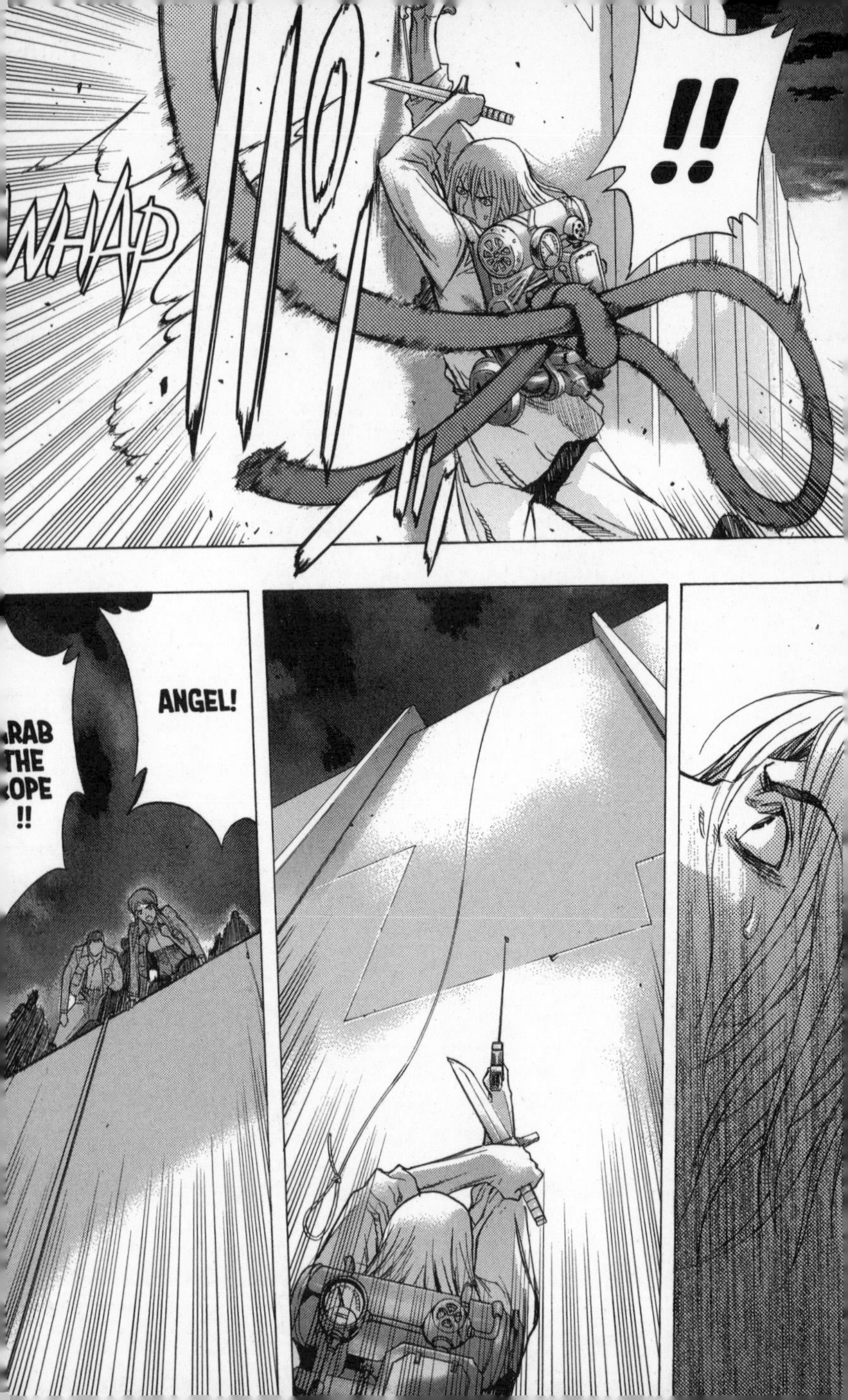
!!
WHAP
ANGEL!
RAB THE OPE !!

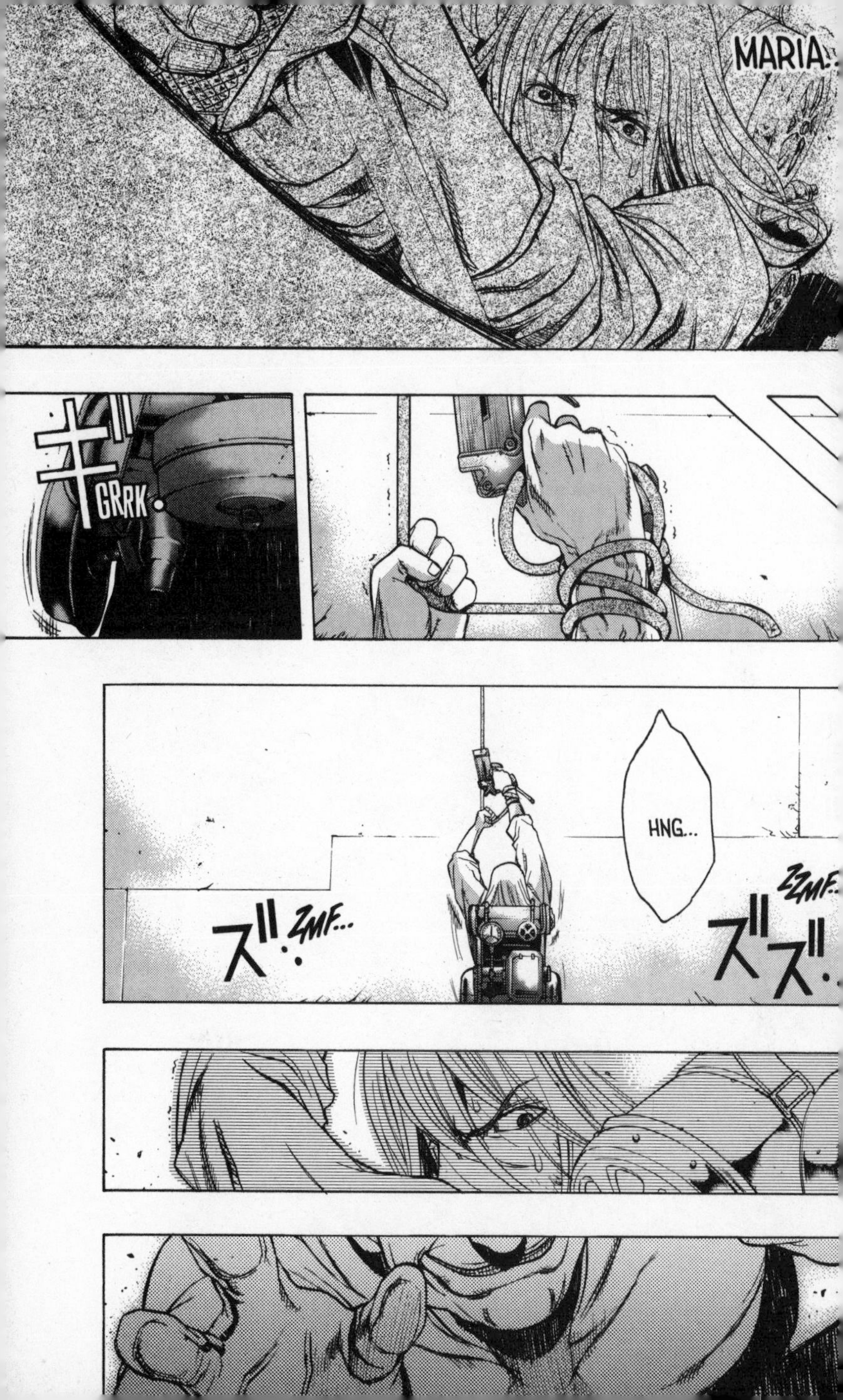
MARIA!
ギ
GRRK
HNG...
ズズ
ZZMF...
ズ
ZMF...

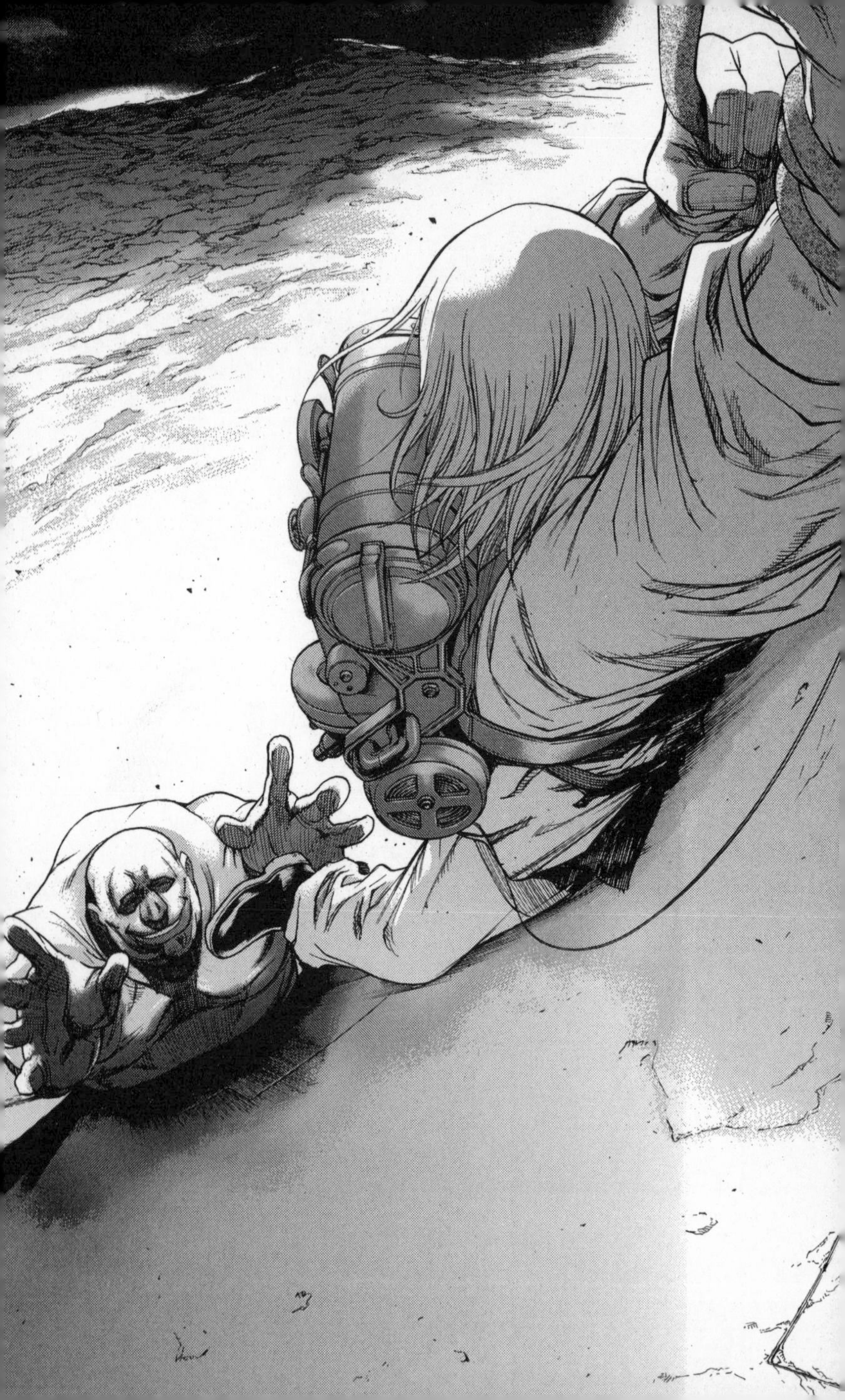

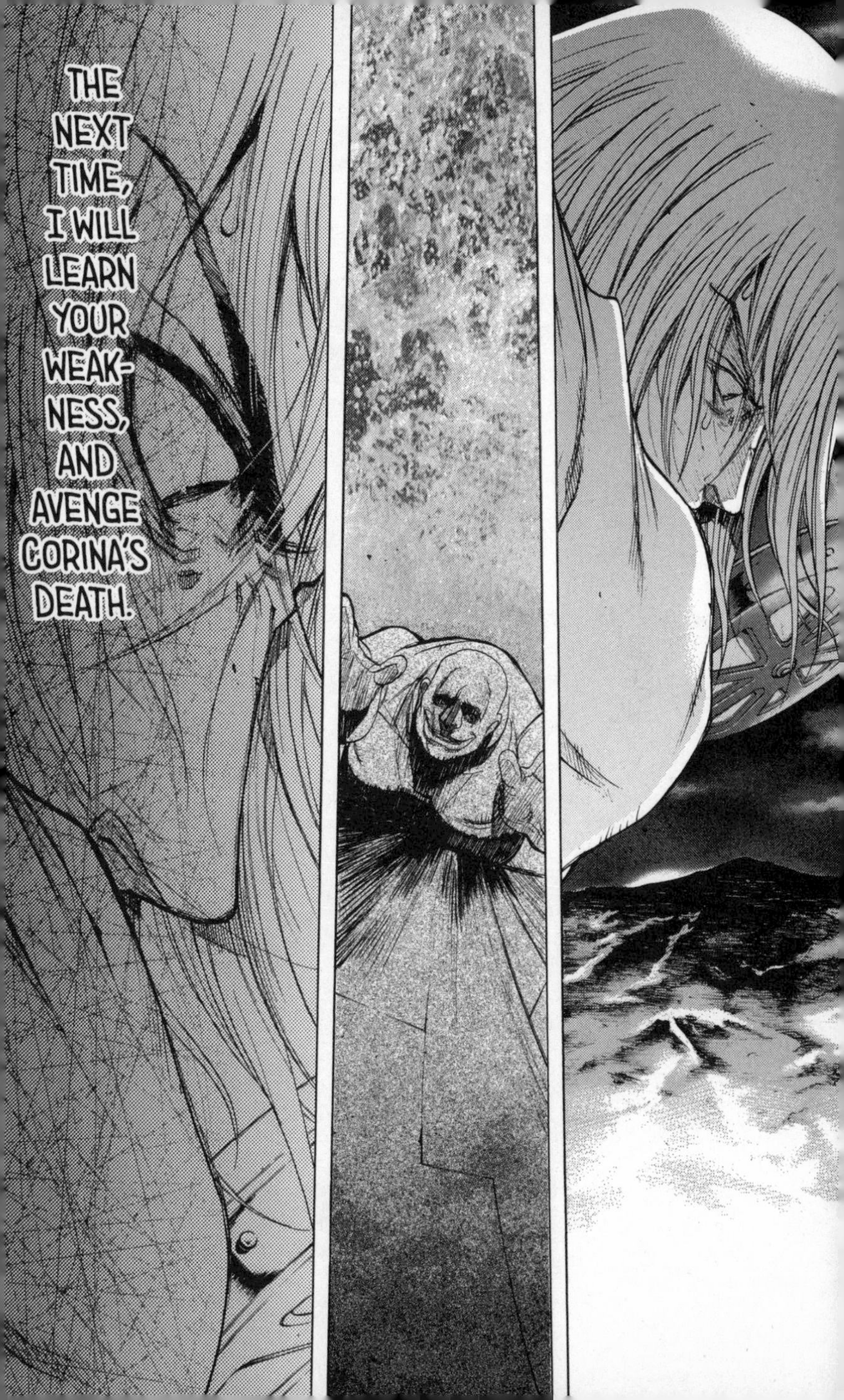
THE NEXT TIME, I WILL LEARN YOUR WEAK-NESS, AND AVENGE CORINA'S DEATH.

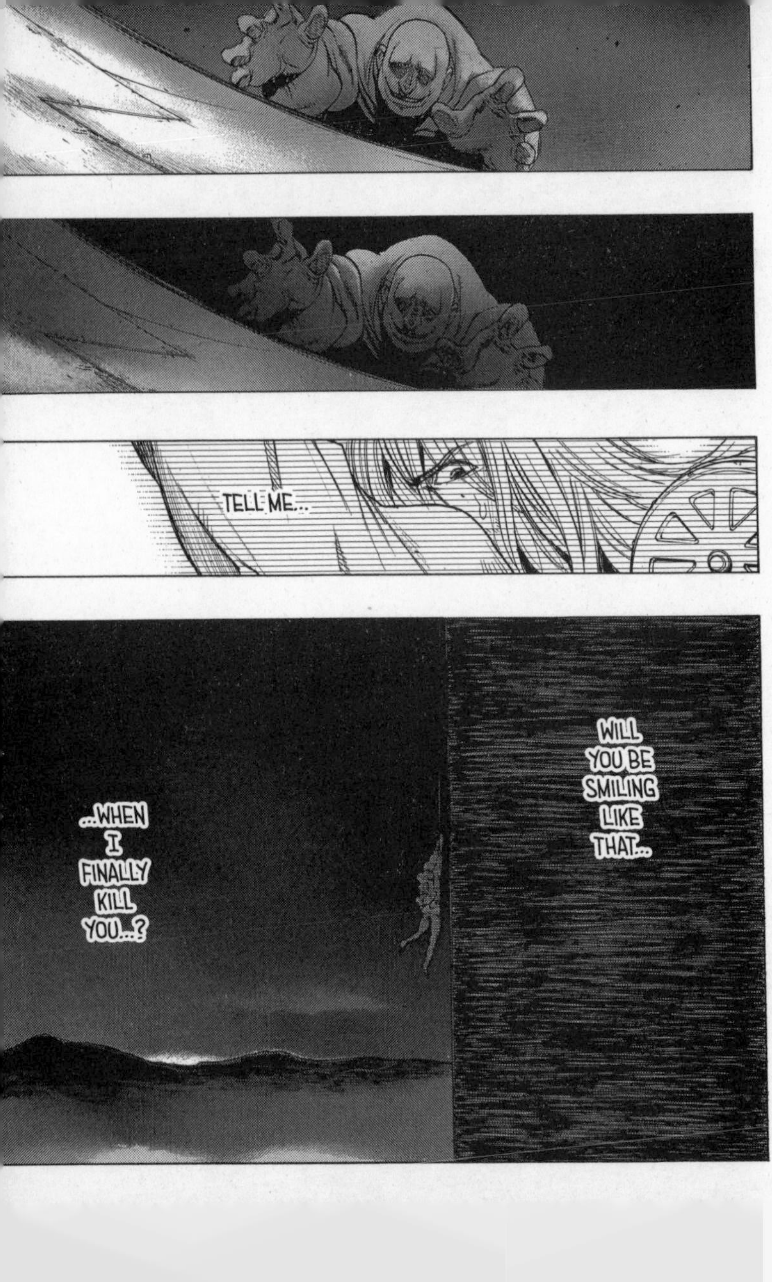
TELL ME...
WILL YOU BE SMILING LIKE THAT...
...WHEN I FINALLY KILL YOU...?

Chapter 38: Warrior of Vengeance · End

ATTACK on TITAN
BEFORE THE FALL

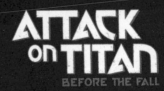

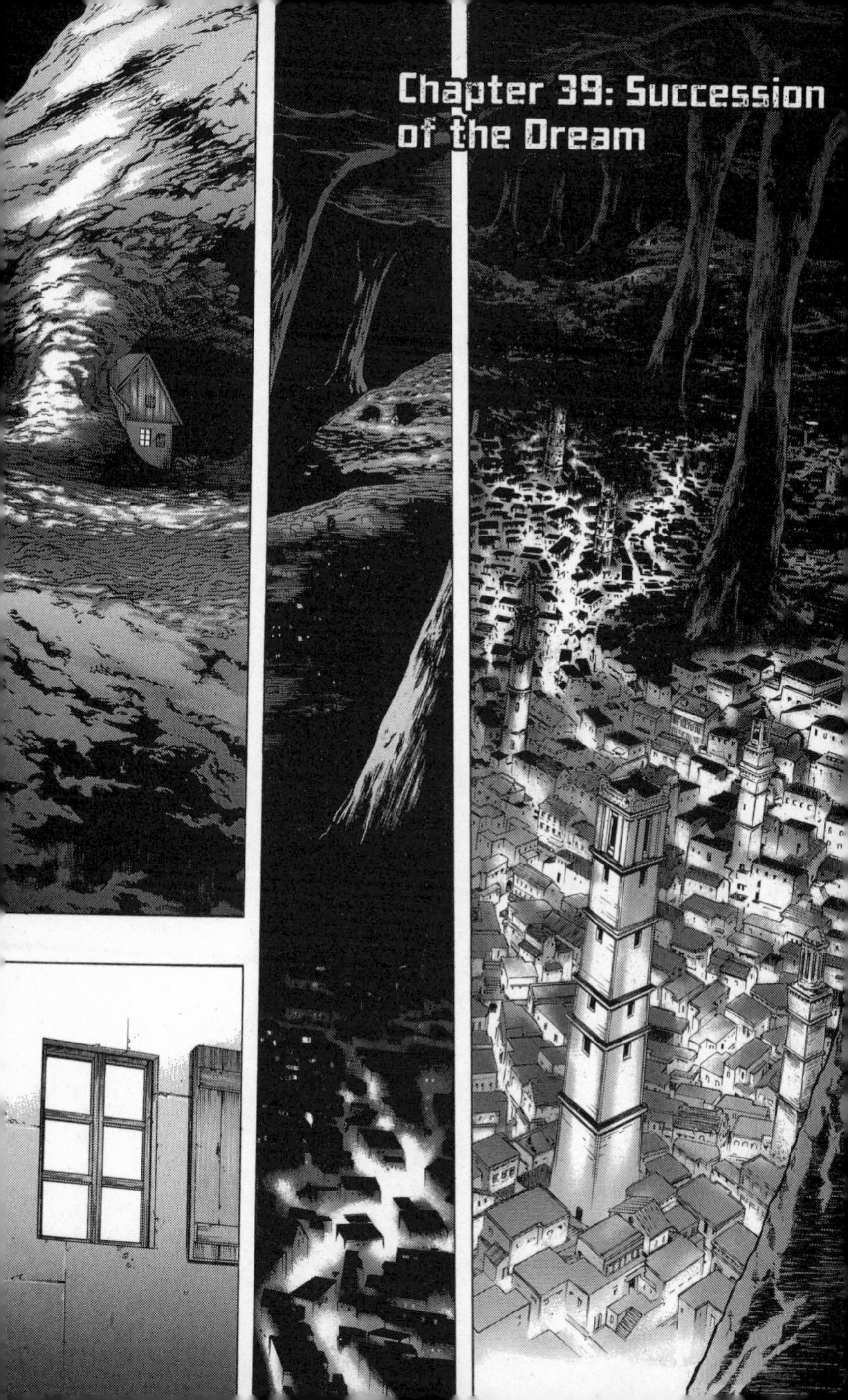
Chapter 39: Succession of the Dream

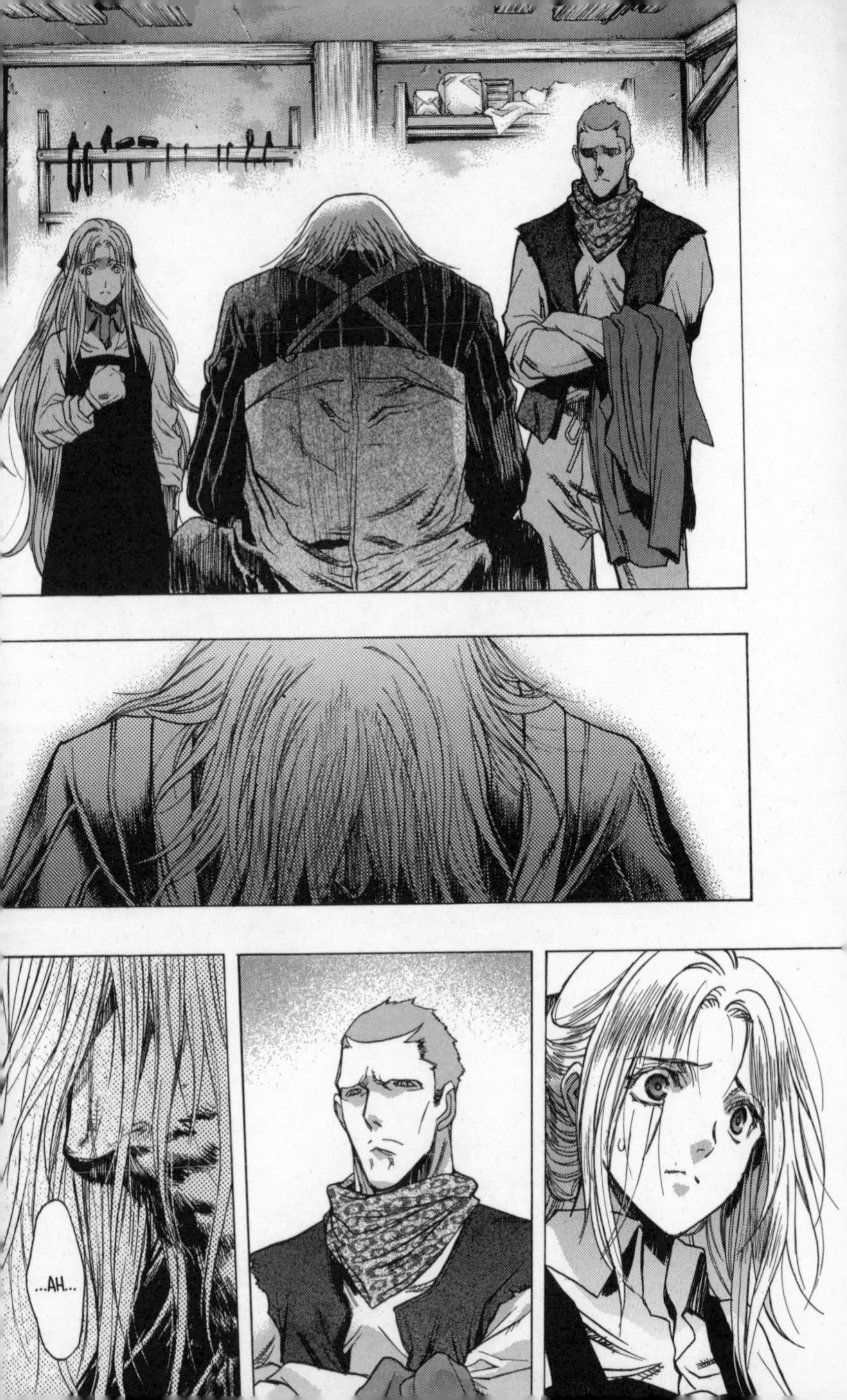
...AH...

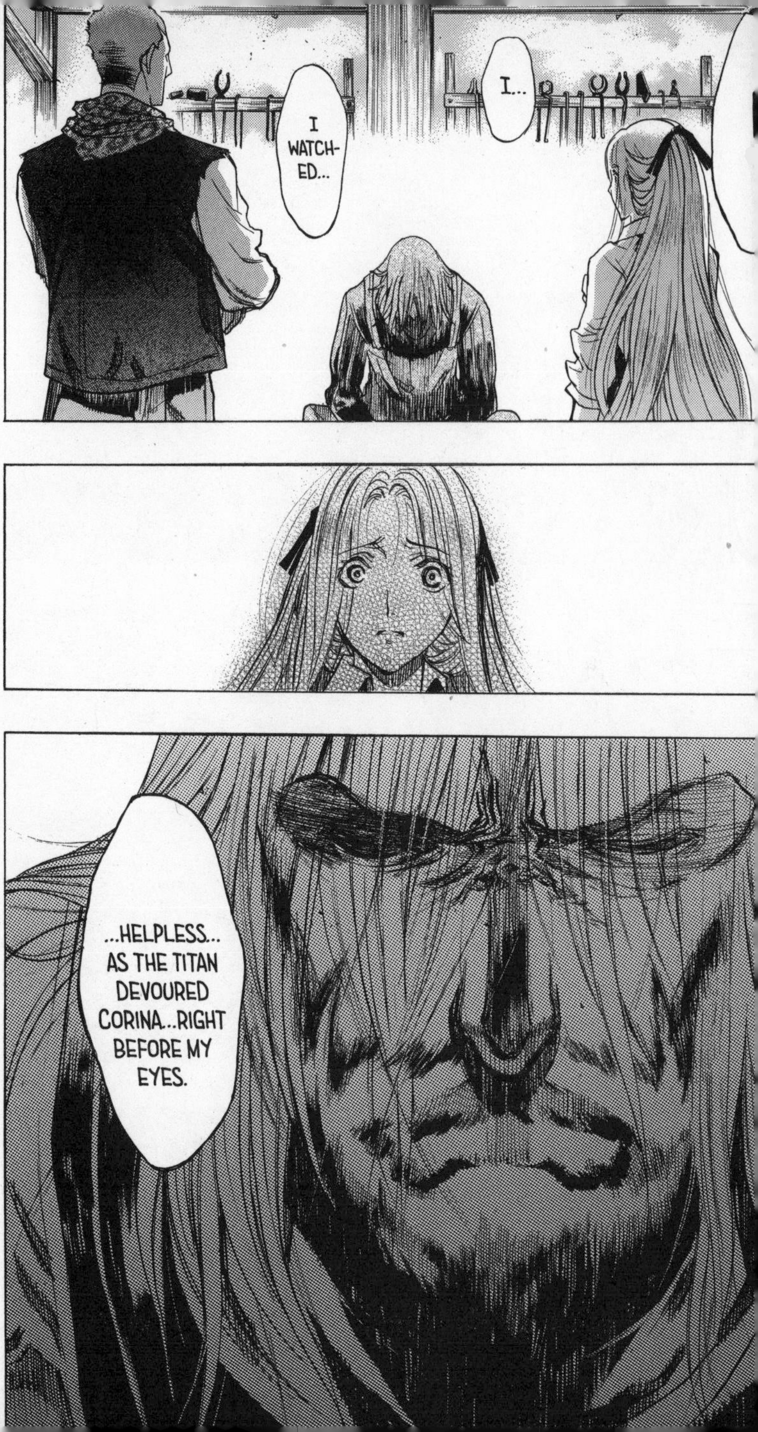
I...
I WATCH-ED...
...HELPLESS... AS THE TITAN DEVOURED CORINA...RIGHT BEFORE MY EYES.

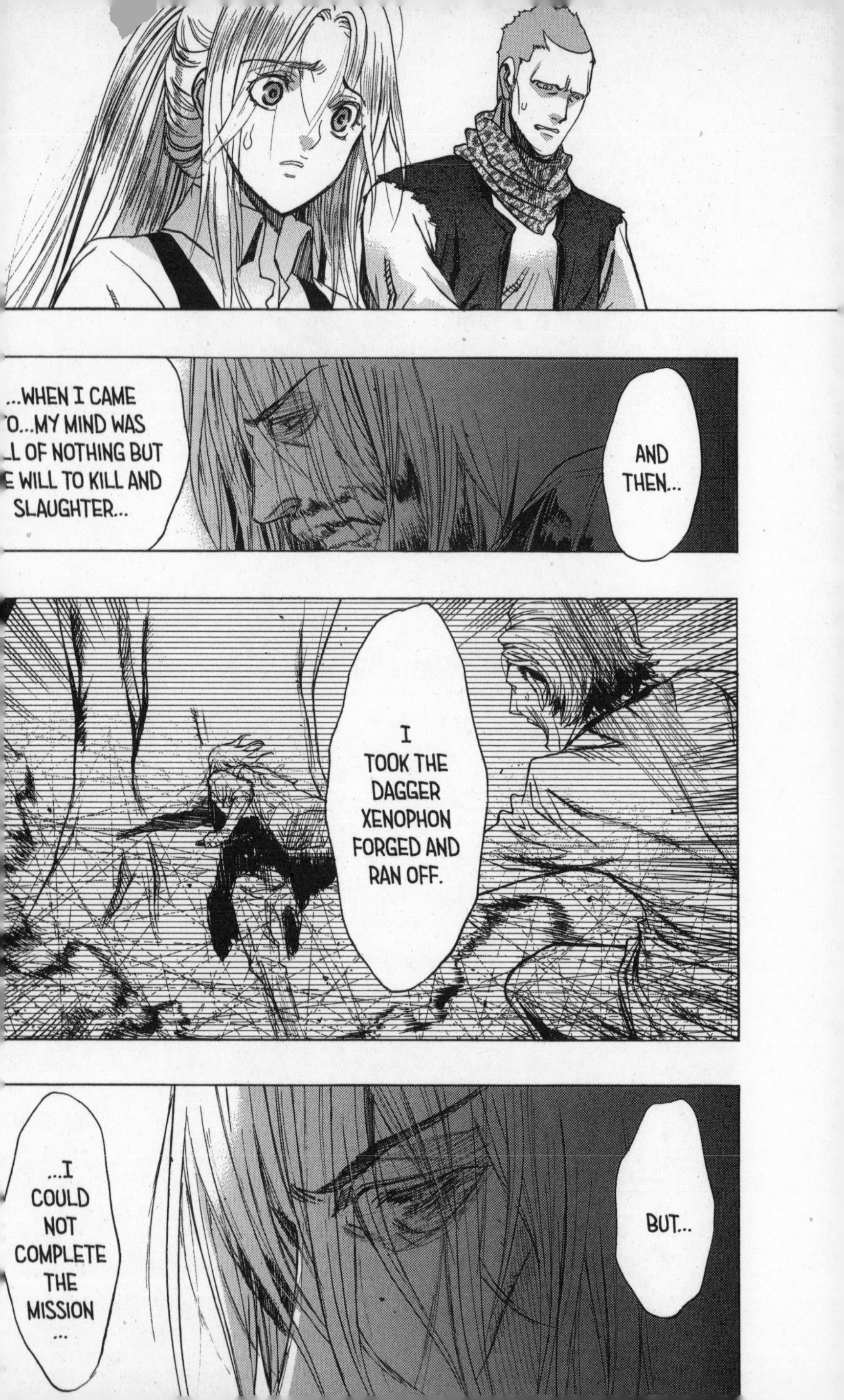
AND THEN...
...WHEN I CAME O...MY MIND WAS L OF NOTHING BUT E WILL TO KILL AND SLAUGHTER...
I TOOK THE DAGGER XENOPHON FORGED AND RAN OFF.
BUT...
...I COULD NOT COMPLETE THE MISSION ...

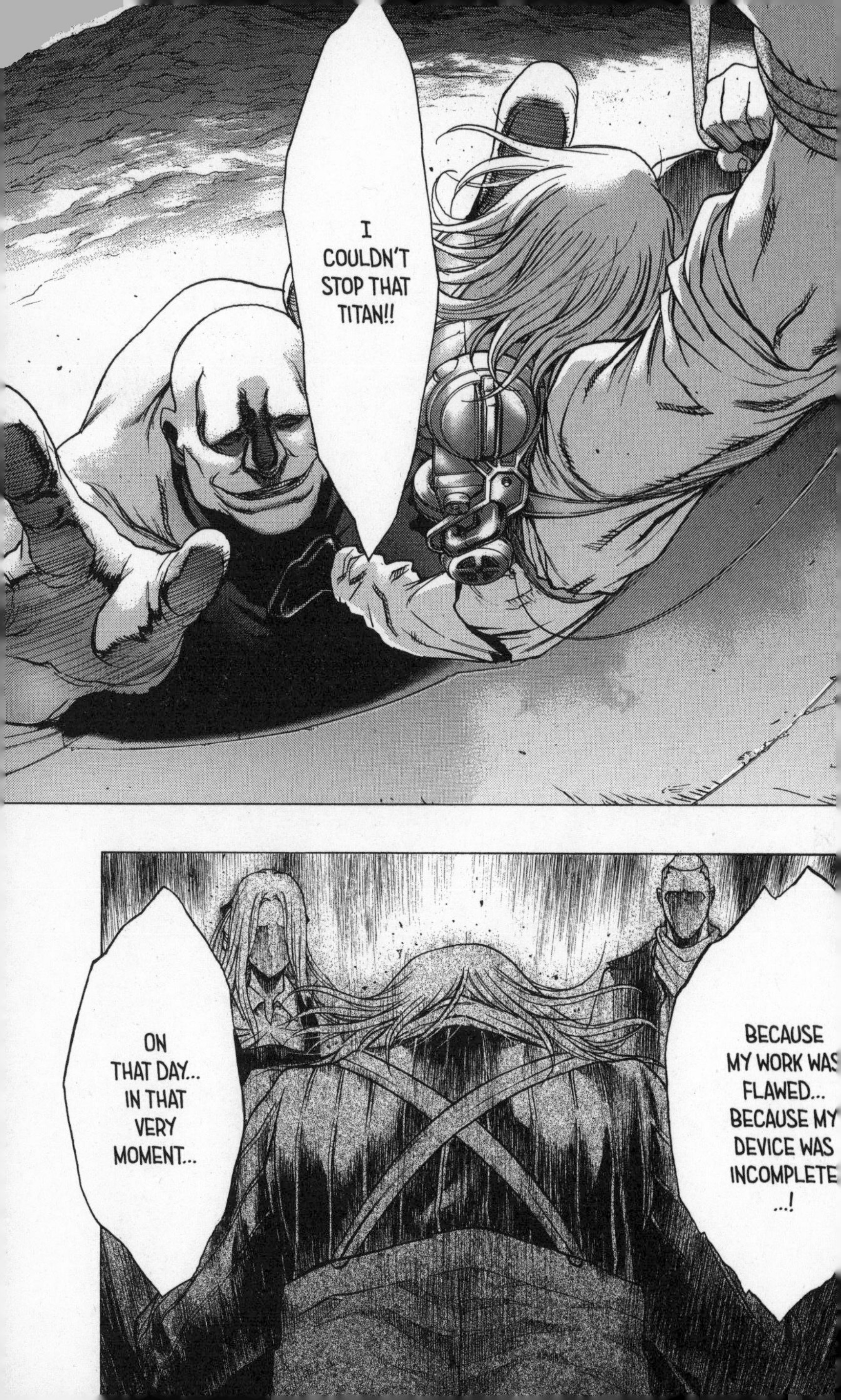
I COULDN'T STOP THAT TITAN!!
BECAUSE MY WORK WAS FLAWED... BECAUSE MY DEVICE WAS INCOMPLETE ...!
ON THAT DAY... IN THAT VERY MOMENT...

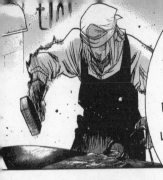

I SWORE VENGEANCE FOR CORINA!
I CHANGED THE CHASSIS AND MANY OF THE PARTS TO IRON BAMBOO IN ORDER TO MAKE IT LIGHTER AND MORE COMPACT.
I RE-EXAMINED EVERY LAST PART OF THE INTERNAL STRUCTURE OF THE DEVICE.
I CHANGED THE WIRES TO USE FILAMENTS FORGED FROM THE FIBERS OF IRON BAMBOO LEAVES.
AND WHEN I WAS DONE...

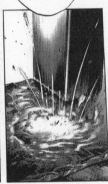

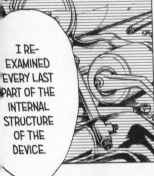

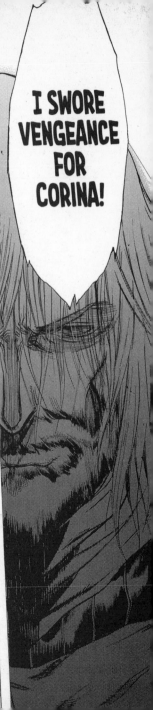

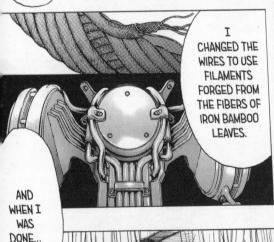

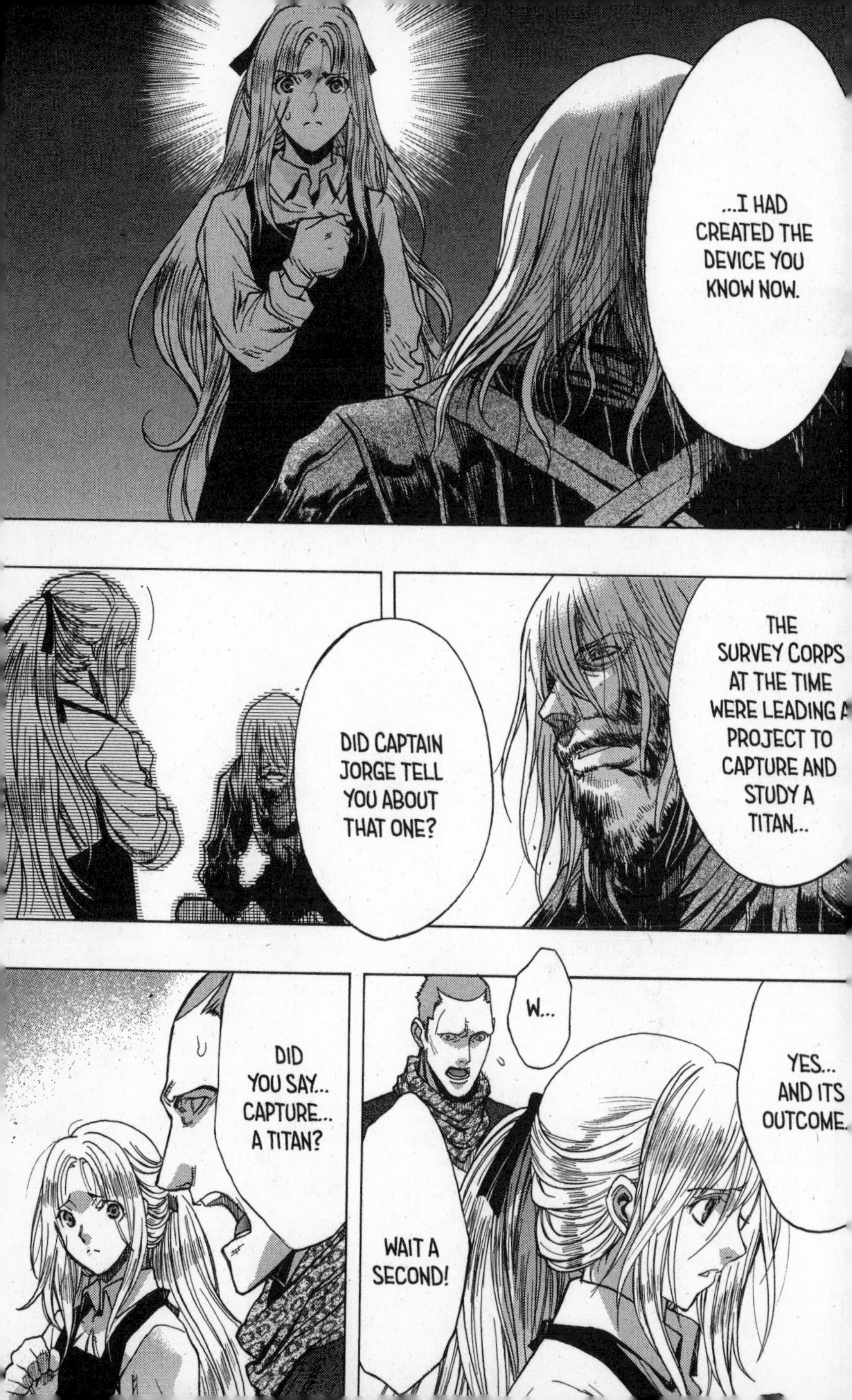
...I HAD CREATED THE DEVICE YOU KNOW NOW.
THE SURVEY CORPS AT THE TIME WERE LEADING A PROJECT TO CAPTURE AND STUDY A TITAN...
DID CAPTAIN JORGE TELL YOU ABOUT THAT ONE?
YES... AND ITS OUTCOME.
W...
WAIT A SECOND!
DID YOU SAY... CAPTURE... A TITAN?

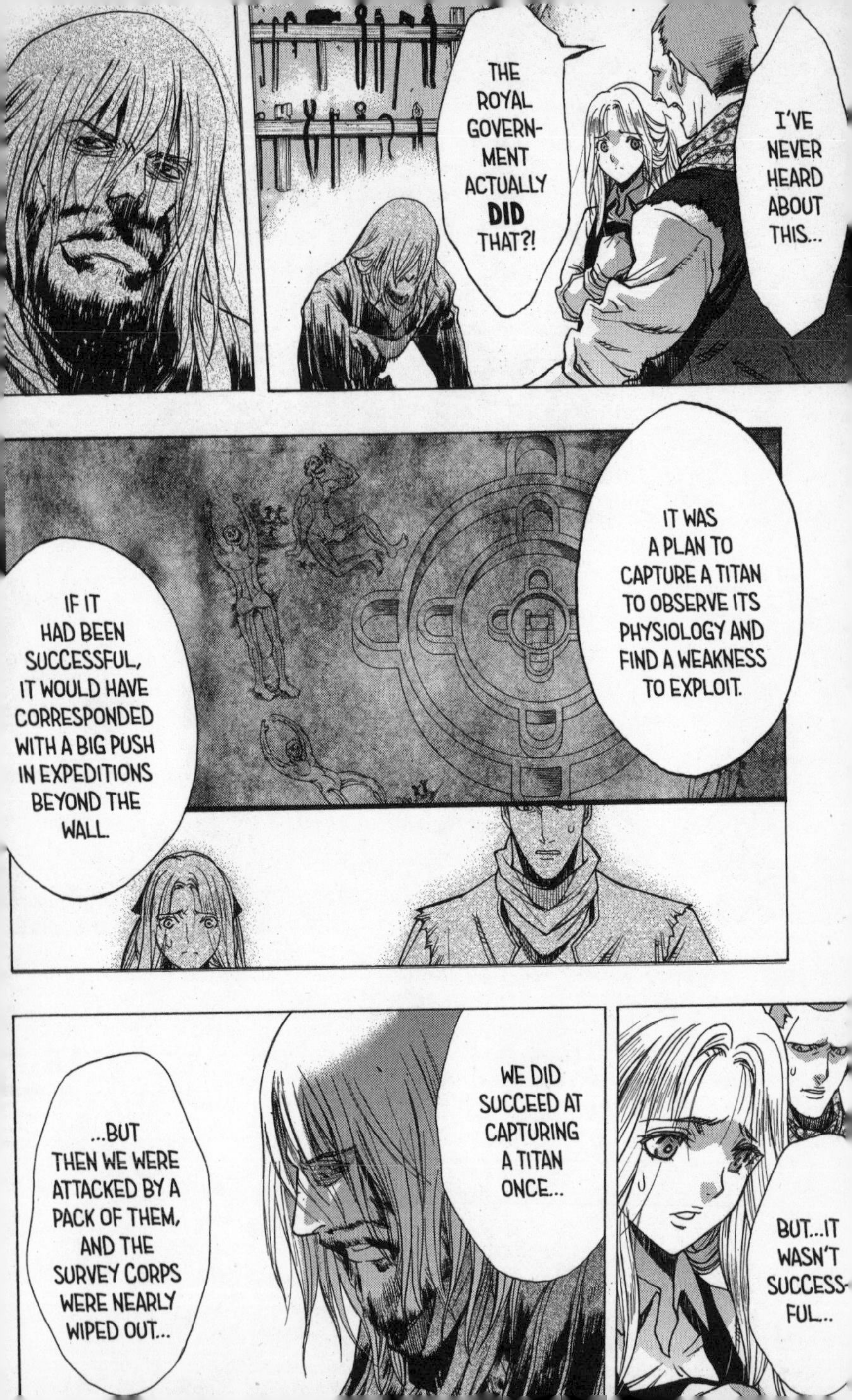
I'VE NEVER HEARD ABOUT THIS...
THE ROYAL GOVERNMENT ACTUALLY **DID** THAT?!
IT WAS A PLAN TO CAPTURE A TITAN TO OBSERVE ITS PHYSIOLOGY AND FIND A WEAKNESS TO EXPLOIT.
IF IT HAD BEEN SUCCESSFUL, IT WOULD HAVE CORRESPONDED WITH A BIG PUSH IN EXPEDITIONS BEYOND THE WALL.
BUT...IT WASN'T SUCCESSFUL...
WE DID SUCCEED AT CAPTURING A TITAN ONCE...
...BUT THEN WE WERE ATTACKED BY A PACK OF THEM, AND THE SURVEY CORPS WERE NEARLY WIPED OUT...

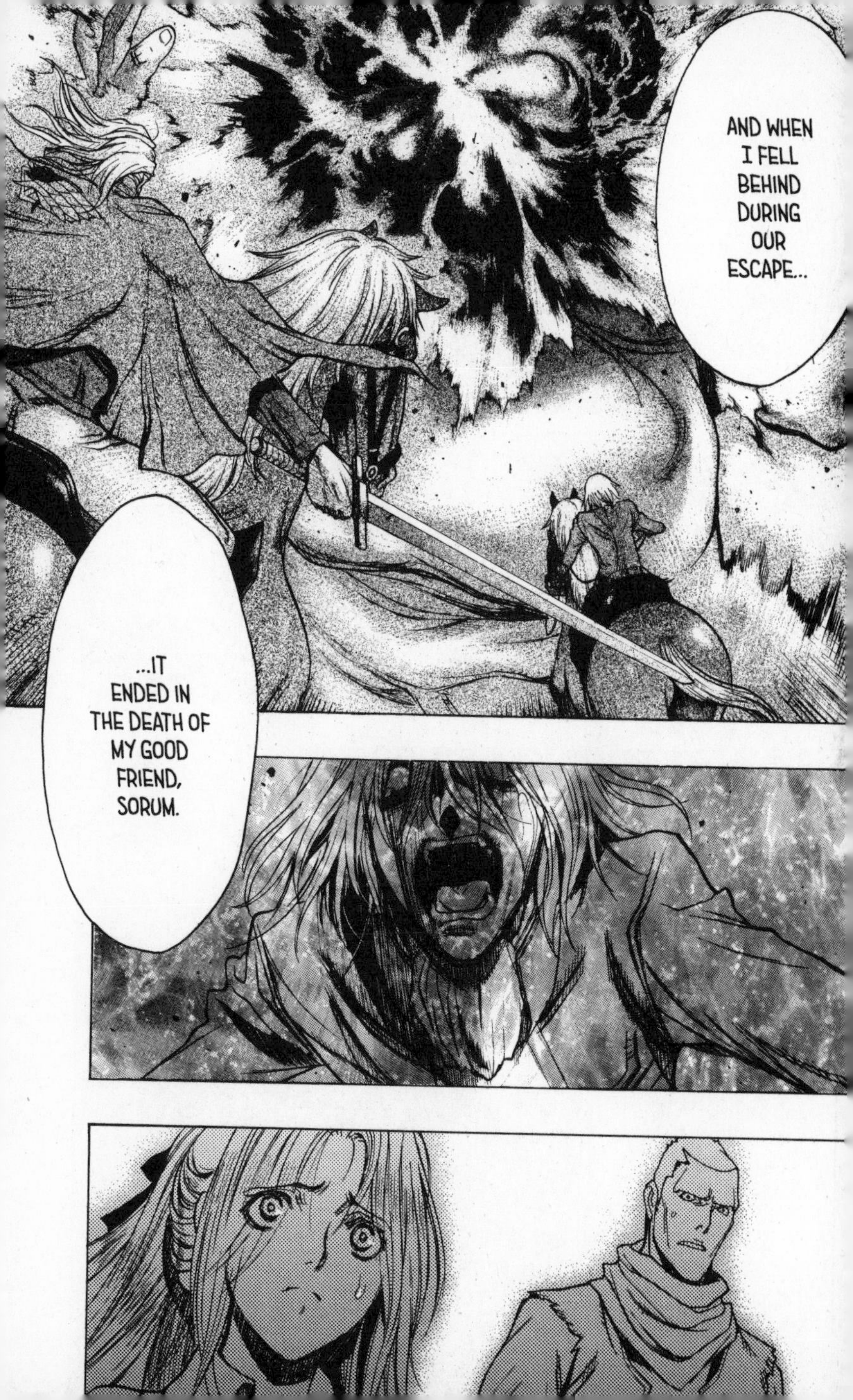
AND WHEN I FELL BEHIND DURING OUR ESCAPE...
...IT ENDED IN THE DEATH OF MY GOOD FRIEND, SORUM.

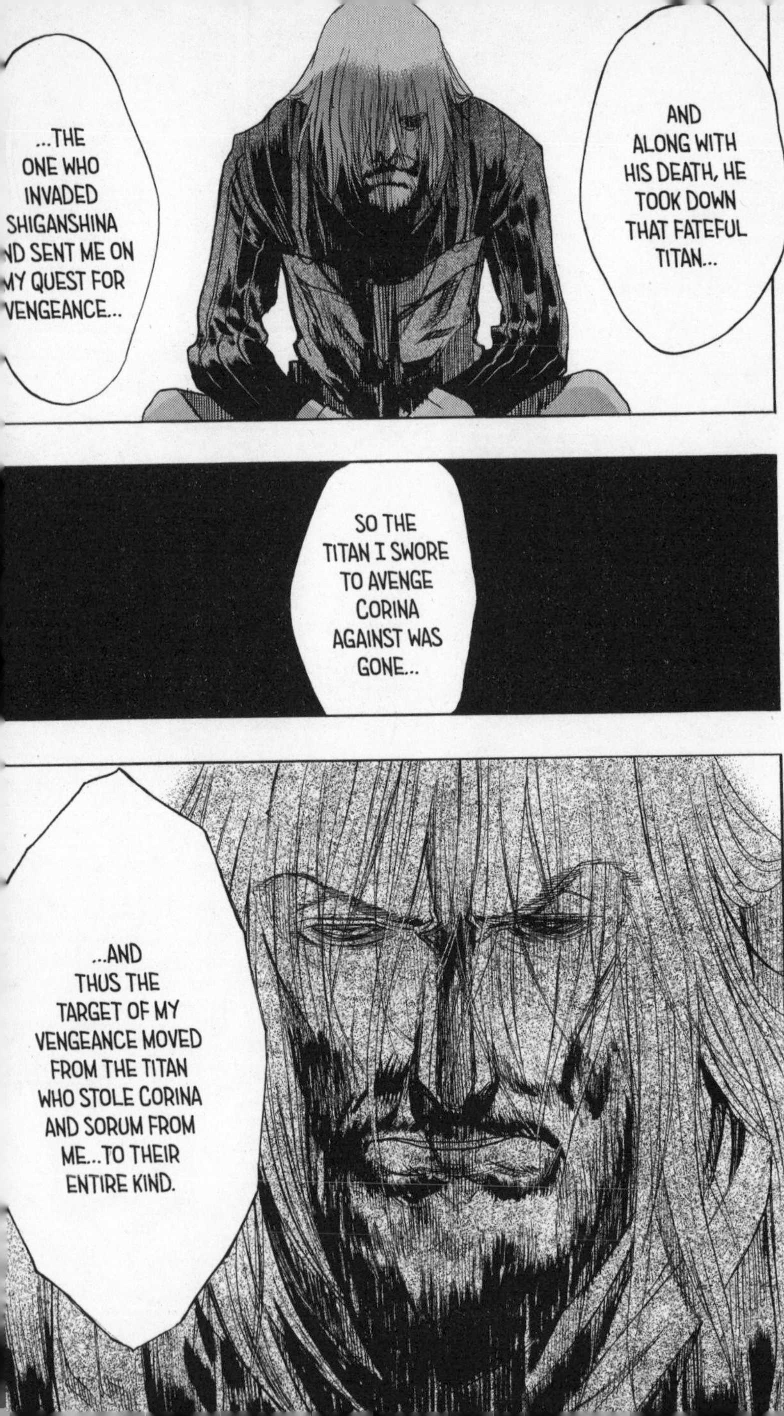
AND ALONG WITH HIS DEATH, HE TOOK DOWN THAT FATEFUL TITAN...
...THE ONE WHO INVADED SHIGANSHINA ND SENT ME ON MY QUEST FOR VENGEANCE...
SO THE TITAN I SWORE TO AVENGE CORINA AGAINST WAS GONE...
...AND THUS THE TARGET OF MY VENGEANCE MOVED FROM THE TITAN WHO STOLE CORINA AND SORUM FROM ME...TO THEIR ENTIRE KIND.

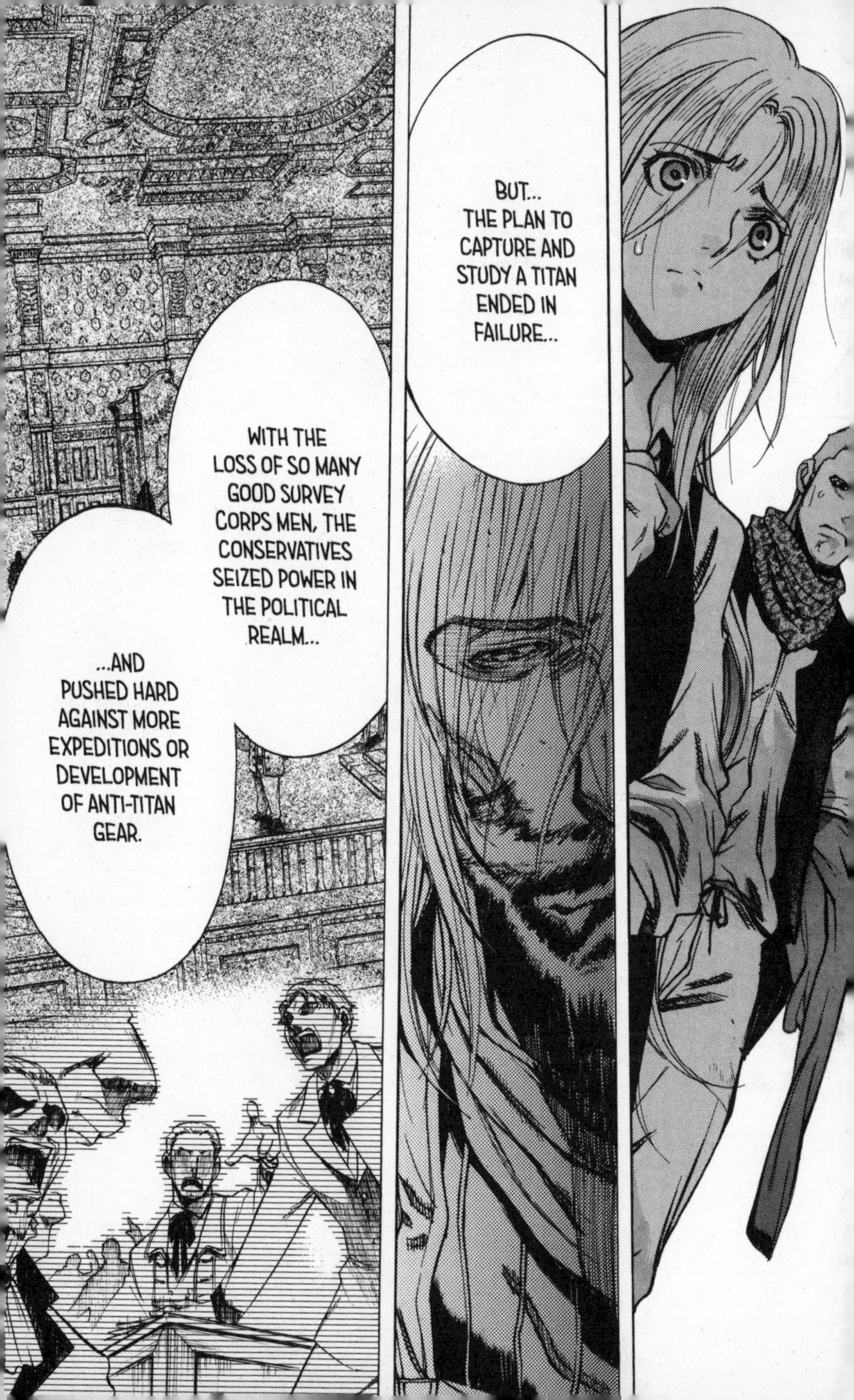
BUT... THE PLAN TO CAPTURE AND STUDY A TITAN ENDED IN FAILURE...
WITH THE LOSS OF SO MANY GOOD SURVEY CORPS MEN, THE CONSERVATIVES SEIZED POWER IN THE POLITICAL REALM...
...AND PUSHED HARD AGAINST MORE EXPEDITIONS OR DEVELOPMENT OF ANTI-TITAN GEAR.

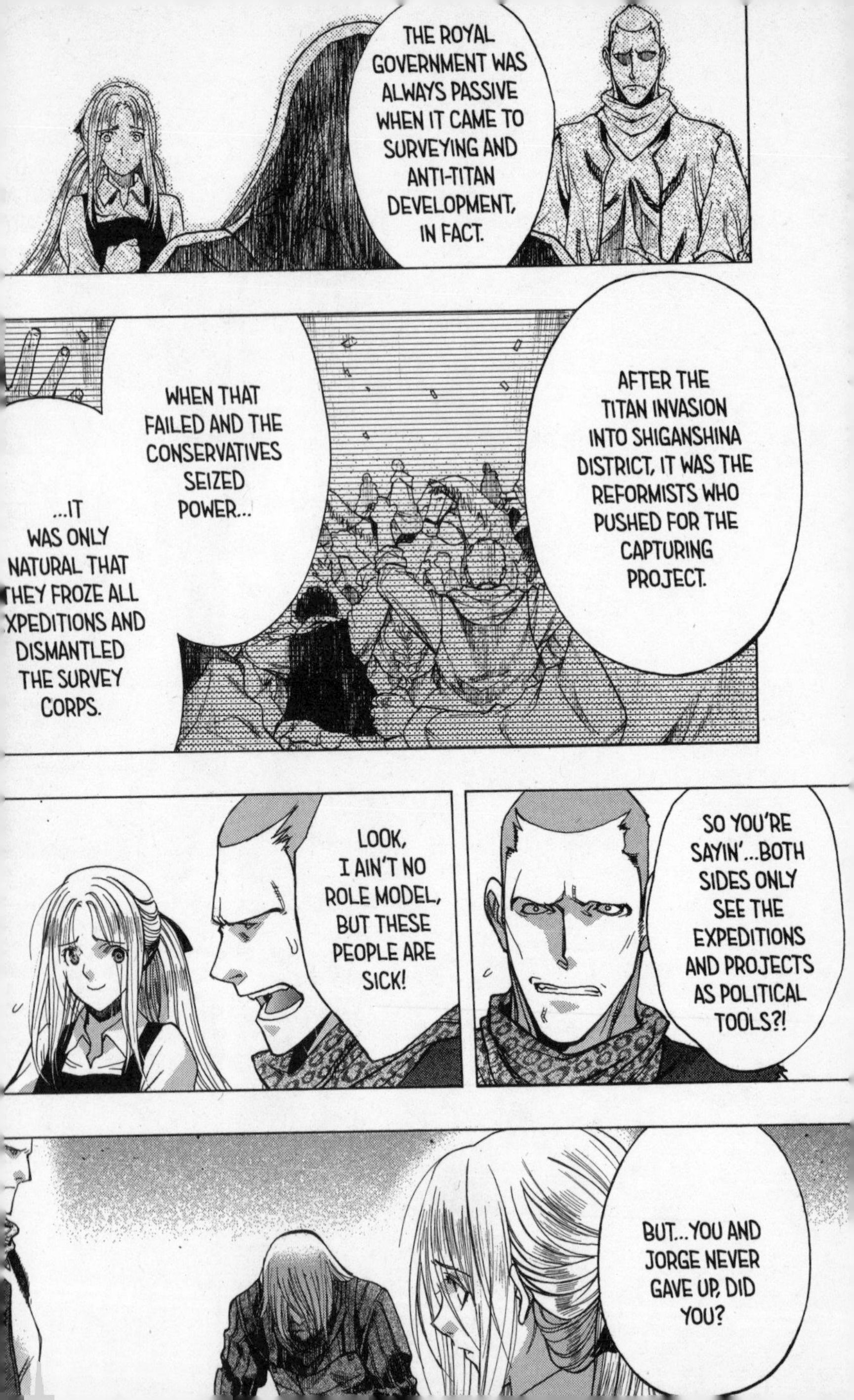
THE ROYAL GOVERNMENT WAS ALWAYS PASSIVE WHEN IT CAME TO SURVEYING AND ANTI-TITAN DEVELOPMENT, IN FACT.
AFTER THE TITAN INVASION INTO SHIGANSHINA DISTRICT, IT WAS THE REFORMISTS WHO PUSHED FOR THE CAPTURING PROJECT.
WHEN THAT FAILED AND THE CONSERVATIVES SEIZED POWER...
...IT WAS ONLY NATURAL THAT THEY FROZE ALL XPEDITIONS AND DISMANTLED THE SURVEY CORPS.
SO YOU'RE SAYIN'...BOTH SIDES ONLY SEE THE EXPEDITIONS AND PROJECTS AS POLITICAL TOOLS?!
LOOK, I AIN'T NO ROLE MODEL, BUT THESE PEOPLE ARE SICK!
BUT...YOU AND JORGE NEVER GAVE UP, DID YOU?

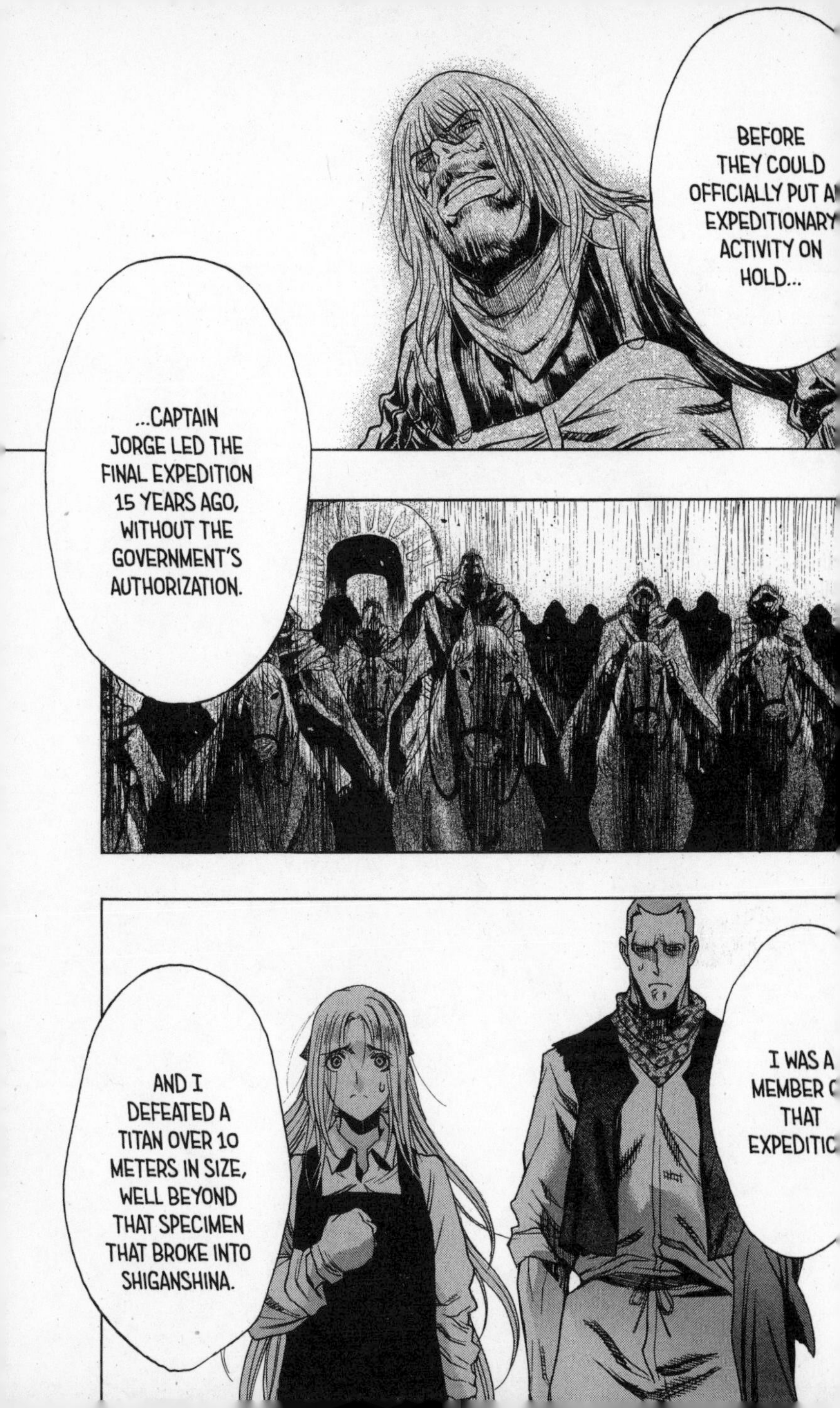
BEFORE THEY COULD OFFICIALLY PUT A EXPEDITIONARY ACTIVITY ON HOLD...
...CAPTAIN JORGE LED THE FINAL EXPEDITION 15 YEARS AGO, WITHOUT THE GOVERNMENT'S AUTHORIZATION.
I WAS A MEMBER THAT EXPEDITI
AND I DEFEATED A TITAN OVER 10 METERS IN SIZE, WELL BEYOND THAT SPECIMEN THAT BROKE INTO SHIGANSHINA.

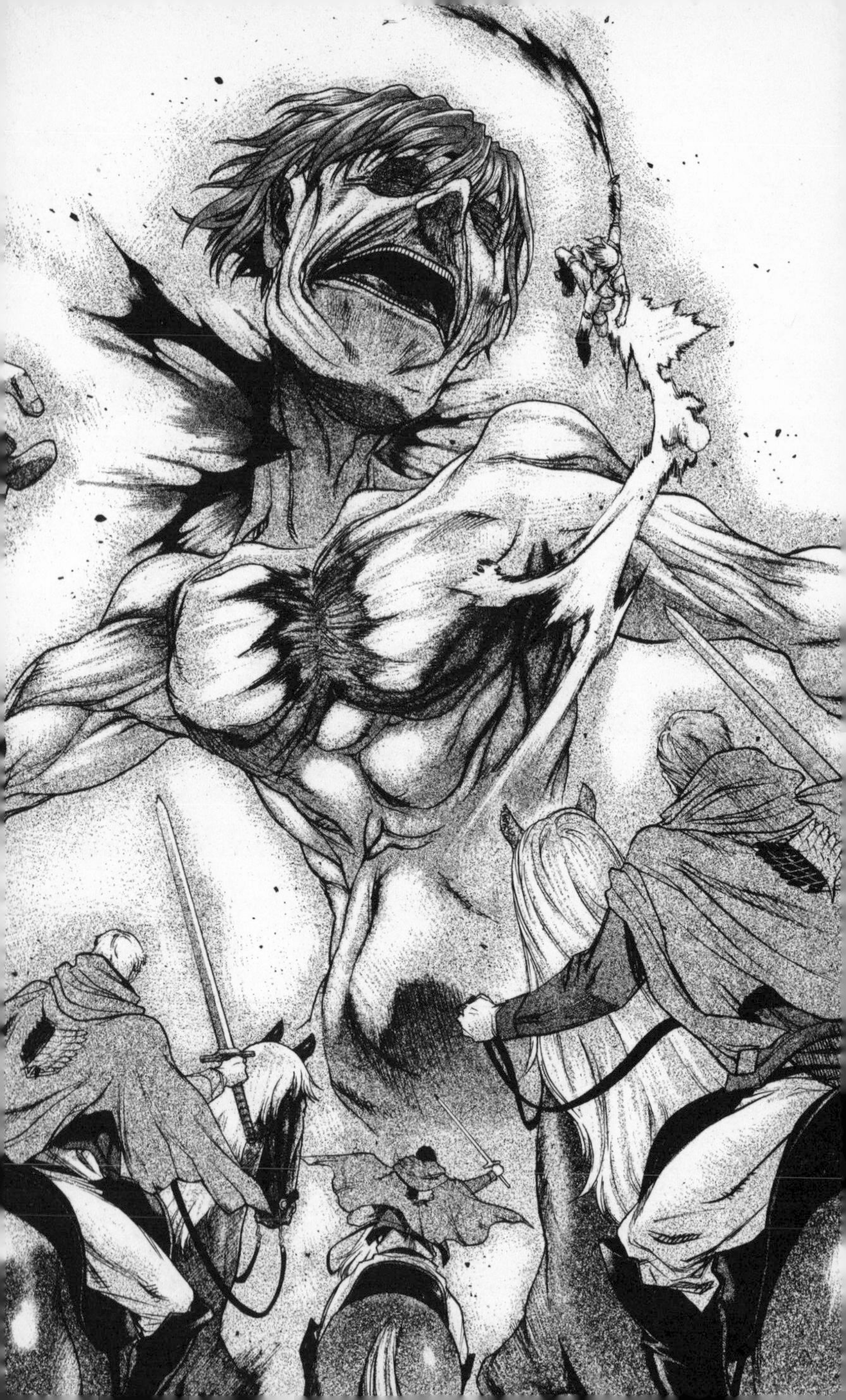

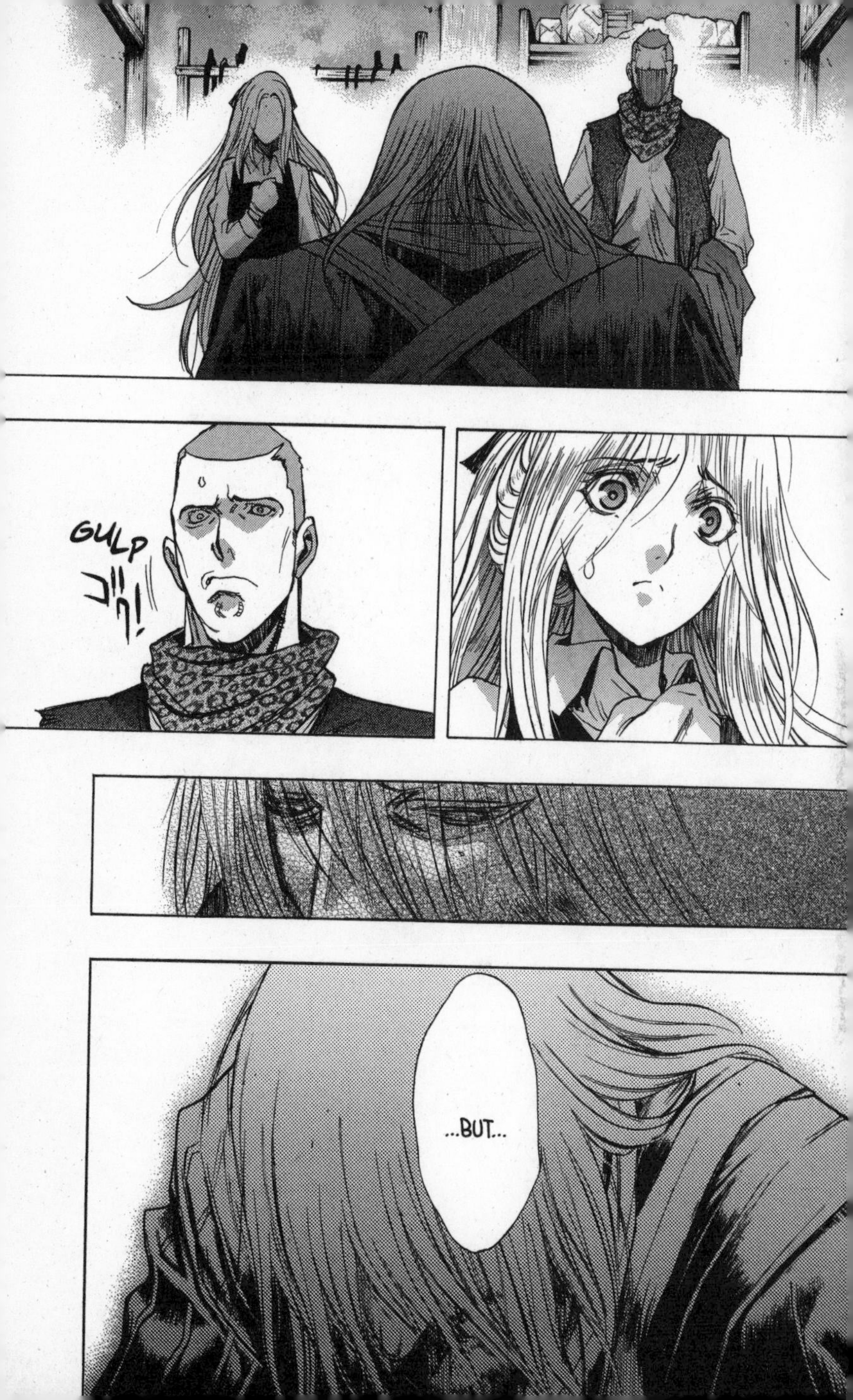
GULP
ゴクッ!
...BUT...

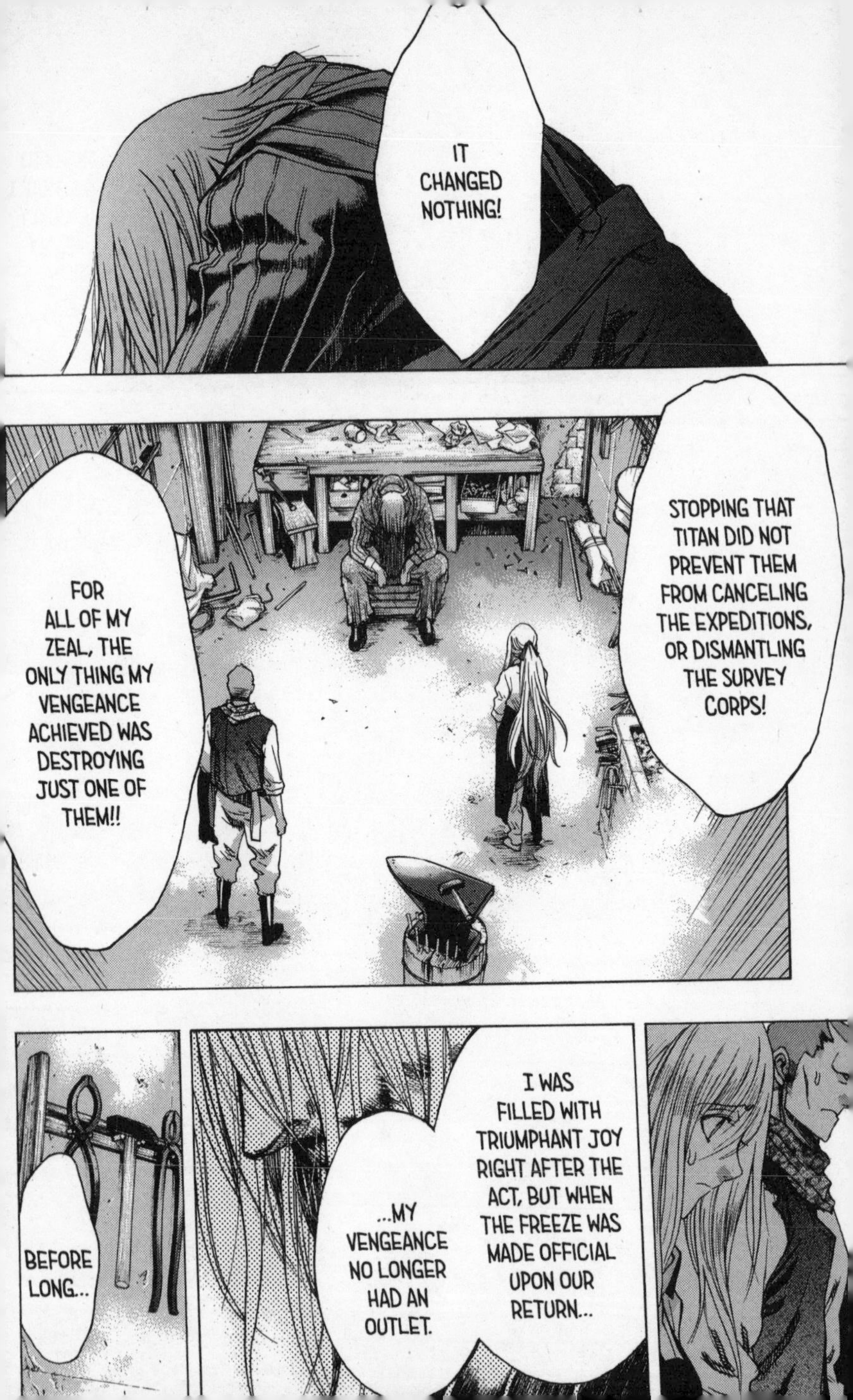
IT CHANGED NOTHING!
STOPPING THAT TITAN DID NOT PREVENT THEM FROM CANCELING THE EXPEDITIONS, OR DISMANTLING THE SURVEY CORPS!
FOR ALL OF MY ZEAL, THE ONLY THING MY VENGEANCE ACHIEVED WAS DESTROYING JUST ONE OF THEM!!
I WAS FILLED WITH TRIUMPHANT JOY RIGHT AFTER THE ACT, BUT WHEN THE FREEZE WAS MADE OFFICIAL UPON OUR RETURN...
...MY VENGEANCE NO LONGER HAD AN OUTLET.
BEFORE LONG...

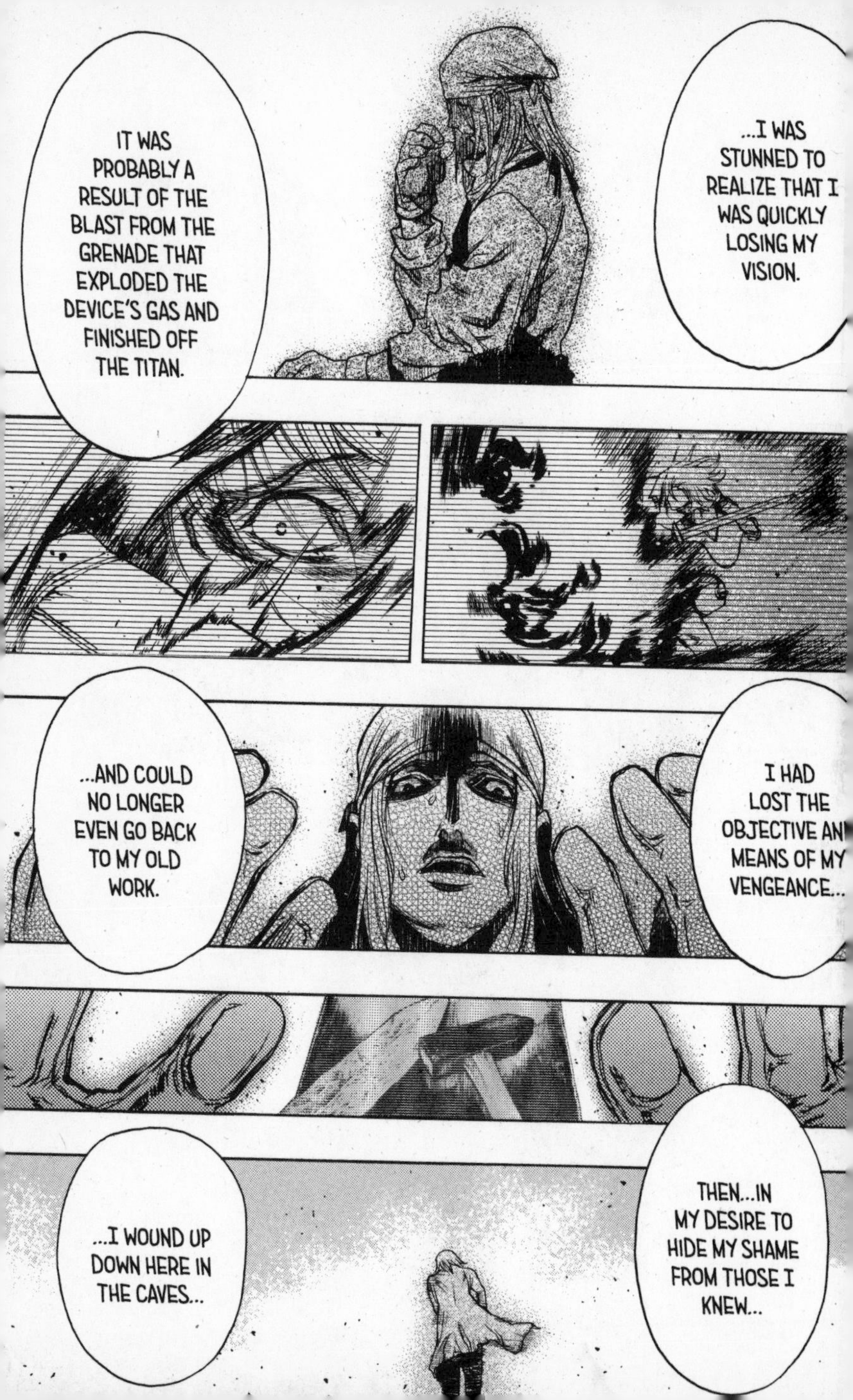
...I WAS STUNNED TO REALIZE THAT I WAS QUICKLY LOSING MY VISION.
IT WAS PROBABLY A RESULT OF THE BLAST FROM THE GRENADE THAT EXPLODED THE DEVICE'S GAS AND FINISHED OFF THE TITAN.
I HAD LOST THE OBJECTIVE AN MEANS OF MY VENGEANCE...
...AND COULD NO LONGER EVEN GO BACK TO MY OLD WORK.
THEN...IN MY DESIRE TO HIDE MY SHAME FROM THOSE I KNEW...
...I WOUND UP DOWN HERE IN THE CAVES...

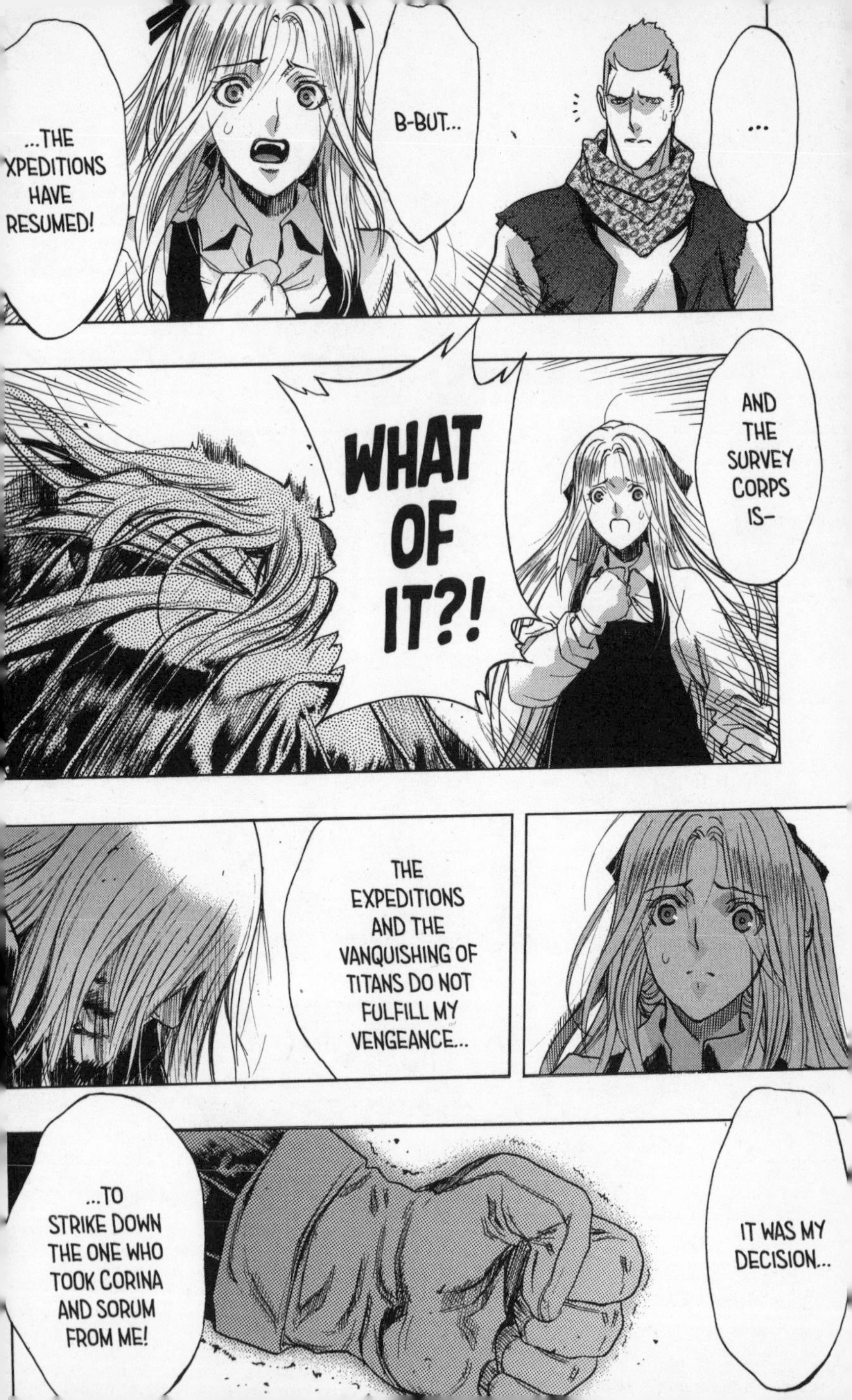
...
B-BUT...
...THE XPEDITIONS HAVE RESUMED!
AND THE SURVEY CORPS IS–
WHAT OF IT?!
THE EXPEDITIONS AND THE VANQUISHING OF TITANS DO NOT FULFILL MY VENGEANCE...
IT WAS MY DECISION...
...TO STRIKE DOWN THE ONE WHO TOOK CORINA AND SORUM FROM ME!

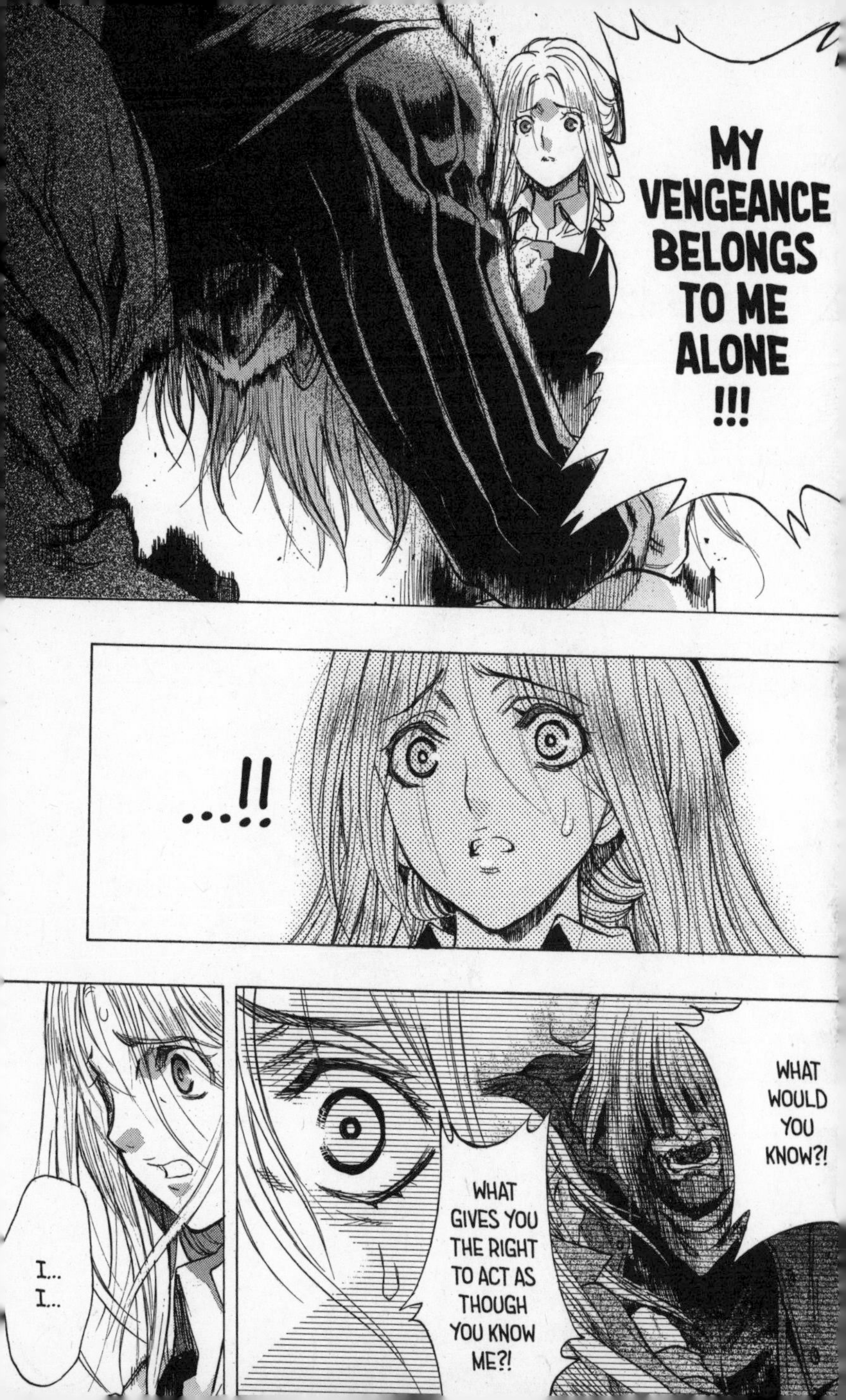
MY VENGEANCE BELONGS TO ME ALONE !!!
...!!
WHAT WOULD YOU KNOW?!
WHAT GIVES YOU THE RIGHT TO ACT AS THOUGH YOU KNOW ME?!
I... I...

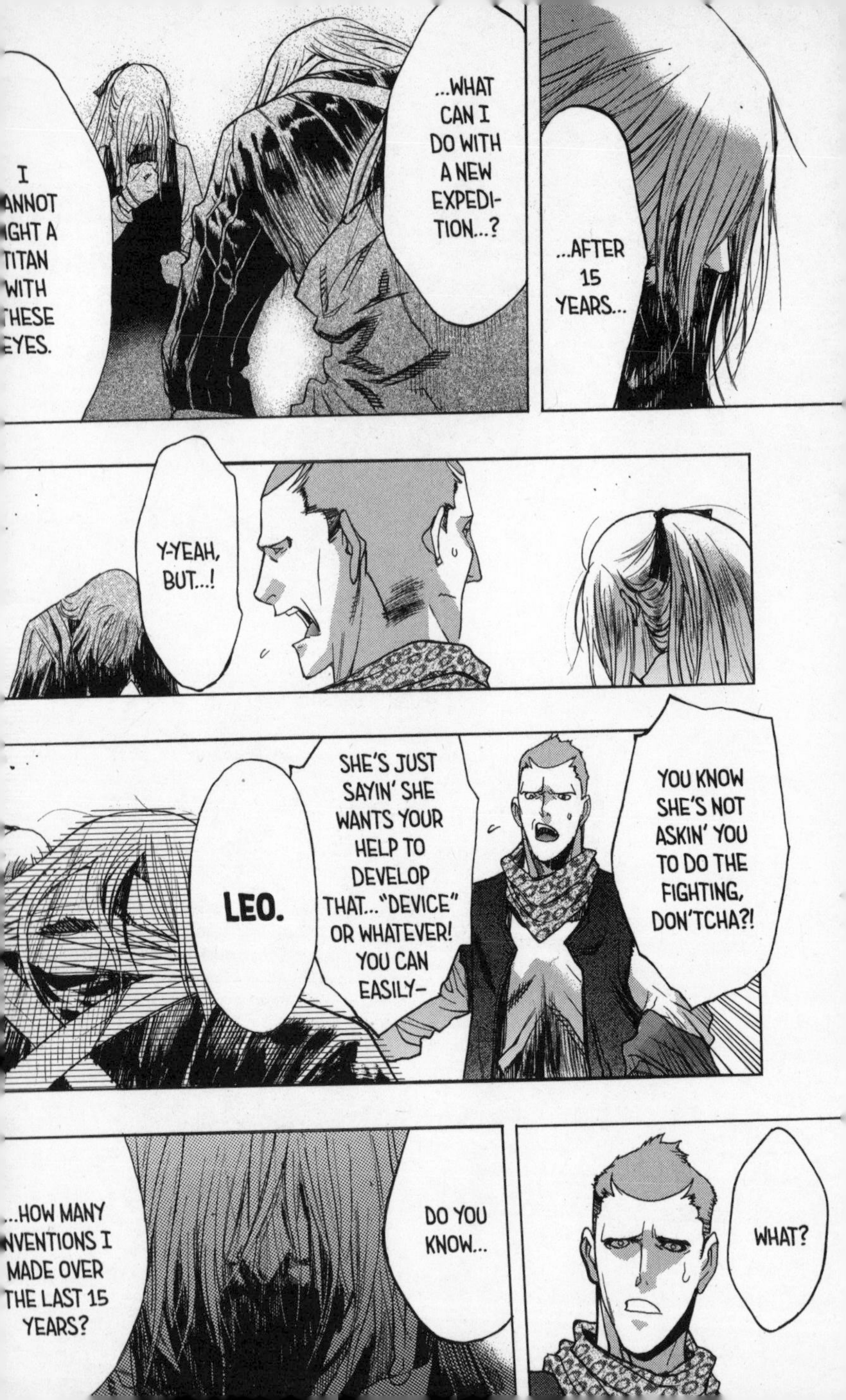
...AFTER 15 YEARS...
...WHAT CAN I DO WITH A NEW EXPEDITION...?
I ANNOT IGHT A TITAN WITH HESE EYES.
Y-YEAH, BUT...!
YOU KNOW SHE'S NOT ASKIN' YOU TO DO THE FIGHTING, DON'TCHA?!
SHE'S JUST SAYIN' SHE WANTS YOUR HELP TO DEVELOP THAT..."DEVICE" OR WHATEVER! YOU CAN EASILY–
LEO.
WHAT?
DO YOU KNOW...
...HOW MANY NVENTIONS I MADE OVER THE LAST 15 YEARS?

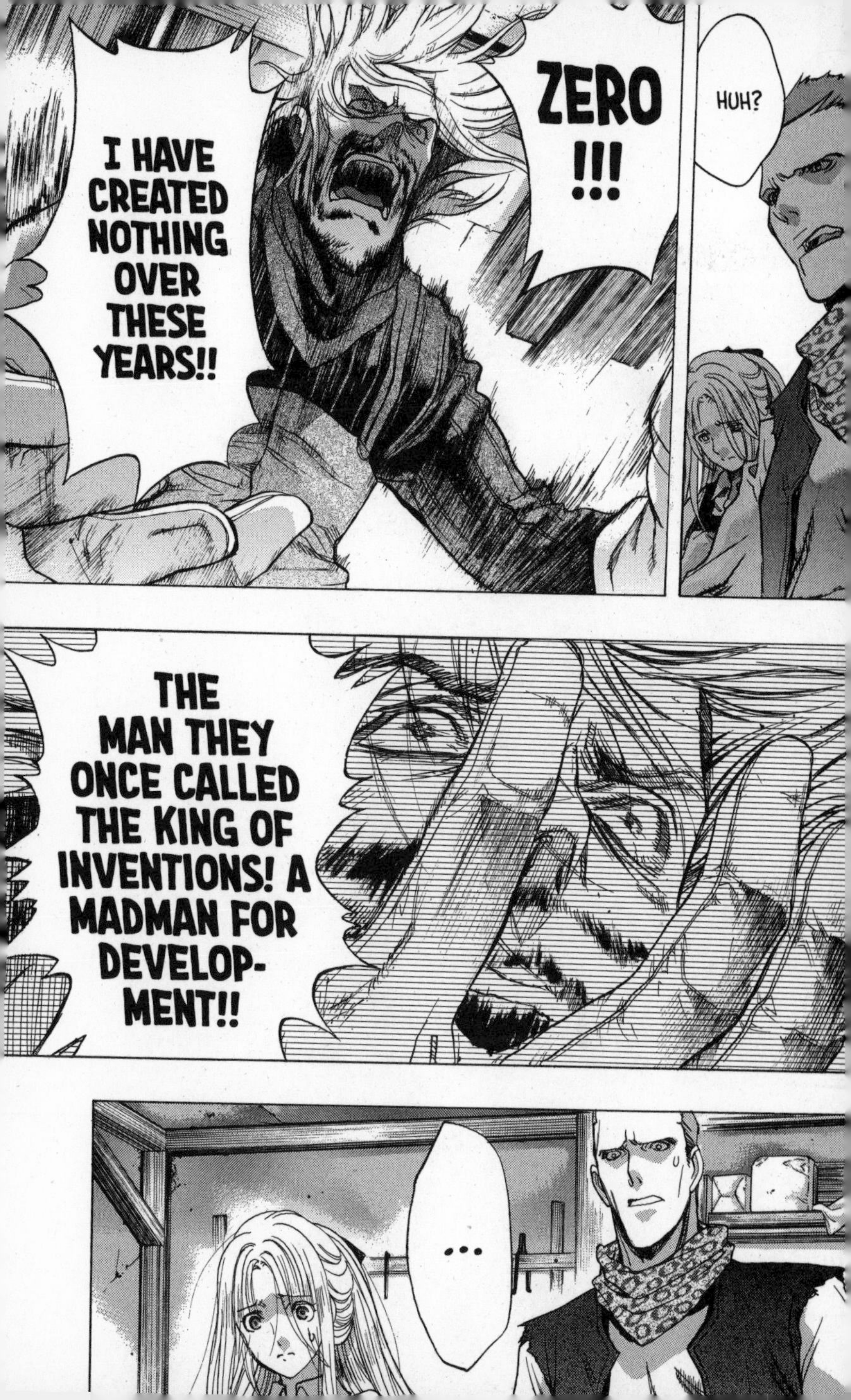
HUH?
I HAVE CREATED NOTHING OVER THESE YEARS!!
ZERO !!!
THE MAN THEY ONCE CALLED THE KING OF INVENTIONS! A MADMAN FOR DEVELOP-MENT!!
...

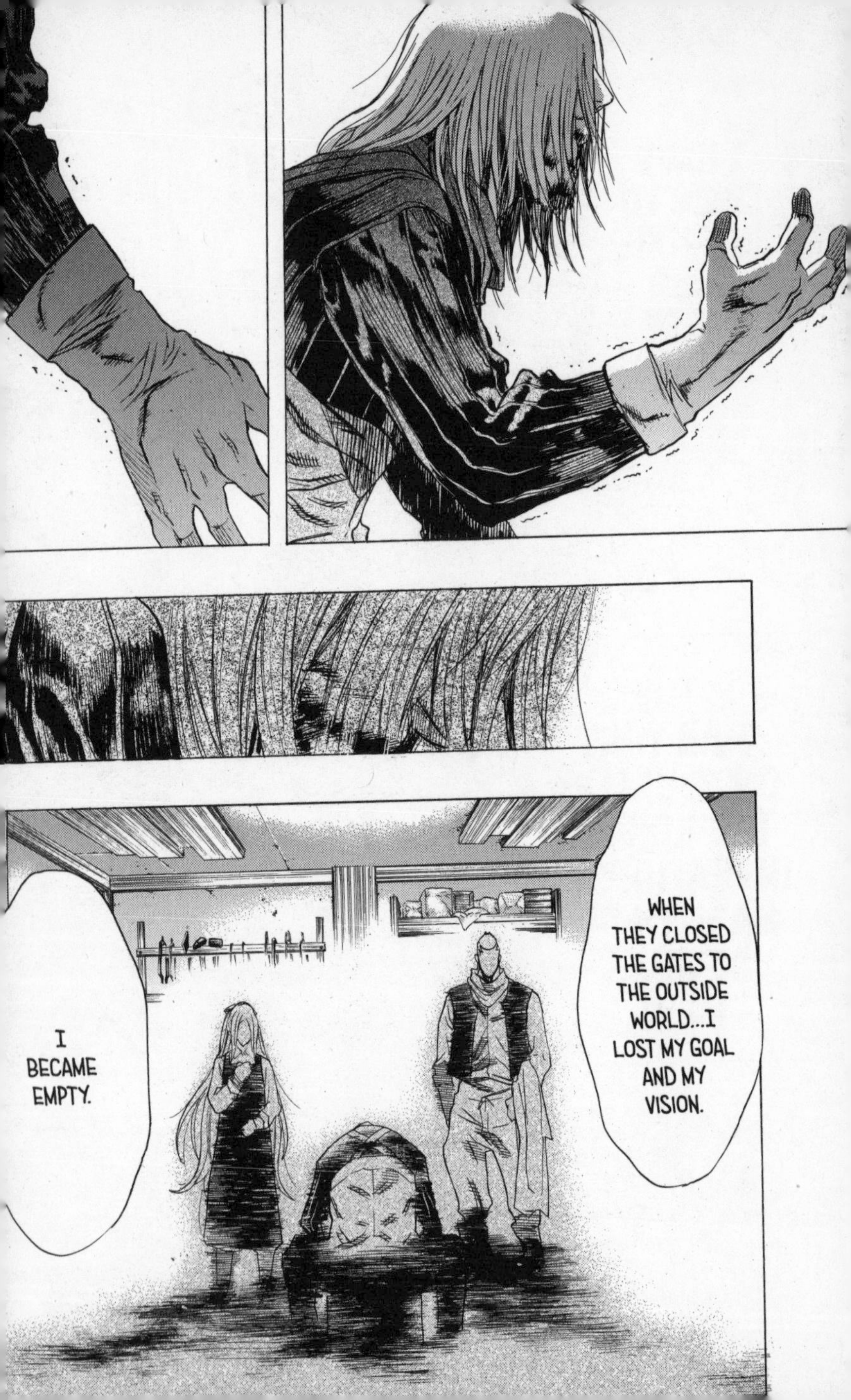
WHEN THEY CLOSED THE GATES TO THE OUTSIDE WORLD...I LOST MY GOAL AND MY VISION.
I BECAME EMPTY.

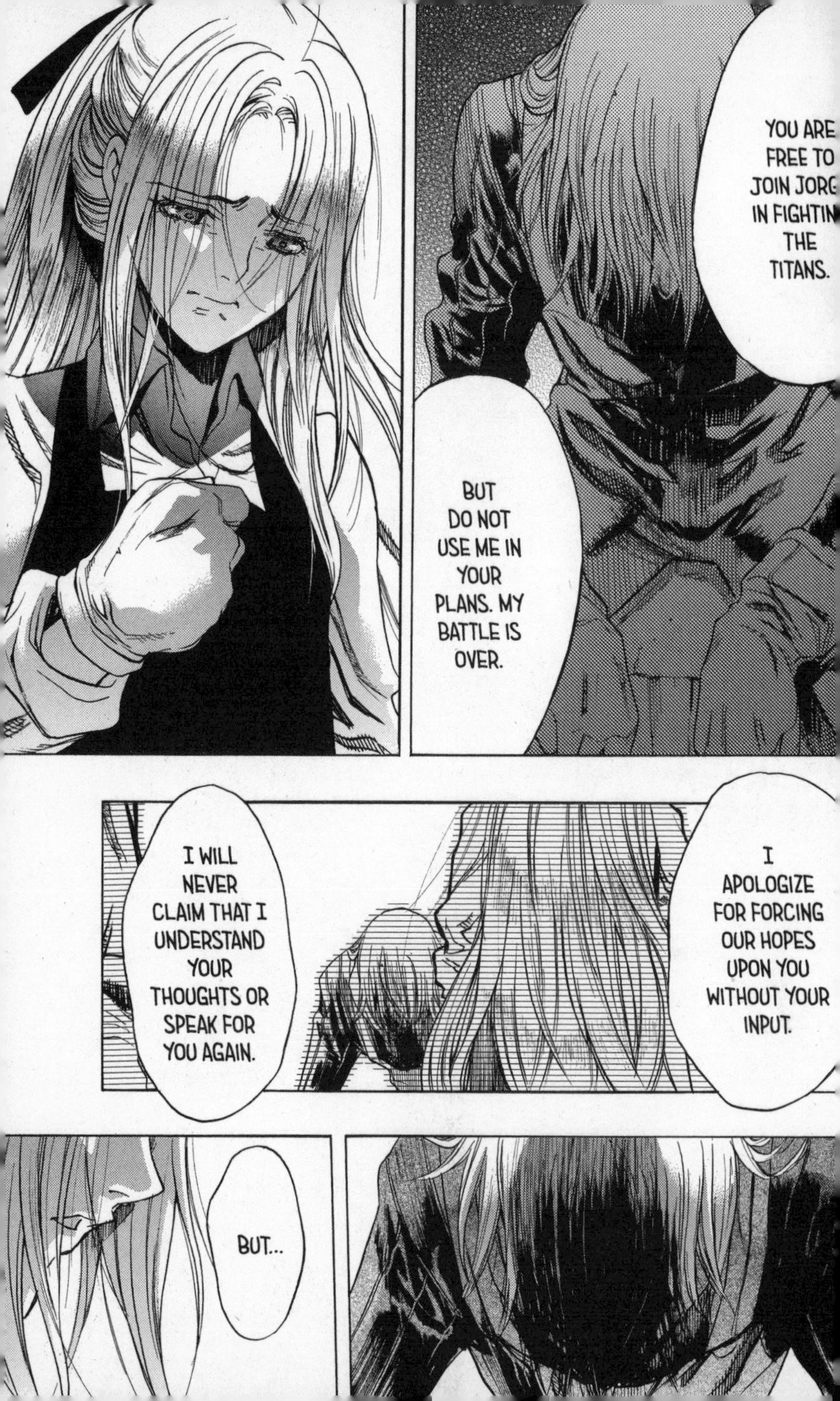
YOU ARE FREE TO JOIN JORG IN FIGHTIN THE TITANS.
BUT DO NOT USE ME IN YOUR PLANS. MY BATTLE IS OVER.
I APOLOGIZE FOR FORCING OUR HOPES UPON YOU WITHOUT YOUR INPUT.
I WILL NEVER CLAIM THAT I UNDERSTAND YOUR THOUGHTS OR SPEAK FOR YOU AGAIN.
BUT...

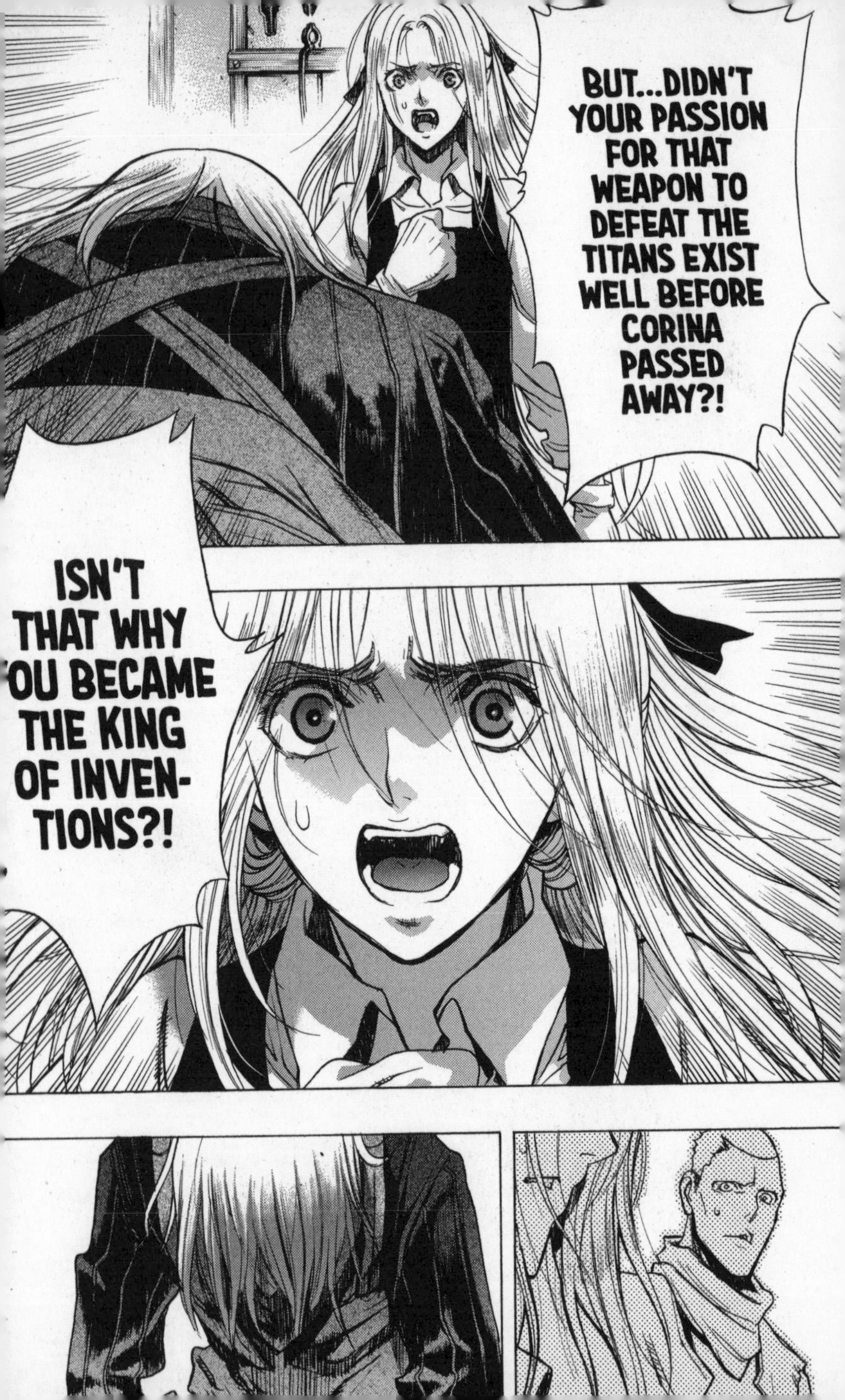
BUT...DIDN'T YOUR PASSION FOR THAT WEAPON TO DEFEAT THE TITANS EXIST WELL BEFORE CORINA PASSED AWAY?!
ISN'T THAT WHY OU BECAME THE KING OF INVEN- TIONS?!

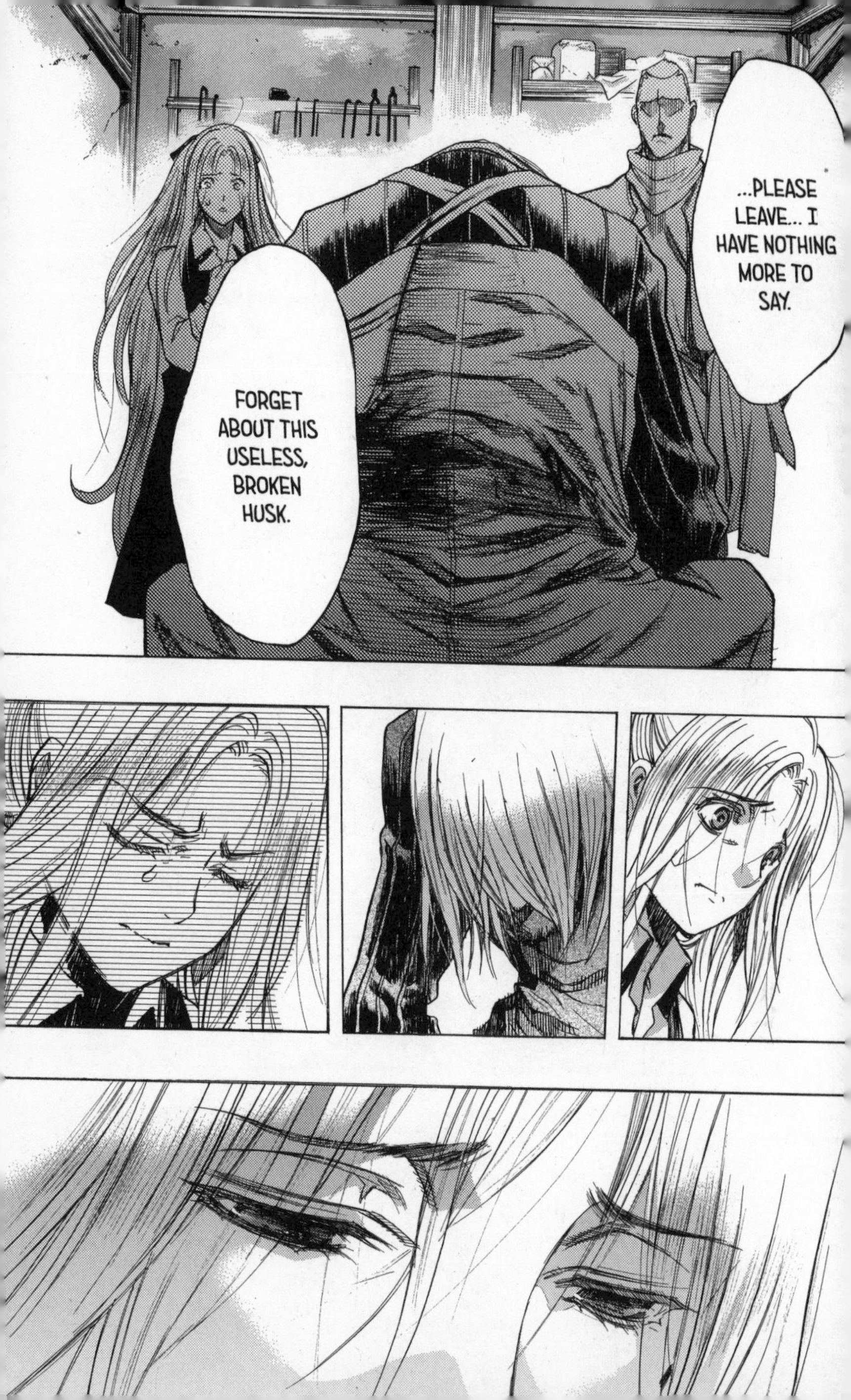
...PLEASE LEAVE... I HAVE NOTHING MORE TO SAY.
FORGET ABOUT THIS USELESS, BROKEN HUSK.

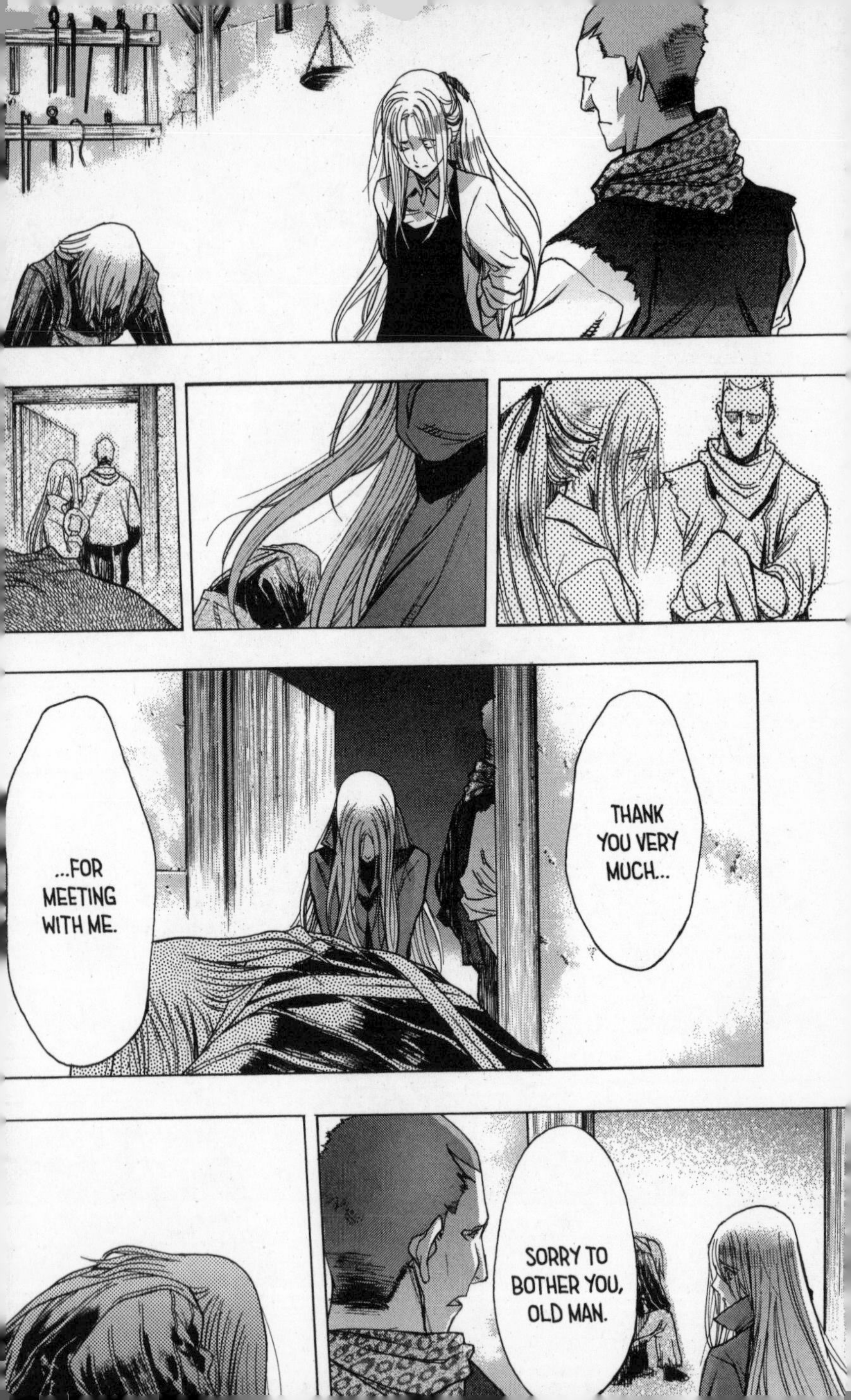
THANK YOU VERY MUCH...
...FOR MEETING WITH ME.
SORRY TO BOTHER YOU, OLD MAN.

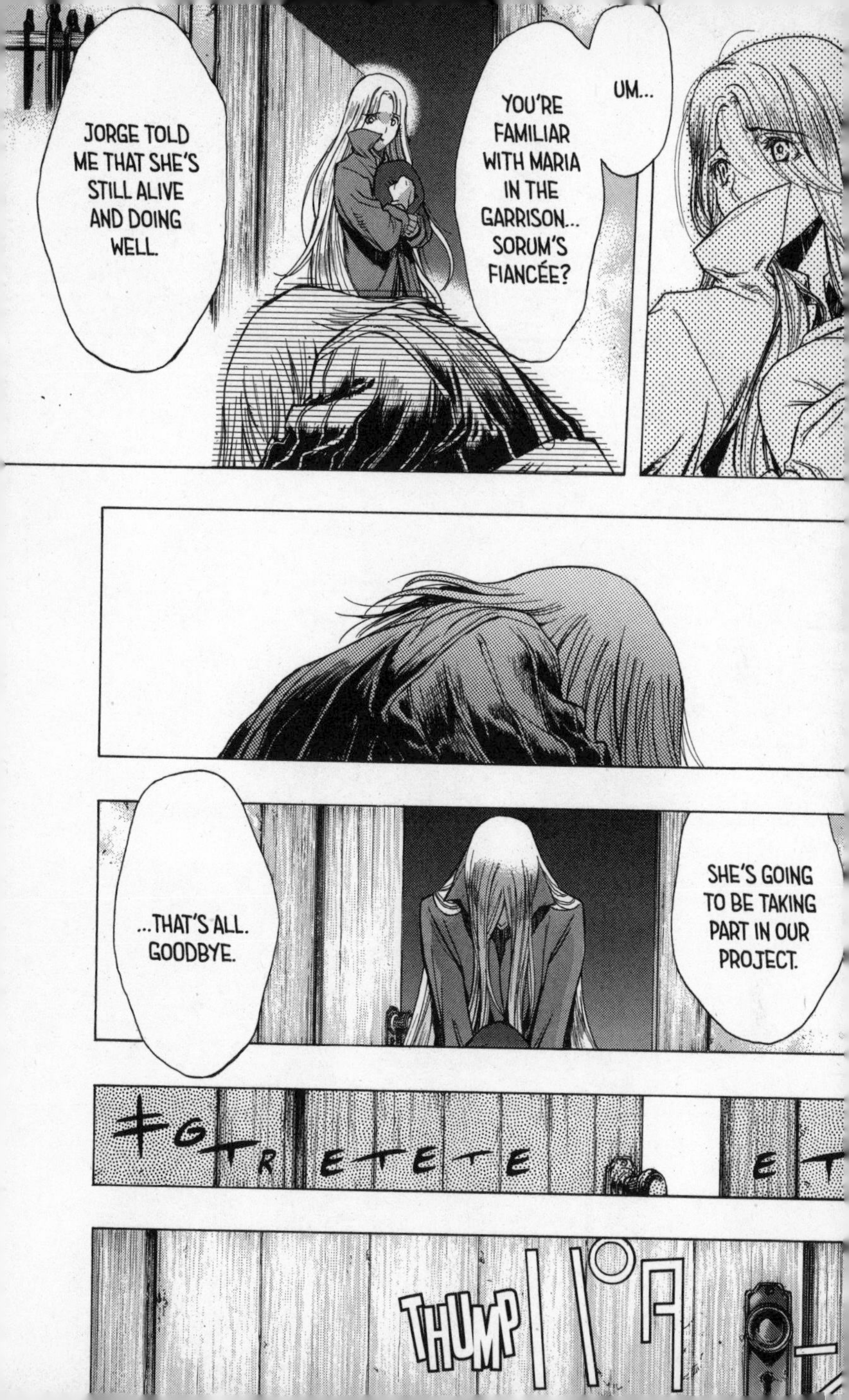
UM...
YOU'RE FAMILIAR WITH MARIA IN THE GARRISON... SORUM'S FIANCÉE?
JORGE TOLD ME THAT SHE'S STILL ALIVE AND DOING WELL.
SHE'S GOING TO BE TAKING PART IN OUR PROJECT.
...THAT'S ALL. GOODBYE.
GTRETETE
THUMP

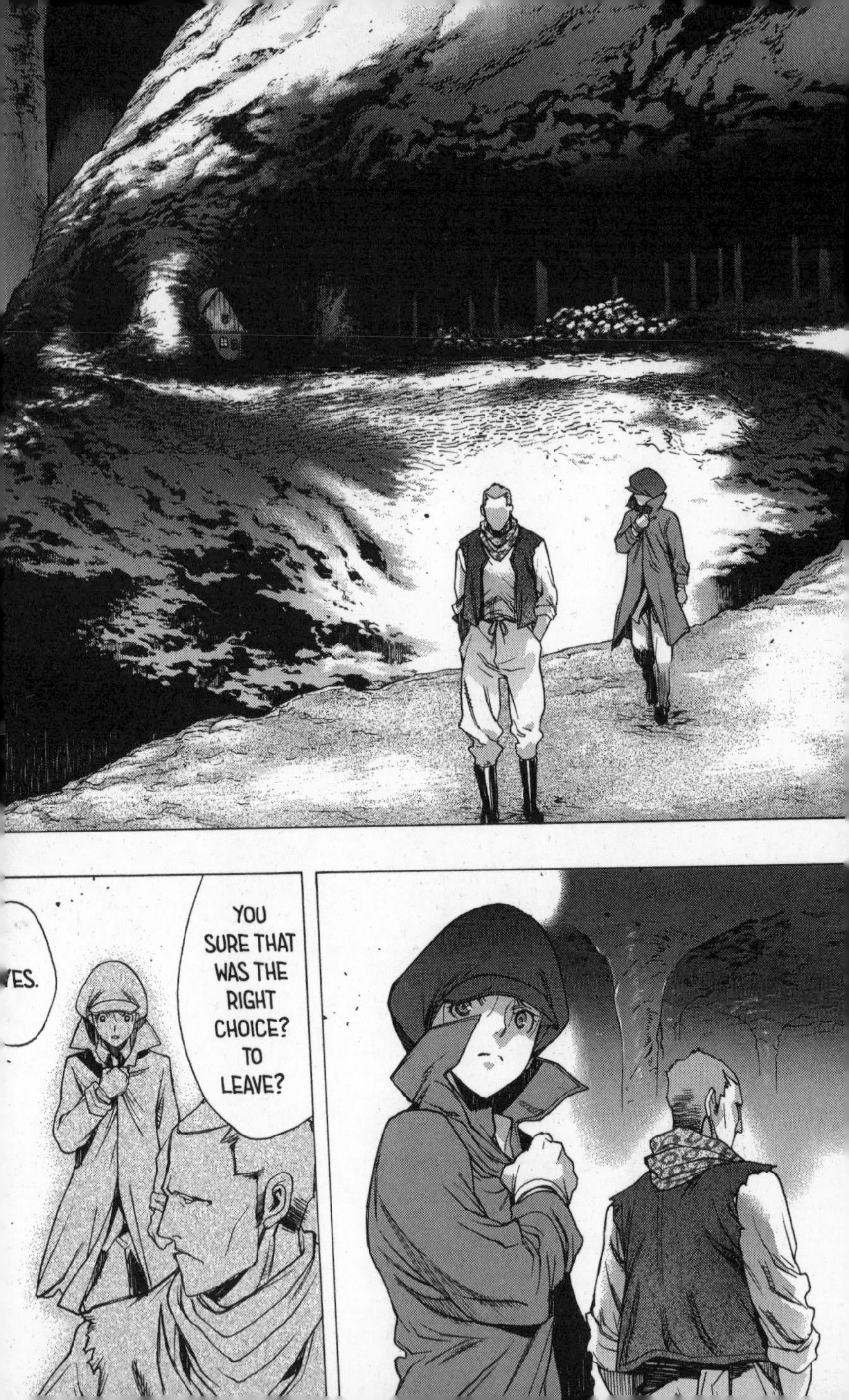
YOU SURE THAT WAS THE RIGHT CHOICE? TO LEAVE?
YES.

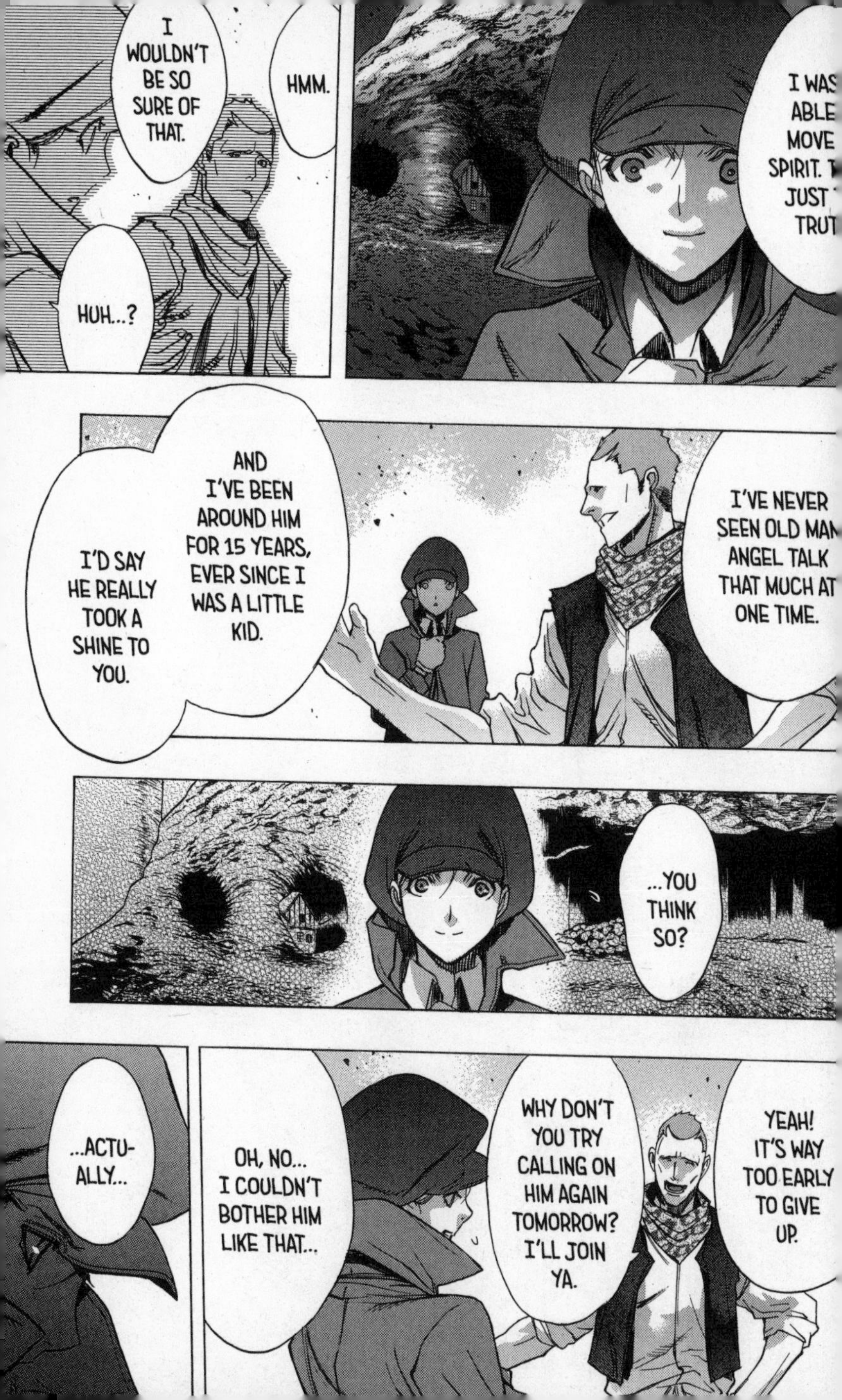
I WAS ABLE MOVE SPIRIT. JUST TRUT
HMM.
I WOULDN'T BE SO SURE OF THAT.
HUH...?
I'VE NEVER SEEN OLD MAN ANGEL TALK THAT MUCH AT ONE TIME.
AND I'VE BEEN AROUND HIM FOR 15 YEARS, EVER SINCE I WAS A LITTLE KID.
I'D SAY HE REALLY TOOK A SHINE TO YOU.
...YOU THINK SO?
YEAH! IT'S WAY TOO EARLY TO GIVE UP.
WHY DON'T YOU TRY CALLING ON HIM AGAIN TOMORROW? I'LL JOIN YA.
OH, NO... I COULDN'T BOTHER HIM LIKE THAT...
...ACTU-ALLY...

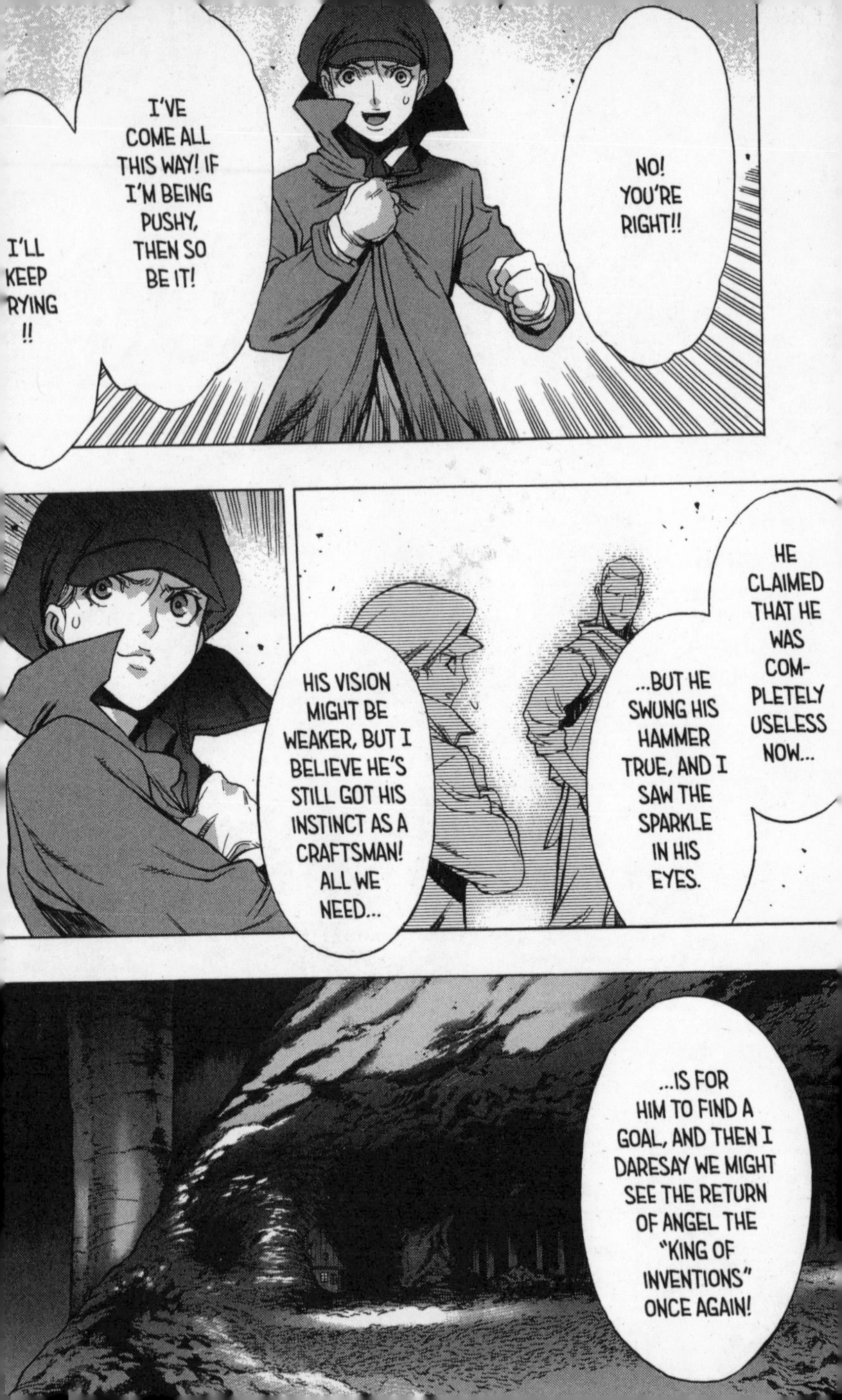
NO! YOU'RE RIGHT!!
I'VE COME ALL THIS WAY! IF I'M BEING PUSHY, THEN SO BE IT!
I'LL KEEP RYING !!
HE CLAIMED THAT HE WAS COM- PLETELY USELESS NOW...
...BUT HE SWUNG HIS HAMMER TRUE, AND I SAW THE SPARKLE IN HIS EYES.
HIS VISION MIGHT BE WEAKER, BUT I BELIEVE HE'S STILL GOT HIS INSTINCT AS A CRAFTSMAN! ALL WE NEED...
...IS FOR HIM TO FIND A GOAL, AND THEN I DARESAY WE MIGHT SEE THE RETURN OF ANGEL THE "KING OF INVENTIONS" ONCE AGAIN!

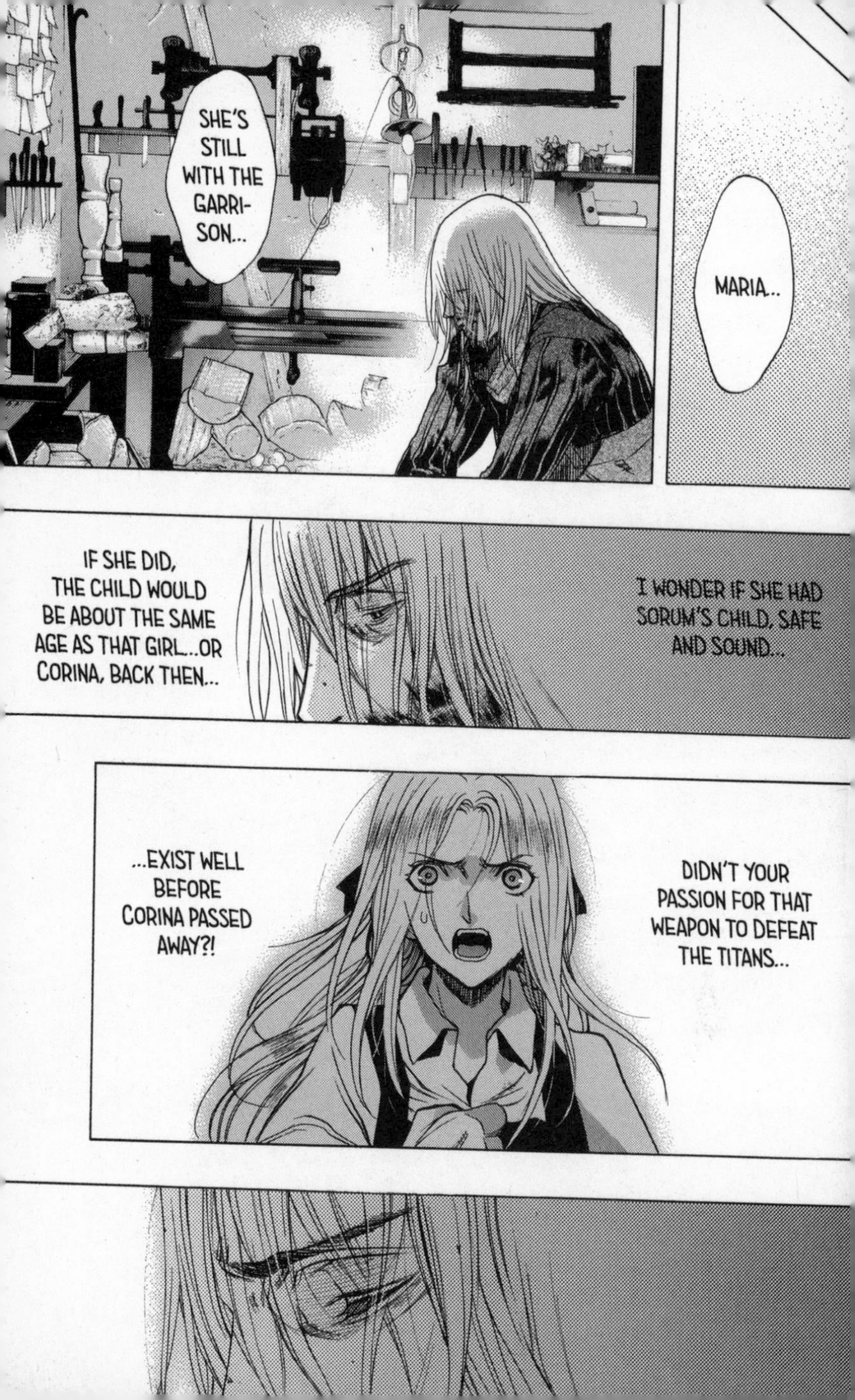
MARIA...
SHE'S STILL WITH THE GARRI-SON...
I WONDER IF SHE HAD SORUM'S CHILD, SAFE AND SOUND...
IF SHE DID, THE CHILD WOULD BE ABOUT THE SAME AGE AS THAT GIRL...OR CORINA, BACK THEN...
DIDN'T YOUR PASSION FOR THAT WEAPON TO DEFEAT THE TITANS...
...EXIST WELL BEFORE CORINA PASSED AWAY?!

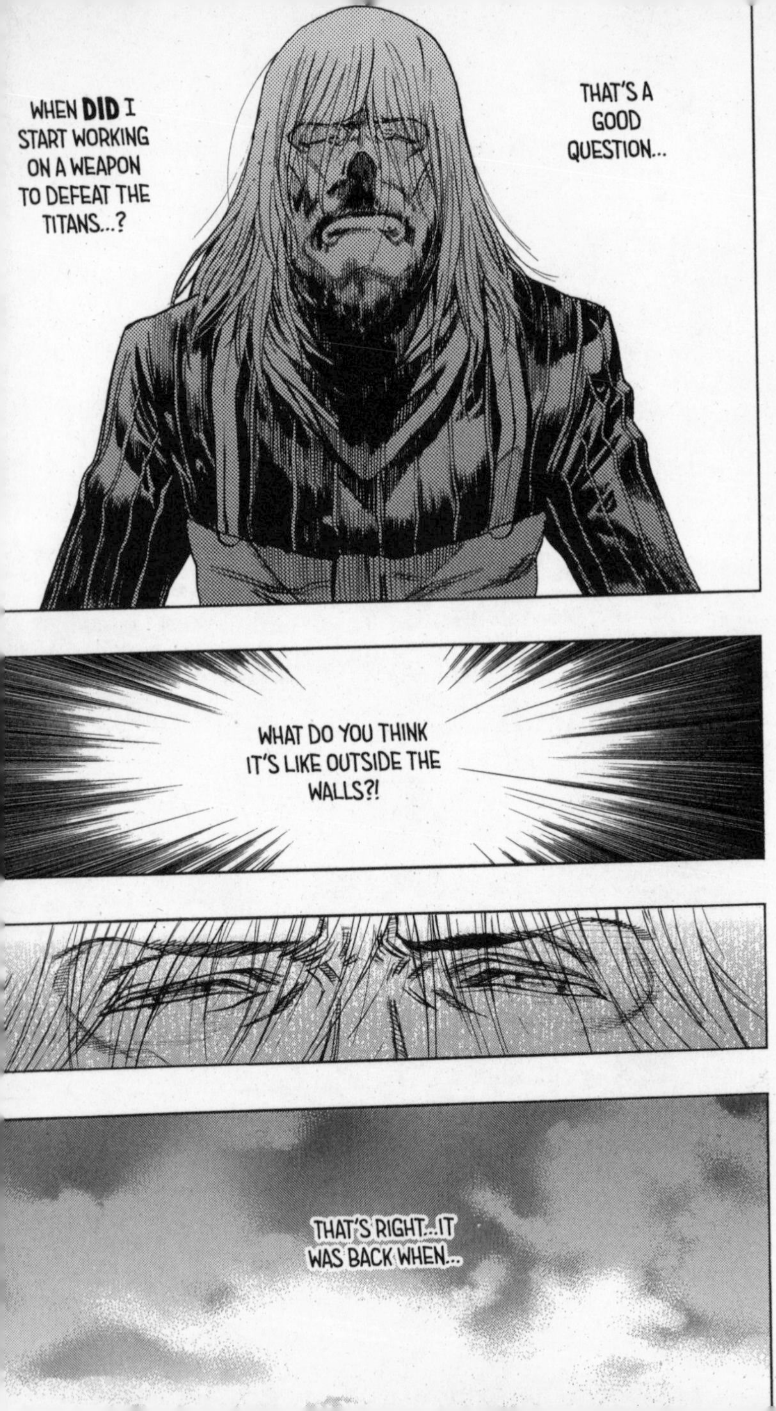
THAT'S A GOOD QUESTION...
WHEN DID I START WORKING ON A WEAPON TO DEFEAT THE TITANS...?
WHAT DO YOU THINK IT'S LIKE OUTSIDE THE WALLS?!
THAT'S RIGHT...IT WAS BACK WHEN...

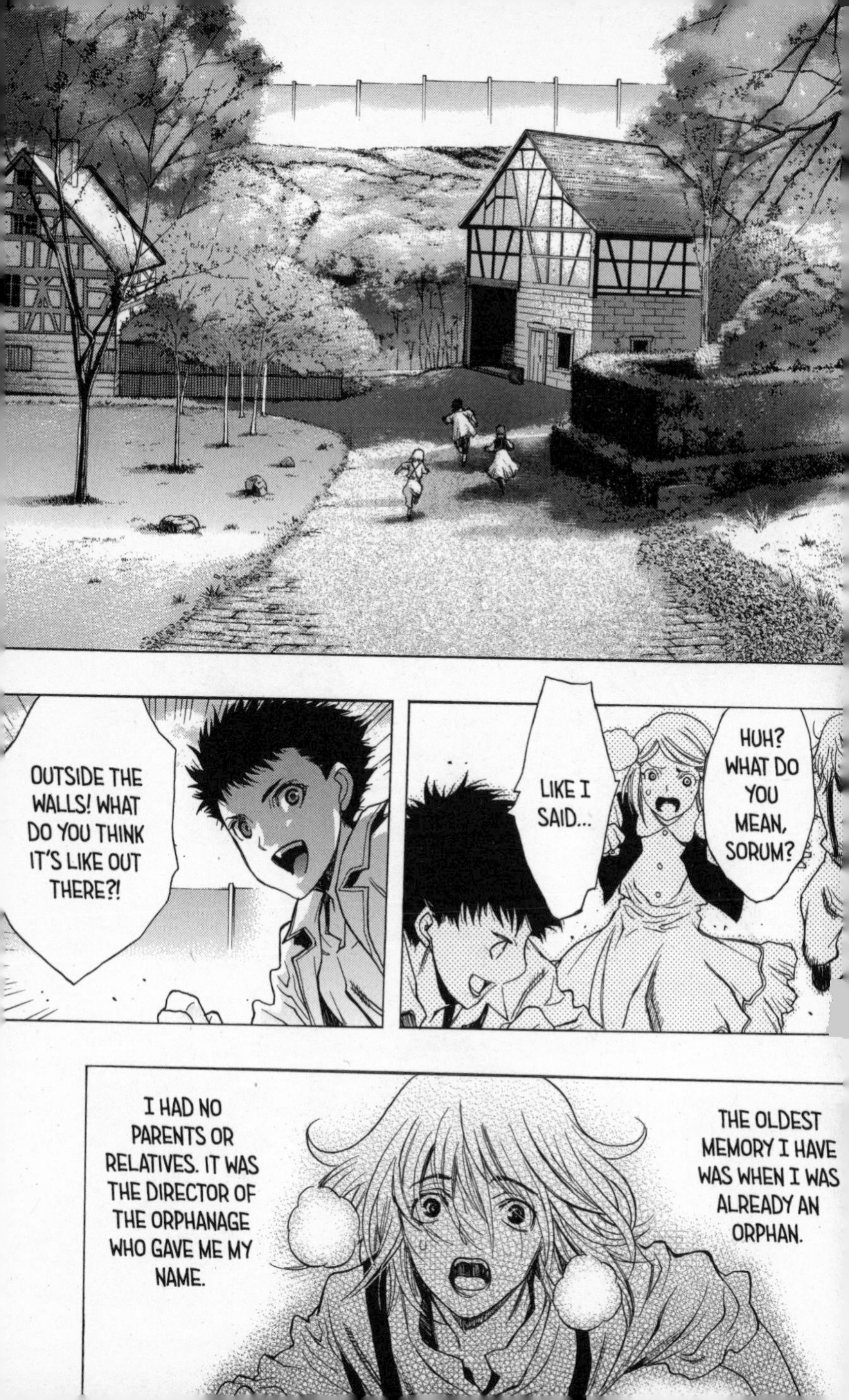
HUH? WHAT DO YOU MEAN, SORUM?
LIKE I SAID...
OUTSIDE THE WALLS! WHAT DO YOU THINK IT'S LIKE OUT THERE?!
THE OLDEST MEMORY I HAVE WAS WHEN I WAS ALREADY AN ORPHAN.
I HAD NO PARENTS OR RELATIVES. IT WAS THE DIRECTOR OF THE ORPHANAGE WHO GAVE ME MY NAME.

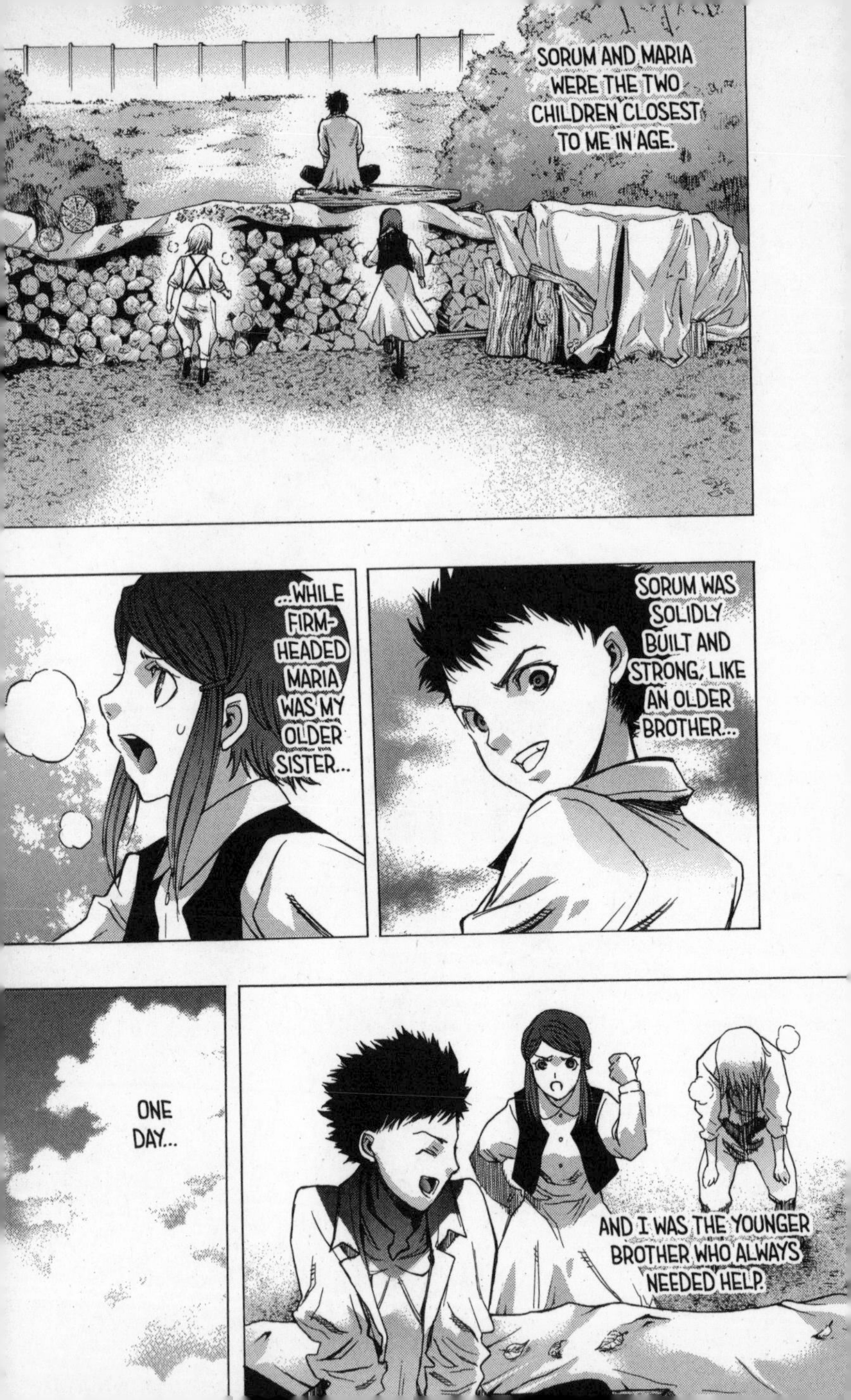
SORUM AND MARIA WERE THE TWO CHILDREN CLOSEST TO ME IN AGE.
SORUM WAS SOLIDLY BUILT AND STRONG, LIKE AN OLDER BROTHER...
...WHILE FIRM-HEADED MARIA WAS MY OLDER SISTER...
AND I WAS THE YOUNGER BROTHER WHO ALWAYS NEEDED HELP.
ONE DAY...

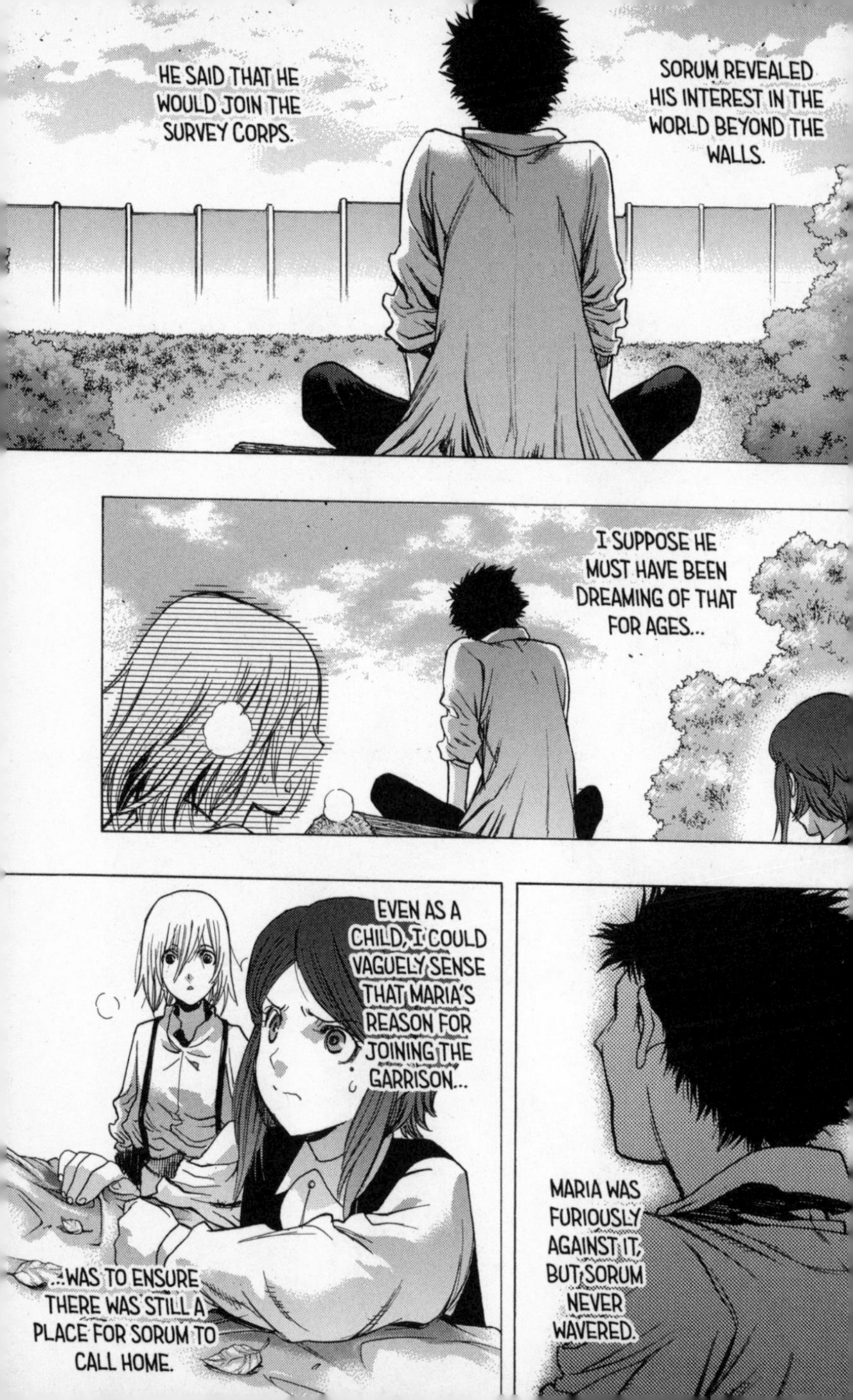
SORUM REVEALED HIS INTEREST IN THE WORLD BEYOND THE WALLS.
HE SAID THAT HE WOULD JOIN THE SURVEY CORPS.
I SUPPOSE HE MUST HAVE BEEN DREAMING OF THAT FOR AGES...
MARIA WAS FURIOUSLY AGAINST IT, BUT SORUM NEVER WAVERED.
EVEN AS A CHILD, I COULD VAGUELY SENSE THAT MARIA'S REASON FOR JOINING THE GARRISON...
...WAS TO ENSURE THERE WAS STILL A PLACE FOR SORUM TO CALL HOME.

SO I DECIDED THAT I WANTED TO HELP ENSURE SORUM'S SAFE RETURN...

...AND THUS, I BECAME A CRAFTSMAN...

WANTED TO HELP MY BROTHER ACHIEVE HIS DREAM.

YES, THAT'S RIGHT.

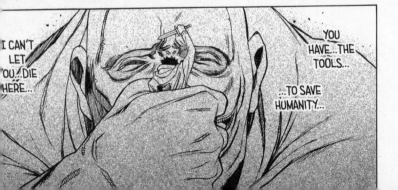

I CAN'T LET YOU DIE HERE...

YOU HAVE...THE TOOLS...

...TO SAVE HUMANITY...

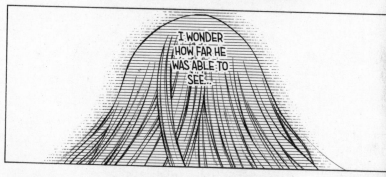

I WONDER HOW FAR HE WAS ABLE TO SEE...

BEYOND THE WALL...

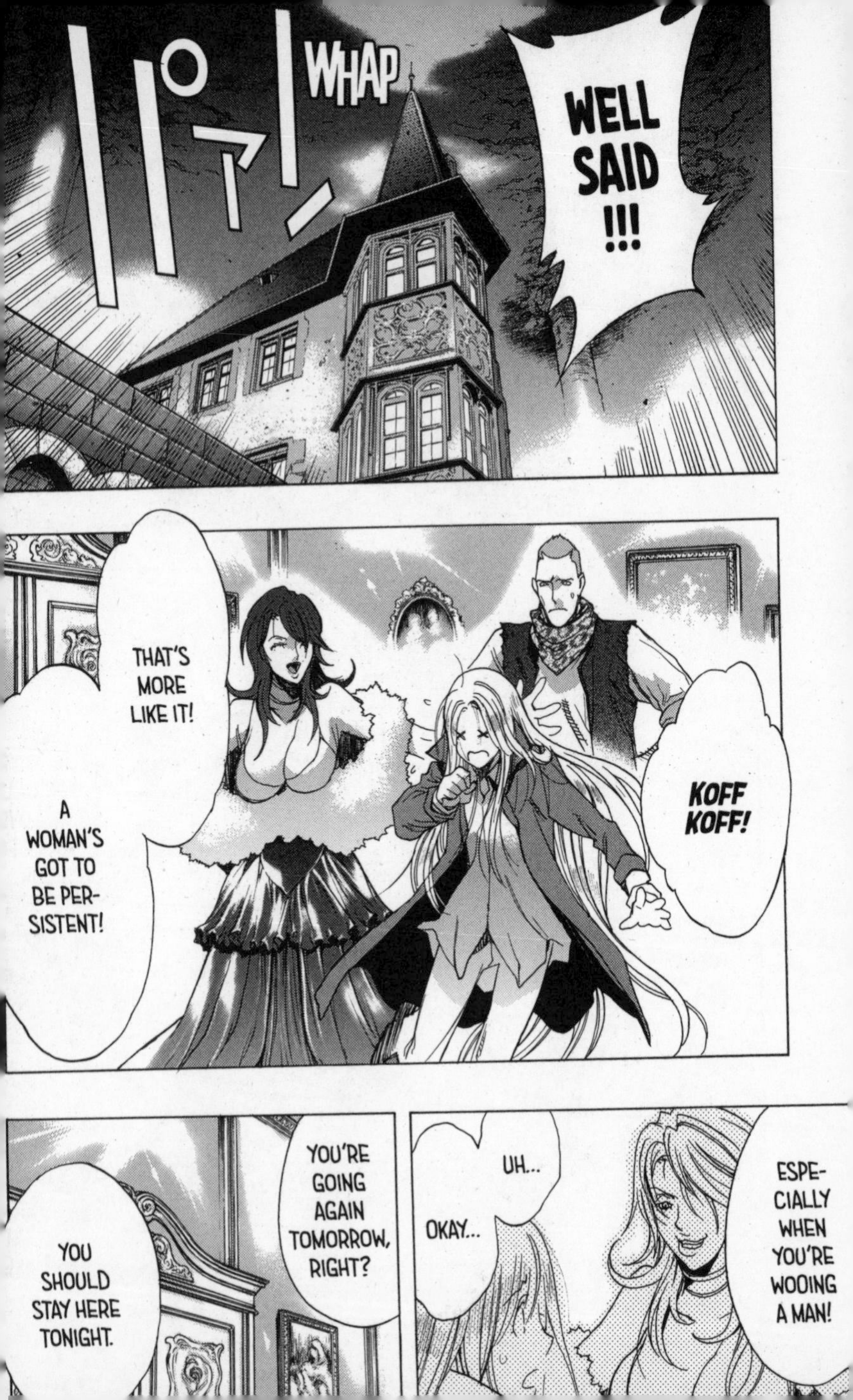
WELL SAID !!!
WHAP
KOFF KOFF!
THAT'S MORE LIKE IT!
A WOMAN'S GOT TO BE PERSISTENT!
ESPECIALLY WHEN YOU'RE WOOING A MAN!
UH...
OKAY...
YOU'RE GOING AGAIN TOMORROW, RIGHT?
YOU SHOULD STAY HERE TONIGHT.

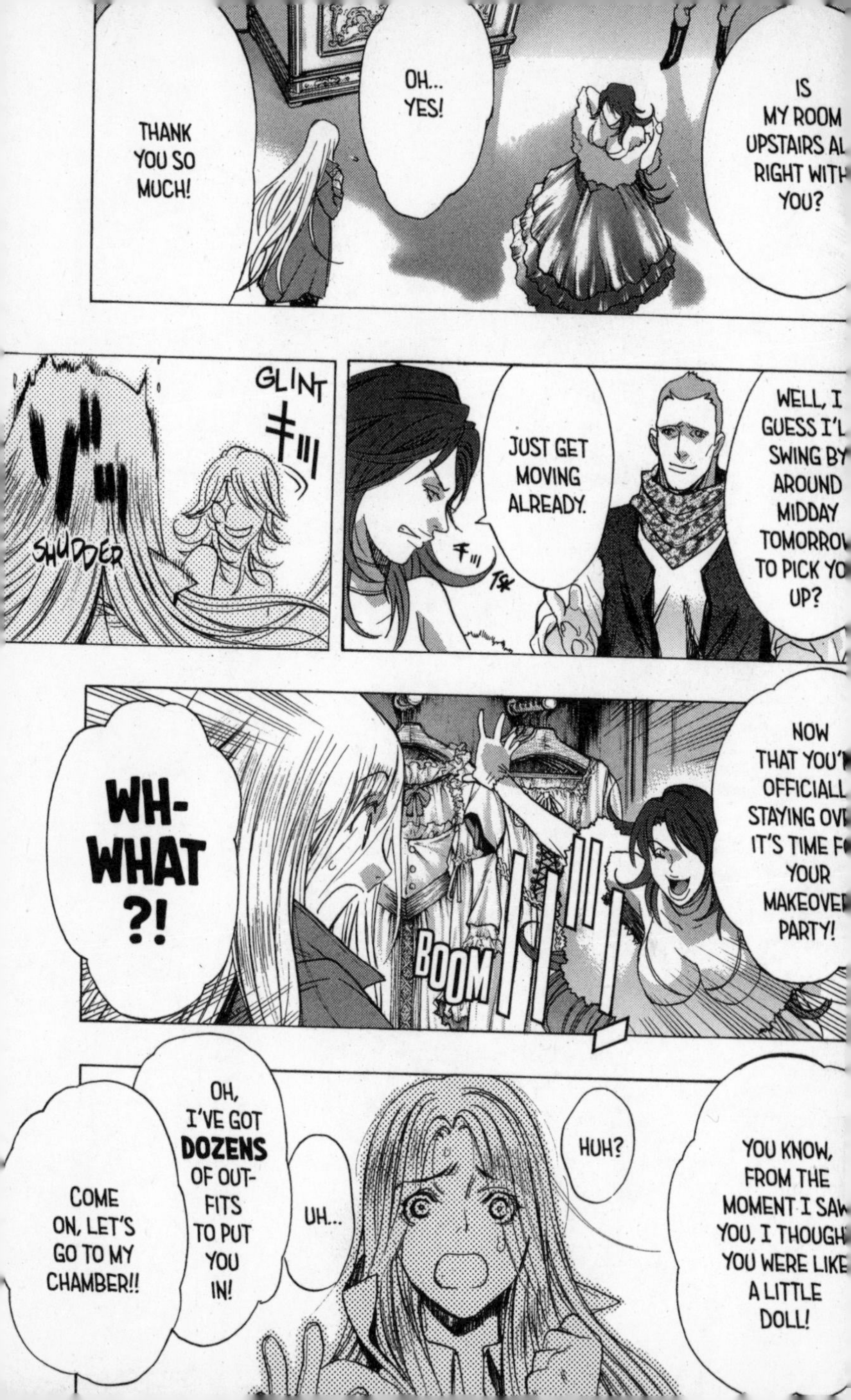

IS MY ROOM UPSTAIRS AL RIGHT WITH YOU?
OH... YES!
THANK YOU SO MUCH!
WELL, I GUESS I'L SWING BY AROUND MIDDAY TOMORRO TO PICK YO UP?
JUST GET MOVING ALREADY.
TSK
GLINT
SHUDDER
NOW THAT YOU' OFFICIALL STAYING OV IT'S TIME F YOUR MAKEOVE PARTY!
BOOM
WH-WHAT?!
YOU KNOW, FROM THE MOMENT I SAW YOU, I THOUGH YOU WERE LIKE A LITTLE DOLL!
HUH?
UH...
OH, I'VE GOT **DOZENS** OF OUT-FITS TO PUT YOU IN!
COME ON, LET'S GO TO MY CHAMBER!!

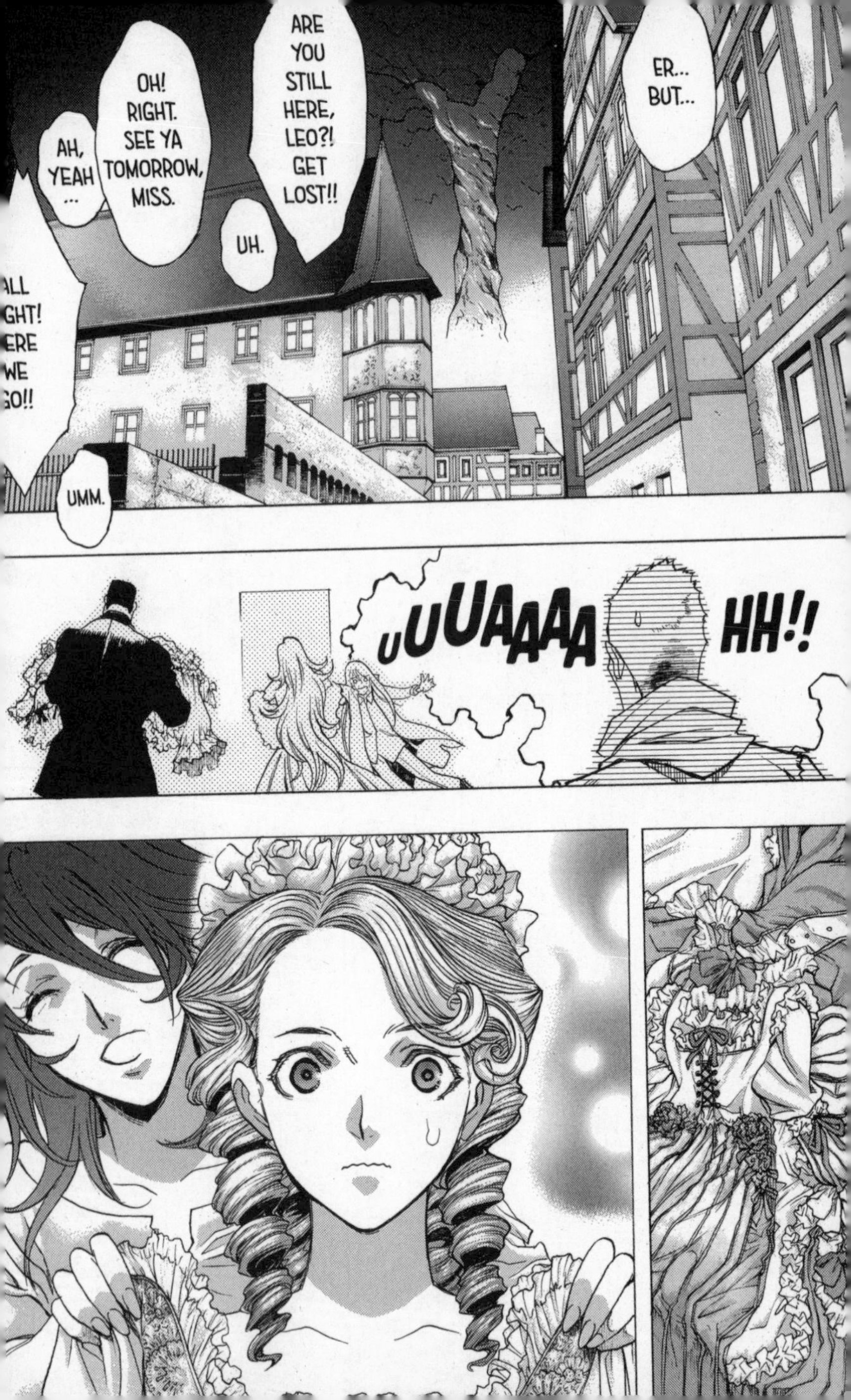
ER... BUT...
ARE YOU STILL HERE, LEO?! GET LOST!!
UH.
OH! RIGHT. SEE YA TOMORROW, MISS.
AH, YEAH ...
ALL GHT! ERE WE GO!!
UMM.
UUUAAAAHH!!

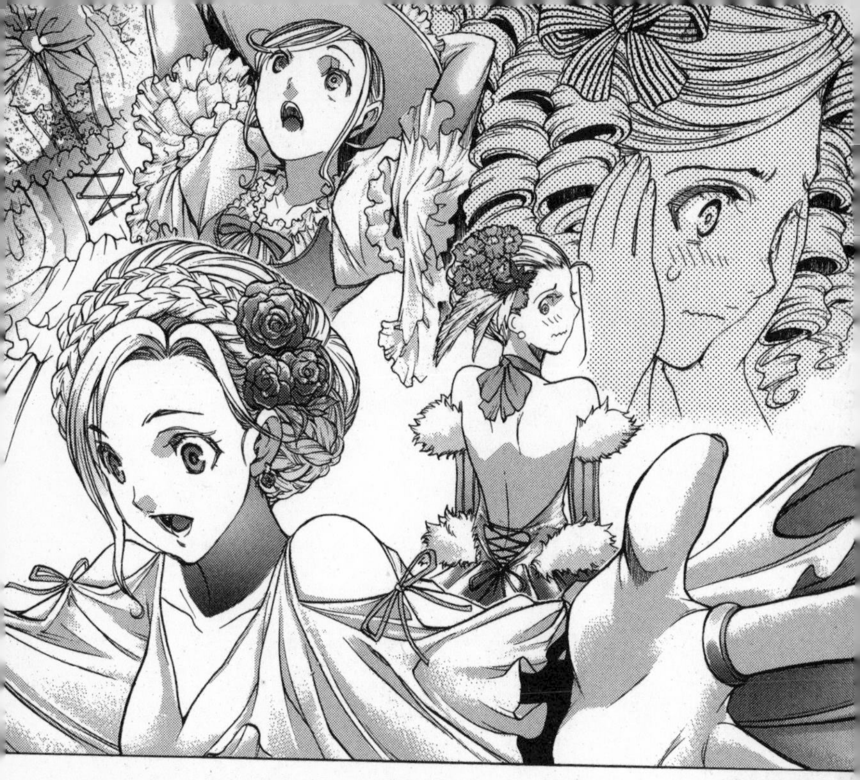
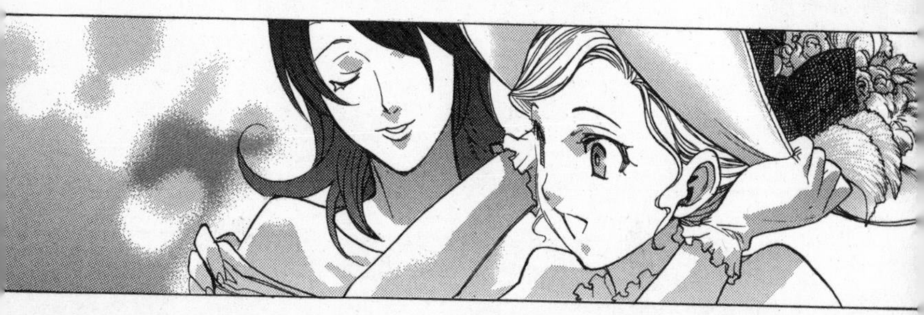
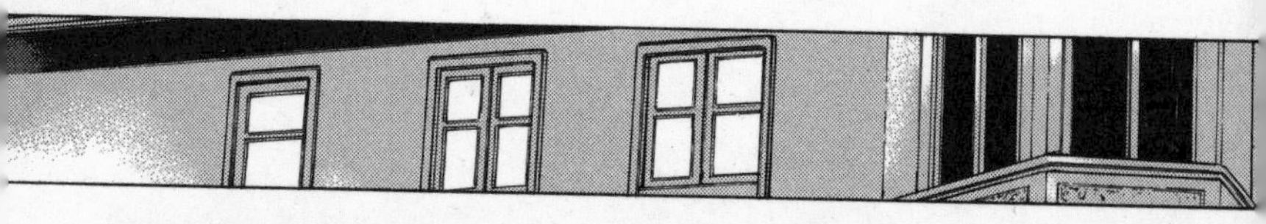
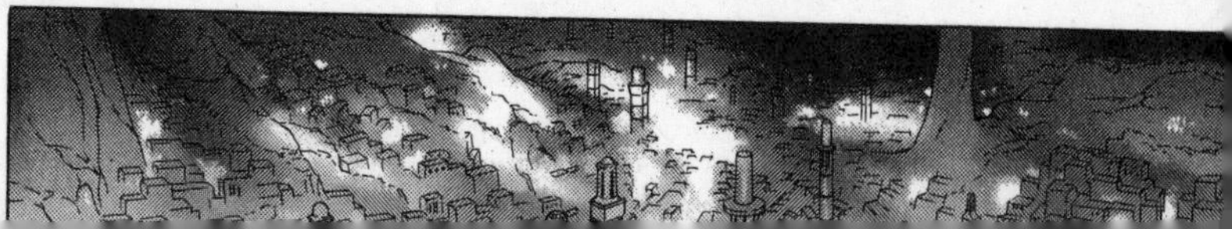

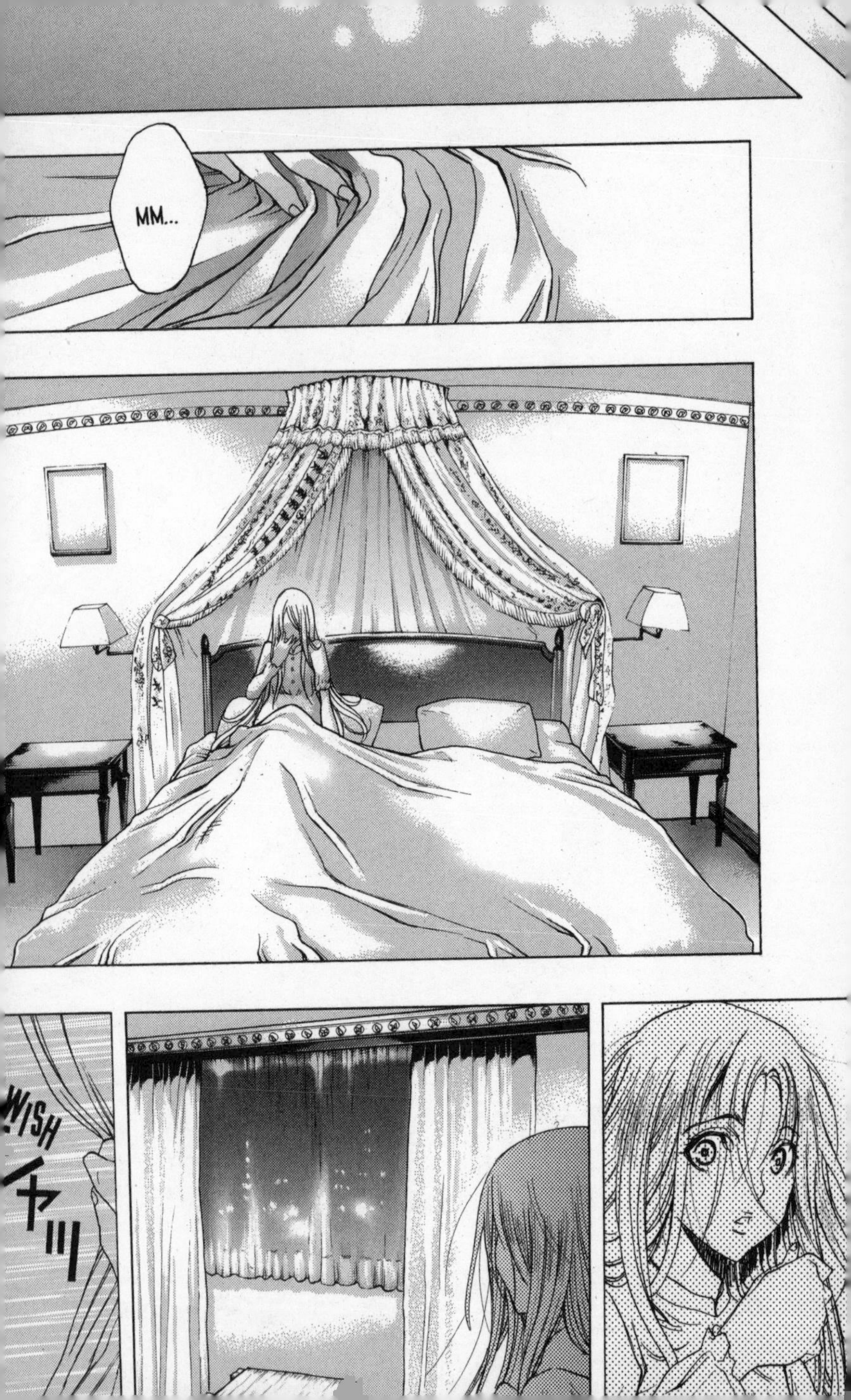
MM...
WISH

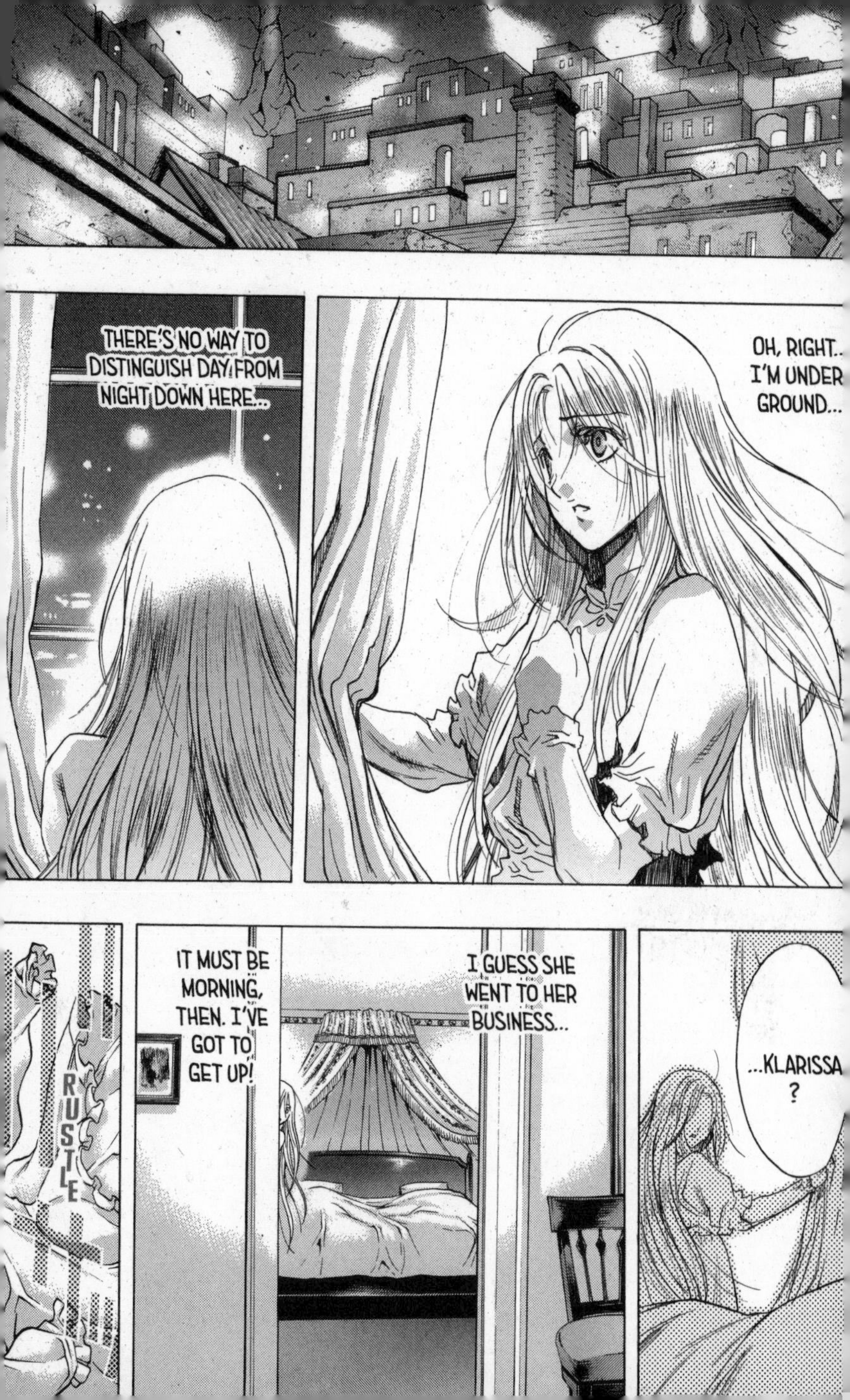
OH, RIGHT.. I'M UNDER GROUND...
THERE'S NO WAY TO DISTINGUISH DAY FROM NIGHT DOWN HERE...
...KLARISSA ?
I GUESS SHE WENT TO HER BUSINESS...
IT MUST BE MORNING, THEN. I'VE GOT TO GET UP!
RUSTLE

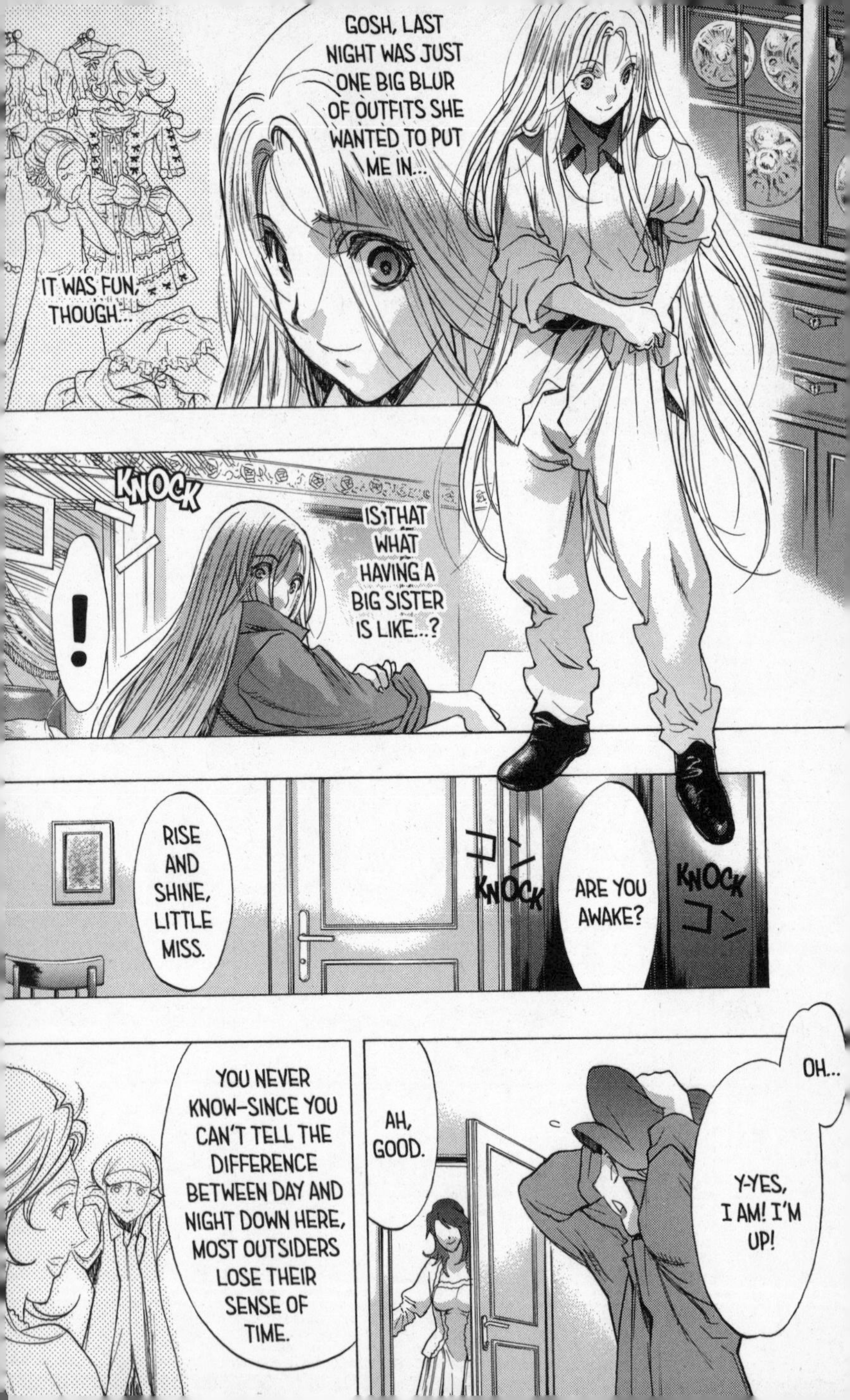
GOSH, LAST NIGHT WAS JUST ONE BIG BLUR OF OUTFITS SHE WANTED TO PUT ME IN...
IT WAS FUN, THOUGH...
IS THAT WHAT HAVING A BIG SISTER IS LIKE...?
KNOCK
!
KNOCK
ARE YOU AWAKE?
KNOCK
RISE AND SHINE, LITTLE MISS.
OH...
Y-YES, I AM! I'M UP!
AH, GOOD.
YOU NEVER KNOW–SINCE YOU CAN'T TELL THE DIFFERENCE BETWEEN DAY AND NIGHT DOWN HERE, MOST OUTSIDERS LOSE THEIR SENSE OF TIME.

I'M SORRY, DID I KEEP YOU WAITING?

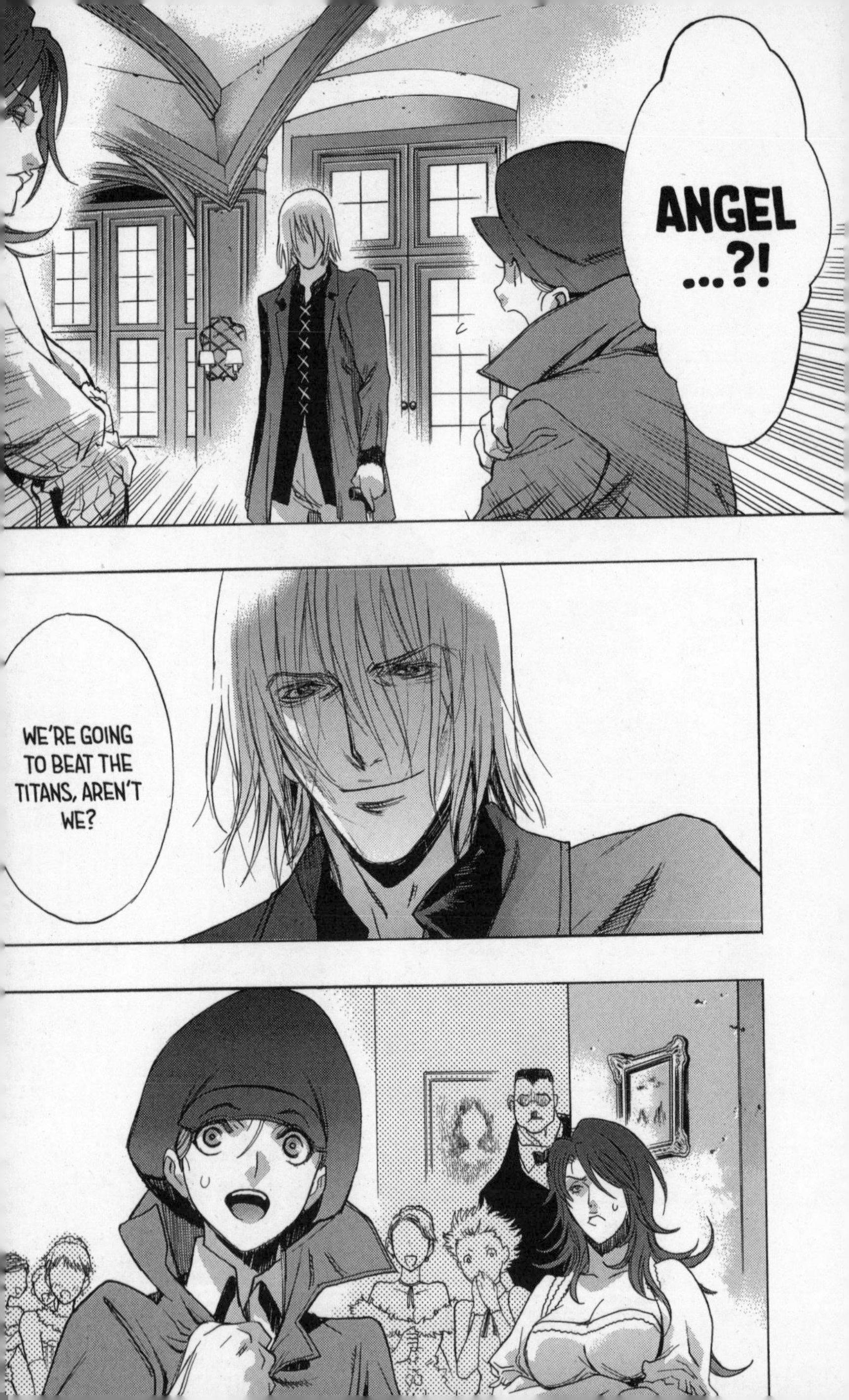
ANGEL ...?!
WE'RE GOING TO BEAT THE TITANS, AREN'T WE?

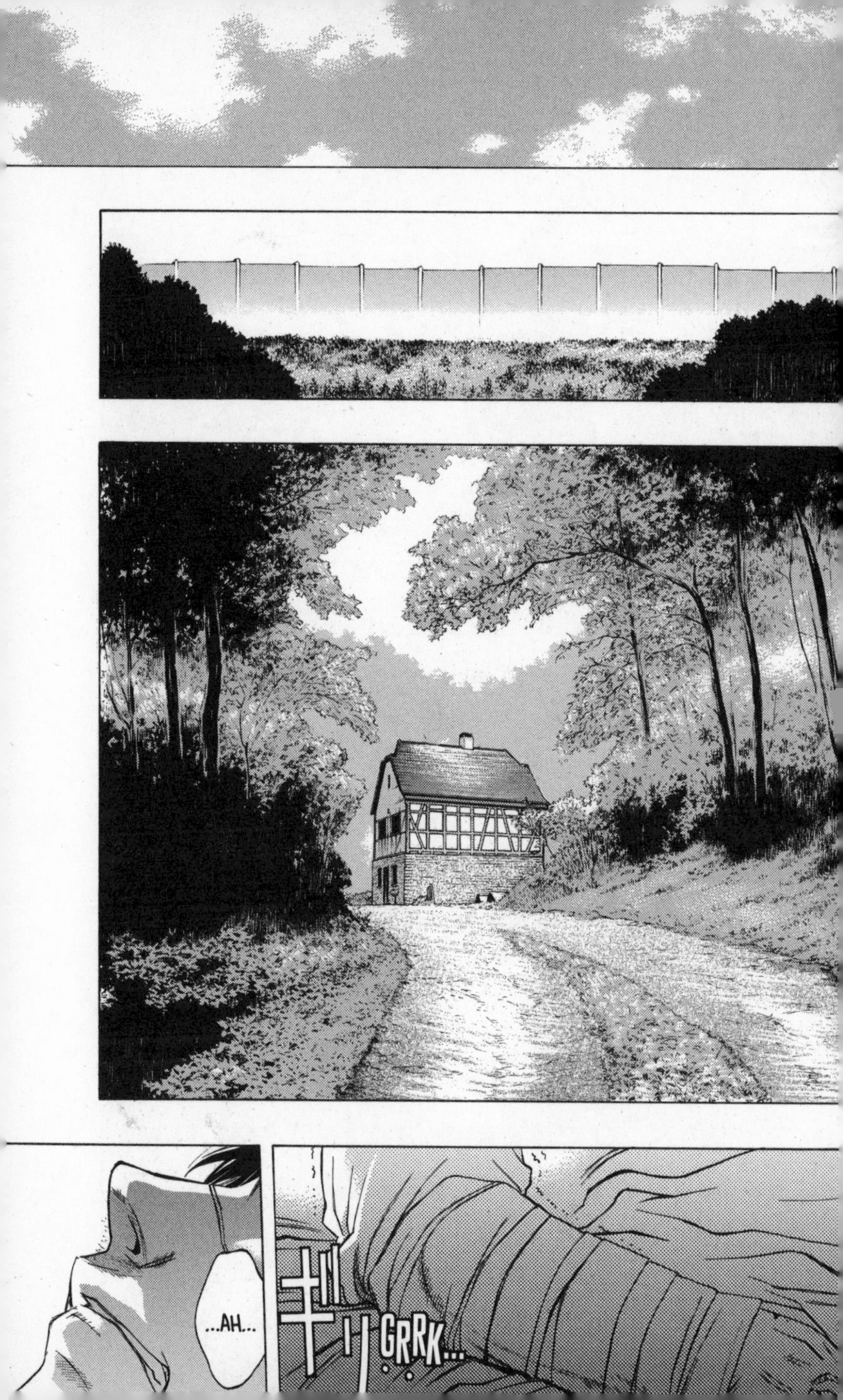
GRRK...
...AH...

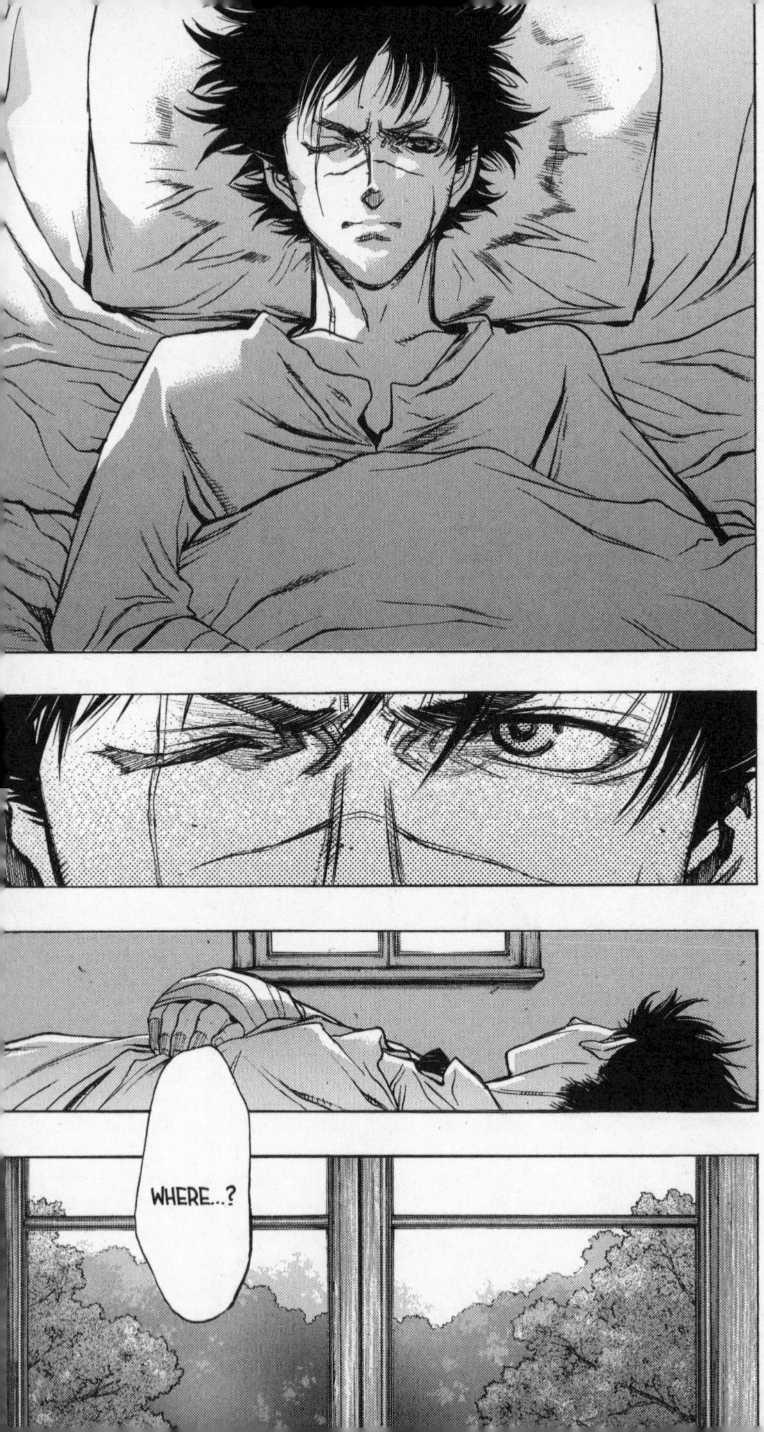
WHERE...?

Chapter 39: Succession of the Dream · End

ATTACK on TITAN
BEFORE THE FALL

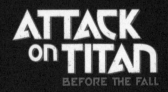

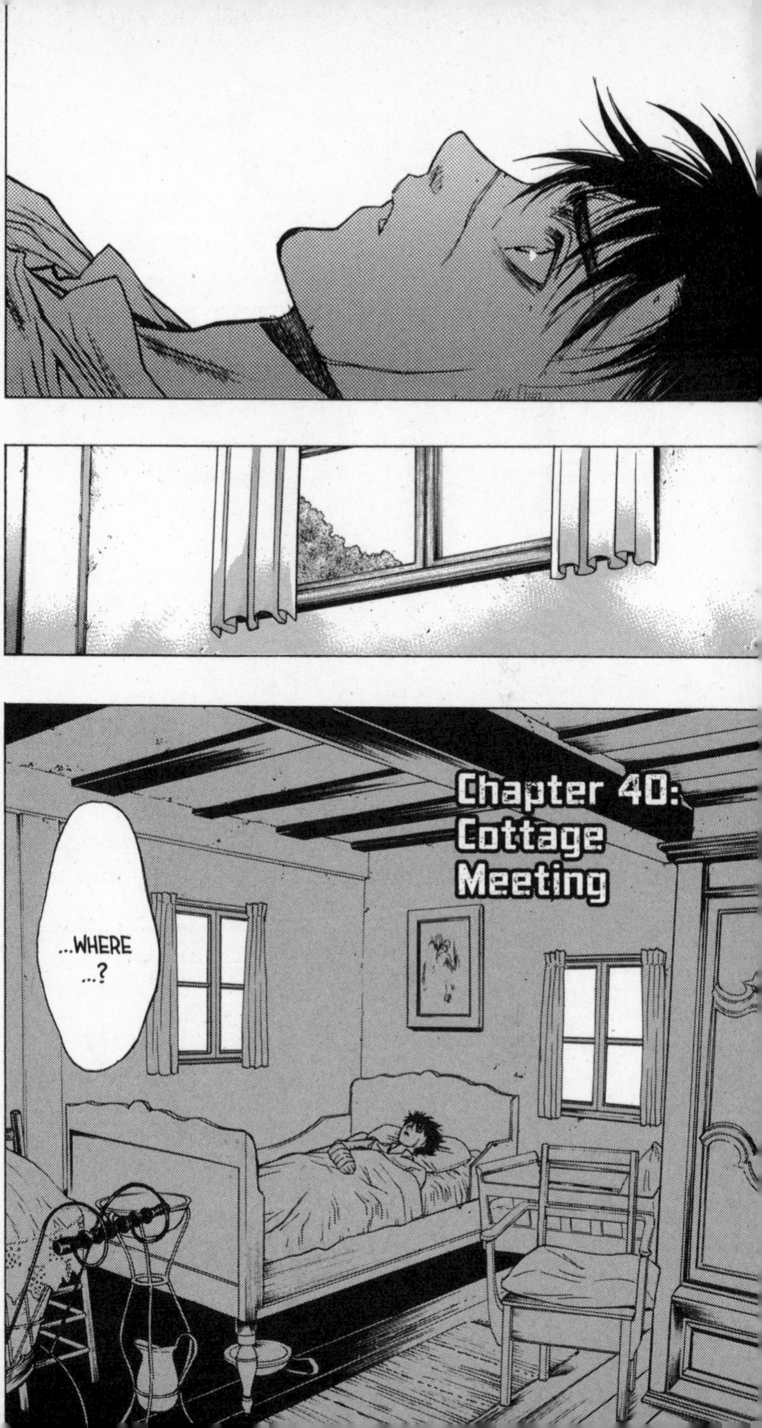
Chapter 40: Cottage Meeting
...WHERE ...?

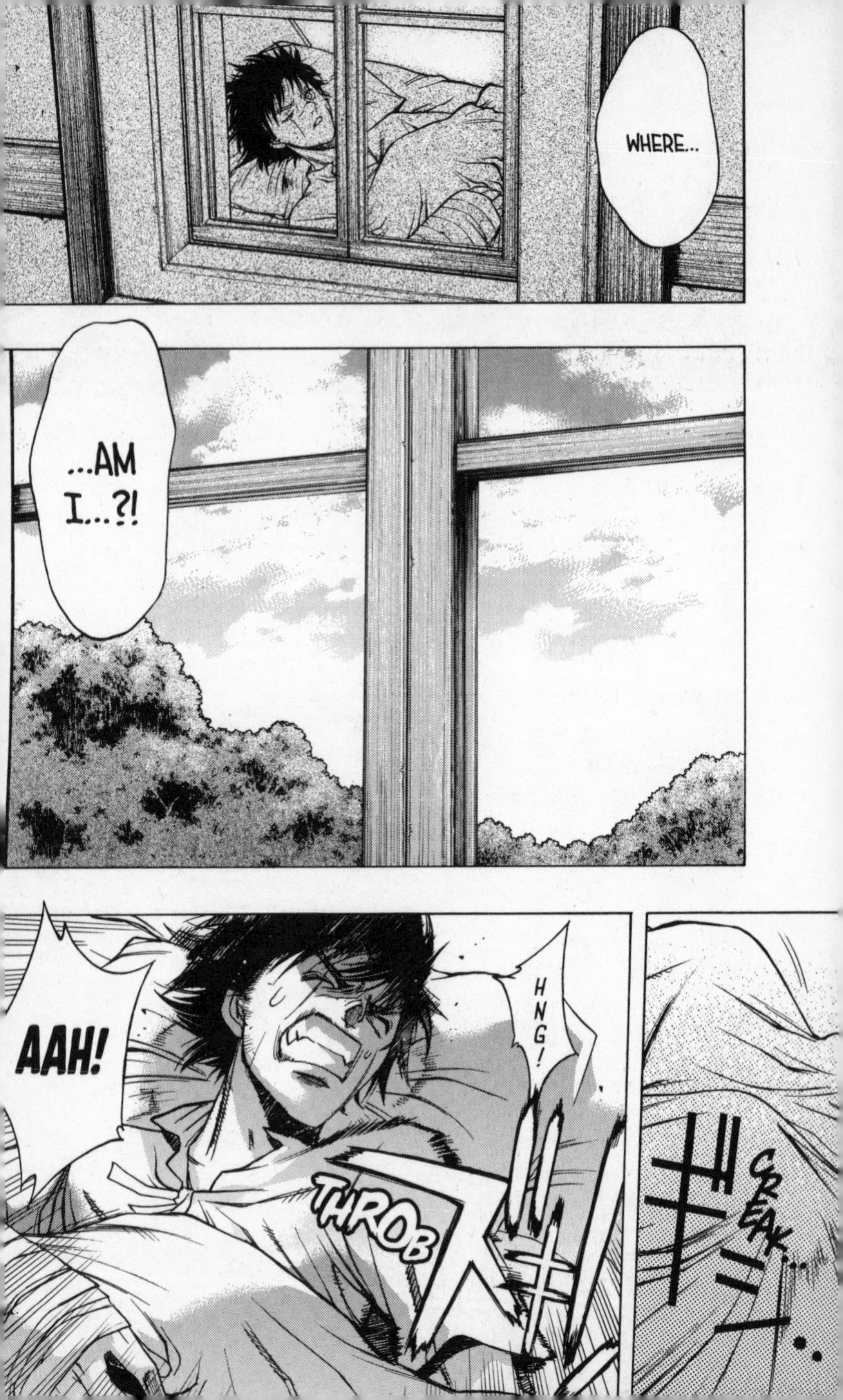
WHERE...
...AM I...?!
CREAK...
HNG!
AAH!
THROB

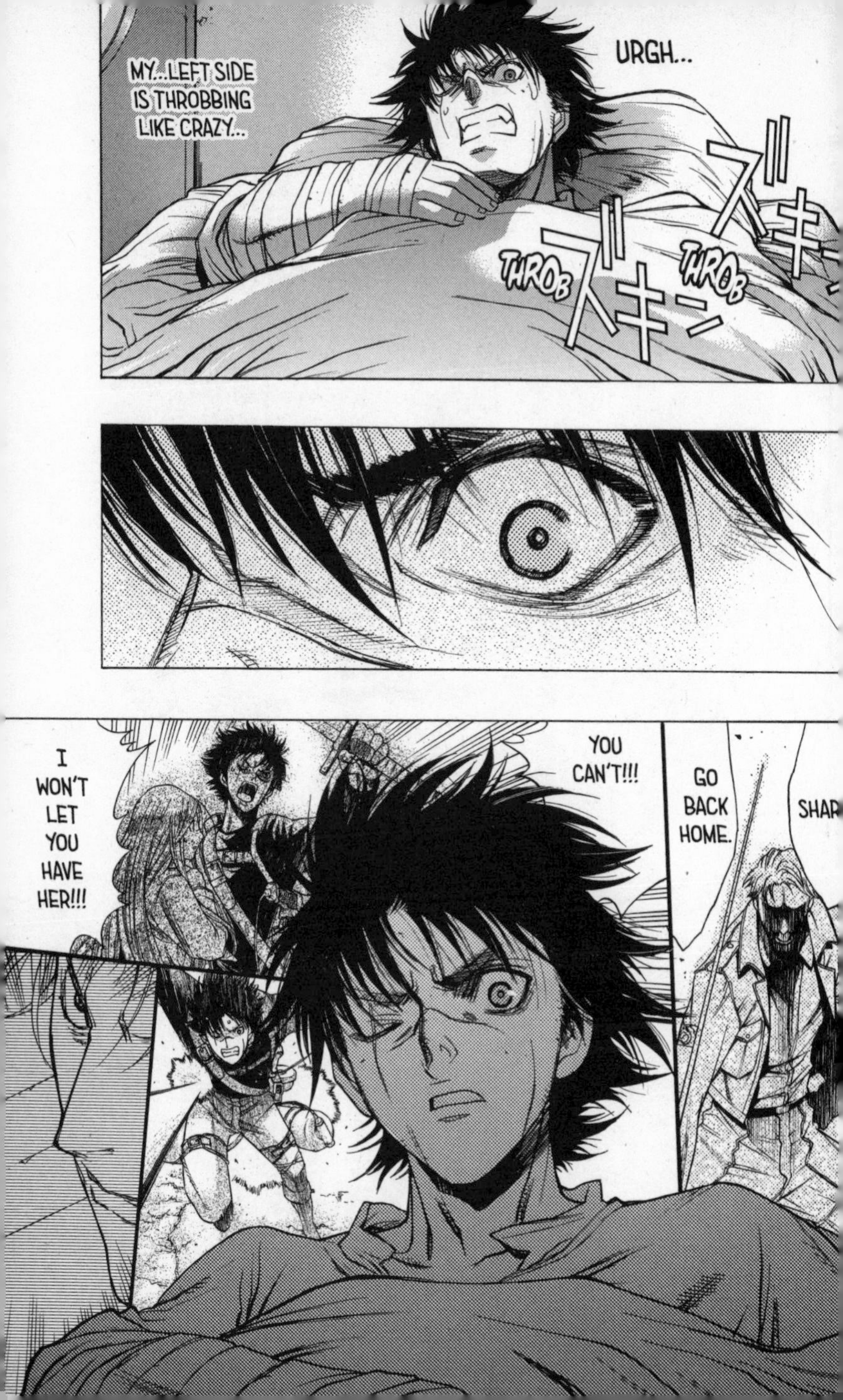
URGH...
MY...LEFT SIDE IS THROBBING LIKE CRAZY...
THROB
THROB
ズキン
SHAR
GO BACK HOME.
YOU CAN'T!!!
I WON'T LET YOU HAVE HER!!!

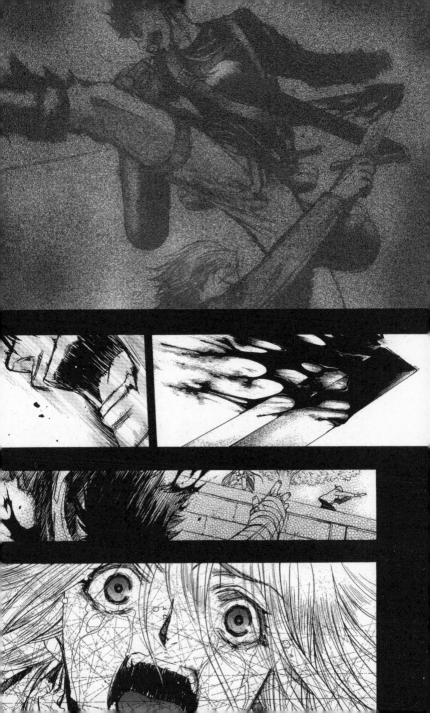

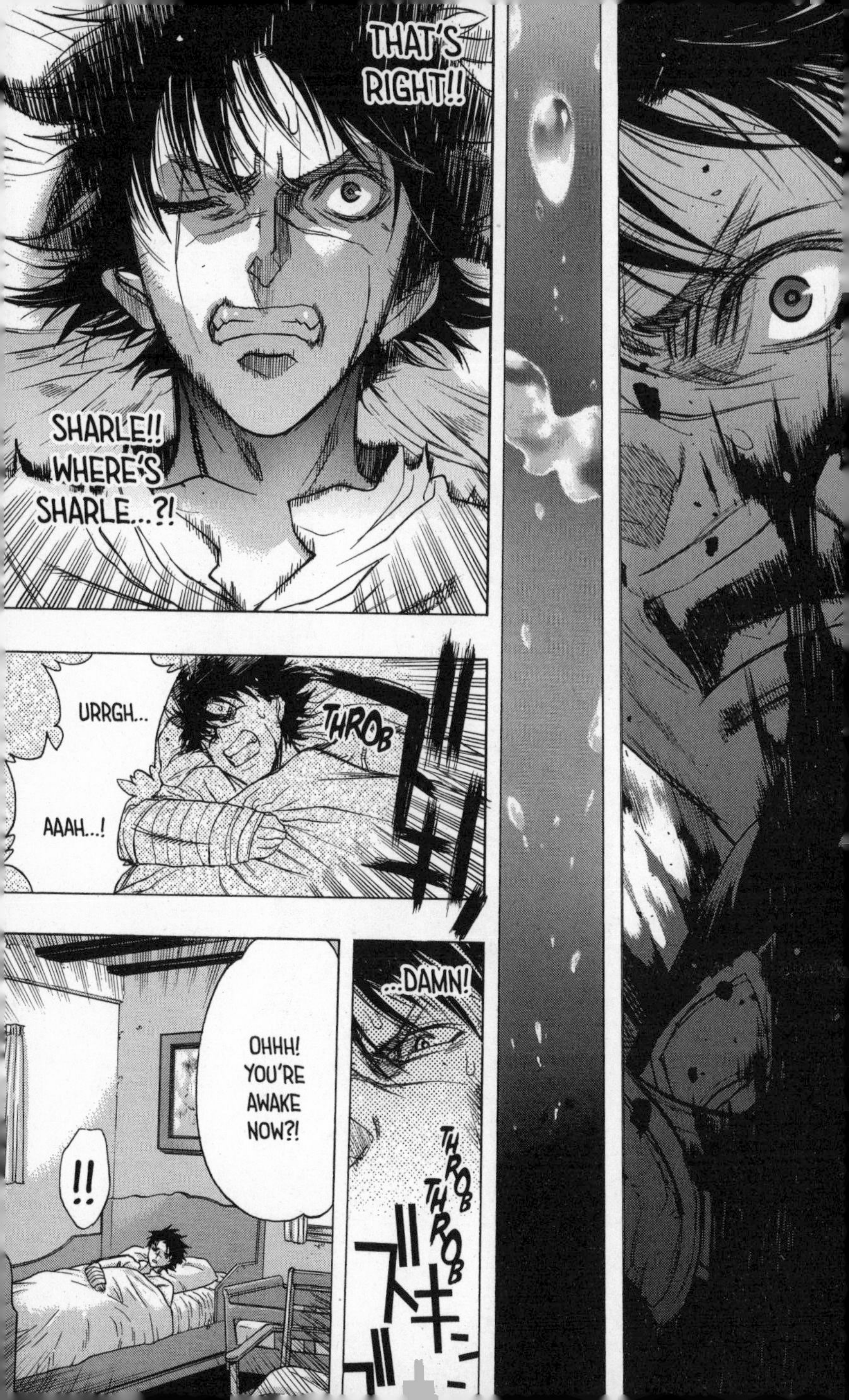
THAT'S RIGHT!!
SHARLE!! WHERE'S SHARLE...?!
THROB
URRGH...
AAAH...!
...DAMN!
THROB THROB
OHHH! YOU'RE AWAKE NOW?!
!!

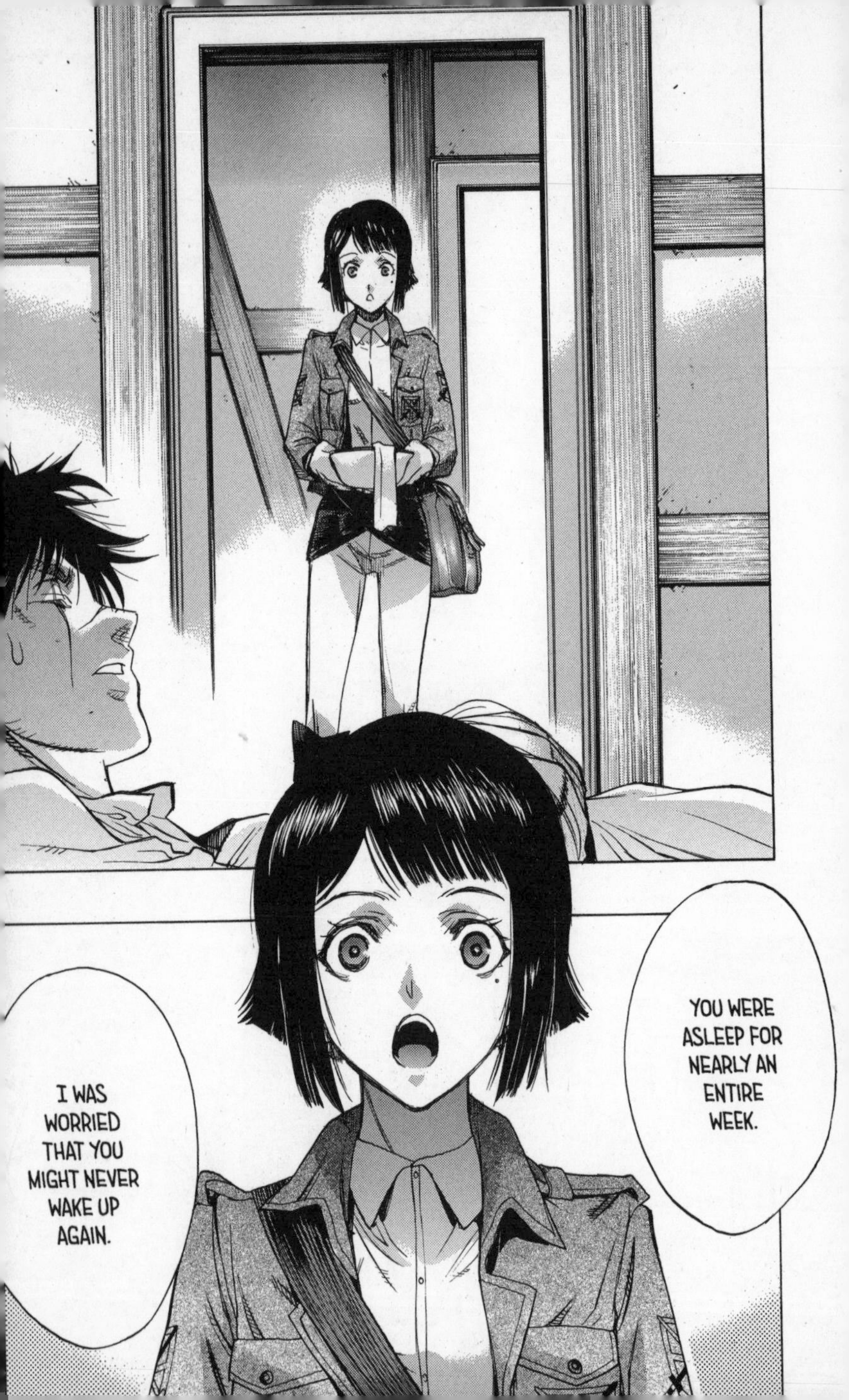
YOU WERE ASLEEP FOR NEARLY AN ENTIRE WEEK.
I WAS WORRIED THAT YOU MIGHT NEVER WAKE UP AGAIN.

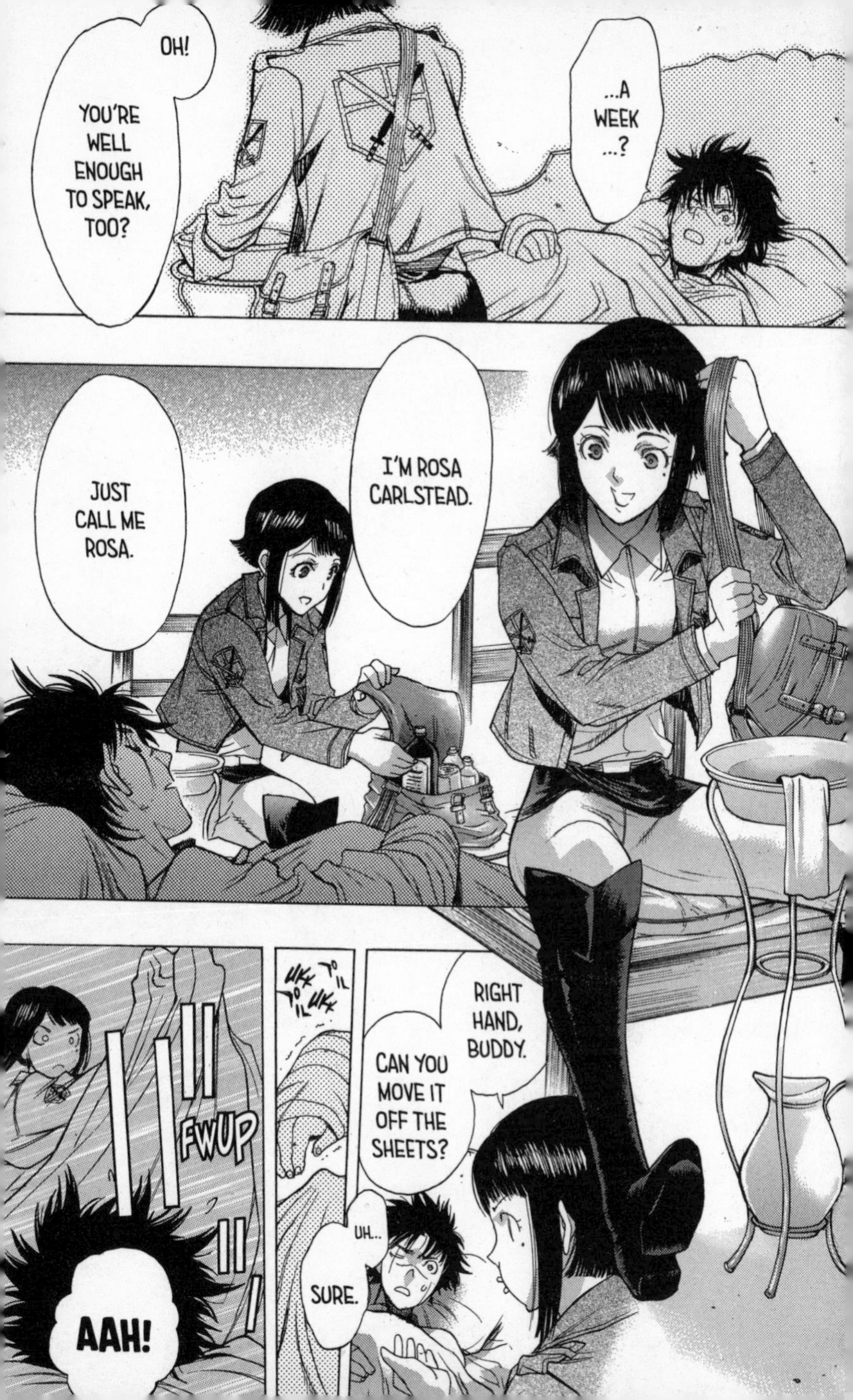
...A WEEK ...?
OH!
YOU'RE WELL ENOUGH TO SPEAK, TOO?
I'M ROSA CARLSTEAD.
JUST CALL ME ROSA.
RIGHT HAND, BUDDY.
CAN YOU MOVE IT OFF THE SHEETS?
UH...
SURE.
UKK
UKK
FWUP
AAH!

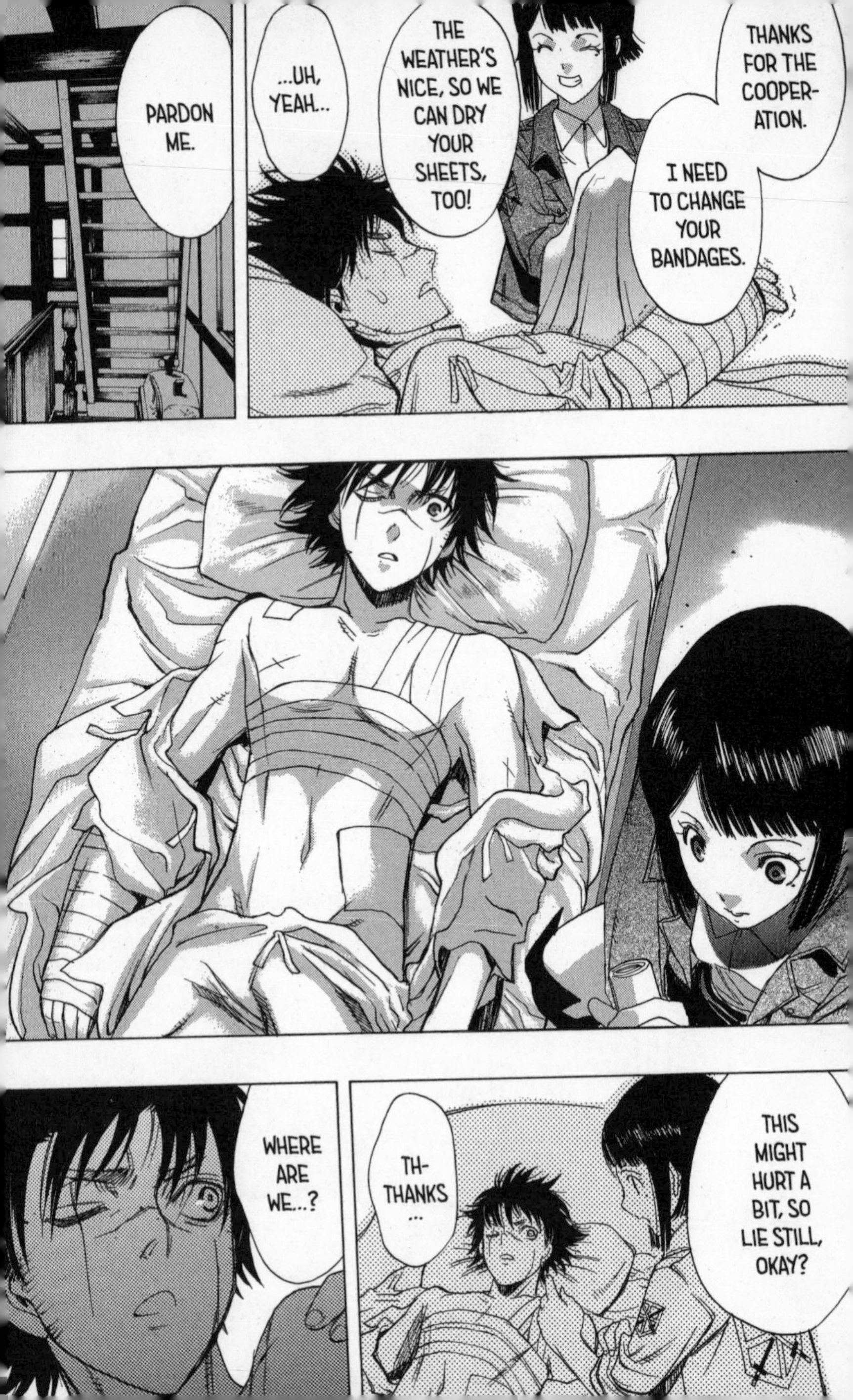
THANKS FOR THE COOPER-ATION.
I NEED TO CHANGE YOUR BANDAGES.
THE WEATHER'S NICE, SO WE CAN DRY YOUR SHEETS, TOO!
...UH, YEAH...
PARDON ME.
THIS MIGHT HURT A BIT, SO LIE STILL, OKAY?
TH-THANKS ...
WHERE ARE WE...?

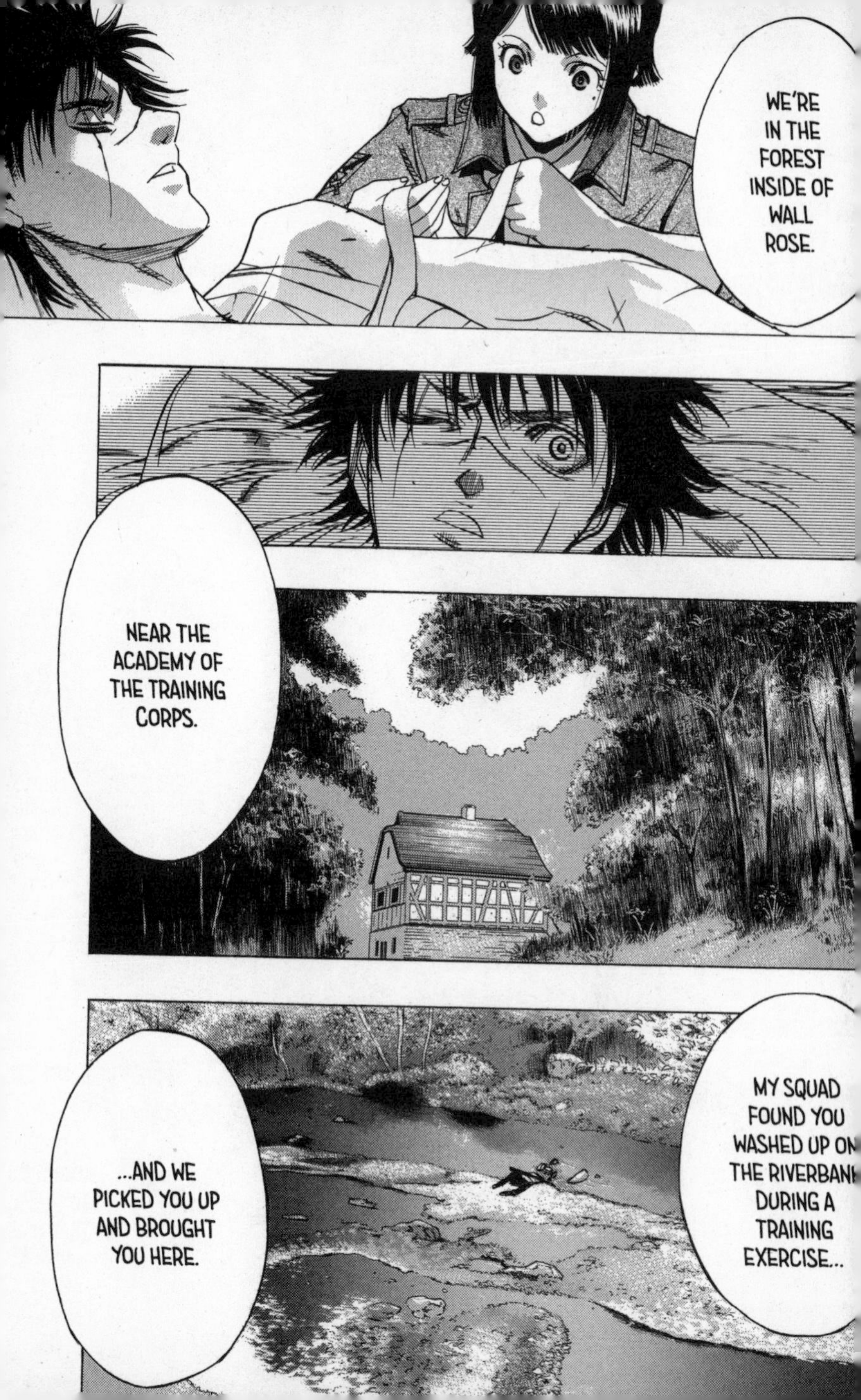
WE'RE IN THE FOREST INSIDE OF WALL ROSE.
NEAR THE ACADEMY OF THE TRAINING CORPS.
MY SQUAD FOUND YOU WASHED UP ON THE RIVERBANK DURING A TRAINING EXERCISE...
...AND WE PICKED YOU UP AND BROUGHT YOU HERE.

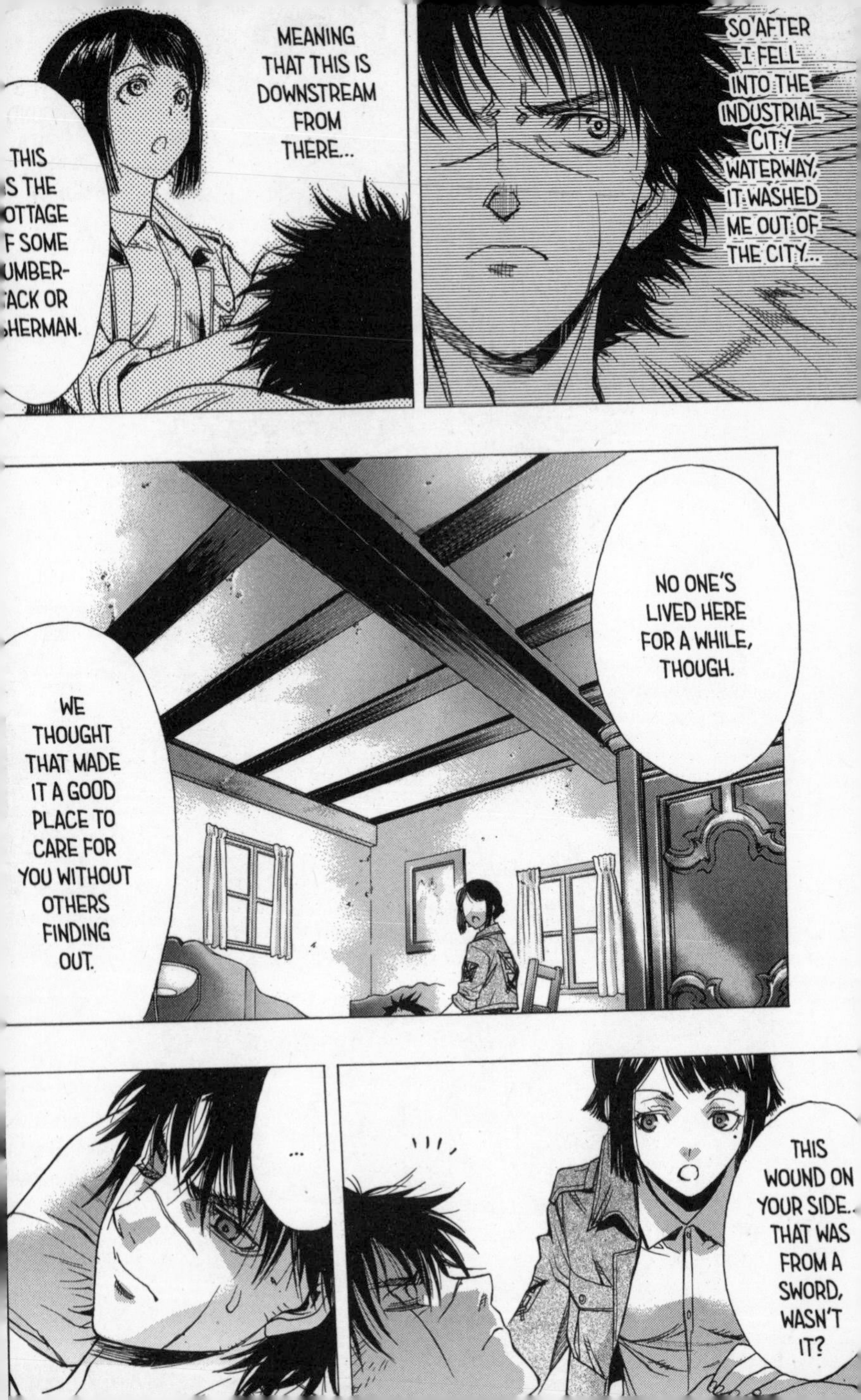
SO AFTER I FELL INTO THE INDUSTRIAL CITY WATERWAY, IT WASHED ME OUT OF THE CITY...
MEANING THAT THIS IS DOWNSTREAM FROM THERE...
THIS S THE OTTAGE F SOME UMBER- ACK OR SHERMAN.
NO ONE'S LIVED HERE FOR A WHILE, THOUGH.
WE THOUGHT THAT MADE IT A GOOD PLACE TO CARE FOR YOU WITHOUT OTHERS FINDING OUT.
THIS WOUND ON YOUR SIDE... THAT WAS FROM A SWORD, WASN'T IT?
...

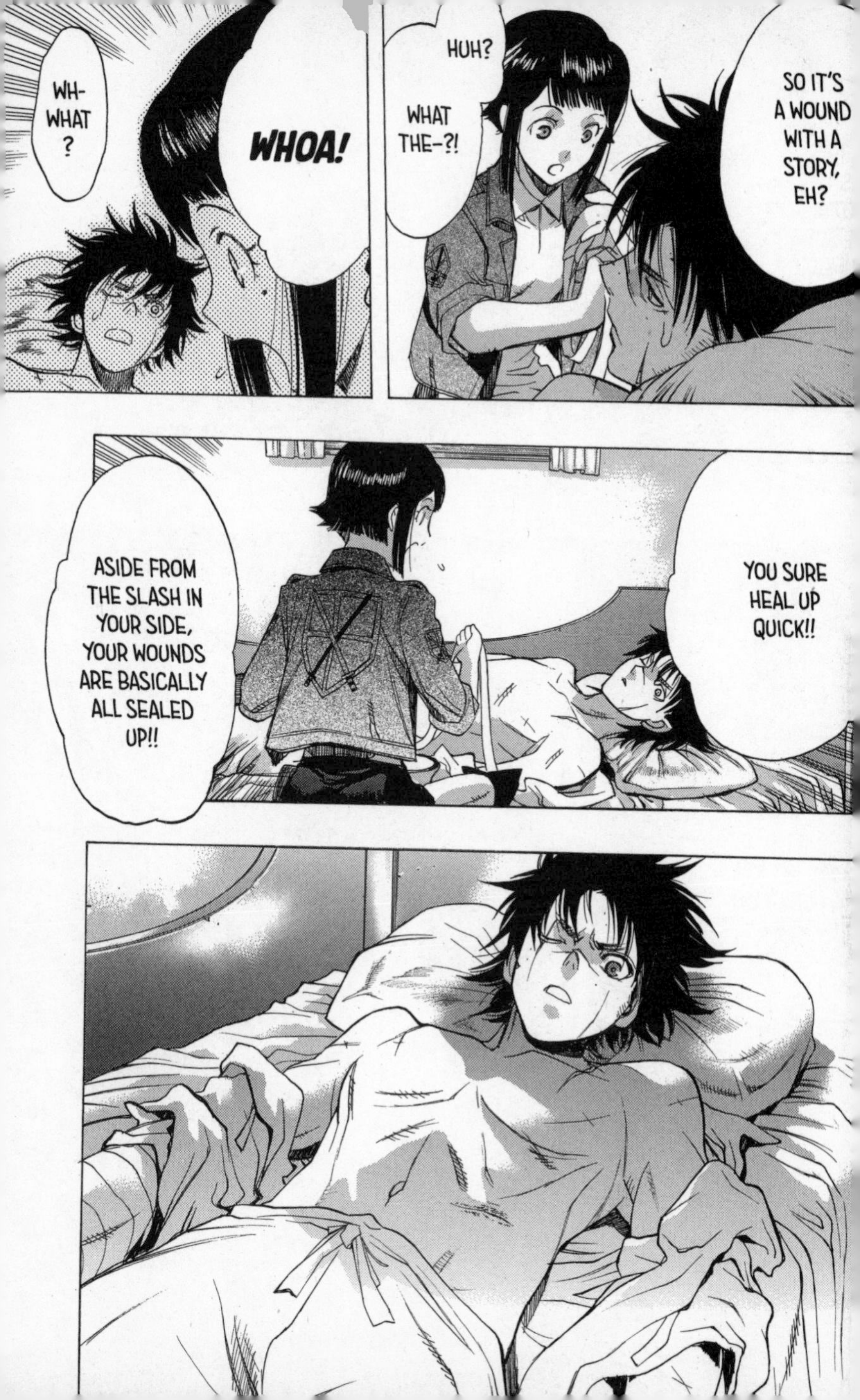
SO IT'S A WOUND WITH A STORY, EH?
HUH?
WHAT THE-?!
WHOA!
WH-WHAT?
YOU SURE HEAL UP QUICK!!
ASIDE FROM THE SLASH IN YOUR SIDE, YOUR WOUNDS ARE BASICALLY ALL SEALED UP!!

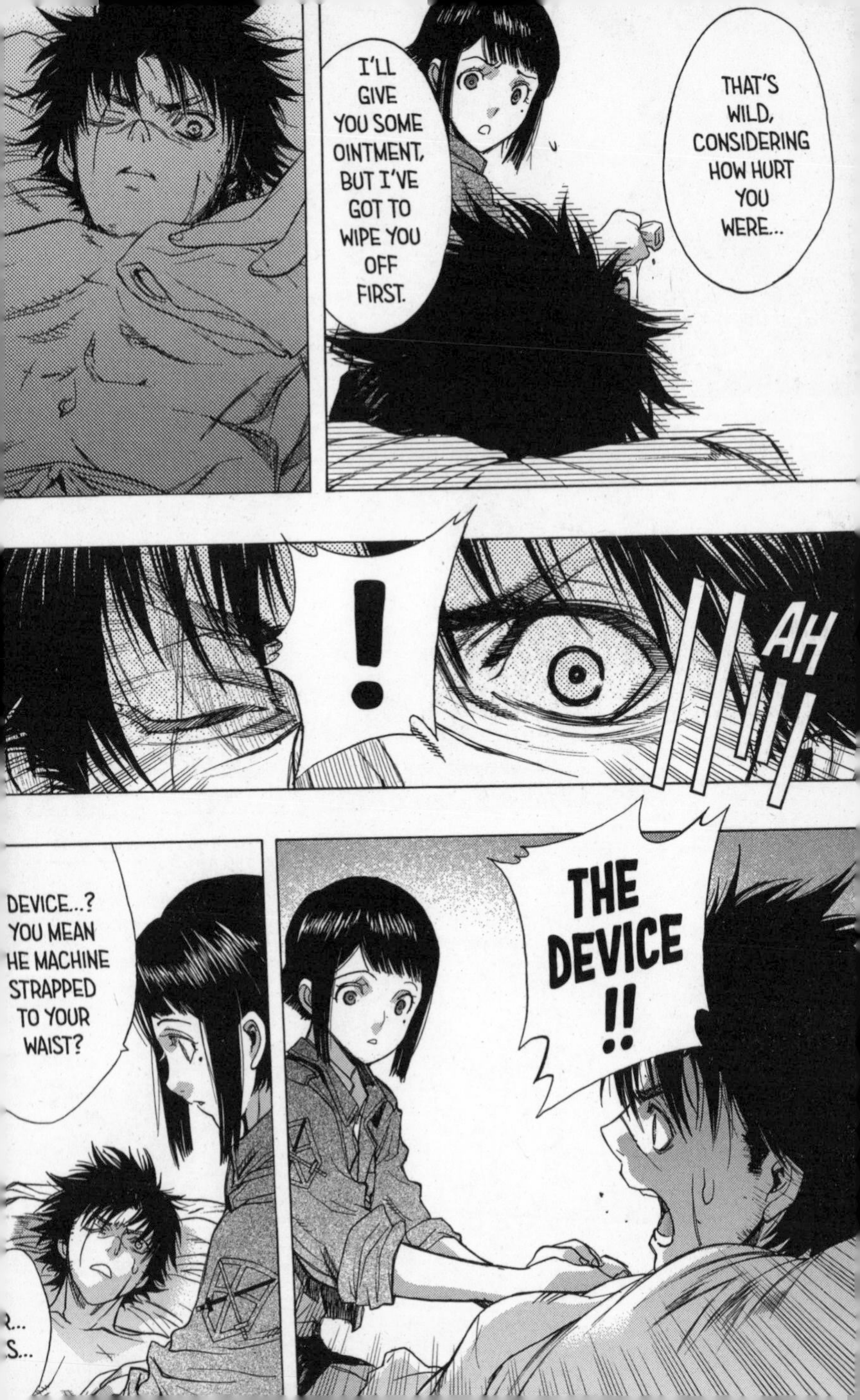
THAT'S WILD, CONSIDERING HOW HURT YOU WERE...
I'LL GIVE YOU SOME OINTMENT, BUT I'VE GOT TO WIPE YOU OFF FIRST.
!
AH
THE DEVICE !!
DEVICE...? YOU MEAN HE MACHINE STRAPPED TO YOUR WAIST?
R...
S...

THAT
SHOULD
BE...

RIGHT
HERE.

IT
MIGHT BE
BUSTED NOW,
SINCE IT WAS
SOAKING IN THE
WATER FOR
QUITE A WHILE,
BUT WE DID
DRAIN IT AND
LET IT DRY
OUT.

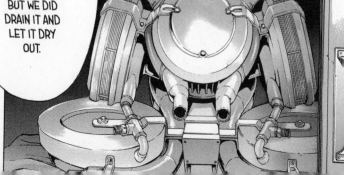

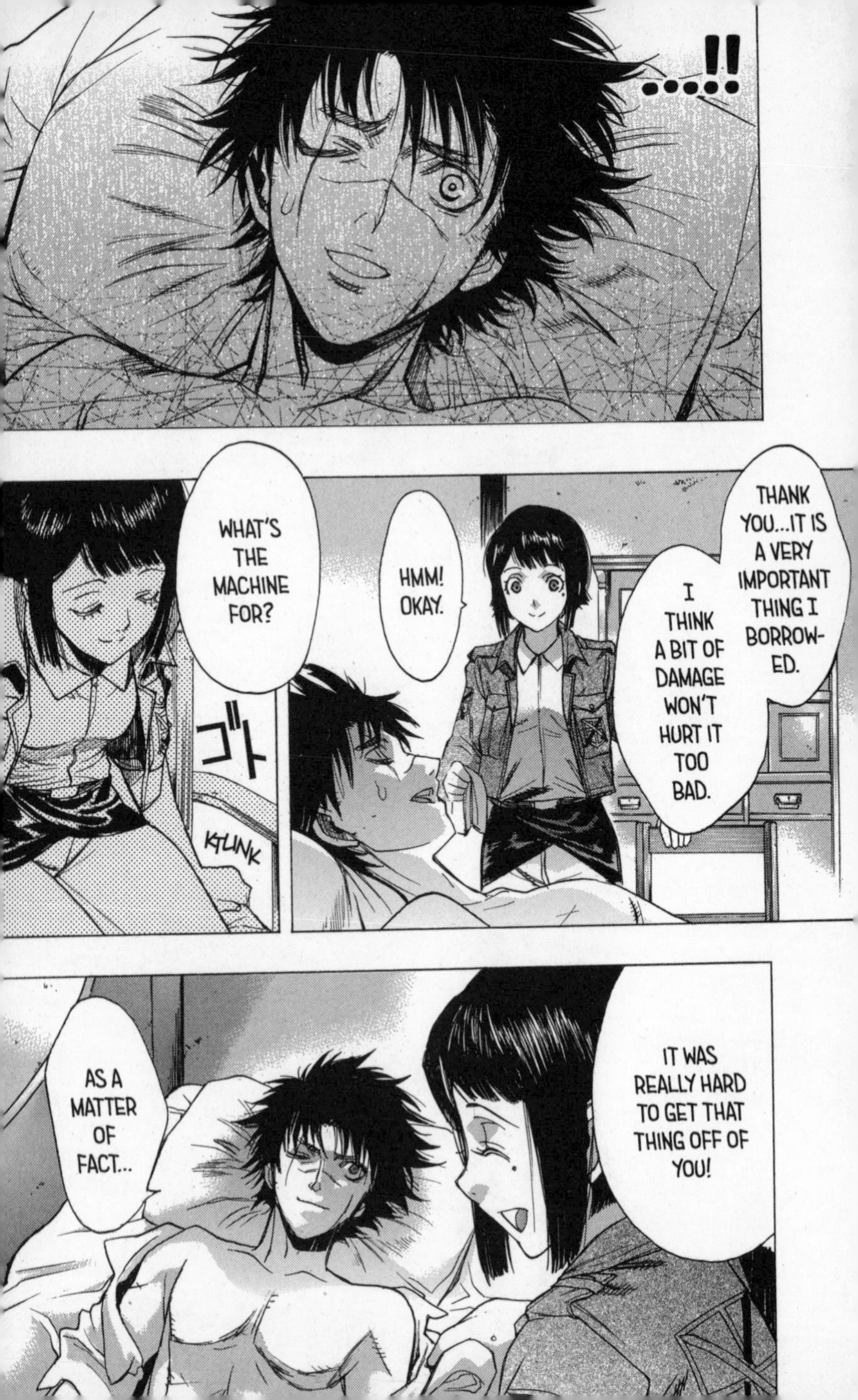
....!!
THANK YOU...IT IS A VERY IMPORTANT THING I BORROWED.
I THINK A BIT OF DAMAGE WON'T HURT IT TOO BAD.
HMM! OKAY.
WHAT'S THE MACHINE FOR?
ゴト
KTUNK
IT WAS REALLY HARD TO GET THAT THING OFF OF YOU!
AS A MATTER OF FACT...

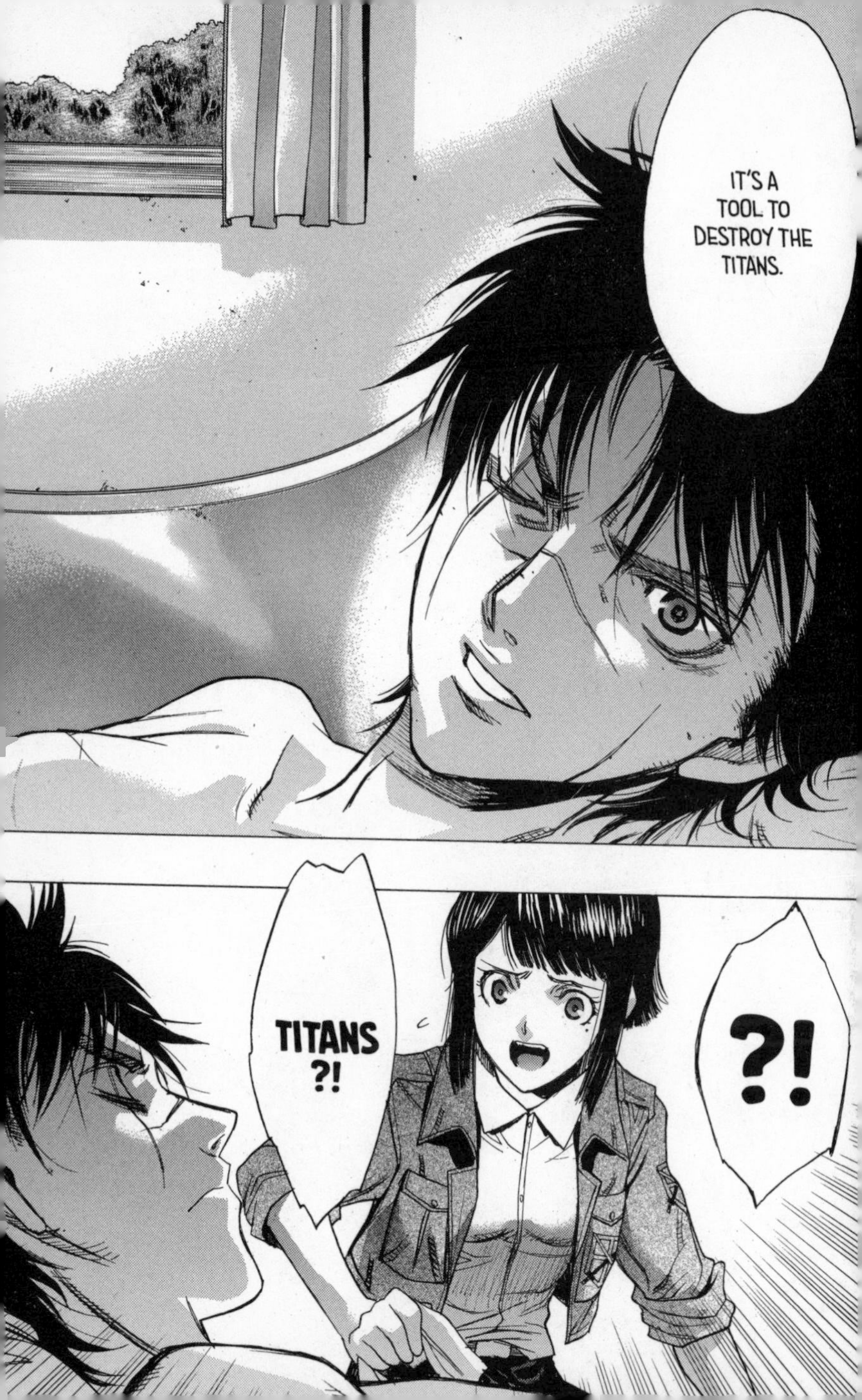
IT'S A TOOL TO DESTROY THE TITANS.
?!
TITANS ?!

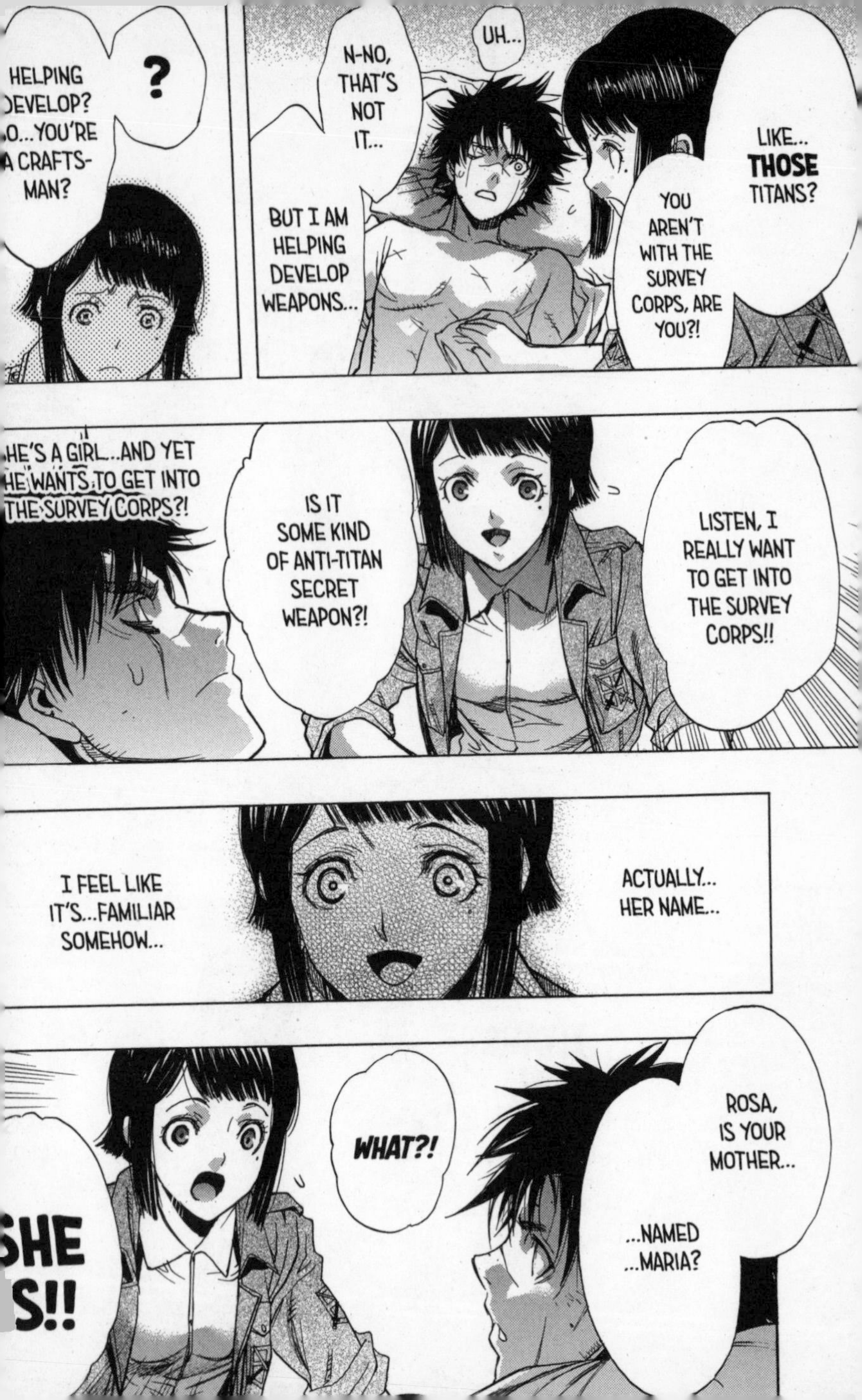
LIKE... THOSE TITANS?
YOU AREN'T WITH THE SURVEY CORPS, ARE YOU?!
UH...
N-NO, THAT'S NOT IT...
BUT I AM HELPING DEVELOP WEAPONS...
?
HELPING EVELOP? O...YOU'RE A CRAFTS-MAN?
LISTEN, I REALLY WANT TO GET INTO THE SURVEY CORPS!!
IS IT SOME KIND OF ANTI-TITAN SECRET WEAPON?!
HE'S A GIRL...AND YET HE WANTS TO GET INTO THE SURVEY CORPS?!
ACTUALLY... HER NAME...
I FEEL LIKE IT'S...FAMILIAR SOMEHOW...
ROSA, IS YOUR MOTHER...
...NAMED ...MARIA?
WHAT?!
SHE S!!

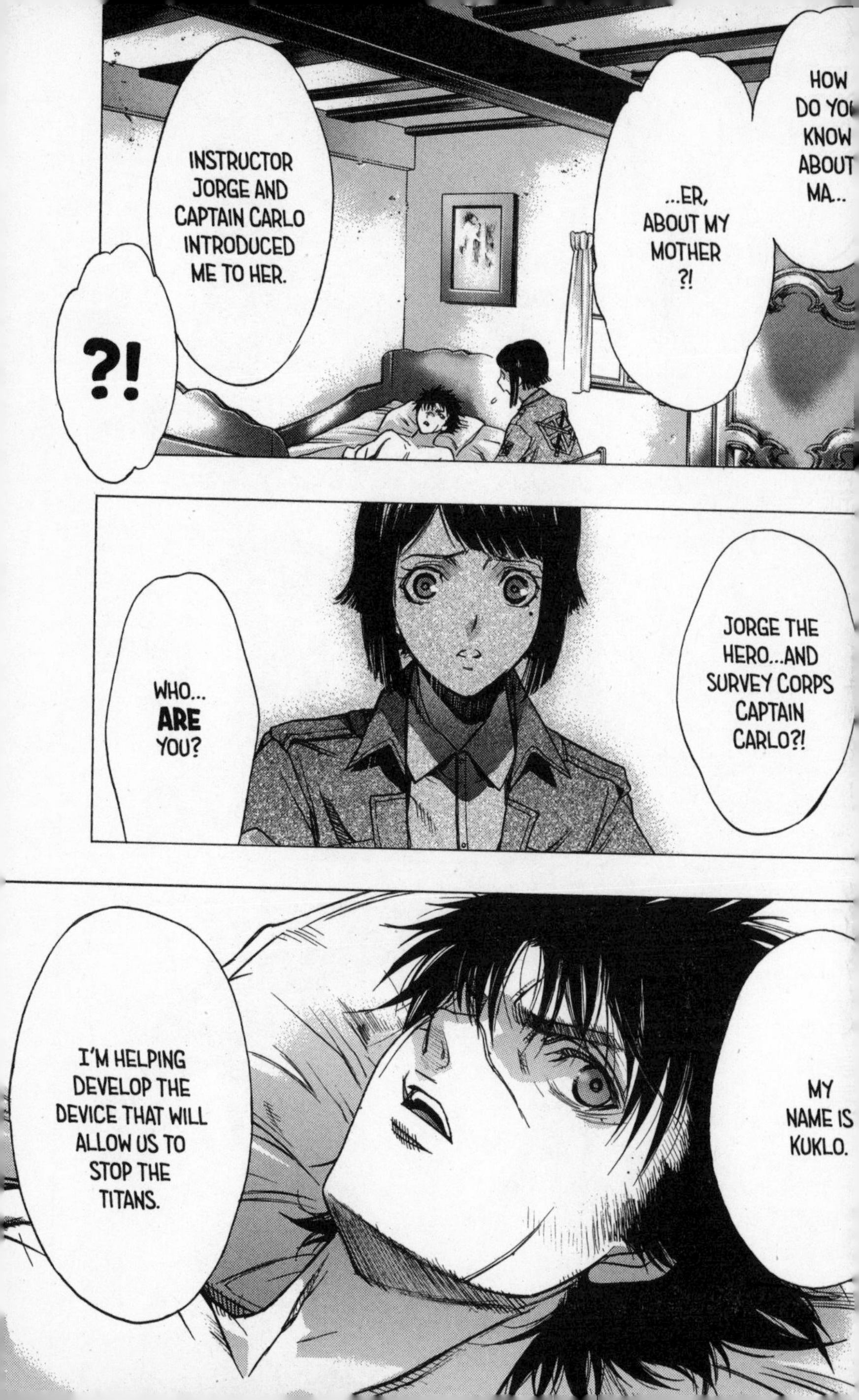
HOW DO YOU KNOW ABOUT MA...
...ER, ABOUT MY MOTHER ?!
INSTRUCTOR JORGE AND CAPTAIN CARLO INTRODUCED ME TO HER.
?!
JORGE THE HERO...AND SURVEY CORPS CAPTAIN CARLO?!
WHO... **ARE** YOU?
MY NAME IS KUKLO.
I'M HELPING DEVELOP THE DEVICE THAT WILL ALLOW US TO STOP THE TITANS.

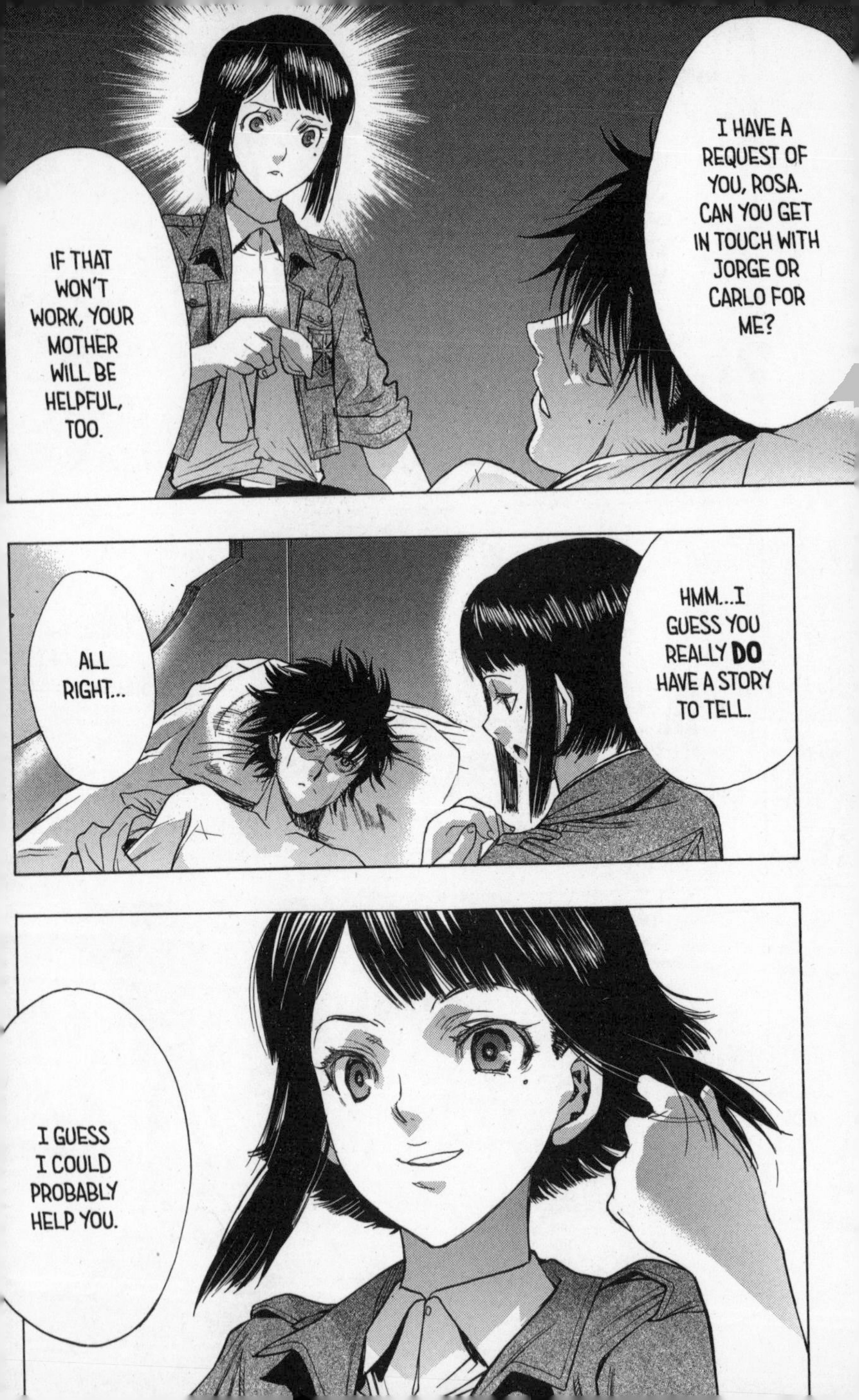
I HAVE A REQUEST OF YOU, ROSA. CAN YOU GET IN TOUCH WITH JORGE OR CARLO FOR ME?
IF THAT WON'T WORK, YOUR MOTHER WILL BE HELPFUL, TOO.
HMM...I GUESS YOU REALLY **DO** HAVE A STORY TO TELL.
ALL RIGHT...
I GUESS I COULD PROBABLY HELP YOU.

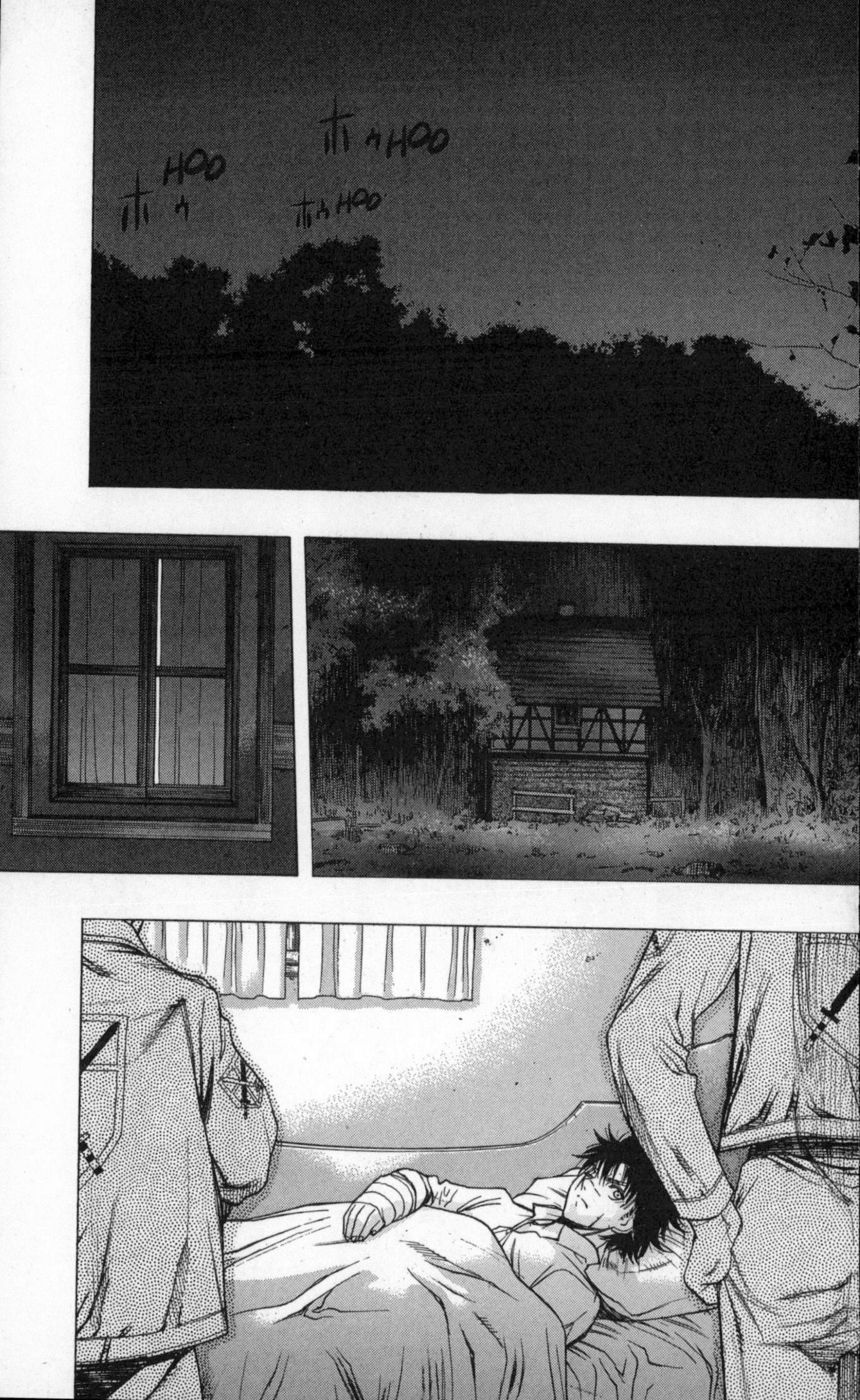
HOO
HOO
HOO

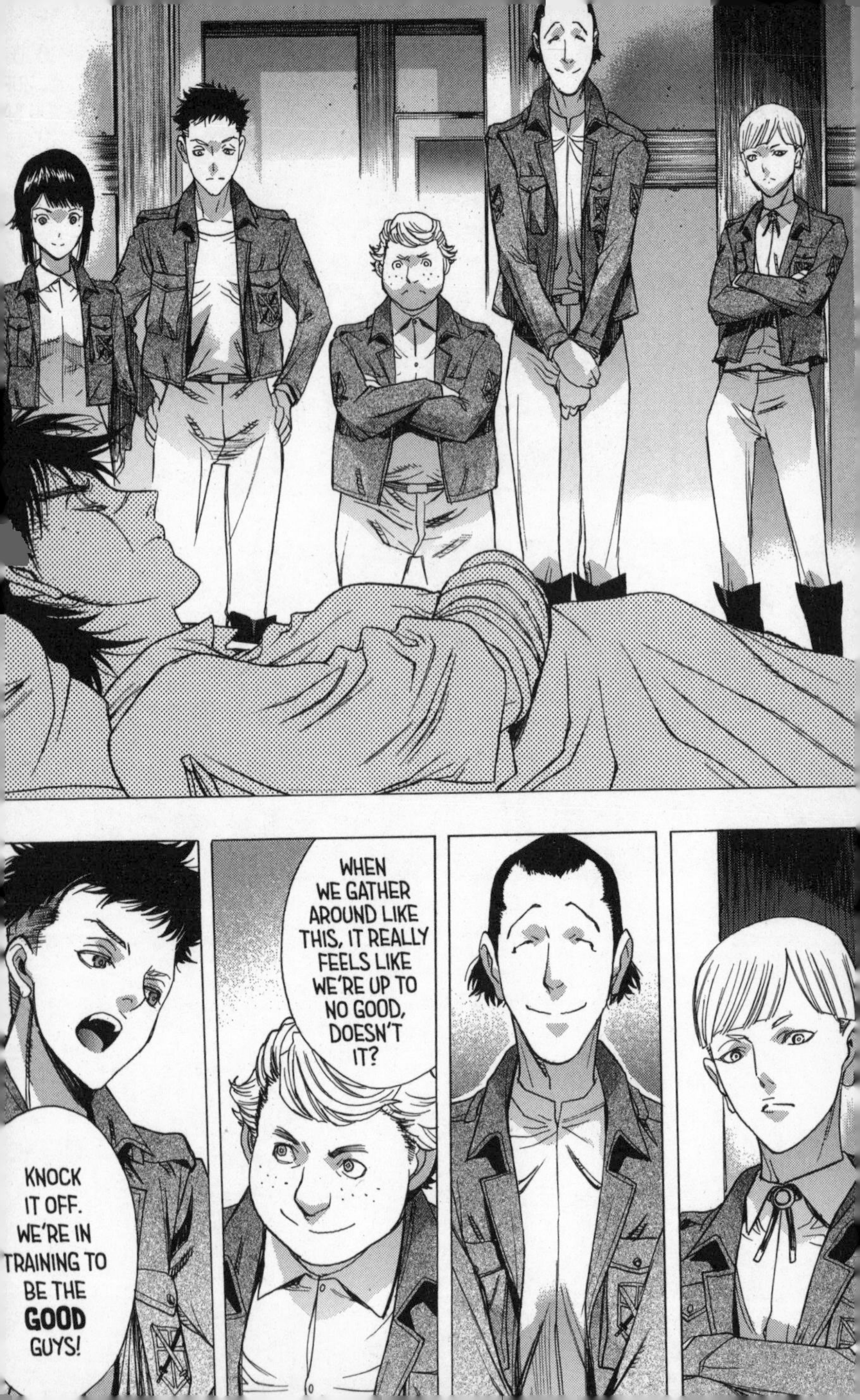
WHEN WE GATHER AROUND LIKE THIS, IT REALLY FEELS LIKE WE'RE UP TO NO GOOD, DOESN'T IT?
KNOCK IT OFF. WE'RE IN TRAINING TO BE THE **GOOD** GUYS!

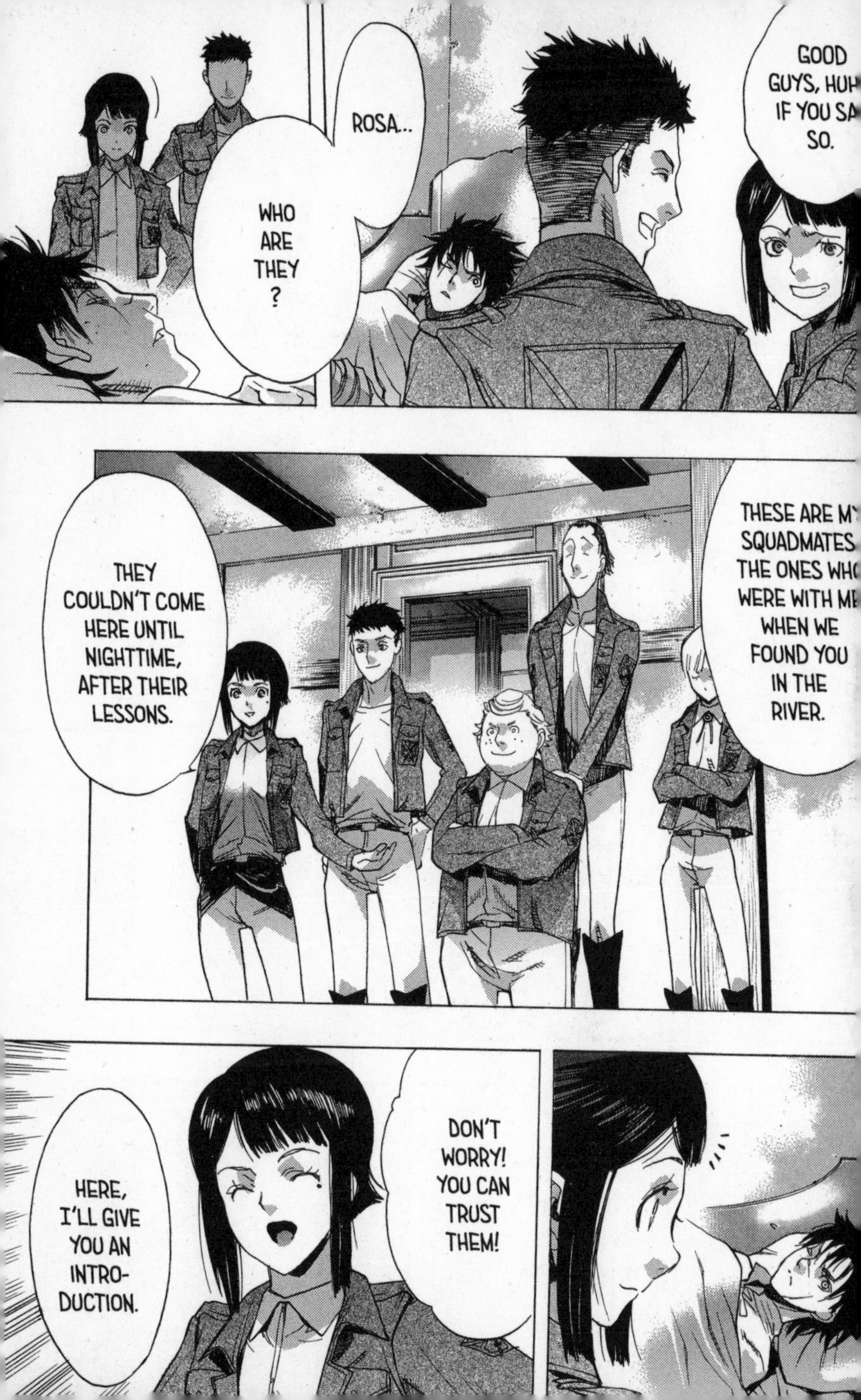
GOOD GUYS, HUH IF YOU SA SO.
ROSA...
WHO ARE THEY ?
THESE ARE M SQUADMATES THE ONES WH WERE WITH M WHEN WE FOUND YOU IN THE RIVER.
THEY COULDN'T COME HERE UNTIL NIGHTTIME, AFTER THEIR LESSONS.
DON'T WORRY! YOU CAN TRUST THEM!
HERE, I'LL GIVE YOU AN INTRO-DUCTION.

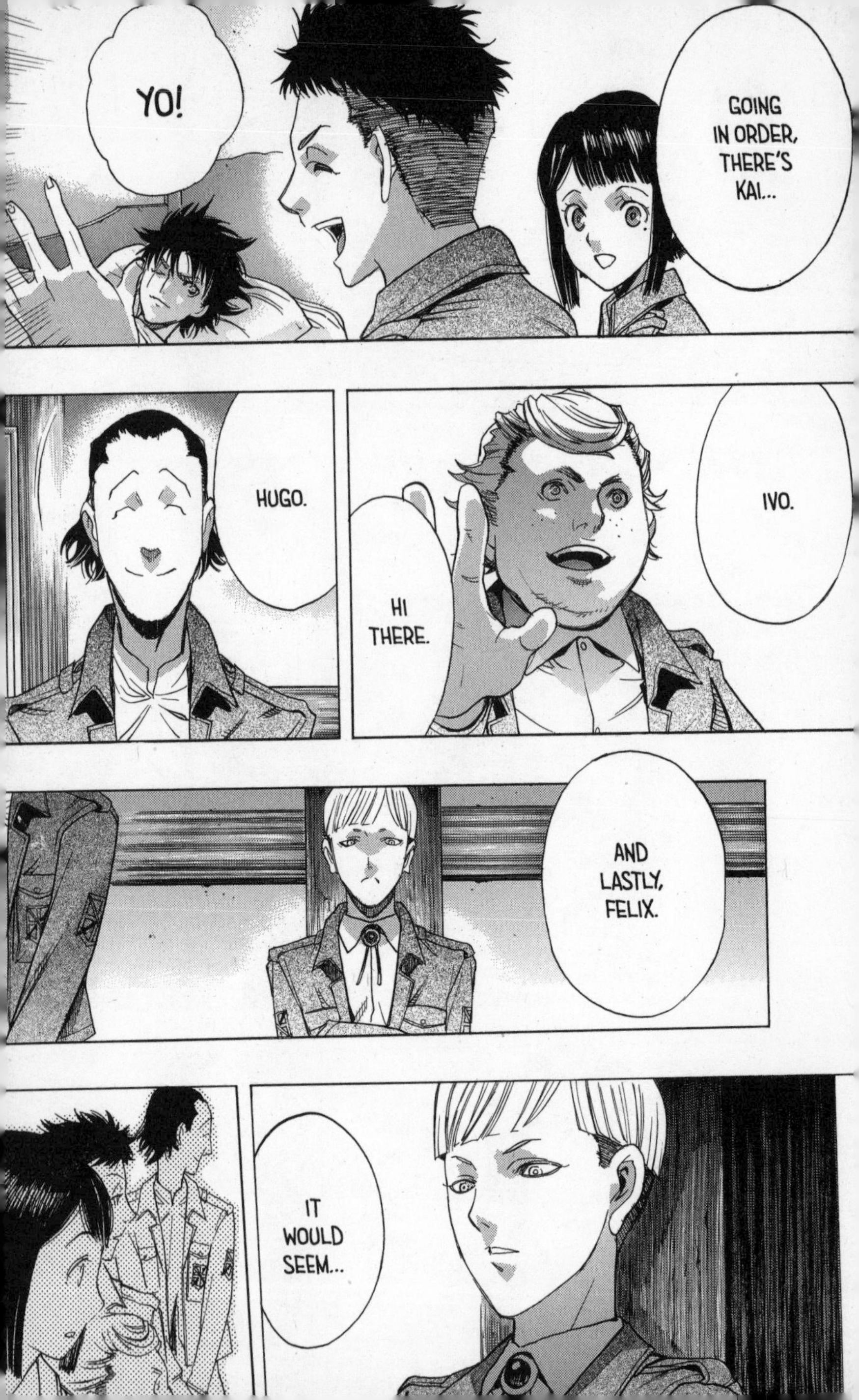
GOING IN ORDER, THERE'S KAI...
YO!
IVO.
HI THERE.
HUGO.
AND LASTLY, FELIX.
IT WOULD SEEM...

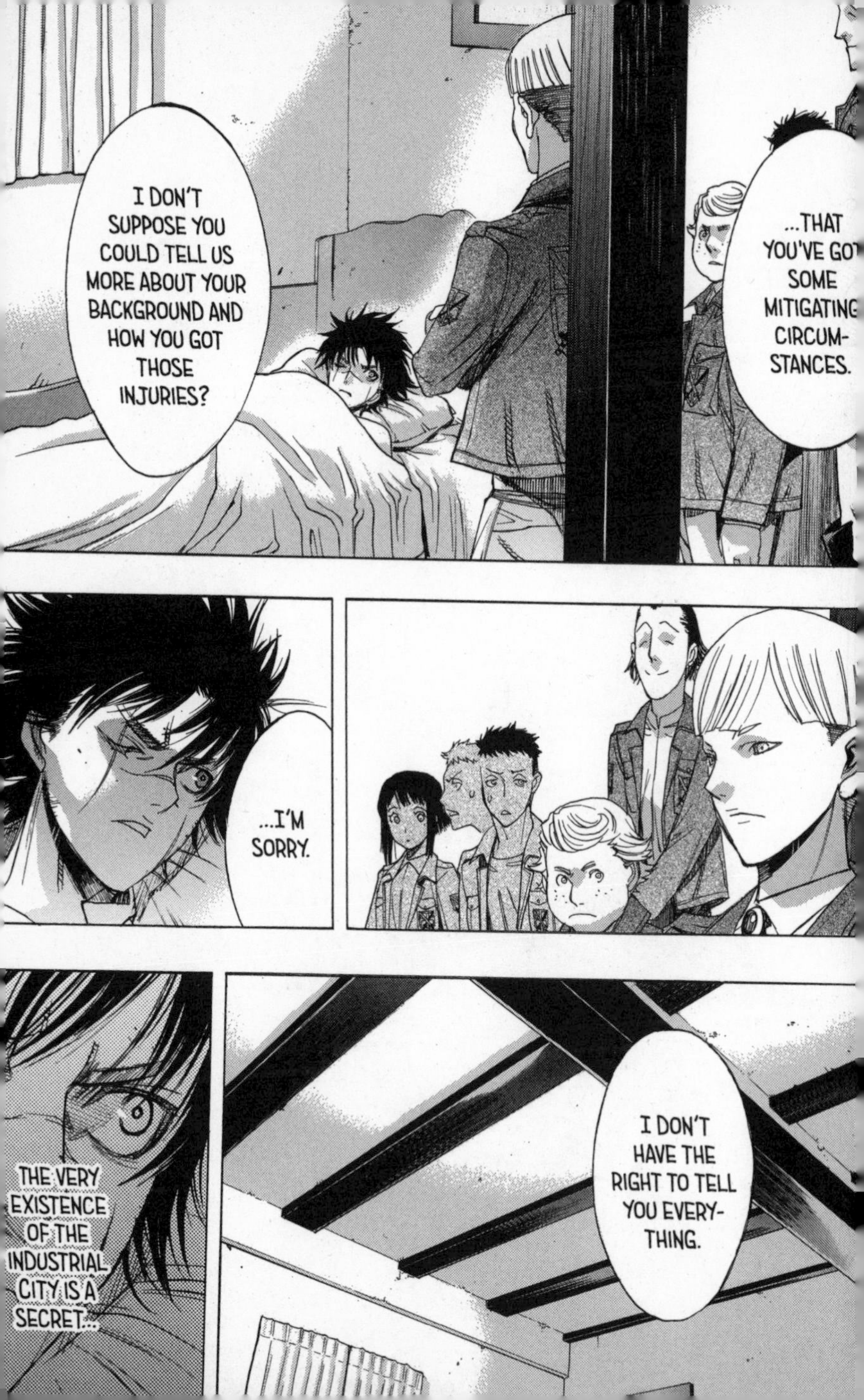
...THAT YOU'VE GOT SOME MITIGATING CIRCUM-STANCES.
I DON'T SUPPOSE YOU COULD TELL US MORE ABOUT YOUR BACKGROUND AND HOW YOU GOT THOSE INJURIES?
...I'M SORRY.
I DON'T HAVE THE RIGHT TO TELL YOU EVERY-THING.
THE VERY EXISTENCE OF THE INDUSTRIAL CITY IS A SECRET...

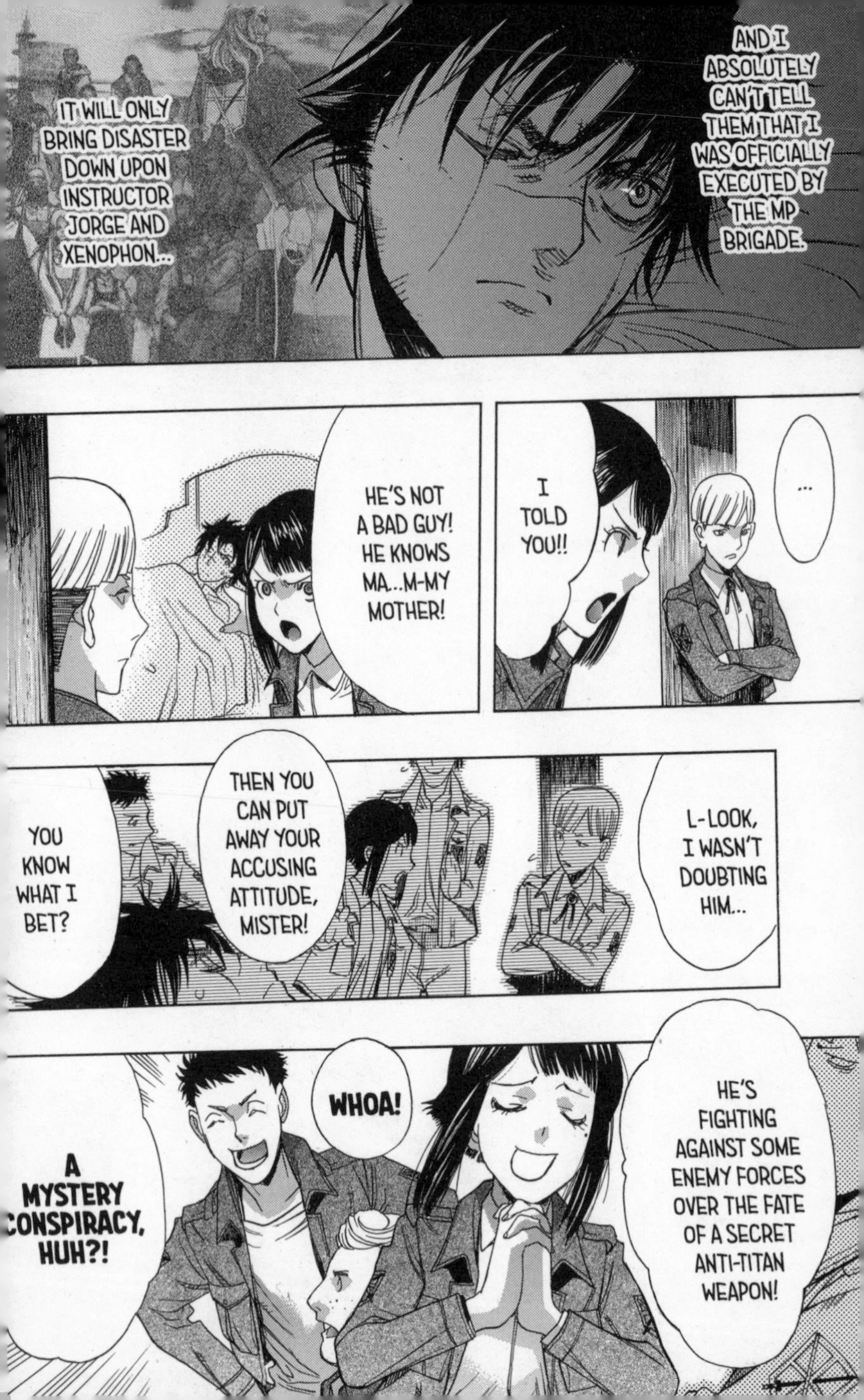
AND I ABSOLUTELY CAN'T TELL THEM THAT I WAS OFFICIALLY EXECUTED BY THE MP BRIGADE.
IT WILL ONLY BRING DISASTER DOWN UPON INSTRUCTOR JORGE AND XENOPHON...
...
I TOLD YOU!!
HE'S NOT A BAD GUY! HE KNOWS MA...M-MY MOTHER!
L-LOOK, I WASN'T DOUBTING HIM...
THEN YOU CAN PUT AWAY YOUR ACCUSING ATTITUDE, MISTER!
YOU KNOW WHAT I BET?
HE'S FIGHTING AGAINST SOME ENEMY FORCES OVER THE FATE OF A SECRET ANTI-TITAN WEAPON!
WHOA!
A MYSTERY CONSPIRACY, HUH?!

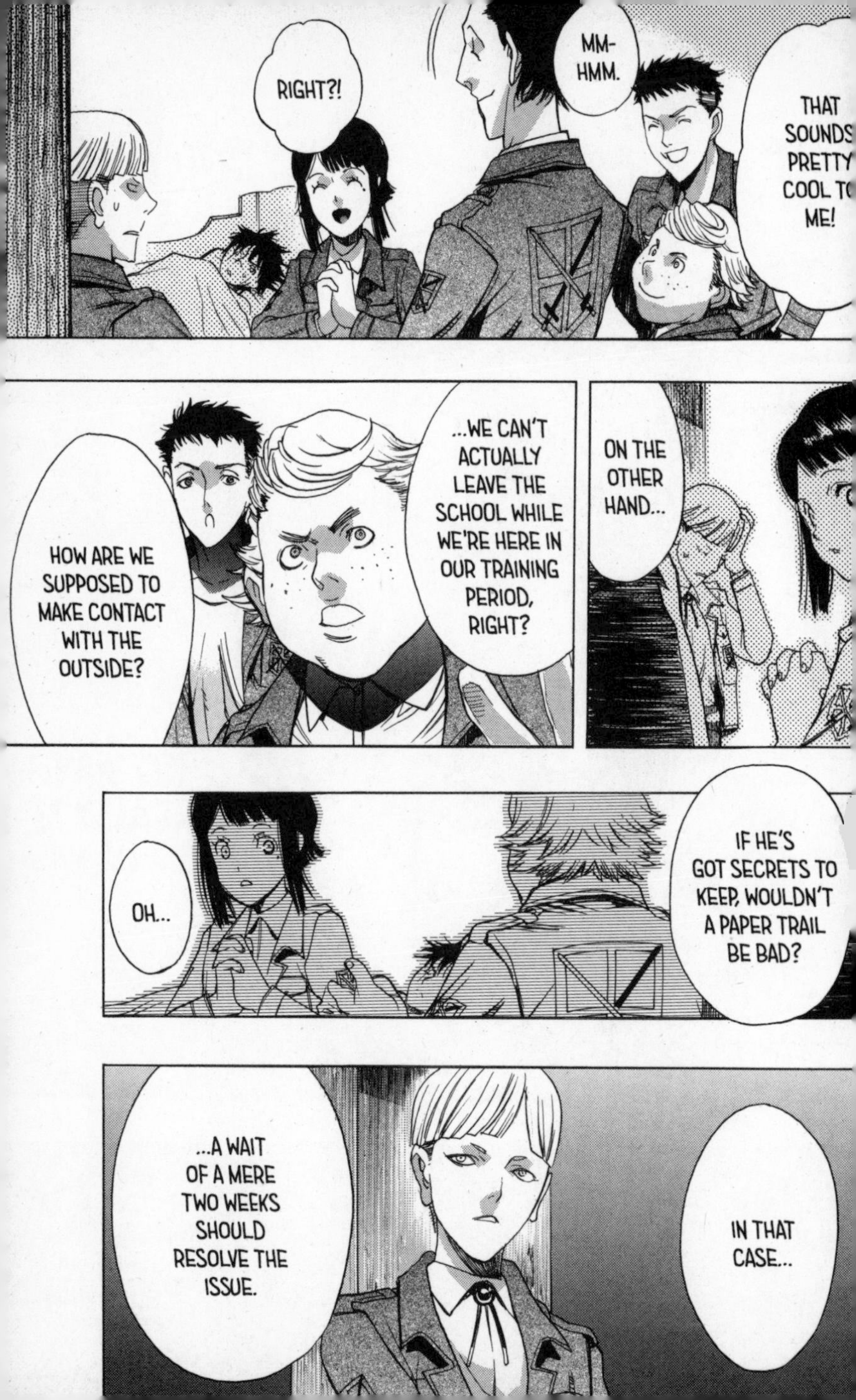
THAT SOUNDS PRETTY COOL TO ME!
MM-HMM.
RIGHT?!
ON THE OTHER HAND...
...WE CAN'T ACTUALLY LEAVE THE SCHOOL WHILE WE'RE HERE IN OUR TRAINING PERIOD, RIGHT?
HOW ARE WE SUPPOSED TO MAKE CONTACT WITH THE OUTSIDE?
IF HE'S GOT SECRETS TO KEEP, WOULDN'T A PAPER TRAIL BE BAD?
OH...
IN THAT CASE...
...A WAIT OF A MERE TWO WEEKS SHOULD RESOLVE THE ISSUE.

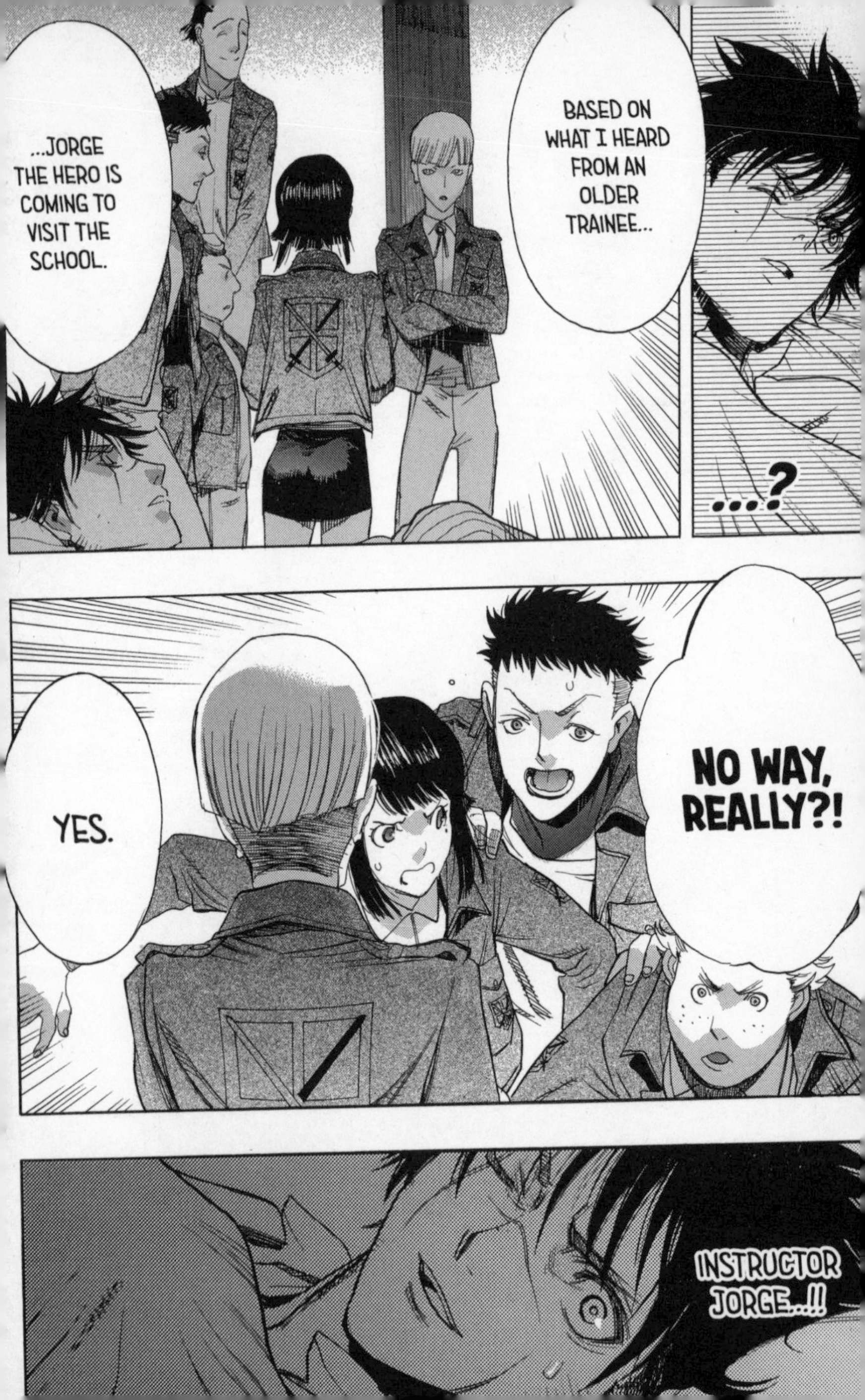
...?
BASED ON WHAT I HEARD FROM AN OLDER TRAINEE...
...JORGE THE HERO IS COMING TO VISIT THE SCHOOL.
NO WAY, REALLY?!
YES.
INSTRUCTOR JORGE...!!

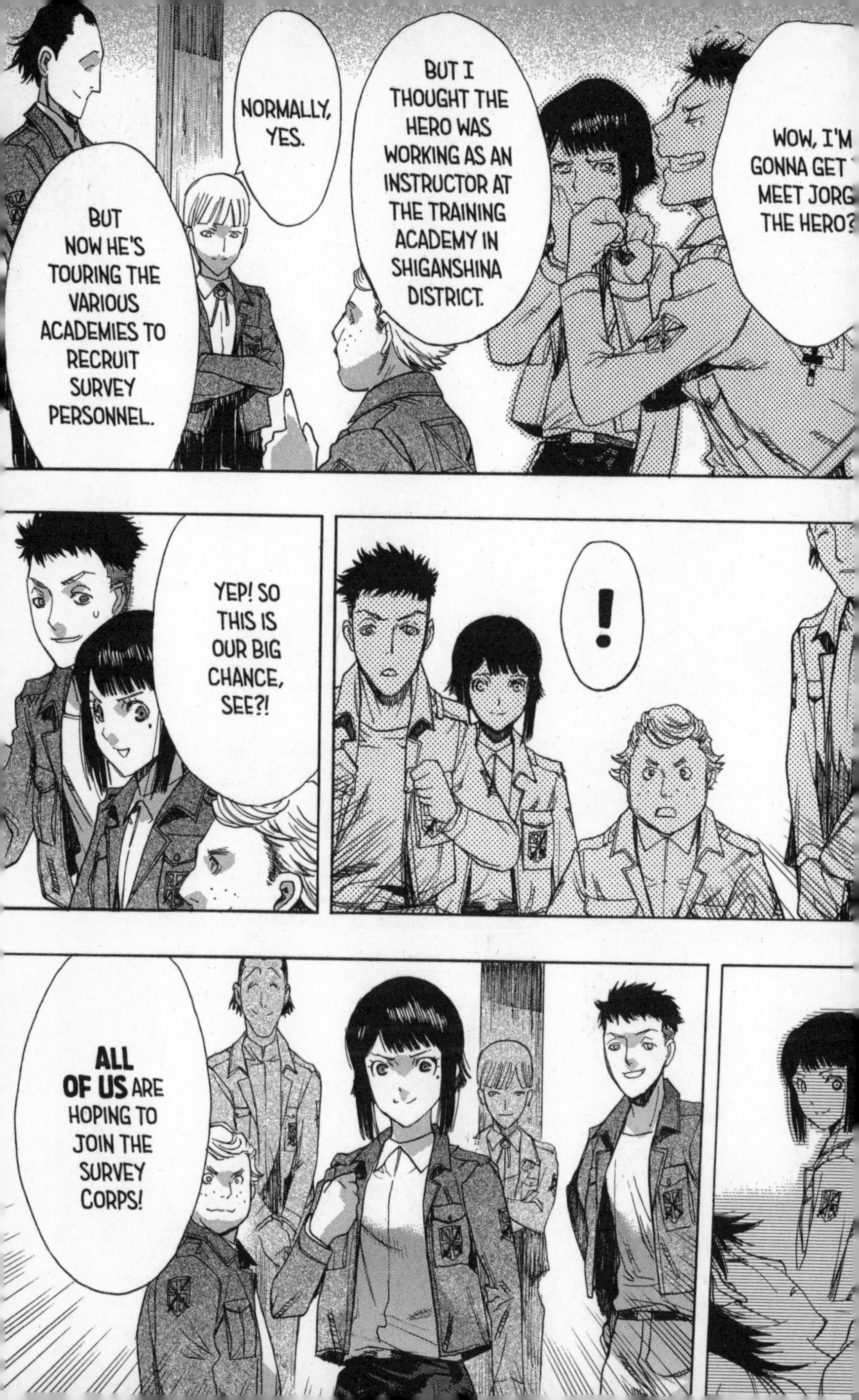
WOW, I'M GONNA GET MEET JORG THE HERO?
BUT I THOUGHT THE HERO WAS WORKING AS AN INSTRUCTOR AT THE TRAINING ACADEMY IN SHIGANSHINA DISTRICT.
NORMALLY, YES.
BUT NOW HE'S TOURING THE VARIOUS ACADEMIES TO RECRUIT SURVEY PERSONNEL.
!
YEP! SO THIS IS OUR BIG CHANCE, SEE?!
ALL OF US ARE HOPING TO JOIN THE SURVEY CORPS!

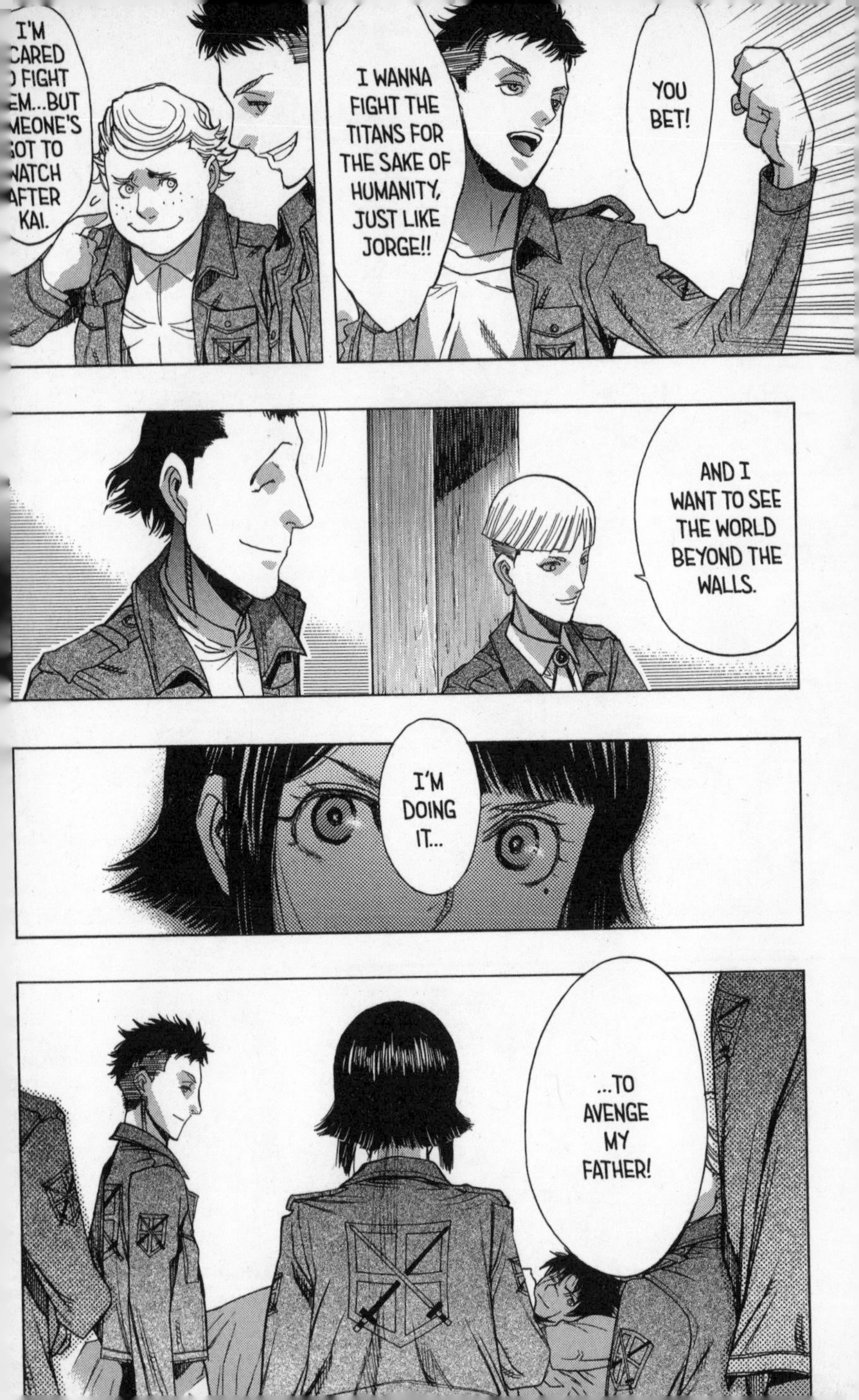
YOU BET!
I WANNA FIGHT THE TITANS FOR THE SAKE OF HUMANITY, JUST LIKE JORGE!!
I'M CARED FIGHT EM...BUT MEONE'S GOT TO WATCH AFTER KAI.
AND I WANT TO SEE THE WORLD BEYOND THE WALLS.
I'M DOING IT...
...TO AVENGE MY FATHER!

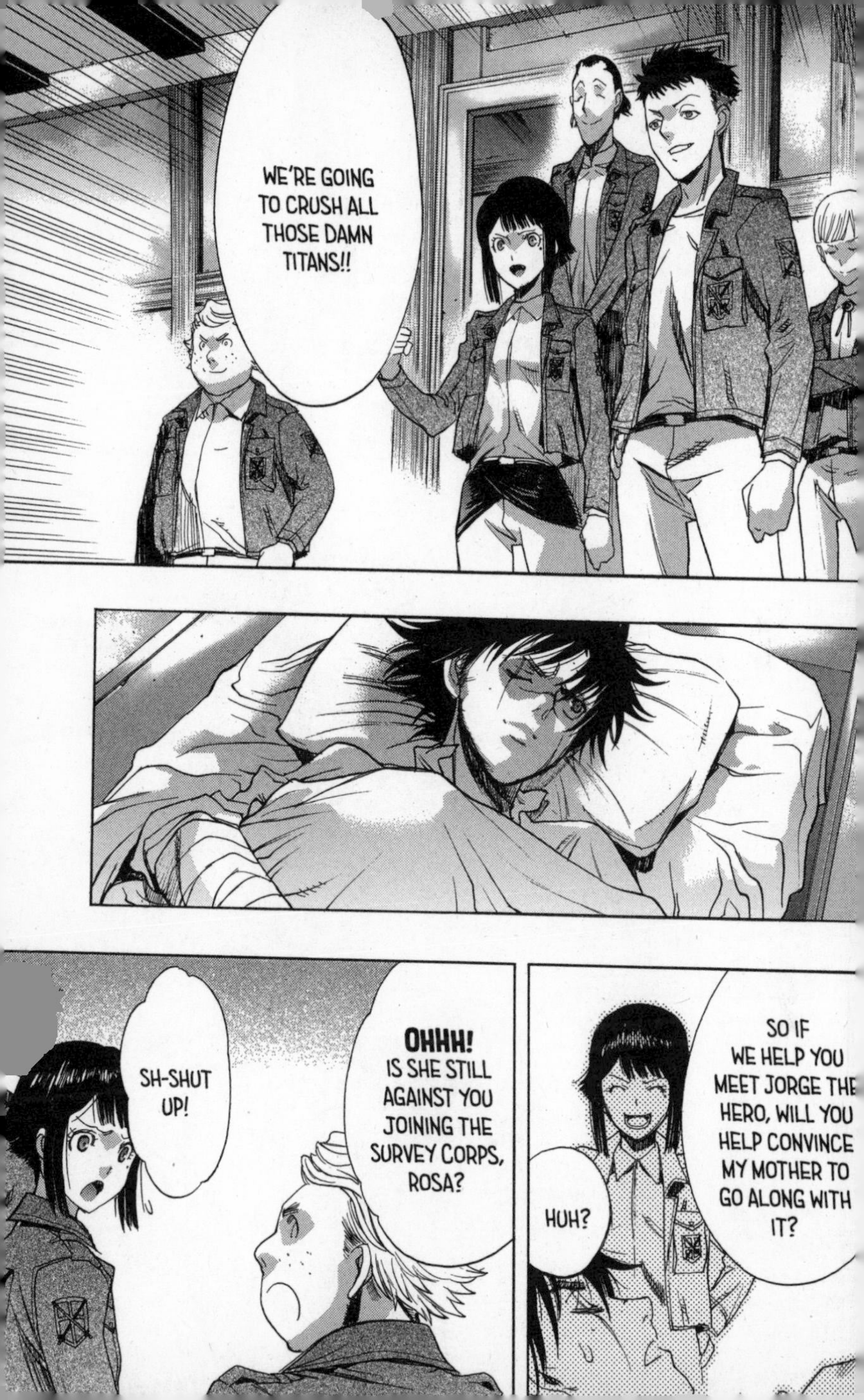
WE'RE GOING TO CRUSH ALL THOSE DAMN TITANS!!
SO IF WE HELP YOU MEET JORGE THE HERO, WILL YOU HELP CONVINCE MY MOTHER TO GO ALONG WITH IT?
HUH?
OHHH! IS SHE STILL AGAINST YOU JOINING THE SURVEY CORPS, ROSA?
SH-SHUT UP!

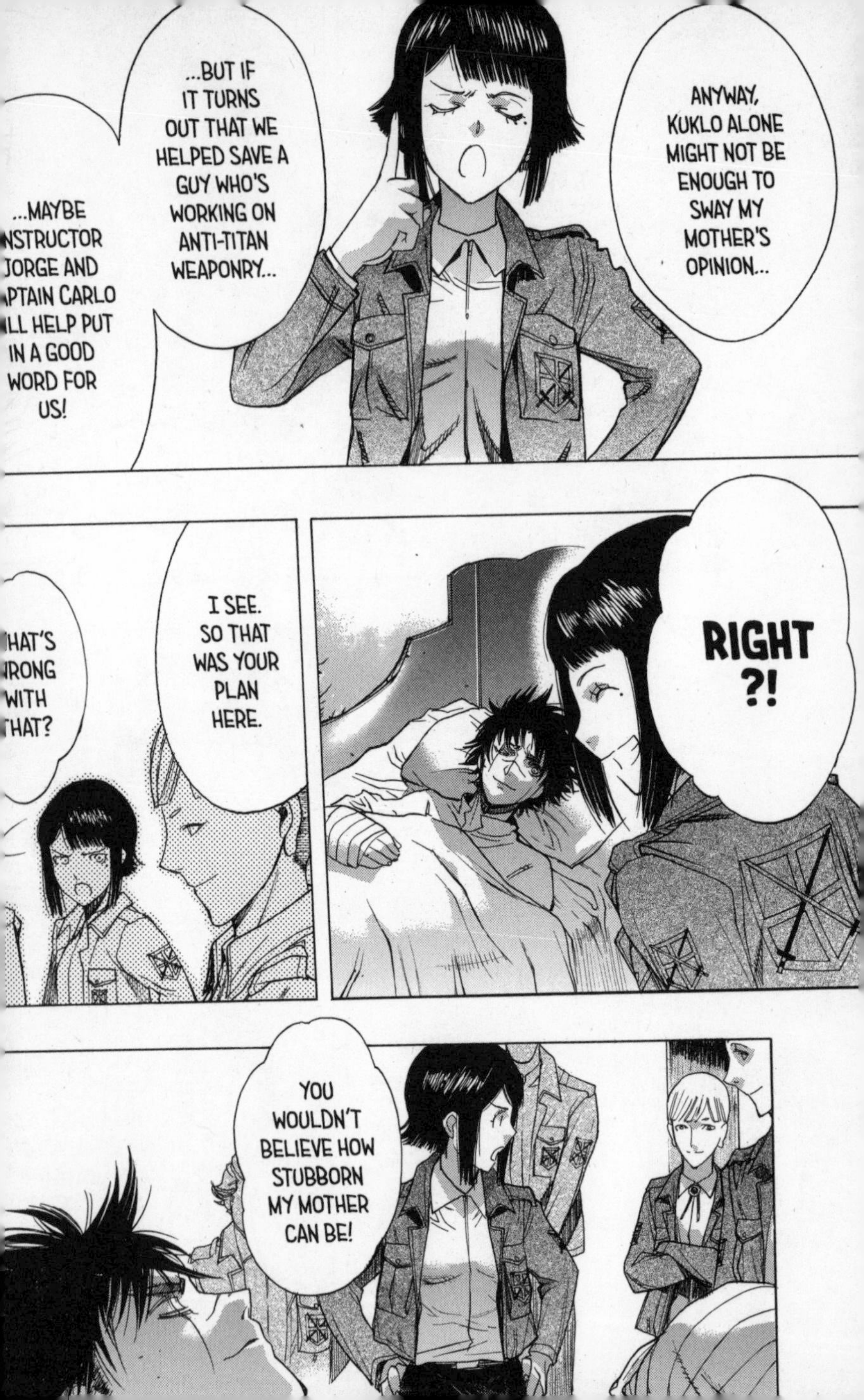
ANYWAY, KUKLO ALONE MIGHT NOT BE ENOUGH TO SWAY MY MOTHER'S OPINION...
...BUT IF IT TURNS OUT THAT WE HELPED SAVE A GUY WHO'S WORKING ON ANTI-TITAN WEAPONRY...
...MAYBE NSTRUCTOR JORGE AND PTAIN CARLO LL HELP PUT IN A GOOD WORD FOR US!
RIGHT ?!
I SEE. SO THAT WAS YOUR PLAN HERE.
HAT'S RONG WITH HAT?
YOU WOULDN'T BELIEVE HOW STUBBORN MY MOTHER CAN BE!

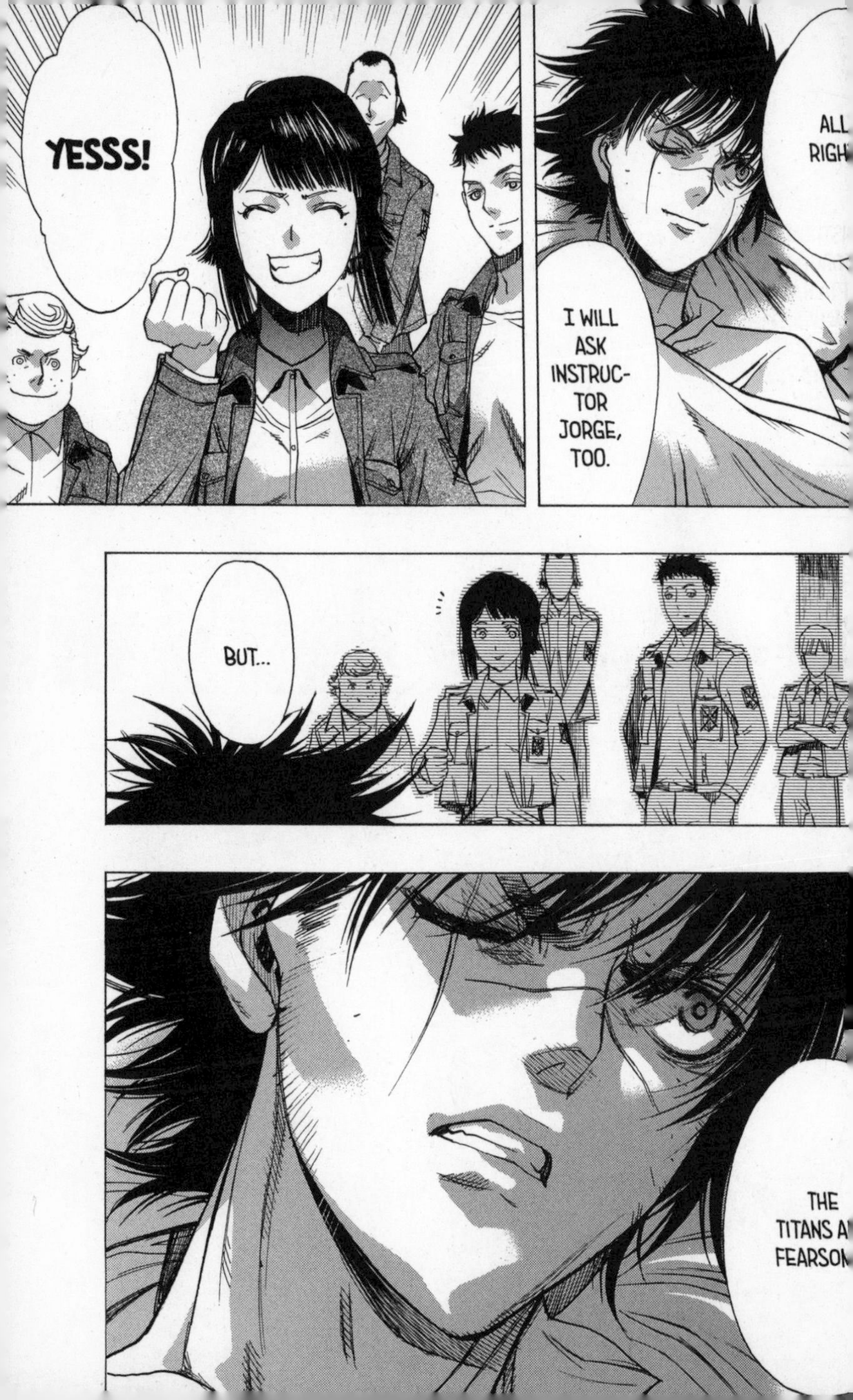
ALL RIGH
I WILL ASK INSTRUCTOR JORGE, TOO.
YESSS!
BUT...
THE TITANS A
FEARSOM

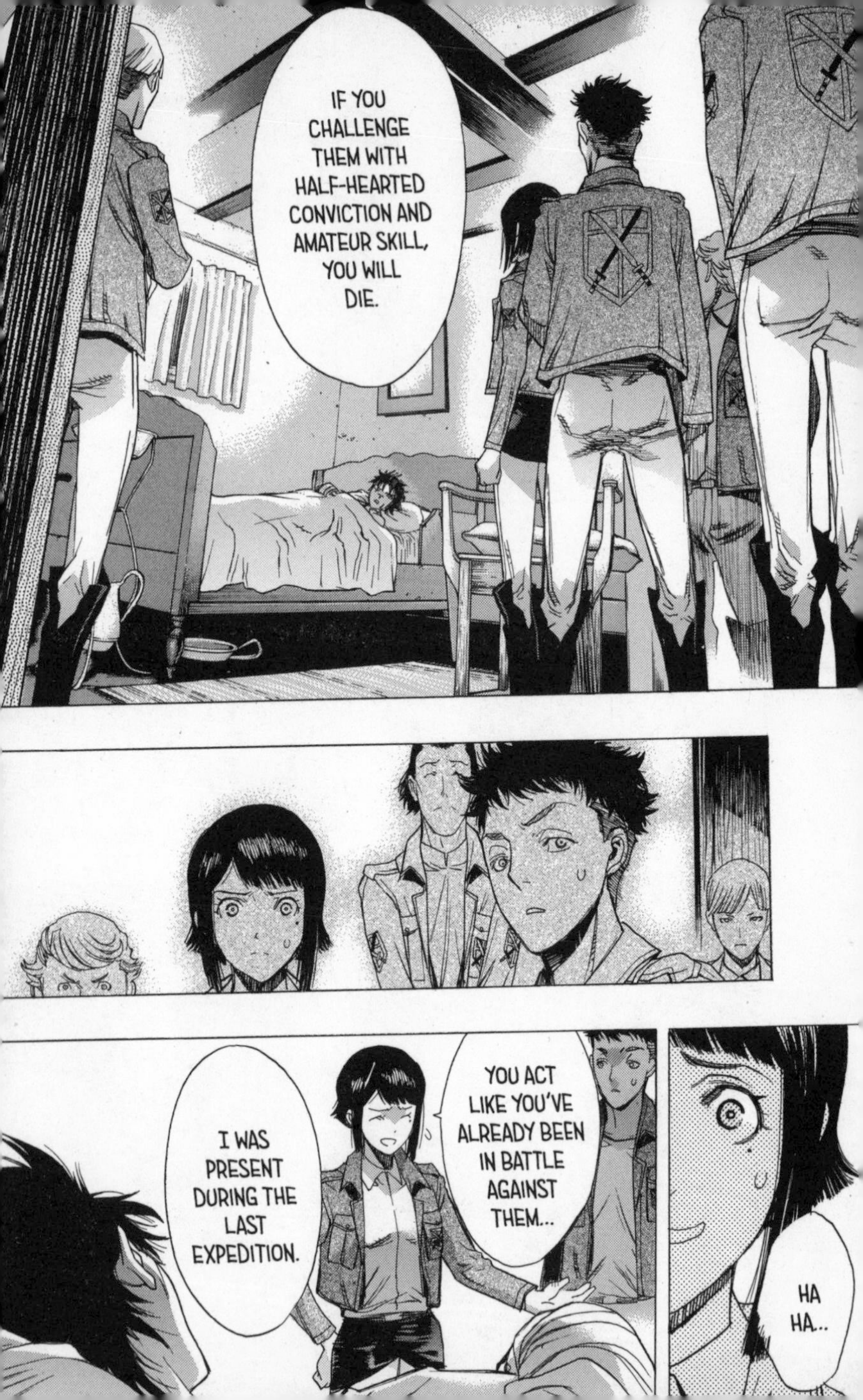
IF YOU CHALLENGE THEM WITH HALF-HEARTED CONVICTION AND AMATEUR SKILL, YOU WILL DIE.
HA HA...
YOU ACT LIKE YOU'VE ALREADY BEEN IN BATTLE AGAINST THEM...
I WAS PRESENT DURING THE LAST EXPEDITION.

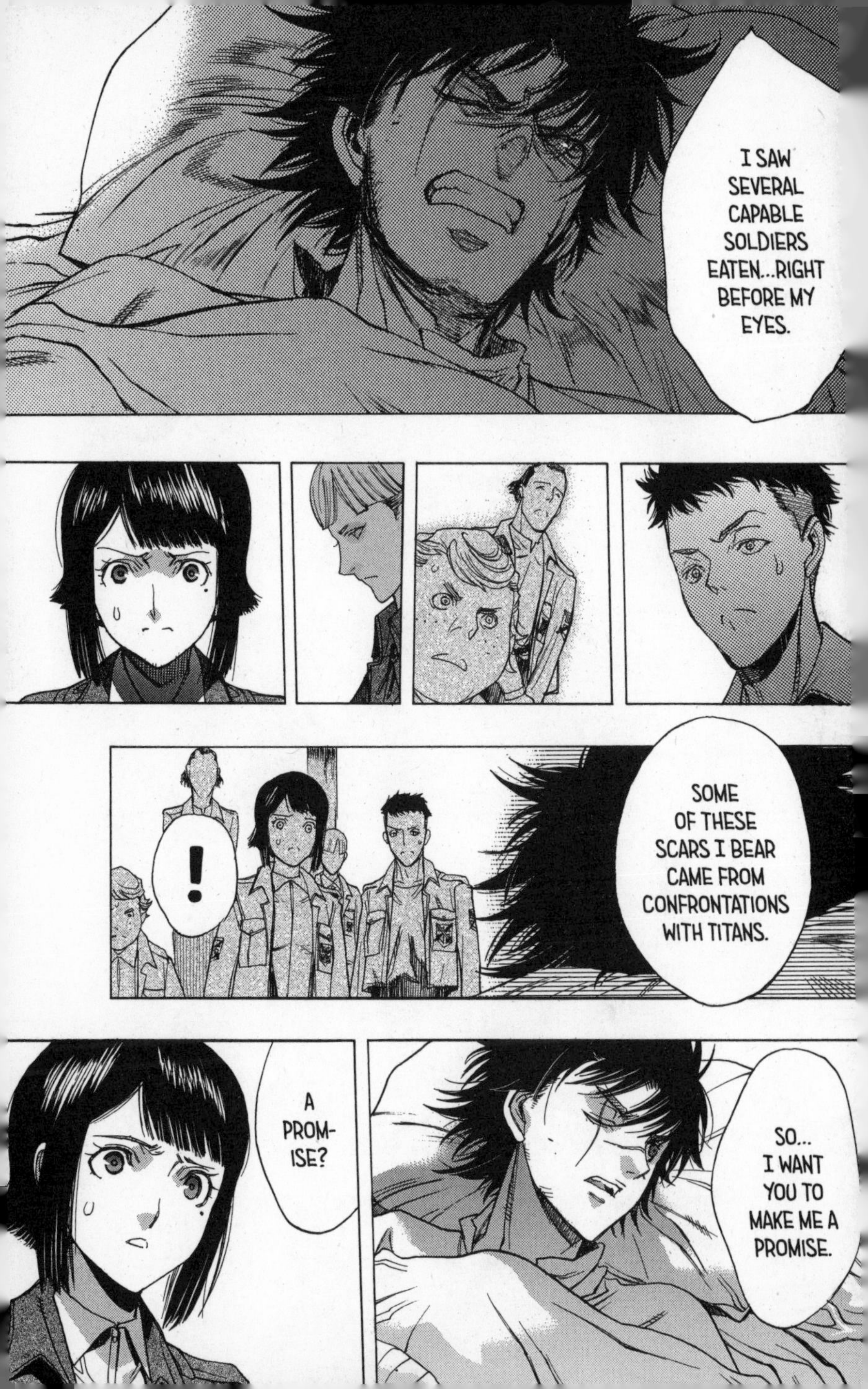
I SAW SEVERAL CAPABLE SOLDIERS EATEN...RIGHT BEFORE MY EYES.
SOME OF THESE SCARS I BEAR CAME FROM CONFRONTATIONS WITH TITANS.
!
SO... I WANT YOU TO MAKE ME A PROMISE.
A PROM-ISE?

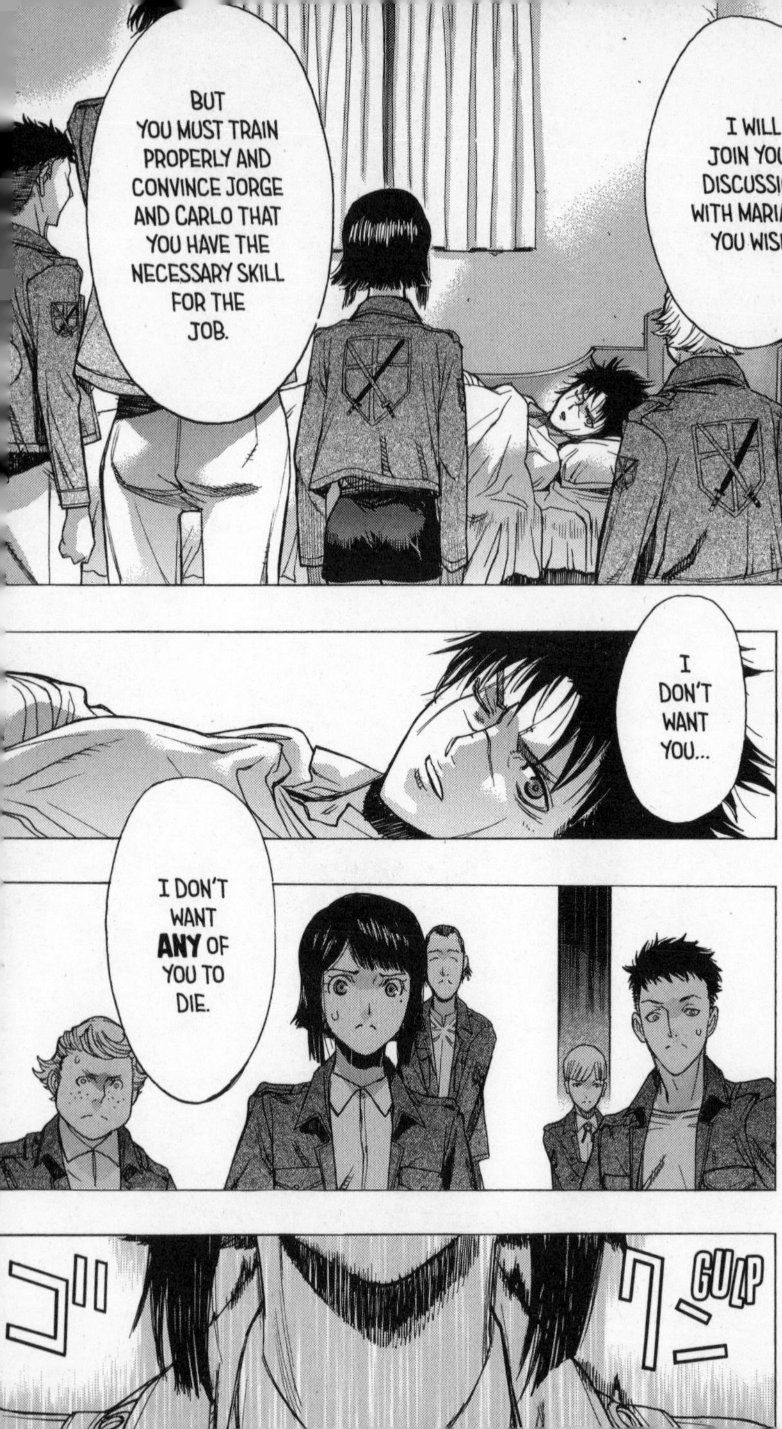
I WILL JOIN YOUR DISCUSSION WITH MARIA, IF YOU WISH.
BUT YOU MUST TRAIN PROPERLY AND CONVINCE JORGE AND CARLO THAT YOU HAVE THE NECESSARY SKILL FOR THE JOB.
I DON'T WANT YOU...
I DON'T WANT **ANY** OF YOU TO DIE.
GULP

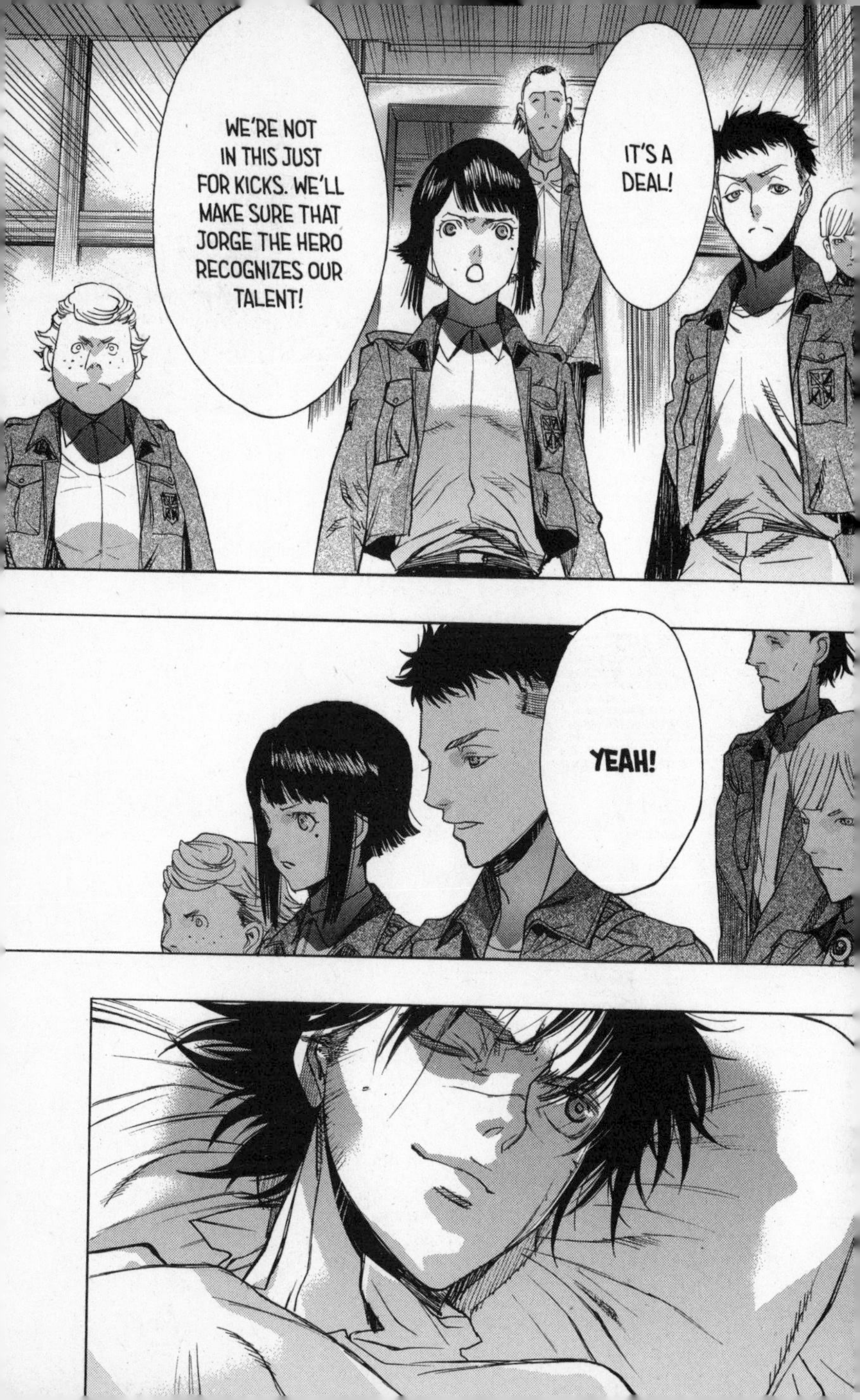
IT'S A DEAL!
WE'RE NOT IN THIS JUST FOR KICKS. WE'LL MAKE SURE THAT JORGE THE HERO RECOGNIZES OUR TALENT!
YEAH!

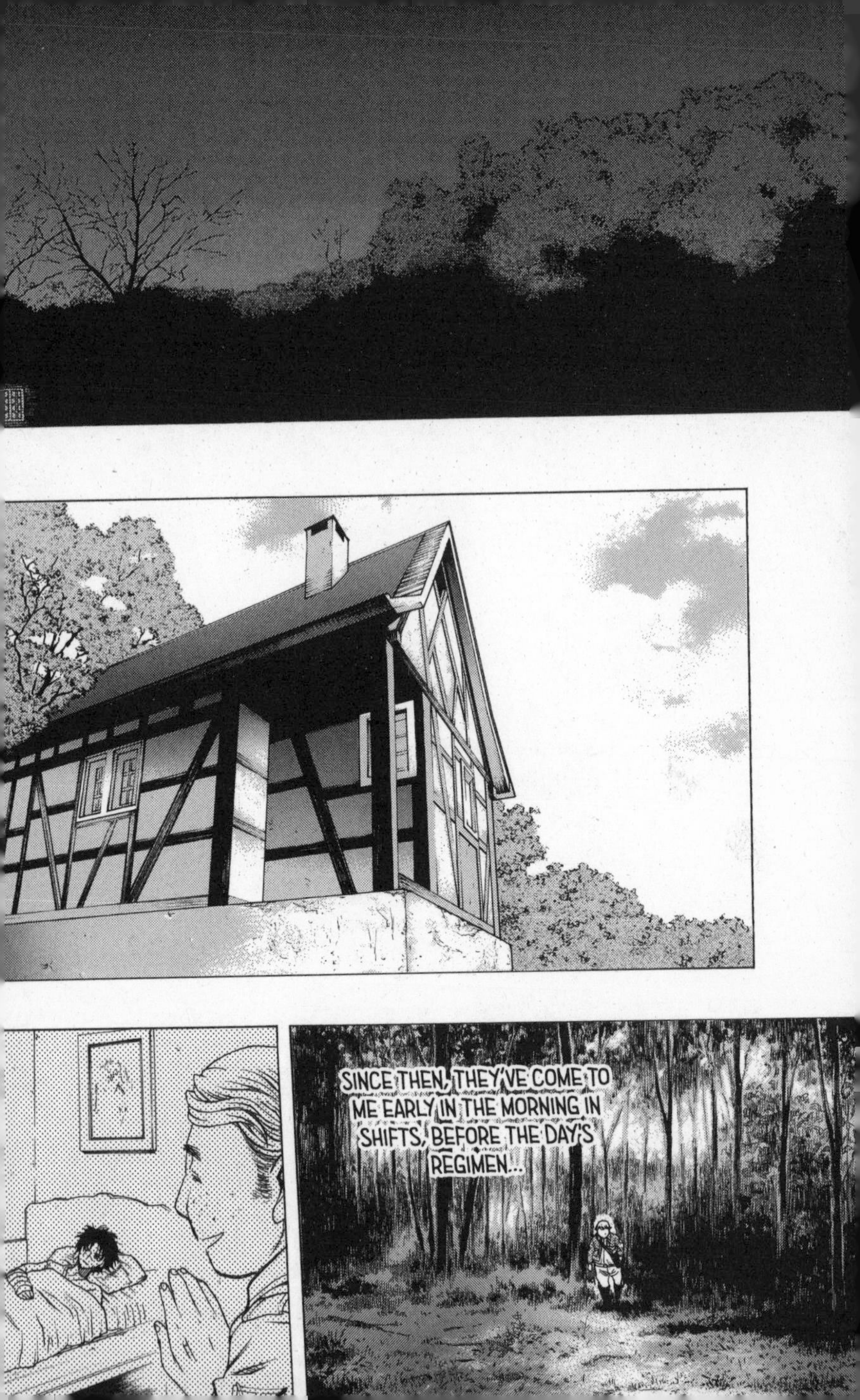
SINCE THEN, THEY'VE COME TO ME EARLY IN THE MORNING IN SHIFTS, BEFORE THE DAY'S REGIMEN...

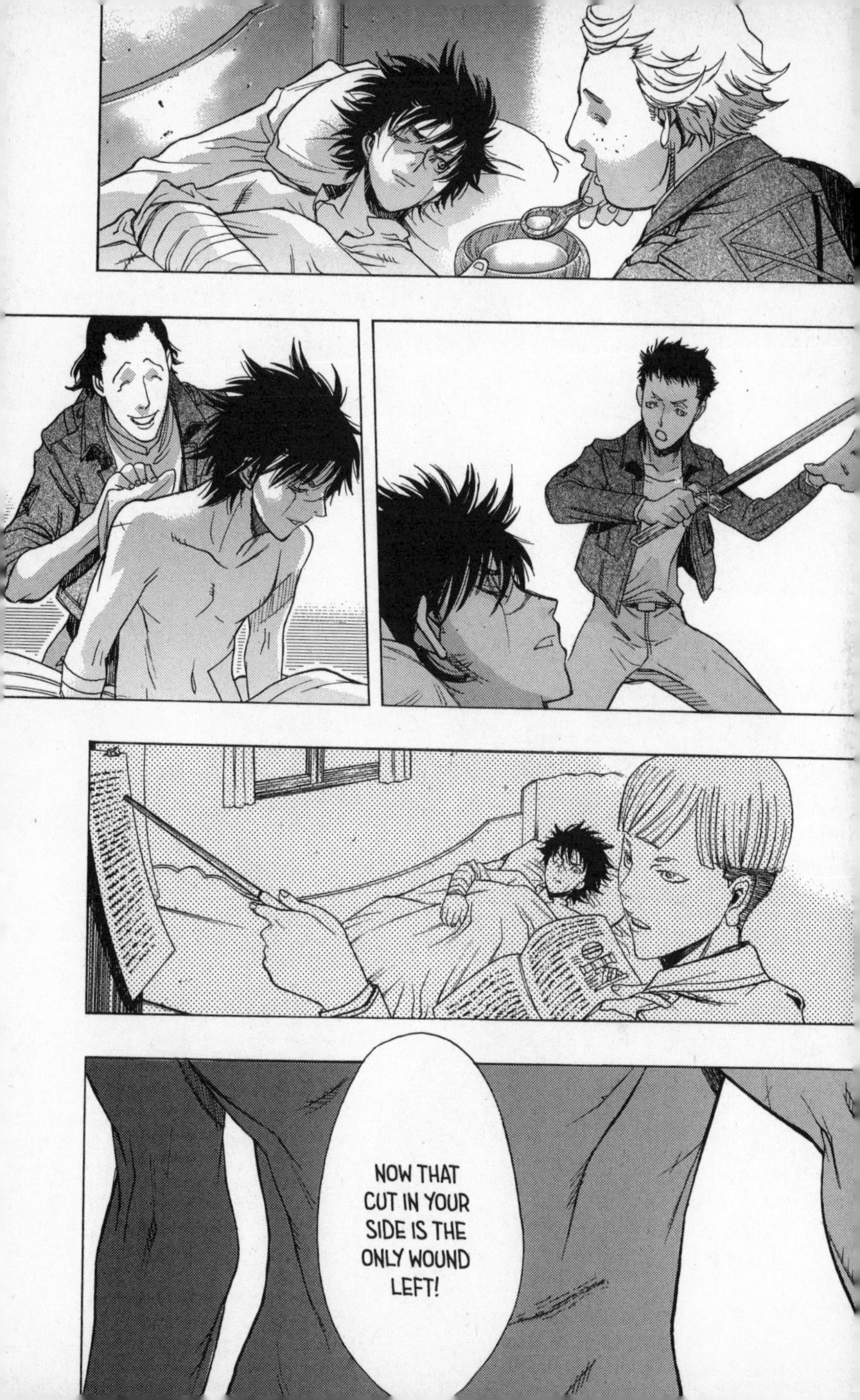
NOW THAT CUT IN YOUR SIDE IS THE ONLY WOUND LEFT!

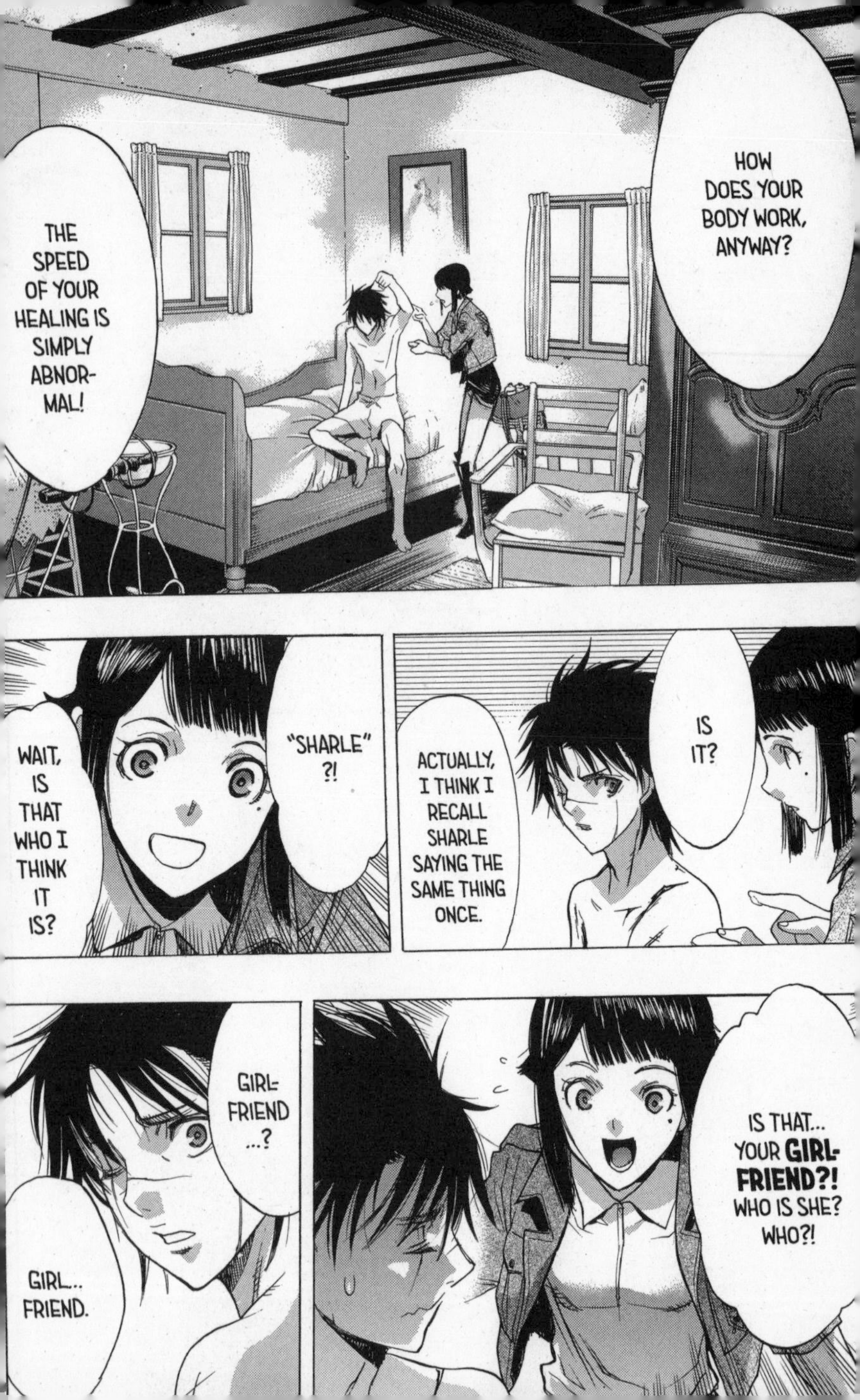
HOW DOES YOUR BODY WORK, ANYWAY?
THE SPEED OF YOUR HEALING IS SIMPLY ABNORMAL!
IS IT?
ACTUALLY, I THINK I RECALL SHARLE SAYING THE SAME THING ONCE.
"SHARLE" ?!
WAIT, IS THAT WHO I THINK IT IS?
IS THAT... YOUR GIRLFRIEND?! WHO IS SHE? WHO?!
GIRLFRIEND ...?
GIRL... FRIEND.

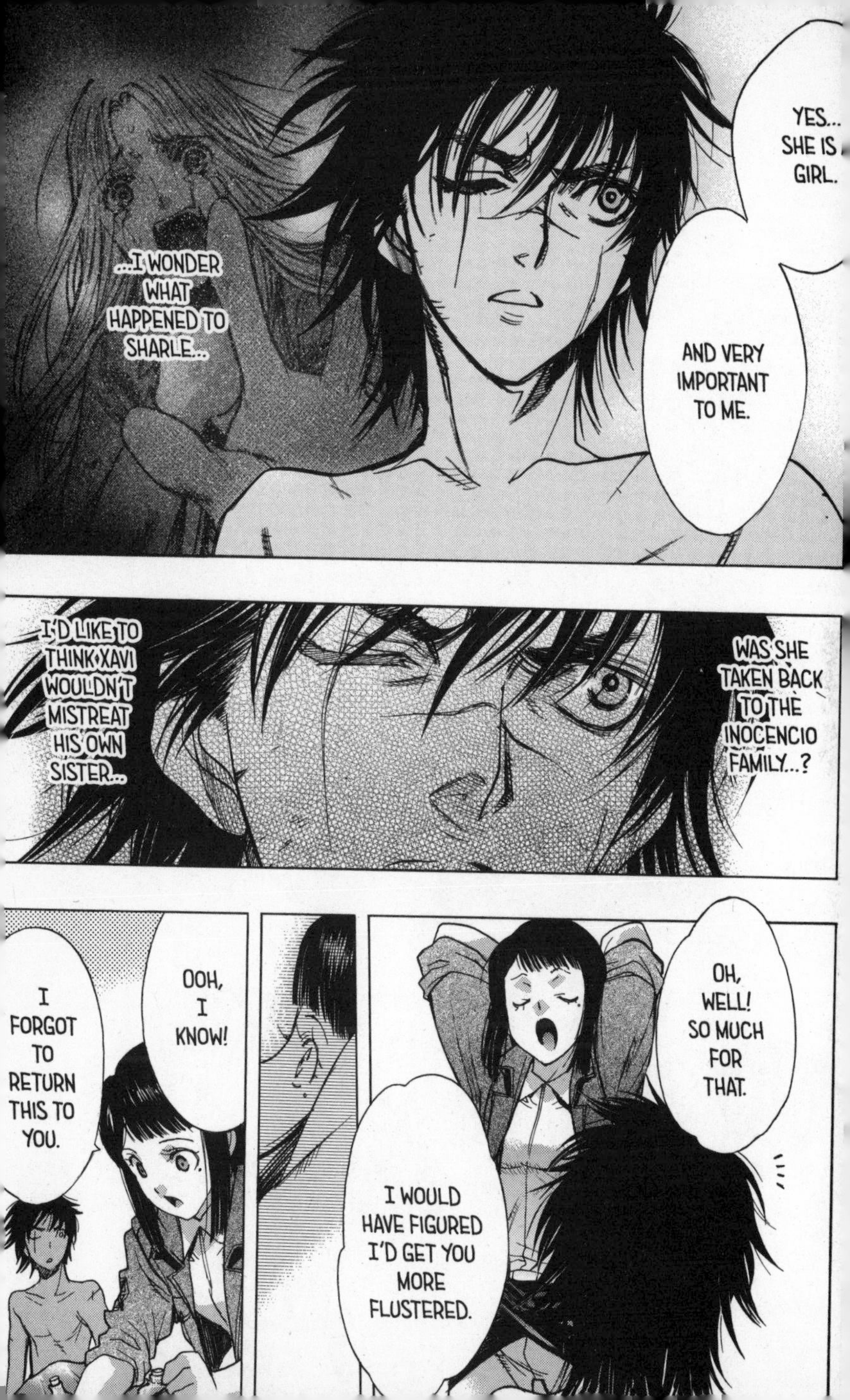
YES... SHE IS A GIRL.
AND VERY IMPORTANT TO ME.
...I WONDER WHAT HAPPENED TO SHARLE...
WAS SHE TAKEN BACK TO THE INOCENCIO FAMILY...?
I'D LIKE TO THINK XAVI WOULDN'T MISTREAT HIS OWN SISTER...
OH, WELL! SO MUCH FOR THAT.
I WOULD HAVE FIGURED I'D GET YOU MORE FLUSTERED.
OOH, I KNOW!
I FORGOT TO RETURN THIS TO YOU.

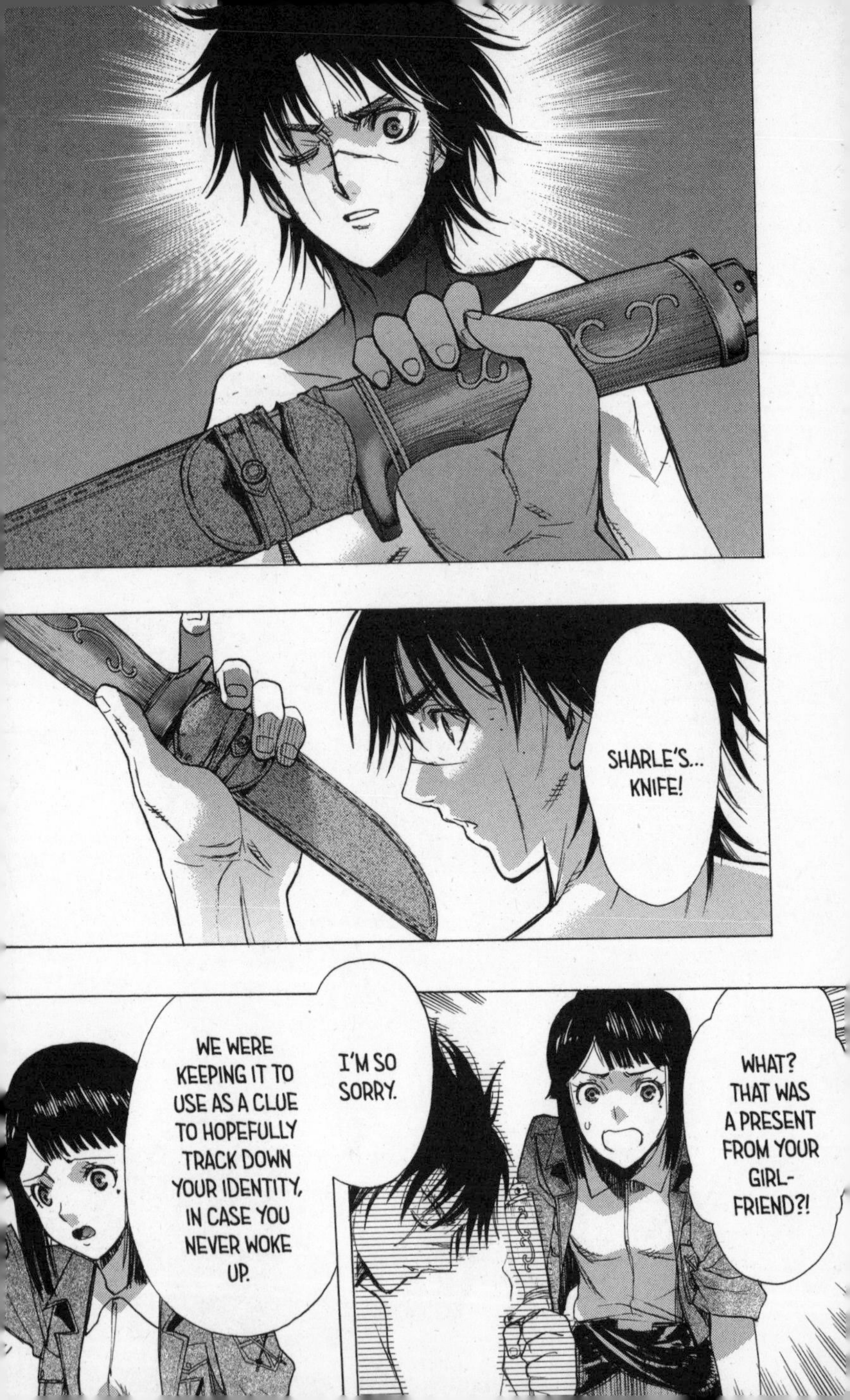
SHARLE'S... KNIFE!
WHAT? THAT WAS A PRESENT FROM YOUR GIRL-FRIEND?!
I'M SO SORRY.
WE WERE KEEPING IT TO USE AS A CLUE TO HOPEFULLY TRACK DOWN YOUR IDENTITY, IN CASE YOU NEVER WOKE UP.

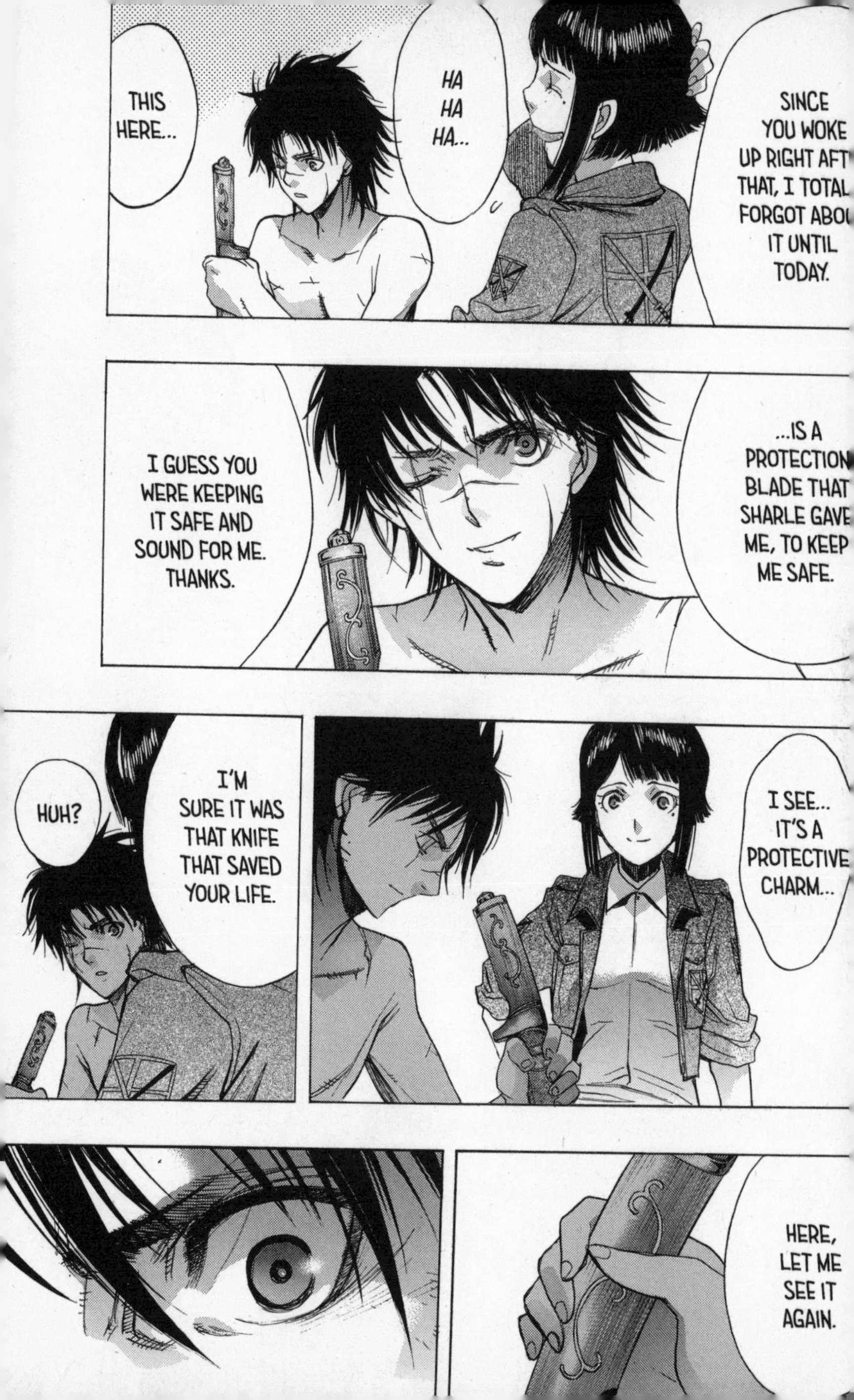
SINCE YOU WOKE UP RIGHT AFT THAT, I TOTAL FORGOT ABO IT UNTIL TODAY.
HA HA HA...
THIS HERE...
...IS A PROTECTION BLADE THAT SHARLE GAVE ME, TO KEEP ME SAFE.
I GUESS YOU WERE KEEPING IT SAFE AND SOUND FOR ME. THANKS.
I SEE... IT'S A PROTECTIVE CHARM...
I'M SURE IT WAS THAT KNIFE THAT SAVED YOUR LIFE.
HUH?
HERE, LET ME SEE IT AGAIN.

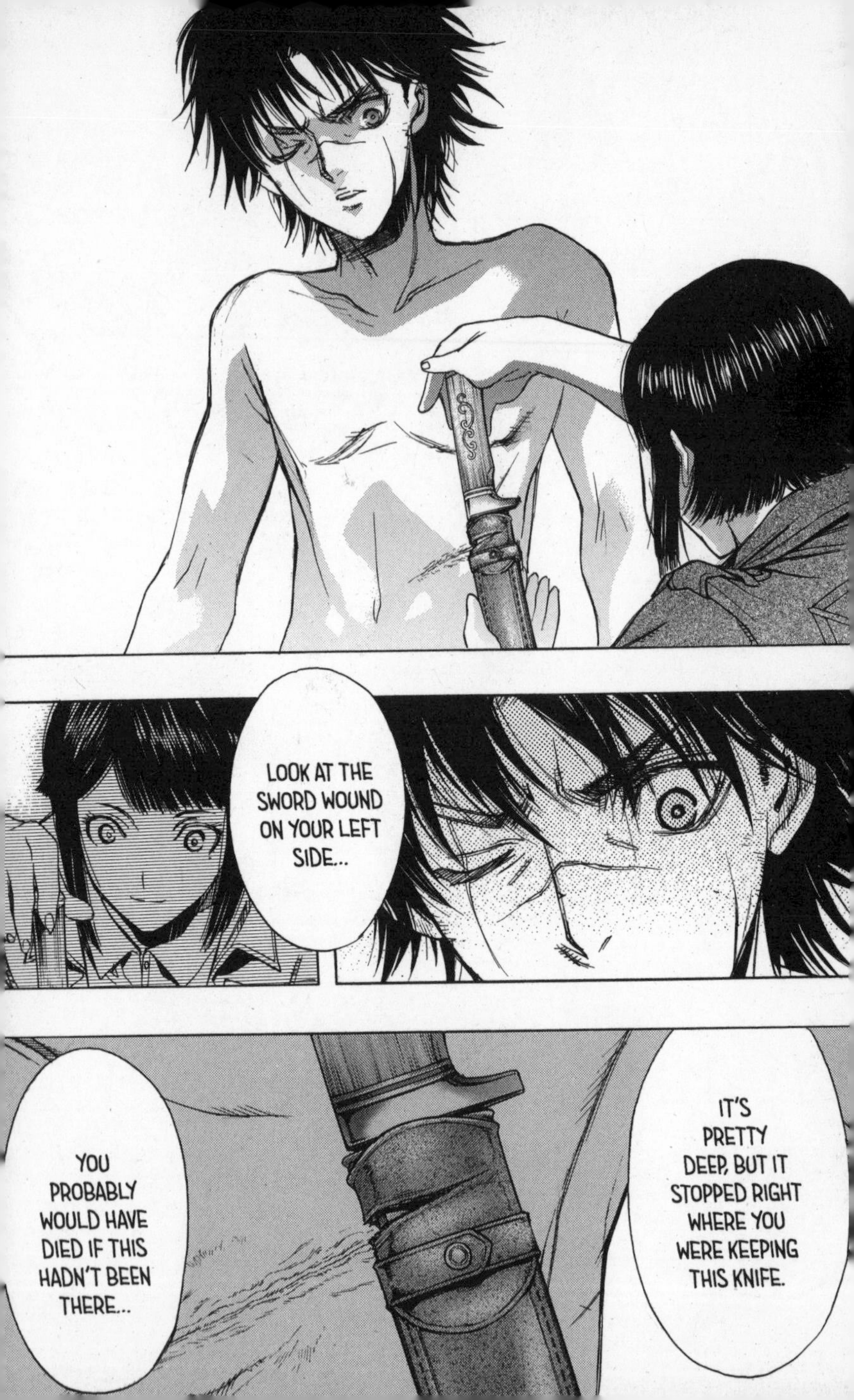
LOOK AT THE SWORD WOUND ON YOUR LEFT SIDE...
IT'S PRETTY DEEP, BUT IT STOPPED RIGHT WHERE YOU WERE KEEPING THIS KNIFE.
YOU PROBABLY WOULD HAVE DIED IF THIS HADN'T BEEN THERE...

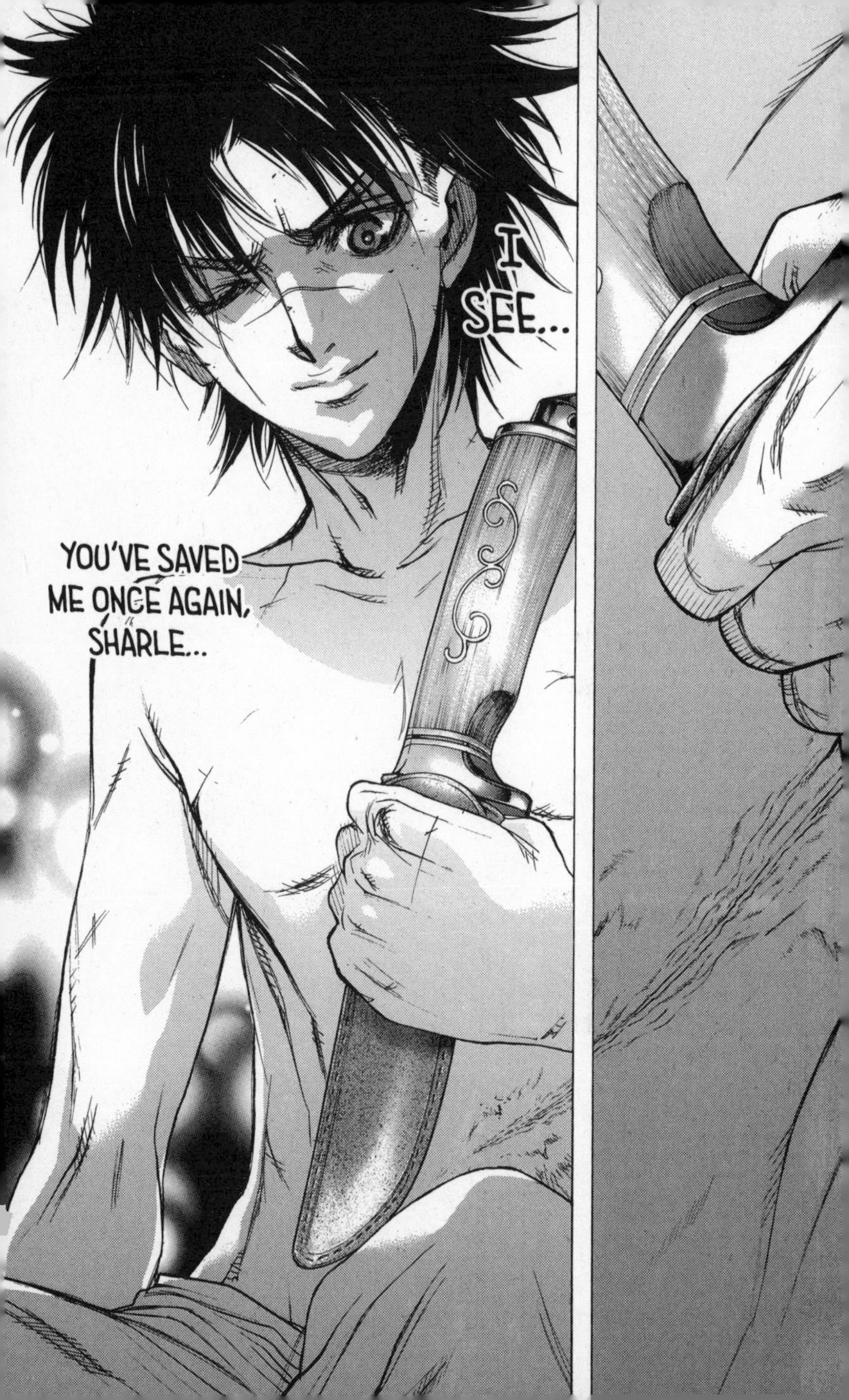
I SEE...
YOU'VE SAVED ME ONCE AGAIN, SHARLE...

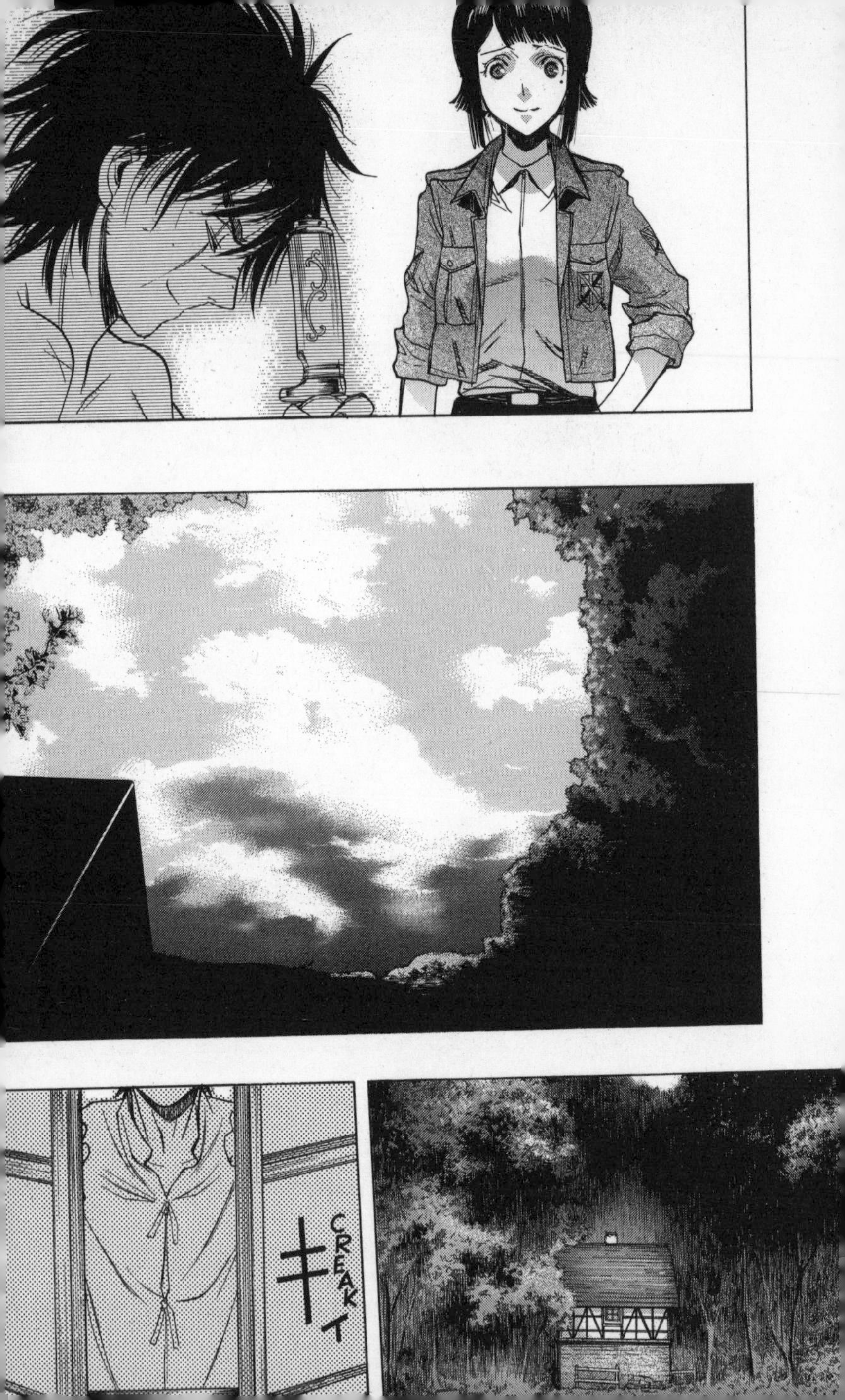
CREAK

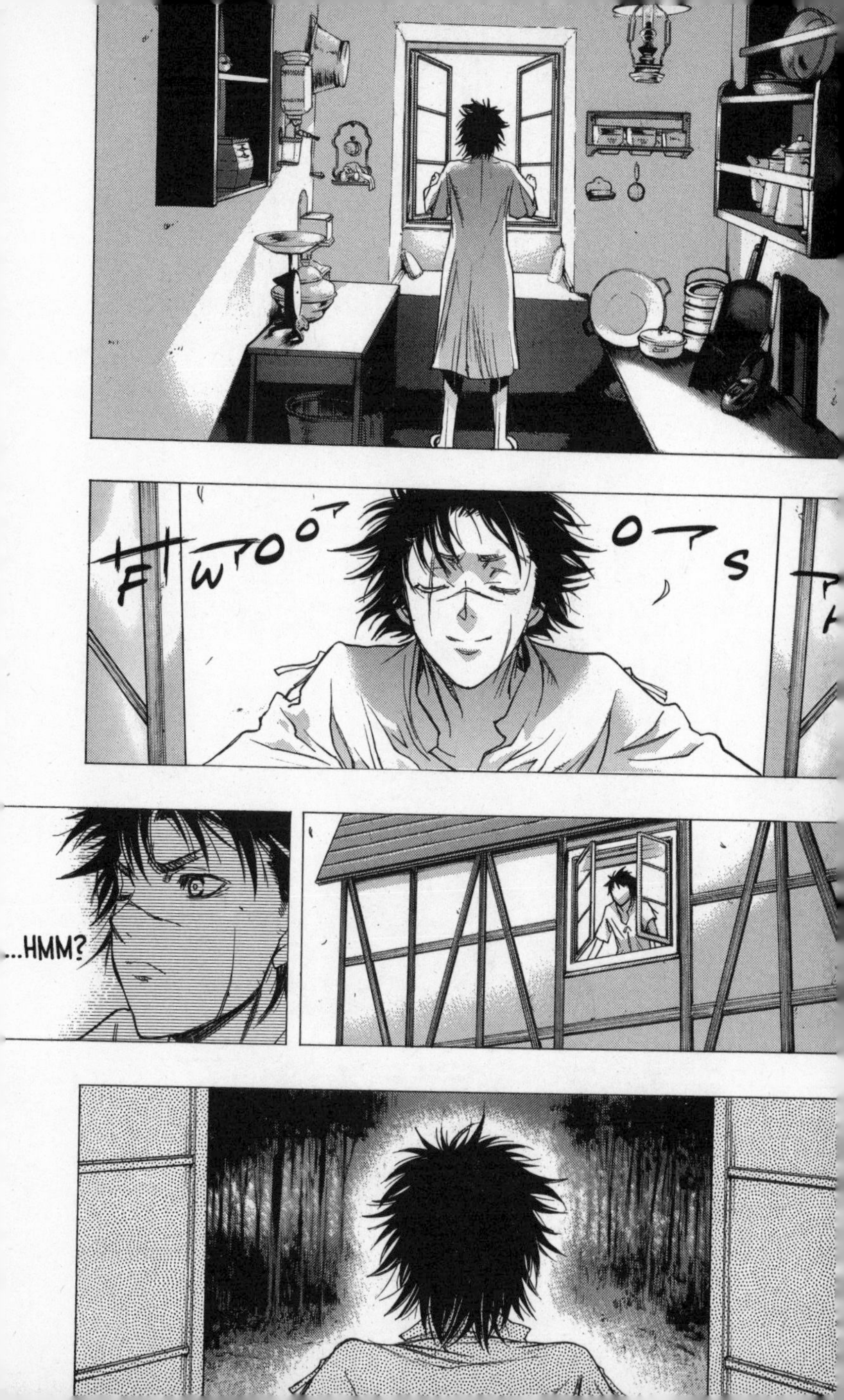
FWOOOOSH
...HMM?

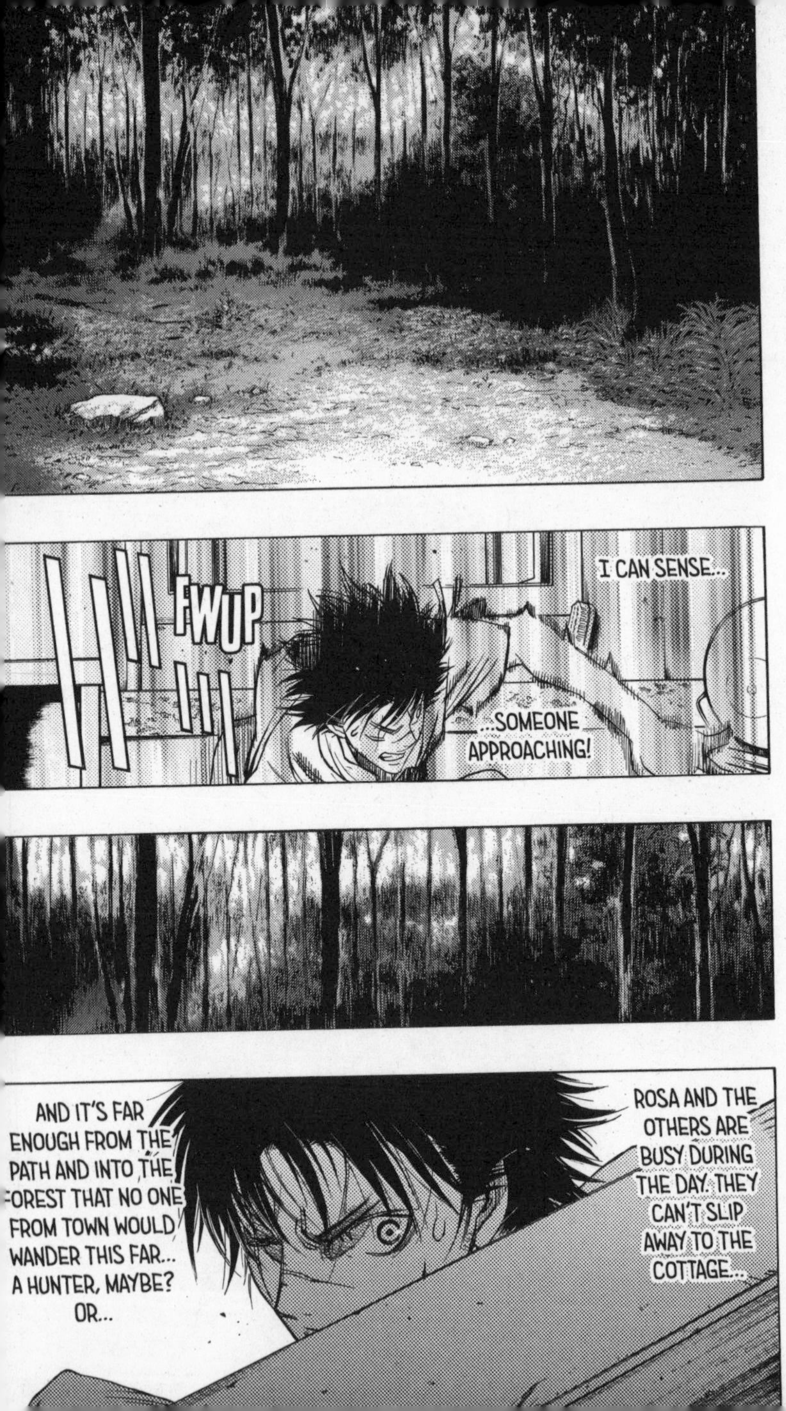
I CAN SENSE...
...SOMEONE APPROACHING!
FWUP
ROSA AND THE OTHERS ARE BUSY DURING THE DAY. THEY CAN'T SLIP AWAY TO THE COTTAGE...
AND IT'S FAR ENOUGH FROM THE PATH AND INTO THE FOREST THAT NO ONE FROM TOWN WOULD WANDER THIS FAR... A HUNTER, MAYBE? OR...

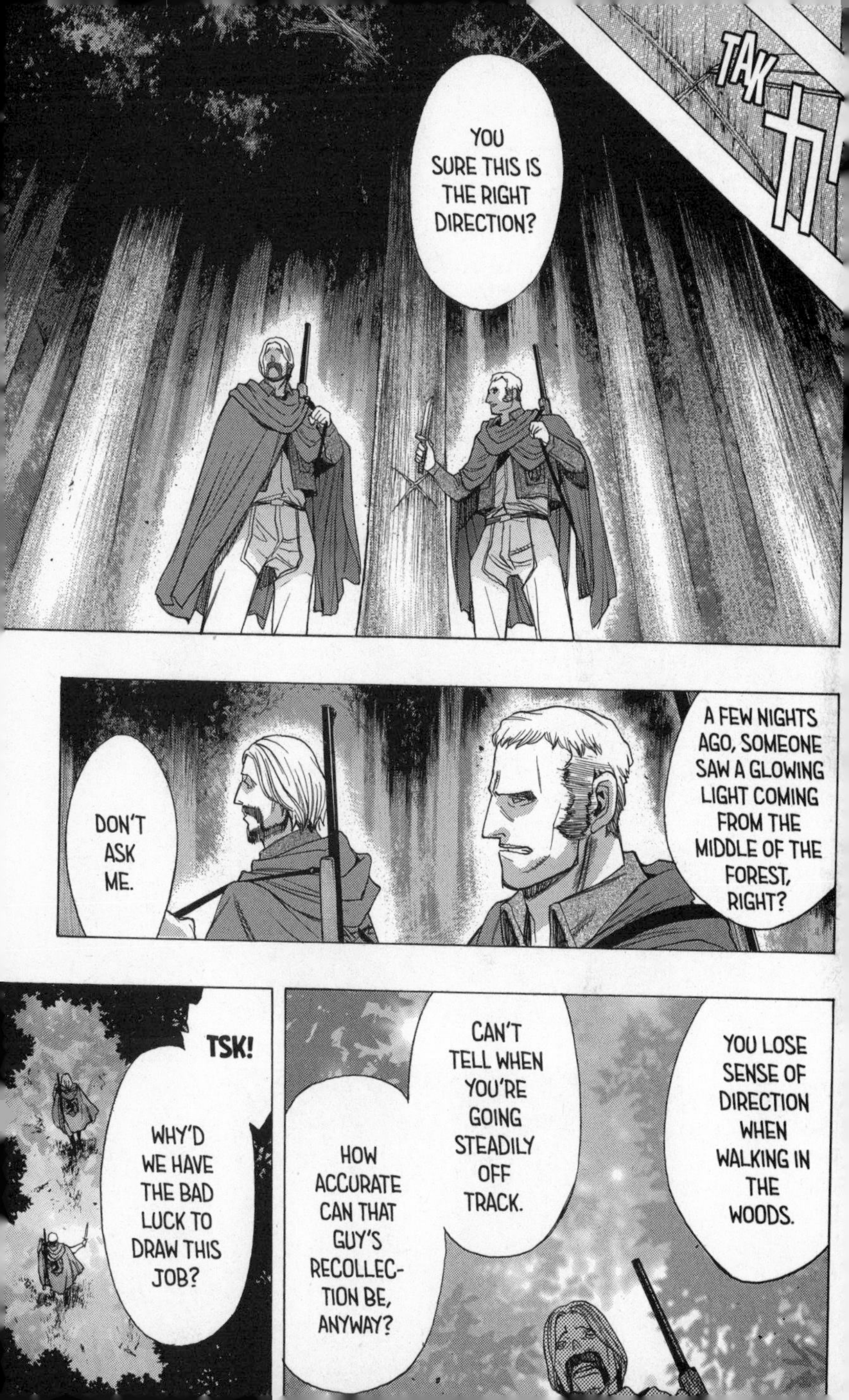
TAK
YOU SURE THIS IS THE RIGHT DIRECTION?
A FEW NIGHTS AGO, SOMEONE SAW A GLOWING LIGHT COMING FROM THE MIDDLE OF THE FOREST, RIGHT?
DON'T ASK ME.
YOU LOSE SENSE OF DIRECTION WHEN WALKING IN THE WOODS.
CAN'T TELL WHEN YOU'RE GOING STEADILY OFF TRACK.
HOW ACCURATE CAN THAT GUY'S RECOLLECTION BE, ANYWAY?
TSK!
WHY'D WE HAVE THE BAD LUCK TO DRAW THIS JOB?

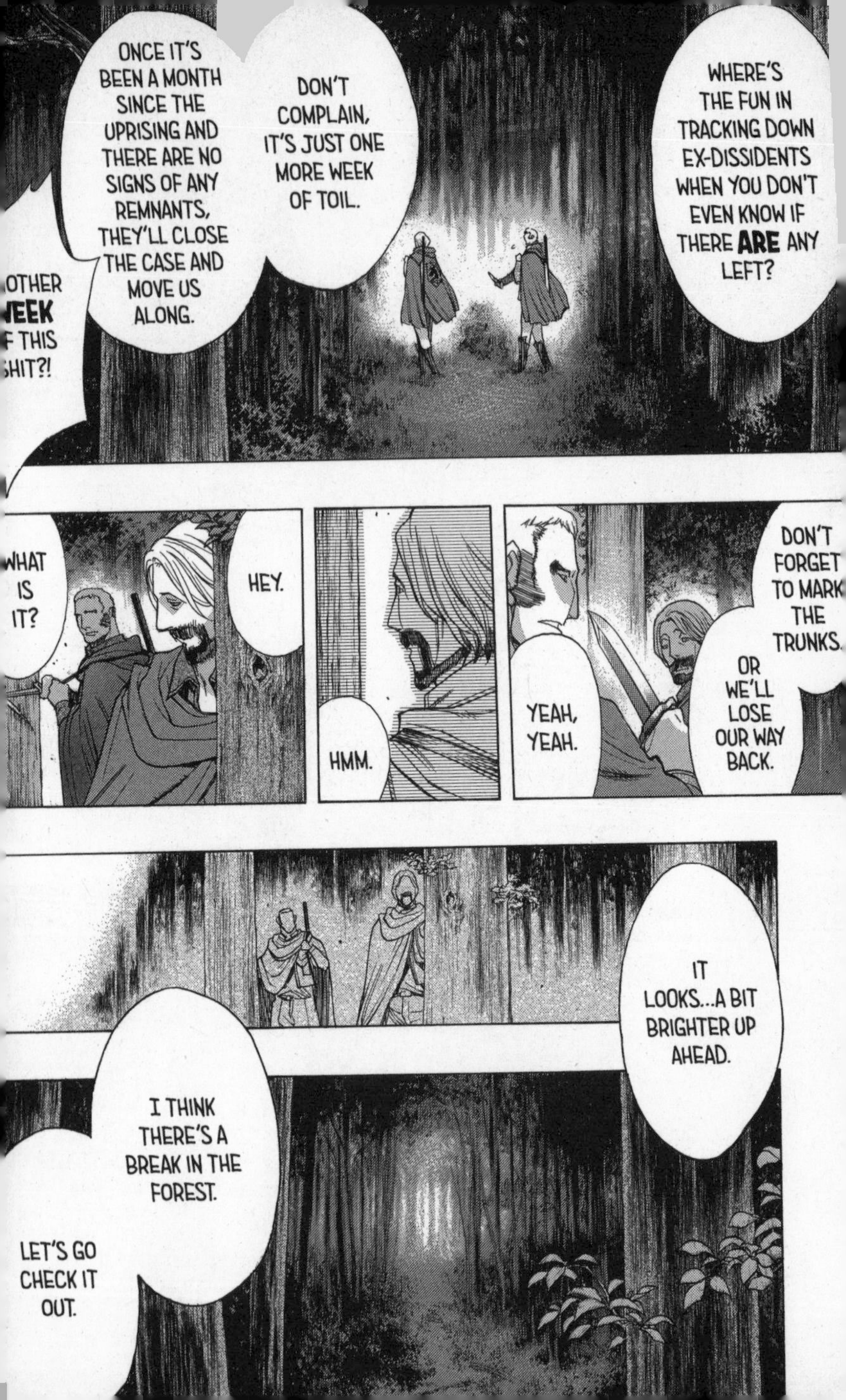
WHERE'S THE FUN IN TRACKING DOWN EX-DISSIDENTS WHEN YOU DON'T EVEN KNOW IF THERE **ARE** ANY LEFT?
DON'T COMPLAIN, IT'S JUST ONE MORE WEEK OF TOIL.
ONCE IT'S BEEN A MONTH SINCE THE UPRISING AND THERE ARE NO SIGNS OF ANY REMNANTS, THEY'LL CLOSE THE CASE AND MOVE US ALONG.
OTHER **WEEK** F THIS HIT?!
DON'T FORGET TO MARK THE TRUNKS.
OR WE'LL LOSE OUR WAY BACK.
YEAH, YEAH.
HMM.
HEY.
WHAT IS IT?
IT LOOKS...A BIT BRIGHTER UP AHEAD.
I THINK THERE'S A BREAK IN THE FOREST.
LET'S GO CHECK IT OUT.

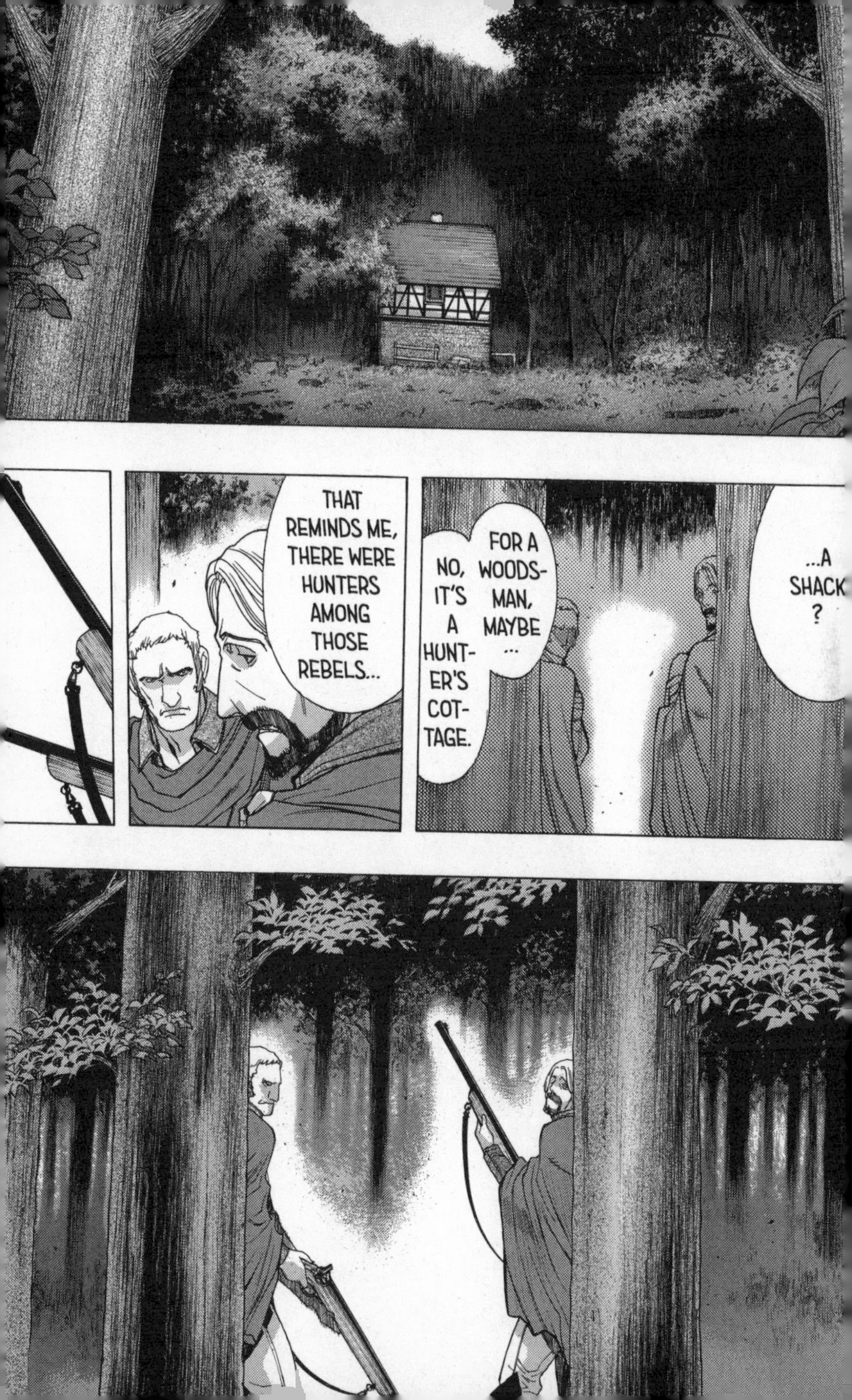
...A SHACK?
FOR A WOODS-MAN, MAYBE...
NO, IT'S A HUNT-ER'S COT-TAGE.
THAT REMINDS ME, THERE WERE HUNTERS AMONG THOSE REBELS...

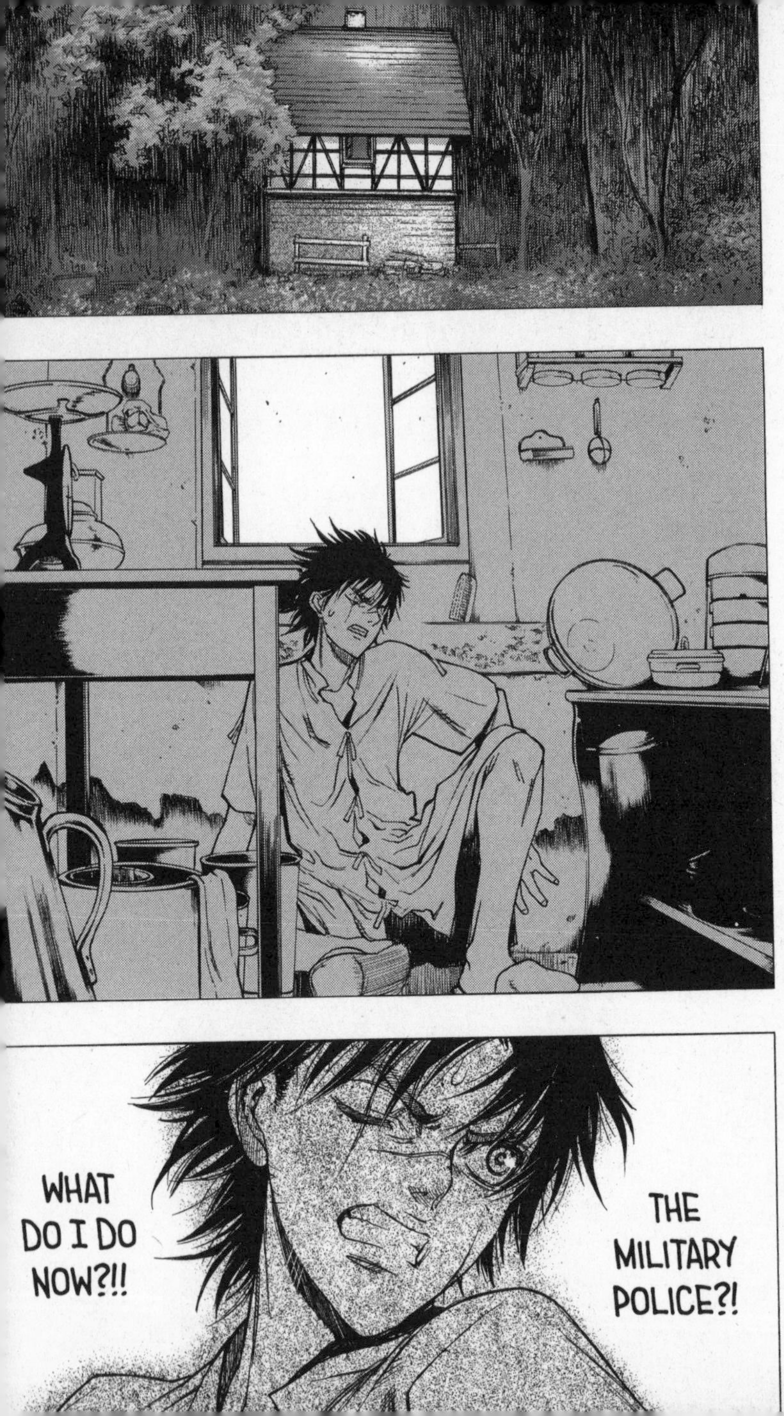
THE MILITARY POLICE?!
WHAT DO I DO NOW?!!

ATTACK on TITAN
BEFORE THE FALL

TO BE CONTINUED

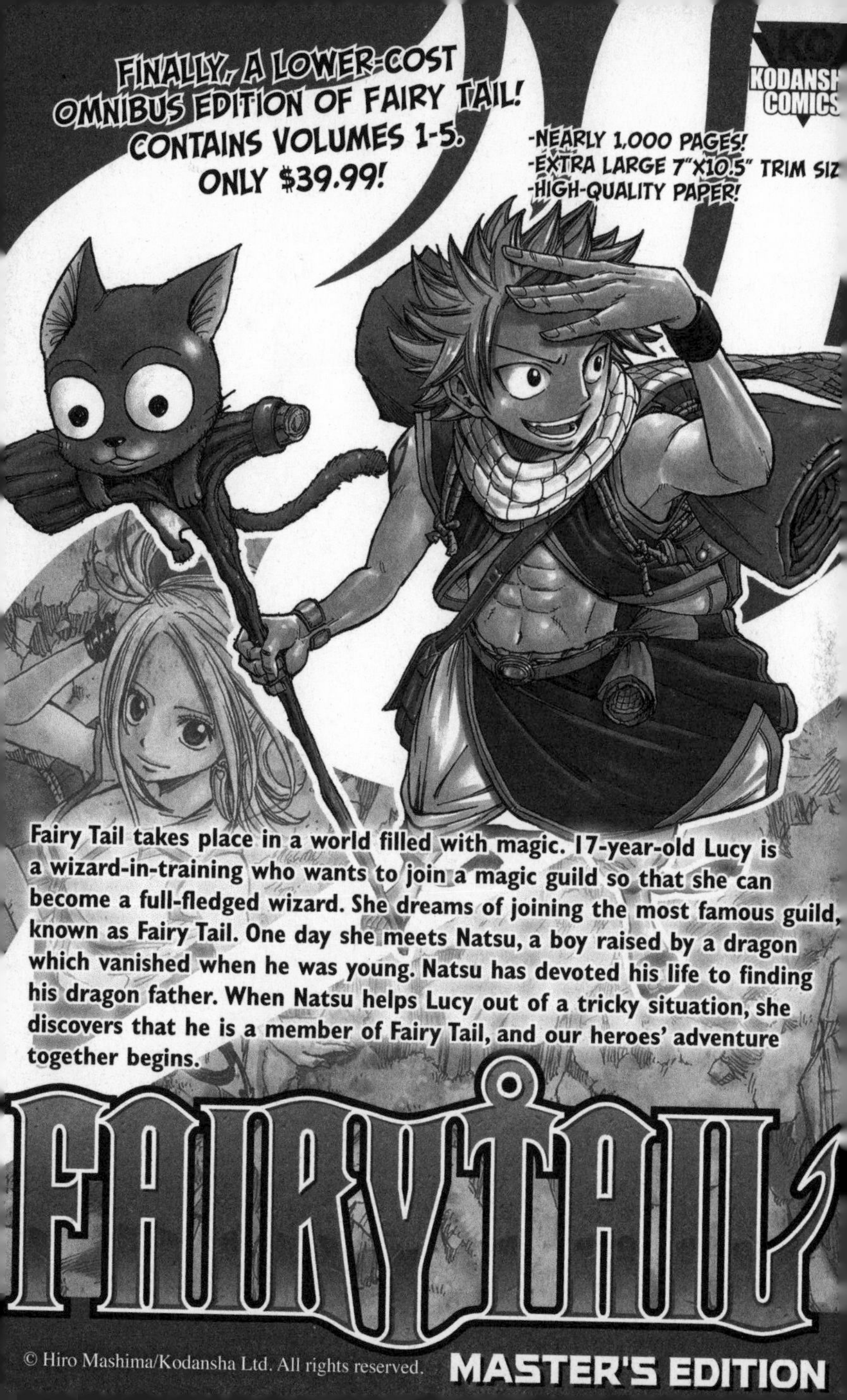
FINALLY, A LOWER-COST
OMNIBUS EDITION OF FAIRY TAIL!
CONTAINS VOLUMES 1-5.
ONLY $39.99!
KODANSHA COMICS
-NEARLY 1,000 PAGES!
-EXTRA LARGE 7"X10.5" TRIM SIZ
-HIGH-QUALITY PAPER!
Fairy Tail takes place in a world filled with magic. 17-year-old Lucy is a wizard-in-training who wants to join a magic guild so that she can become a full-fledged wizard. She dreams of joining the most famous guild, known as Fairy Tail. One day she meets Natsu, a boy raised by a dragon which vanished when he was young. Natsu has devoted his life to finding his dragon father. When Natsu helps Lucy out of a tricky situation, she discovers that he is a member of Fairy Tail, and our heroes' adventure together begins.
FAIRY TAIL
© Hiro Mashima/Kodansha Ltd. All rights reserved.
MASTER'S EDITION

ving lost his wife, high school teacher Kōhei Inuzuka is doing his best to raise his young
ughter Tsumugi as a single father. He's pretty bad at cooking and doesn't have a huge
petite to begin with, but chance brings his little family together with one of his students, the
ely Kotori. The three of them are anything but comfortable in the kitchen, but the healing
wer of home cooking might just work on their grieving hearts.

his season's number-one feel-good anime!" —Anime News Network

beautifully-drawn story about comfort food and family and grief. Recommended." —Otaku
SA Magazine

sweetness & lightning

By Gido Amagakure

KC
KODANSHA
COMICS

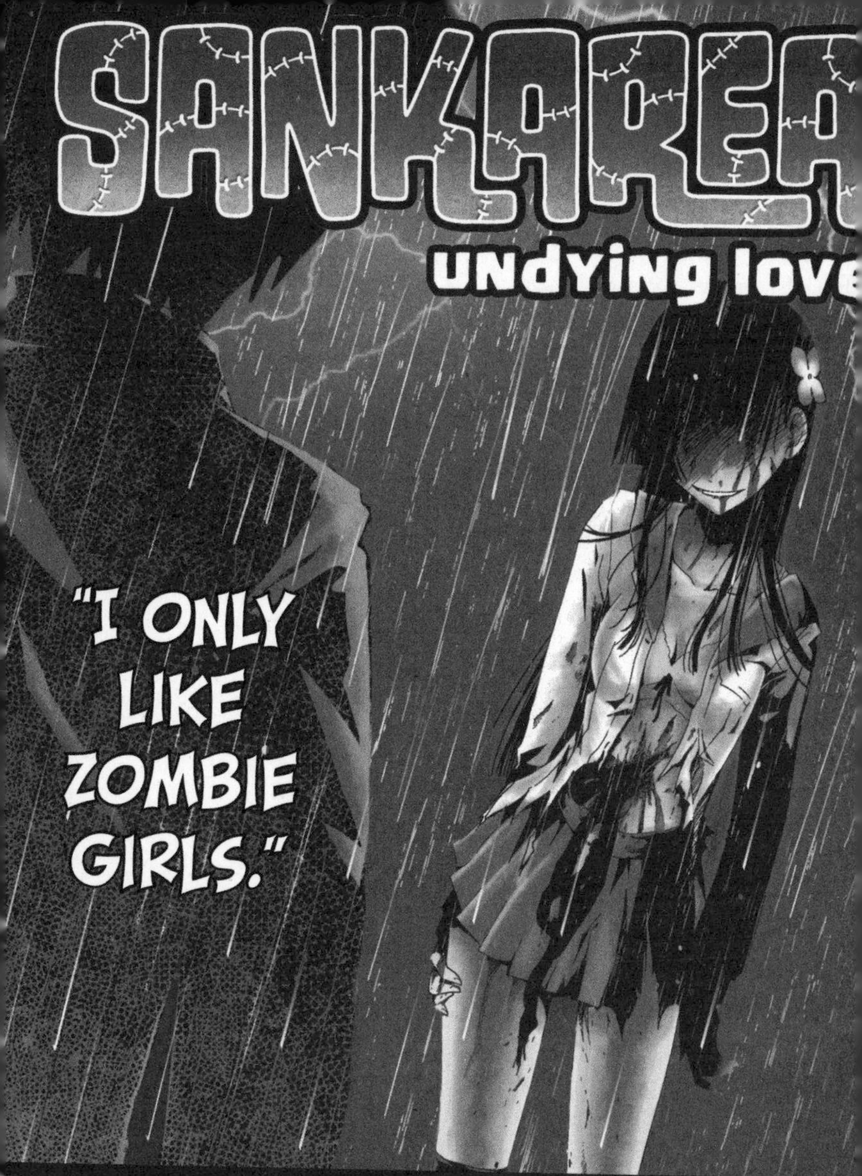

SANKAREA

UNDYING love

"I ONLY LIKE ZOMBIE GIRLS."

Chihiro has an unusual connection to zombie movies. He doesn't feel bad fo the survivors – he wants to comfort the undead girls they slaughter! When his pet passes away, he brews a resurrection potion. He's discovered by local heiress Sanka Rea, and she serves as his first test subject!

"I'm pleasantly surprised to find modern shojo using cross-dressing as a dramatic device to deliver social commentary... Recommended."

-Otaku USA Magazine

The prince in his dark days

By **Hico Yamanaka**

A drunkard for a father, a household of poverty... For 17-year-old Atsuko, misfortune is all she knows and believes in. Until one day, a chance encounter with Itaru–the wealthy heir of a huge corporation–changes everything. The two look identical, uncannily so. When Itaru curiously goes missing, Atsuko is roped into being his stand-in. There, in his shoes, Atsuko must parade like a prince in a palace. She encounters many new experiences, but at what cost...?

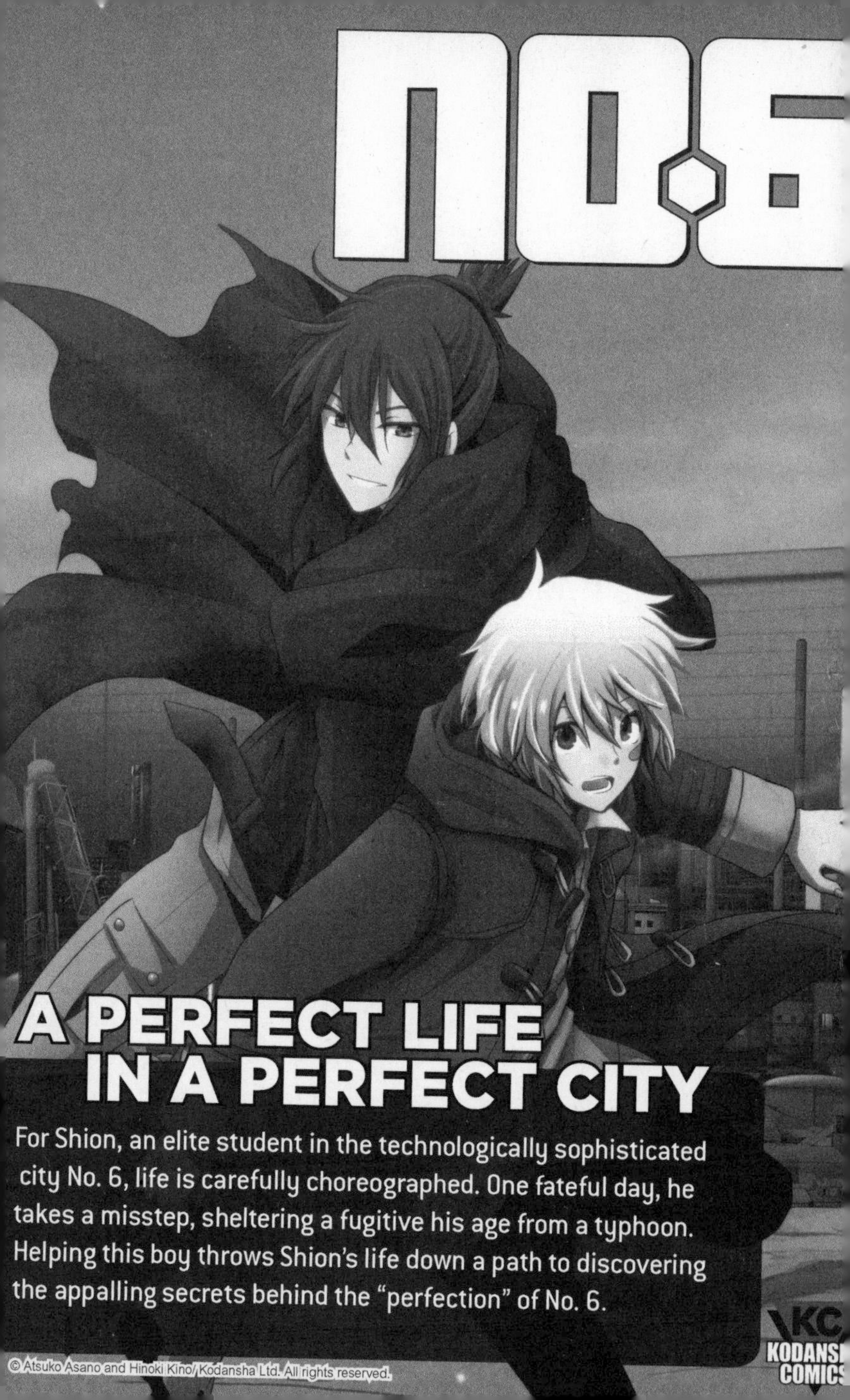
NO.6
A PERFECT LIFE IN A PERFECT CITY
For Shion, an elite student in the technologically sophisticated city No. 6, life is carefully choreographed. One fateful day, he takes a misstep, sheltering a fugitive his age from a typhoon. Helping this boy throws Shion's life down a path to discovering the appalling secrets behind the "perfection" of No. 6.
© Atsuko Asano and Hinoki Kino/ Kodansha Ltd. All rights reserved.

By

Hiroyuki Takei

Japan's most powerful spirit medium delves into the ghost world's greatest mysteries!

Story by Kyo Shirodaira, famed author of mystery fiction and creator of *Spiral*, *Blast of Tempest*, and *The Record of a Fallen Vampire*.

Both touched by spirits called yôkai, Kotoko and Kurô have gained unique superhuman powers. But to gain her powers Kotoko has given up an eye and a leg, and Kurô's personal life is in shambles. So when Kotoko suggests they team up to deal with renegades from the spirit world, Kurô doesn't have many other choices, but Kotoko might just have a few ulterior motives...

IN/SPECTRE

STORY BY KYO SHIRODAIRA
ART BY CHASHIBA KATASE

H·A·P·P·I·N·E·S·S

——ハピネス——

By Shuzo Oshimi

From the creator of *The Flowers of Evil*

Nothing interesting is happening in Makoto Ozaki's first year of hig
school. HIs life is a series of quiet humiliations: low-grade bullie
unreliable friends, and the constant frustration of his adolescent lust. B
one night, a pale, thin girl knocks him to the ground in an alley and offe
him a choice.

Now everything is different. Daylight is searingly bright. Food taste
awful. And worse than anything is the terrible, consuming thirst...

Praise for Shuzo Oshimi's *The Flowers of Evil*

"A shockingly readable story that vividly—one might even say queasily—evokes the fea
and confusion of discovering one's own sexuality. Recommended." —The Manga Critic

"A page-turning tale of sordid middle school blackmail." —Otaku USA Magazine

"A stunning new horror manga." —Third Eye Comics

A new series from the creator of *Soul Eater*, the megahit manga and anime seen on Toonami!

"Fun and lively... great start!"
-Adventures in Poor Taste

FIRE FORCE

By Atsushi Ohkubo

The city of Tokyo is plagued by a deadly phenomenon: spontaneous human combustion! Luckily, a special team is there to quench the inferno: The Fire Force! The fire soldiers at Special Fire Cathedral 8 are about to get a unique addition. Enter Shinra, a boy who possesses the power to run at the speed of a rocket, leaving behind the famous "devil's footprints" (and destroying his shoes in the process). Can Shinra and his colleagues discover the source of this strange epidemic before the city burns to ashes?

The award-winning manga about what happens inside you!

"Far more entertaining than it ought to be... wha kid doesn't want to think that every time the sneeze a torpedo shoots out their nose?"
—Anime News Networ

Strep throat! Hay fever! Influenz The world is a dangerous place fo a red blood cell just trying to get he deliveries finished. Fortunately she's not alone...she's got whole human body's worth o cells ready to help out! The mysterious white bloo cells, the buff and bras killer T cells, even th cute little platelets— everyone's got t come together they want to keep yo healthy!

Cells at Work!

はたらく細胞

By Akane Shimizu

WELCOME TO THE BALLROOM

By Tomo Takeuchi

Feckless high school student Tatara Fujita wants to be good at something—anything. Unfortunately, he's about as average as a slouchy teen can be. The local bullies know this, and make it a habit to hit him up for cash, but all that changes when the debonair Kaname Sengoku sends them packing. Sengoku's not the neighborhood watch, though. He's a professional ballroom dancer. And once Tatara Fujita gets pulled into the world of ballroom, his life will never be the same.

KC
KODANSHA COMICS

A Kodansha Comics Trade Paperback Original

Attack on Titan: Before the Fall volume 11 copyright © 2017 Hajime Isayama/
Ryo Suzukaze/Satoshi Shiki
English translation copyright © 2017 Hajime Isayama/Ryo Suzukaze/Satoshi Shiki

Published in the United States by Kodansha Comics, an imprint of
Kodansha USA Publishing, LLC, New York.

Publication rights for this English edition arranged through
Kodansha Ltd, Tokyo.

First published in Japan in 2017 by Kodansha Ltd., Tokyo
as *Shingeki no kyojin Before the fall*, volume 11.

ISBN 978-1-63236-382-4

Character designs by Thores Shibamoto
Original cover design by Takashi Shimoyama (Red Rooster)

Printed in the United States of America.

www.kodanshacomics.com

9 8 7 6 5 4 3 2 1
Translation: Stephen Paul
Lettering: Steve Wands
Editing: Haruko Hashimoto and Lauren Scanlan
Kodansha Comics edition cover design by Phil Balsman

STOP!

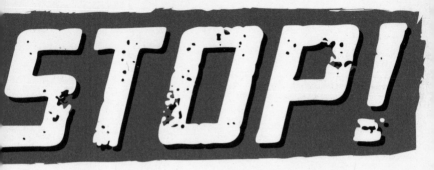

You are going the *wrong way!*

Manga is a *completely* different type of reading experience.

To start at the *BEGINNING*, go to the *END!*

That's right! Authentic manga is read the traditional Japanese way—from right to left, exactly the opposite of how American books are read. It's easy to follow: just go to the other end of the book, and read each page—and each panel—from the right side to the left side, starting at the top right. Now you're experiencing manga as it was meant to be.